The Presidency of
DWIGHT D.
EISENHOWER

AMERICAN PRESIDENCY SERIES

Donald R. McCoy, Clifford S. Griffin, Homer E. Socolofsky
General Editors

George Washington, Forrest McDonald
John Adams, Ralph Adams Brown
Thomas Jefferson, Forrest McDonald
James Madison, Robert Allen Rutland
John Quincy Adams, Mary W. M. Hargreaves
Martin Van Buren, Major L. Wilson
William Henry Harrison & John Tyler, Norma Lois Peterson
James K. Polk, Paul H. Bergeron
Zachary Taylor & Millard Fillmore, Elbert B. Smith
Franklin Pierce, Larry Gara
James Buchanan, Elbert B. Smith
Andrew Johnson, Albert Castel
Rutherford B. Hayes, Ari Hoogenboom
James A. Garfield & Chester A. Arthur, Justus D. Doenecke
Grover Cleveland, Richard E. Welch, Jr.
Benjamin Harrison, Homer E. Socolofsky & Allan B. Spetter
William McKinley, Lewis L. Gould
Theodore Roosevelt, Lewis L. Gould
William Howard Taft, Paolo E. Coletta
Woodrow Wilson, Kendrick A. Clements
Warren G. Harding, Eugene P. Trani & David L. Wilson
Herbert C. Hoover, Martin L. Fausold
Harry S. Truman, Donald R. McCoy
Dwight D. Eisenhower, Chester J. Pach, Jr., & Elmo Richardson
John F. Kennedy, James N. Giglio
Lyndon B. Johnson, Vaughn Davis Bornet

The Presidency of

DWIGHT D. EISENHOWER

Revised Edition

*Chester J. Pach, Jr.,
and Elmo Richardson*

UNIVERSITY PRESS OF KANSAS

Published by the University Press of Kansas (Lawrence,
Kansas 66049), which was organized by the Kansas
Board of Regents and is operated and funded by Emporia
State University, Fort Hays State University,
Kansas State University, Pittsburg State University, the
University of Kansas, and Wichita State University

Library of Congress Cataloging-in-Publication Data

Pach, Chester J.
The presidency of Dwight D. Eisenhower.—Rev. ed. / Chester J.
Pach, Jr., Elmo Richardson.
p.   cm. — (American presidency series)
Rev. ed. of: The presidency of Dwight D. Eisenhower / by Elmo
Richardson. c1979.
Includes bibliographical references and index.
ISBN 0-7006-0436-7 (cloth)—ISBN 0-7006-0437-5 (paper)
1. United States—Politics and government—1953–1961.
2. Eisenhower, Dwight D. (Dwight David), 1890–1969. 3. Presidents—
United States—Biography. I. Richardson, Elmo. II. Richardson,
Elmo. Presidency of Dwight D. Eisenhower. III. Title. IV. Series.
E835.P26   1991
973.921′092—dc20   90-45952
                                                                              CIP

British Library Cataloguing in Publication data is available.

Printed in the United States of America
10 9 8 7 6 5 4 3 2

The paper used in this publication meets the minimum requirements
of the American National Standard for Permanence of Paper for
Printed Library Materials Z39.48–1984.

For
Donald R. McCoy

CONTENTS

FOREWORD

The aim of the American Presidency Series is to present historians and the general reading public with interesting, scholarly assessments of the various presidential administrations. These interpretive surveys are intended to cover the broad ground between biographies, specialized monographs, and journalistic accounts. As such, each will be a comprehensive, synthetic work which will draw upon the best in pertinent secondary literature, yet leave room for the author's own analysis and interpretation.

Volumes in the series will present the data essential to understanding the administration under consideration. Particularly, each book will treat the then current problems facing the United States and its people and how the president and his associates felt about, thought about, and worked to cope with these problems. Attention will be given to how the office developed and operated during the president's tenure. Equally important will be consideration of the vital relationships between the president, his staff, the executive officers, Congress, foreign representatives, the judiciary, state officials, the public, political parties, the press, and influential private citizens. The series will also be concerned with how this unique American institution—the presidency—was viewed by the presidents, and with what results.

All this will be set, insofar as possible, in the context not only of contemporary politics but also of economics, international relations, law, morals, public administration, religion, and thought. Such a broad approach is necessary to understanding, for a presidential administration is more than the elected and appointed officers composing it, since its work so often reflects the major problems, anxieties, and glories of the nation. In short, the authors in this series will strive to recount and evaluate the record of each administration and to identify its distinctiveness and relationships to the past, its own time, and the future.

The General Editors

PREFACE

"Poor Ike," President Harry S. Truman exclaimed gleefully as he contemplated the fate of his successor, "it won't be a bit like the Army." "He'll sit there," Truman predicted, "and he'll say, 'Do this! Do that!' *And nothing will happen.*"[1] Truman turned out to be a prophet, but not in the way he imagined. He anticipated not how Eisenhower would conduct his presidency, but the way many observers would evaluate it.

Much of the early writing on Eisenhower came to the conclusion that the general was beyond his depth in the presidency. Lacking political experience and abhorring politics, he failed to grasp the complexities of national issues. His wide grin and engaging demeanor could scarcely conceal his befuddlement when addressing tax policy, civil rights, or farm subsidies. When speaking extemporaneously, his statements, even on simple matters, were often so baffling that an assistant had to offer clarification so that listeners would understand the president's point, if indeed there was one beneath the verbiage. Rather than grapple with matters that puzzled or bored him, he acted as any general would—he delegated the task to a subordinate. John Foster Dulles thus handled foreign affairs; George M. Humphrey shaped economic policy; Sherman Adams took responsibility for a host of domestic matters. While his assistants governed, Eisenhower reserved his energies for golf, bridge, and fishing. The president presided over his administration, but he did not run it. As a result, the country simply drifted. Fortunately, though, the Eisenhower torpor coincided with a time in which there were few critical issues and little public desire to confront them. Eisenhower's only achievement, according to this view, was his ability to provide inertia at a time of national complacency.

During the 1970s, revisionists began to challenge these caustic conclusions, and by the end of the decade they had constructed a radically different interpretation of the Eisenhower presidency. Eisenhower, these scholars argued, only appeared to be a passive chief executive. He actually used his power vigorously and deftly, but often behind the scenes, to achieve his goals. Although he frequently let his associates take responsibility for decisions, in the Oval Office and the Cabinet Room he was an energetic and thoughtful leader who not only knew what his subordinates were doing, but also took charge of shaping the policies that they implemented. In addition to praising the president's methods of using power, the Eisenhower revisionists lauded the results the president achieved, especially in foreign affairs. Particularly notable was his success in extricating the United States from the Korean War and restraint in avoiding intervention in other conflicts, such as Indochina and Suez. The main tenets of revisionism dominated scholarship on the Eisenhower presidency throughout the 1980s. So powerful was their influence that Eisenhower's ranking in polls of presidential performance shot up from twenty-second in 1962 to as high as ninth in 1982.

A confluence of circumstances accounted for the emergence and appeal of Eisenhower revisionism. The opening of collections of official records and personal papers previously closed by security classification or donor restriction multiplied the sources available for the study of the Eisenhower presidency. Scholars gained access to new information that showed that the president's performance in meetings of the National Security Council or gatherings with congressional leaders was far more impressive than his obtuse responses to reporters' questions or his uninspiring speeches. Comparison of Eisenhower's actions with those of his successors also accounted for the favorable assessments of his presidency during the 1970s. At a time of widespread discontent with the "imperial presidency," restraint in the exercise of presidential power looked far more attractive than it had a decade earlier. After the disaster of Vietnam, the ability to avoid war seemed an achievement that had been far too little appreciated. After the travesty of Watergate, modesty and integrity in public officials had become virtues that could no longer be taken for granted. In many ways, then, Eisenhower looked far better a generation later simply because he had managed to avoid the excesses of those who succeeded him.

The new perspectives of revisionism rapidly made the first edition of this book outdated. Elmo Richardson published *The Presidency of Dwight D. Eisenhower* in 1979, a time when the openings at the Eisenhower Library were only beginning and the scholarship on the thirty-fourth president was still rather thin. Because of the subsequent explosion in writings on the Eisenhower presidency, a new edition seemed desirable so that the American Presidency Series, in accordance with its basic purpose, would again have a volume on Eisenhower that drew "upon the best in pertinent secondary literature."

Also in conformity with the goals of this series, this revised edition provides "the author's own analysis and interpretation." Many of those judgments take issue with the conclusions of the Eisenhower revisionists. Too often, it seems, revisionists mistook Eisenhower's cognizance of policies for brilliance and his avoidance of war for the promotion of peace. This edition, then, is part of a small but growing body of postrevisionist scholarship that argues that the Eisenhower presidency was more complex and not as successful as many revisionists have maintained. Yet it also accepts the basic revisionist argument that Eisenhower was a thoughtful and skillful leader.

Although two authors have their names on the title page of this book, their responsibilities in producing it were separate and distinct. Elmo Richardson alone wrote the first edition; Chester Pach alone drafted the revised edition. In producing this volume, I have preserved much of Richardson's organization. But many of the conclusions are new, and the narrative is almost entirely different.

Several people were particularly helpful in the writing of the revised edition of this book. I am indebted to Tom Branigar and Kathleen Struss of the Dwight D. Eisenhower Library. Special thanks go to Dan Barkley and Ingeburg Starr for help in finding government documents. Paula Malone and Pam LeRow typed the manuscript, and Donna Eades copyedited it. The staff at the University Press of Kansas was friendly, cooperative, and extremely efficient.

Beth Bailey always makes things easier for me simply by being the best of friends. While I was writing, she was always there whenever I needed sympathy or encouragement.

For more than two years, Mary Jane Kelley lived not only with me but also with the presence of Eisenhower while I was absorbed in research and writing. She put up with the intrusion and somehow made daily life run smoothly. Her understanding, help, and love mean more than I can ever express. I hope that it is some small consolation that the Eisenhower presidency—at least, in our household—is once again an event of the past.

For several years, Donald R. McCoy has been a wonderful friend and colleague. He has shared his counsel, wisdom, and lively conversation, often at his luncheon table, which justly deserves its fame as a local institution. The dedication is an expression of thanks for his exceptional generosity.

Chester J. Pach, Jr.

Lawrence, Kansas
July 1990

1

★ ★ ★ ★ ★

DUTY AND AMBITION

"I do not want to be president of the United States," Gen. Dwight
D. Eisenhower told a stream of prominent visitors to Supreme Headquarters Allied Powers, Europe, near Paris during the last half of 1951,
"and I want no other political office or political connection of any
kind."[1] While emphatic and sincere, Eisenhower's oft-repeated declaration did not discourage the American business leaders and politicians
who called upon him and urged a run for the White House. They told
him that the stalemated war in Korea and scandals in Washington had
divided the American people and besmirched the nation's prestige.
Federal controls on the economy, they cried, had taken the nation far
down the road to socialism. Yet these callers insisted that despite the
failings of the Truman administration, the only Republican who could
end the Democrats' twenty years of control of the White House was
Eisenhower. At stake in the next election, then, was nothing less than
the preservation of individual freedom, capitalism, and the two-party
system. These visitors implored Eisenhower to declare his candidacy for
the GOP presidential nomination in 1952.

The general was courteous but somewhat impatient with these
callers. Eisenhower's uneasiness came not from any disagreement with
his visitors' criticism of the Truman administration or doubts about his
ability to be a good president. Rather it arose from his reservations about
politics and his fidelity to duty. Eisenhower loathed the partisanship of
the political arena and lacked any burning desire to hold public office.
Furthermore, as supreme commander of North Atlantic Treaty Organi-

1

zation (NATO) military forces, he believed that he already had "a job of transcendent importance to the United States."[2] Most important, however, was his conviction that a military officer had no right to seek political office while still in uniform. So strong was this conviction that by late 1951 Eisenhower made a standard reply to those who urged him to declare his interest in the presidency. "For me to admit, while in this post, or to imply or even to leave open for interpretation by others a partisan political loyalty," he told advocates of an Eisenhower candidacy, "would properly be resented by thinking Americans and would be doing a disservice to our country, for it would interfere with the job to which the country has assigned me."[3]

Yet despite his scruples about the obligations of duty, Eisenhower did not categorically rule out a run for the White House. Seeking the nomination was improper, since it violated Eisenhower's long-standing principle that soldiers ought not to mix in politics. Accepting the summons of the nation to political office, however, accorded with Eisenhower's belief that the first obligation of a military officer was to serve. In late 1951, Eisenhower's admirers and associates labored to persuade the general that the American people were genuinely calling him to a higher, political service. Tempted but hesitant, Eisenhower struggled to reconcile conflicting thoughts about duty and ambition, politics and the military. By early 1952, Eisenhower had made up his mind. At age sixty-one, he entered politics, but he brought to this new endeavor the values and outlook he had forged during a remarkable military career.

Born 14 October 1890, in Denison, Texas, Eisenhower grew up in Abilene, Kansas, a small farm town located on the eastern edge of the Great Plains. His father, David, a quiet but stern man, worked as an engineer in a creamery; his mother, born Ida Stover in Virginia, was a religious pacifist whose firm but loving rearing of six sons made her, in Eisenhower's recollection, "by far the greatest personal influence in our lives."[4] Along with nightly family Bible readings, the brothers found a framework of certainty in their father's firm instructions and their mother's favorite axioms. Each child also learned to accept a share of responsibility for the running of the household by performing chores in the kitchen, garden, and barn. Dwight, or "Little Ike"—his next older brother, Edgar, was nicknamed "Big Ike"—at an early age showed a deliberate cast of mind, a seriousness leavened by the delight he took in hunting and fishing and playing competitive sports. Dwight also developed such a passion for historical epics—especially those about generals and battles—that in his high school yearbook it was predicted that he would become a professor of history. Edgar, this oracle prophesied, would be the president of the United States. In 1911, an appointment to the United States Military Academy at West Point, New York, provided Dwight with the opportunity for a free college education. Despite her religious convictions, his mother did not object.

Eisenhower was anything but a model cadet. Stubborn, mischievous, and possessed of a ferocious temper, he fell to the bottom of his class in discipline as a plebe and hardly improved his ranking during subsequent years. A heavy smoker, he routinely disregarded the academy's restrictions on cigarettes and paid heavily in demerits. He also had a fondness for lampooning the many academy rules that he considered unnecessary or silly. Once he and a friend obeyed an order to report to an upperclassman's room in full dress coats all too literally; they wore nothing else. If Eisenhower was something of a good-natured rebel against West Point's rigorous code of discipline, he was by no means a loner. He was always ready to flash an appealing smile and join in the comradeship of the barracks. He relished card games with a wide circle of friends, but football was his real love while he was a cadet. Just when he demonstrated enough skill on the gridiron to attract outside notice, however, he suffered a leg injury that ended his athletic career. From then on, he had to be content with expressing his enthusiasm for the sport by organizing and coaching football teams at posts where he was stationed.

Eisenhower graduated in 1915 with a commendable but by no means distinguished record. His disciplinary problems kept his overall ranking near the middle of his class, even though he did well in some academic subjects. One such area was English, in which he earned high grades for clear and logical writing. In other subjects that constituted the bulk of the West Point curriculum, such as engineering and military science, Eisenhower's performance was average. Yet even though Eisenhower generally did not excel in the classroom or on the training field, he left West Point steeped in the canons of professional officership. He learned to value not individual heroics or personal glory, but teamwork—disciplined and efficient management of the tasks of modern war. Politics, which, according to contemporary thought, was little more than the clash of narrow, partisan interests, was at odds with this corporate, scientific model of professional officership. Those who knew Eisenhower expected competence in living up to these values, but not greatness. "We saw in Eisenhower a not uncommon military type," one of his instructors recollected, "a man who would thoroughly enjoy his army life," but not one "who would throw himself into his job so completely that nothing else would matter."[5]

After securing a second lieutenant's commission in the infantry, Eisenhower experienced a mixture of disappointment and success in his personal and professional life. While stationed at Fort Sam Houston in San Antonio, Texas, he met and married Mamie Doud, a native Iowan whose family had moved to Denver. The early death of their first child, a son named Doud who was fondly known as Icky, haunted Eisenhower's thoughts until the last years of his life. A second son, John, was born in 1922 and raised not only with considerable affection, but also with all of the discipline of an army child. By then, Eisenhower had held a series of duty assignments that frustrated his ambitions and even threatened his career. His desire for combat duty in World War I was thwarted when the armistice was signed a week before he was scheduled to go overseas. At army training camps in the East, however, he developed important friendships with officers who had had wartime battle experience. One of them was George S. Patton, who preached the revolutionary advantages of the new weapons called tanks. Eisenhower shared this perspective and, like Patton, published an article in 1920 that advocated the development of more powerful tanks that could prevent a recurrence of the static trench warfare that had slaughtered millions of soldiers in the First World War. Such thinking, however, transgressed official doctrine, which relegated tanks to a supporting role in the infantry, and earned Eisenhower the enmity of the army hierarchy.

Eisenhower's career soon turned sharply upward, thanks to the assistance of Gen. Fox Conner. Impressed by Eisenhower's theories of tank warfare, Conner arranged for Eisenhower to serve as his executive officer in the Panama Canal Zone. Under Conner's tutelage, Eisenhower's enthusiasm for life and career revived after the twin blows of Icky's death and the controversy over the tank article. Eisenhower venerated Conner and much later called him "the ablest man I ever knew." He learned from Conner a maxim that he quoted repeatedly throughout his career, "Always take your job seriously, never yourself."[6] With Conner's recommendation, Eisenhower was assigned to the Command and General Staff School at Fort Leavenworth, Kansas, to study war-games theory. The appointment was a plum; Eisenhower was part of a group of the army's best officers selected for advanced study of warfare. Eisenhower seized the opportunity and graduated first in his class in 1925. Yet his reward for such excellent performance was a job as football coach at Fort Benning, Georgia. Again Conner intervened, and Eisenhower went to Washington, D.C., to serve first as an aide to Gen.

John J. Pershing and then as a student at the Army War College, an institution that trained the army's future leaders. After a year in France writing a guide to the battlefields on which American soldiers had fought during World War I, Eisenhower returned to Washington in 1929 and held a series of staff positions, culminating in an assignment as a personal aide to the chief of staff, Gen. Douglas MacArthur.

For seven years, and for better or worse, MacArthur was a major influence on Eisenhower's career. Brilliant, flamboyant, and tempestuous, MacArthur was one of the greatest—and most controversial—military leaders in American history. Eisenhower learned simply by watching the chief of staff in action and later recollected that without the administrative experience he gained while serving under MacArthur, he "would not have been ready for the great responsibilities of the war period."[7] MacArthur, in turn, lavishly praised his aide. Yet differing views on the boundary between military and political affairs placed strain on the relationship between the major and the general. By training and inclination, Eisenhower abhorred partisanship and stood aloof from political conflict. MacArthur, on the other hand, had presidential aspirations and relished political controversy. Eisenhower was disgusted by MacArthur's conduct during the Bonus March of 1932, when the chief of staff took personal command of troops and led a rout of the unemployed veterans who were camped near the Capitol. MacArthur believed that he had quelled an uprising by a dangerous army of Communist revolutionaries—an assertion for which there was no credible evidence—while Eisenhower believed that the general had taken himself and his staff perilously close to "the edge of partisan politics."[8]

Despite such friction, Eisenhower stayed with MacArthur when the general took up a new command in the Philippines in 1935. MacArthur's mission was to organize and train the army of the Philippine Commonwealth. Eisenhower would have preferred a troop assignment but decided not to protest when, as he recollected, MacArthur "lowered the boom on me." During the next four years, his duties ranged from making plans for the recruitment of Filipino soldiers to polishing the general's speeches and correspondence. MacArthur valued Eisenhower's dedication and staff abilities but privately denigrated his aide as lacking toughness. Eisenhower appreciated MacArthur's "determination and optimism" but often became enraged by his chief's inability to appreciate the practical problems of building an army from scratch.[9] Relations between the two deteriorated, and Eisenhower became all too familiar with MacArthur's "regular shouting tirades."[10] By the time war broke out in Europe in September 1939, Eisenhower was ready for reassignment. At the end of the year, he left Manila for Fort Lewis, Washington, and command of an infantry battalion of the Third Division.

As the Second World War engulfed Europe and Asia, Eisenhower began a spectacular rise to the top of the army hierarchy. In mid-1941, he went back to Fort Sam Houston as chief of staff of the Third Army and played a leading role in the largest peacetime maneuvers ever held by the army. Occurring in Louisiana and involving more than 400,000 soldiers, this field exercise tested the army's combat capabilities and revealed some deficiencies. (Among the most glaring was a lack of equipment that led to the use of trucks with signs that said "tank.") The maneuvers also demonstrated the brilliance of some officers, including Patton, who commanded an armored division, and Eisenhower, who helped prepare the plans for the victorious Third Army. For that achievement, Eisenhower earned his first star. This promotion to brigadier general, however, did not lead immediately to further field duties. Instead, five days after the Japanese attack on Pearl Harbor, Eisenhower was summoned to Washington by the chief of staff, Gen. George C. Marshall.

For several years, Marshall had followed Eisenhower's career and believed that he had acquired the knowledge and maturity to help shape the strategic plans for the defeat of Germany and Japan. When Eisenhower arrived at the War Department, Marshall greeted him with a somber description of the grave military situation in the Pacific and then abruptly asked, "What should be our general line of action?" Such directness was characteristic of Marshall, a man known for being blunt, austere, and demanding. After reflecting for several hours, Eisenhower reported that even though it would be impossible to send significant reinforcements, the army should still do everything within its capabilities to save MacArthur's garrison in the Philippines. Such a recommendation accorded with Marshall's thinking, but rarely did the chief of staff express praise; his approval came in the form of bigger assignments and promotion.[11] Eisenhower repeatedly passed Marshall's tests and within four months gained a second star and command of the Operations Division. He also absorbed Marshall's managerial philosophy, the two most important tenets of which were these: first, the decision maker must not be distracted by problems that subordinates should resolve for themselves; and second, the assistants must have ready the precise information needed to make decisions. Eisenhower never had a better teacher. "I wouldn't trade one Marshall for fifty MacArthurs," he confided to an aide.[12]

Despite his success as a staff planner, Eisenhower still coveted a field command—an assignment that Marshall seemed determined to deny him. "You are going to stay right here on this job and you'll probably never move," Marshall warned him soon after he arrived in Washington. Marshall finally did allow his subordinate to escape Washington in May 1942, but only on temporary duty to London to serve as the liaison between American and British strategists. What Eisenhower did not realize was that this brief assignment was another test—one he passed most impressively. Winston Churchill, the British prime minister, was extravagant in his praise and agreed with Marshall that Eisenhower would be a good choice to take charge of the buildup of American troops in Great Britain in preparation for an assault on Nazi-occupied Europe.[13] When the cross-channel attack that Marshall hoped would occur in 1942 was postponed in favor of an Allied invasion of North Africa, the British and American Combined Chiefs of Staff named Eisenhower the overall commander of the operation. In less than two years, Eisenhower had risen from an unknown lieutenant colonel in charge of a peacetime battalion to a renowned lieutenant general in command of an Allied invasion force in the greatest war in history.

Wartime command was Eisenhower's political education. Eisenhower quickly became skilled in selecting subordinates for field and staff positions and effective at bringing together people of many nationalities and differing perspectives to work for the common cause of victory. Even the most notoriously egocentric war leaders, such as Gen. Charles de Gaulle and Winston Churchill, yielded to the force of Eisenhower's logic and the charm of his personality. Eisenhower also used diplomatic skills to help lessen the persistent tensions between British officials, who favored an indirect strategy of tightening the ring around Nazi-occupied Europe, and American planners, who preferred a direct thrust across the English Channel into the heart of German military power. The differences continued as Eisenhower directed an invasion of Sicily in July 1943 and then an Allied campaign in Italy. A resolution finally occurred in November at the first meeting of the Big Three in Tehran, when President Franklin D. Roosevelt, Soviet Premier Josef Stalin, and Churchill agreed to open a second front against Hitler by launching a cross-channel assault. The most likely choice for supreme commander of operation OVERLORD was Marshall, but Roosevelt protested that he could not spare his organizer of victory. "Well, Ike," the president informed him when they met after the Tehran Conference, "you are going to command Overlord."[14]

In that high position, Eisenhower was no solitary leader, deciding grand strategy while surrounded by obsequious lieutenants. Instead he insisted that teamwork was the key to planning the greatest amphibious operation in military history. Eisenhower had little patience with "the intense personal outlook that most officers have upon even such a critical thing as war." He himself had to set aside his personal preferences at times to conform to the stipulations of Roosevelt and Churchill. He also realized that the success of OVERLORD depended on smooth relations with the Combined Chiefs of Staff, who allocated resources among the many theaters of a global war, and a phalanx of field commanders, who made their own on-the-spot tactical judgments within the framework of approved strategy. Teamwork also necessitated cooperation among armies, navies, and air forces. While this last requirement caused him some of his greatest headaches, Eisenhower ultimately achieved unity of command by extending his authority over all the armed forces that participated in OVERLORD.[15]

By dealing sympathetically with military and political leaders of many countries, Eisenhower encouraged the most important kind of teamwork. Problems arose between even the closest of allies, he recognized, and their resolution sometimes required "a great deal of patience and negotiation." Eisenhower applied this formula to his dealings with Bernard L. Montgomery, the British general who commanded the ground forces in operation OVERLORD. A hero of the North African campaign, Montgomery was temperamentally Eisenhower's opposite—aloof, prickly, and condescending. When difficulties arose after Allied troops landed on the Normandy beaches, Eisenhower suffered Montgomery's rudeness, checked his own temper, and repeatedly asked for cooperation. Some critics thought Eisenhower unwisely appeased Montgomery, but Eisenhower did not want personal friction to jeopardize Allied unity. Eisenhower also worked hard to smooth relations with the leader of the Free French, Gen. Charles de Gaulle. Although Eisenhower could be tough about essential matters, he appreciated that he could not merely give orders to many of his subordinates without offending national sensibilities. That the Americans, British, Canadians, French, Poles, and others worked together so smoothly in such a demanding military operation as OVERLORD was one of Eisenhower's greatest triumphs.

In handling recalcitrant American subordinates, such as George Patton, Eisenhower was far more blunt and direct, although ultimately forebearing. Upon learning that his old comrade had slapped a hospitalized enlisted man in Italy in mid-1943, he sternly, but privately, rebuked the general by pointing out that any further lapse of self-control might force him to relieve Patton of his command. He secured the silence of war correspondents who knew of the slapping incident by telling them that Patton's reassignment would hurt the Allied cause.

After Eisenhower selected him as one of his chief lieutenants in OVERLORD, Patton again caused a scandal by delivering a speech in which he predicted that the British and Americans would rule the world. Eisenhower exploded, and Patton apologized and promised to hold his tongue. Eisenhower endured heavy criticism in the newspapers for not firing his intemperate subordinate. But the subsequent bold actions of the Third Army in sweeping through the Nazi defenses in France ultimately justified, in Eisenhower's view, Patton's retention.

Despite his emphasis on teamwork, Eisenhower took final responsibility for the most important decisions. Collective effort on an unprecedented scale made possible the Allied invasion of Europe on D-Day, 6 June 1944, but it was up to just one man to determine when the plan would be set in motion. Eisenhower's terse "O.K., let's go" was the most admired of all his wartime decisions. In contrast, he never heard the end of criticism about his refusal to order Anglo-American units to try to capture Berlin before the Russians. Eisenhower believed that he had sound military reasons to justify his action. The Soviets, he argued, were much closer to the city. Furthermore, an advanced striking force of Anglo-American troops would have been vulnerable to flank attacks and to the severing of their supply lines. Berlin had symbolic importance, he conceded, but not enough to warrant action that seemed to him militarily unwise. Finally, the decision was in keeping with an agreement made by Roosevelt, Churchill, and Stalin at the Yalta Conference in February 1945, to divide Germany and Berlin into postwar occupation zones. Eisenhower thus concluded that the Americans and the British had little to gain and much to lose by making a race for Berlin and raising Soviet suspicions about future cooperation among the victors. Whether the issue was taking Berlin or launching OVERLORD, Eisenhower's foremost consideration was doing what would most effectively contribute to victory.

When the forces of Nazi Germany surrendered on 7 May 1945, Eisenhower gladly put down the grim burden of making life-and-death decisions. He savored the triumph of "the forces of human freedom." He also enjoyed the adulation not only of the American people when he returned home briefly in June, but also of the British, Soviets, and French when he visited the capitals of the victorious Allied nations. He was the greatest military hero of the war.[16]

The coming of peace in Europe, however, did not bring an end to his command responsibilities, only a change in them. As the leader of American occupation forces in Germany, Eisenhower performed onerous duties that often plunged him into political controversy. Following the Nazi surrender, newspaper and radio commentators repeatedly charged that the United States lacked a policy to guide its occupation of Germany. Eisenhower complained to Marshall that "much of this criticism arises from unthinking and uninformed people" who thought that because "the shooting has stopped," there was no reason for delay in establishing the "perfect democratic organization in Germany." The complex task of rooting out Nazi influence was made more difficult by a few of Eisenhower's subordinates, including Patton, the military governor of Bavaria. In defiance of Eisenhower's orders, Nazis continued to hold positions in local government in Bavaria, a practice that Patton insisted was necessary to prevent the complete breakdown of public order and the seizure of power by German Communists. In early October, Eisenhower finally relieved his insubordinate deputy, a step that enraged Patton's many admirers, including some who insisted that the Communists, not the Nazis, were now the real enemy of the United States. Another action that drew fire from those at home concerned about communism was Eisenhower's order, which complied with agreements made at the Yalta Conference, to repatriate displaced Soviet citizens found in the American occupation zone in Germany.[17]

Yet no issue that Eisenhower confronted at war's end had greater implications for Soviet-American relations or postwar security than whether to use the atomic bomb. Eisenhower had little, if any, influence on President Harry S. Truman's decision. Not until the final Big Three conference at Potsdam in mid-July did he even learn that scientists and engineers working under the direction of the army had been trying to develop a bomb since the beginning of the war. Secretary of War Henry L. Stimson informed him that the first bomb had just been successfully tested and that this revolutionary new weapon would be used to force the surrender of Japan. Eisenhower strenuously objected. Japan was already defeated and making overtures for peace, he protested, and the use of such a devastating weapon might tarnish the image of the United States at the moment of its greatest international triumph. Truman's mind was made up, however, before hearing Eisenhower's arguments. Truman believed that the bomb would shorten the war and save the lives of American soldiers. Furthermore, accepting the advice of Stimson, he believed that the bomb could be a "master card" in international relations, a weapon of such awesome force that it would give the United States a decisive advantage in peace negotiations with the Soviets.[18]

When Japan surrendered after the atomic bombing of Hiroshima and Nagasaki, Eisenhower informed Marshall that he yearned to escape "the headaches and the headlines." Marshall, who had served for six years as chief of staff, proposed to Truman that his one-time protegé become his successor. Such a position, Marshall asserted, was the only one "suitable to . . . [Eisenhower's] present rank and prestige." "The most 'suitable' position for me," Eisenhower replied, "is unquestionably a remotely situated cottage in a state of permanent retirement." Neither Marshall nor Truman, however, agreed with Eisenhower's assessment. In November 1945, Truman consented to Marshall's retirement and nominated Eisenhower as chief of staff.[19]

Eisenhower accepted his new position with little enthusiasm and soon found it "as bad as I always thought it would be." The job of chief of staff was far less satisfying and much more complicated than that of a theater commander, Eisenhower complained. To get almost anything done, he found, one had to overcome "personal hatreds, political and partisan prejudices, ignorance, [and] opposing ideologies." Furthermore, there seemed no respite from the duties of the office. In late 1946, Eisenhower confided in his diary that he was "arthritic, . . . overweight, and soft" and had had "no real exercise since the shooting stopped in Europe."[20] Several months later, he wrote to his wartime driver, Kay Summersby, that the only way he was able to get the time for the physical activity prescribed by his doctors was by "just walking out and letting things wait until I get back." Deluged with speaking invitations, Eisenhower found that he could accept only a minuscule portion of the offers, yet still seemed to "have the feeling that I am talking all the time."[21] The only reason he stayed on as chief of staff was "straight duty."[22]

For the army as well as for Eisenhower, peace brought difficult readjustment and fundamental change. Within two years, the army shrank from eight million to one million men and women. Demobilization, however, did not occur fast enough—at least at first—to please many Americans. Community groups organized "Bring Daddy Home" clubs, and soldiers rioted at several foreign posts. To calm the protests, Eisenhower repeatedly intervened to accelerate the return of overseas service personnel, while making sure that the army maintained the strength and expertise to carry out its occupation duties in Germany and Japan. In presiding over demobilization, Eisenhower stressed efficiency, a goal that also made him champion an important—and controversial— reform, the unification of the armed services. Only after lengthy and sometimes acrimonious negotiations among military and naval leaders did Congress approve the National Security Act in mid-1947, which separated the air force from the army and created the office of secretary of defense to coordinate the three services. Eisenhower hailed the legislation as a major step toward the teamwork among the army, navy, and air force that he considered essential to national defense. Also for reasons of efficiency, Eisenhower advocated—although unsuccessfully—

a program of universal military training to ensure that the United States would be able to mobilize rapidly in the event of war.

Eisenhower's greatest disappointment as chief of staff was the emergence of the Cold War with the Soviet Union. While commanding American occupation forces in Germany, Eisenhower established very friendly relations with Marshal Georgi Zhukov, the head of Soviet forces. After meeting Stalin in Moscow in August 1945, he predicted that the wartime cooperation between the United States and the Soviet Union would continue in peacetime. During his first months as chief of staff, he dismissed suggestions from his colleagues in the Pentagon that Russia would be the next enemy of the United States. The Soviets, he said, did not want war; they would need years to recover from the devastation of World War II, and they desired American economic aid. But by early 1947, Eisenhower's outlook had changed. Following the imposition of Communist regimes in Eastern Europe and Cold War crises over Iran, Greece, and Turkey, Eisenhower sadly concluded that "Russia is definitely out to communize the world." Because noncommunist nations were "under deadly, persistent, and constant attack," Eisenhower believed that the United States had to muster its moral, material, and military strength to meet the assault.[23]

Eisenhower insisted that the United States could meet the Soviet challenge only by using its resources wisely and efficiently. Even though he feared that the Russians aspired to world domination, Eisenhower doubted that war was imminent or inevitable. He reminded those who thought war likely that not only was the Soviet Union still suffering from the enormous losses of World War II, but also that it was achieving its goals quite effectively through much less risky tactics, such as subversion and political intimidation. In July 1947, for example, he chided a planning committee of the Joint Chiefs of Staff for recommending "a . . . virtual mobilization for war" to counter Soviet ambitions. Instead he advocated a program of preparedness that focused on "strengthening the economic and social dikes against Soviet communism rather than . . . preparing for a possibly eventual, but not yet inevitable, war." After President Harry S. Truman declared in March 1947 that "it must be the policy of the United States to support free peoples who are resisting attempted subjugation by armed minorities or by outside pressures," Eisenhower worried about the consequences of the Truman Doctrine. He thought that the United States should try to head off international crises through "positive, forehanded, and preventative action." Otherwise a series of costly international emergencies would overtax the American economy as well as increase Soviet power.

Meeting the Soviet challenge, in short, required balancing military strength against economic capacity.[24]

After a little more than two years of contending with international crises and interservice conflicts, Eisenhower gladly retired from his position as chief of staff in February 1948. No longer on active duty for the first time in thirty-three years, he savored the release from the daily pressures and responsibilities that he had known all his adult life. Eisenhower, however, did not relax; instead he immediately began writing a memoir of his experiences in World War II. Assisted by a small staff of editors and secretaries, Eisenhower completed a book of five hundred pages in an astounding two months. He was driven by the importance of the story he had to tell, which he summarized in the title, *Crusade in Europe.* He was also motivated by the financial rewards of the project, which provided him with the monetary security that he had never known on soldier's pay. Only after finishing the manuscript did he allow himself a vacation—golfing in Georgia and visiting his brother Milton in Kansas.

Eisenhower did not escape the Pentagon for long. In early 1949, Secretary of Defense James V. Forrestal persuaded him to serve as temporary presiding officer of the Joint Chiefs of Staff until Congress enacted legislation providing for a permanent chair. Forrestal made his request of Eisenhower because of deep and persistent divisions within the Joint Chiefs over the roles and missions of the army, navy, and air force and the share of each service in the defense budget. The quarreling disgusted Eisenhower, who found it "personal as well as organizational" with "all the earmarks of a vehicle by which rival personalities are struggling for prestige and power." He accepted the assignment mainly because of his great respect for Forrestal but worried that both the secretary of defense and the president believed that he had "some miraculous power to make some of these warring elements lie down in peace together."[25] At times Eisenhower actually exacerbated service divisions, since he tended to support the air force, usually at the expense of the navy, out of conviction that "we . . . must not fail to provide a respectable long range strategic bombing force" as a deterrent to war.[26] Difficult choices were unavoidable; Truman and his advisers in the Bureau of the Budget had imposed strict limits on defense spending—at first, $15 billion for fiscal year 1951, later reduced to $13 billion. Although the service chiefs bridled at these limitations, Eisenhower agreed with the president that to avoid deficits and inflation, national security expenditures had to be weighed against the requirements of a sound economy. He continually urged the chiefs not to use the size of their service's budget as the sole "measure [of] its importance to the country."[27] By mid-1949, Eisenhower had demonstrated no miraculous powers, but he did hammer out an agreement on defense spending for fiscal year 1951.

For Eisenhower, presiding officer of the Joint Chiefs was not just a temporary job that he relinquished in July 1949, but a secondary responsibility he held while serving as president of Columbia University. Eisenhower was installed in that academic position in October 1948, a year and a half after a group of the university's trustees headed by Thomas J. Watson, the president of International Business Machines Corporation, approached him with the offer. Eisenhower at first demurred. He believed that he was not even the most qualified member of his family for the job; Milton, the president of Kansas State College, certainly seemed a better choice. He also wanted to avoid tying himself down after his service as chief of staff was over. For that reason, he declined a simultaneous offer to head the Boy Scouts of America. But within a few weeks, Eisenhower changed his mind, mainly because of his interest in promoting "basic concepts of education in a democracy with particular emphasis upon the *American* system of democracy."[28]

As Columbia's president, Eisenhower was not generally successful in communicating with the university population. Although he defended faculty and academic integrity in that time of loyalty oaths and urged students to seek opportunity rather than security, he was unable to establish strong ties with the university's academics. No intellectual, he was not at home in a world of ideas. Limiting himself to the most important policy and administrative matters, Eisenhower remained aloof from Columbia's intellectual community, even inaccessible, some faculty members complained. Yet he was remarkably successful in presenting the university's best features to the public and in soliciting funds for its growth. Traveling across the country, he met with hundreds of alumni, most of them wealthy and prominent. They usually reacted enthusiastically to his portrayal of the university as one of the most important institutions of democracy.

So favorable was the response to his public speeches that many friends, associates, and even strangers urged Eisenhower to run for the presidency. Such advice was not new; it began when he was commanding Allied forces in North Africa. While fighting the Axis, Eisenhower curtly dismissed any talk about his presidential aspirations. "Once this war is won," he wrote to a friend in 1943, "I hope never again to hear the word 'politics.' "[29] But after the war, the question of his political aspirations followed Eisenhower as he made a hero's tour of cities across the United States. Truman even offered in June 1945 to help him secure the presidency in the next election, an offer that Eisenhower did not take seriously. Two years later, with the Democratic party deeply divided, Truman told Eisenhower that he was willing to accept the *second* spot on the national ticket if only the general would rescue the Democrats by accepting the top position.[30] Eisenhower rejected this extraordinary proposal. Repeatedly Eisenhower said that he had no political aspirations, although he left open the very slim possibility that duty to country might require him to accept a genuine draft.

Finally, he took himself out of the race categorically in January 1948 by making public a letter to Leonard Finder, a New Hampshire newspaper publisher who was drumming up support for him in the Republican party. "I am not available for and could not accept nomination to high public office," he wrote. "It is my conviction that the necessary and wise subordination of the military to civil power will be best sustained . . . when lifelong professional soldiers, in the absence of some obvious and overriding reasons, abstain from seeking high public office." Eisenhower expected that this letter would end speculation about his candidacy not just in 1948, but for the rest of his life. He believed that New York Governor Thomas E. Dewey, the leading Republican contender, would secure the nomination and the presidency. By the end of the Dewey administration in 1956, Eisenhower, who would be sixty-six, thought he would be too old to run for the White House.[31]

Dewey's unexpected defeat in November upset these calculations. Very quickly Eisenhower's boosters renewed their efforts. Their interest was whetted by the distinctly political overtones of Eisenhower's speeches and writings as a university president. He referred to an "ever-expanding federal government" and to extremist appeals to "selfish advantage" that ignored "the enduring truth that no part of our society may prosper permanently" unless the whole nation does. There were some citizens, he said, who believed themselves to be liberals but who, in fact, worked "unceasingly" for ideas that would advance American civilization "one more step toward total socialism, just beyond which lies total dictatorship."[32]

Eisenhower was undoubtedly giving serious thought during 1949 to the possibilities of political life. In July, Dewey told him that he was "a public possession" because of the popular affection that he enjoyed. Dewey also argued that Eisenhower was the only one who could prevent the country from going to hell in a "handbasket of paternalism, socialism, [and] dictatorship."[33] Dewey suggested that Eisenhower take

15

the first step toward the presidency by running as a Republican to succeed him as governor of New York. At the same time, Democratic leaders tried to induce Eisenhower, who had not publicly announced a party affiliation, to declare his candidacy as a Democrat for United States senator from New York. Eisenhower rejected both overtures but found it increasingly difficult to withstand the pressure that he enter the political arena. At the end of the year, he wrote emphatically in his diary, "I am not, now or in the future, going willingly into politics." Yet Eisenhower's callers kept telling him a run for the presidency was his duty. And as he conceded, "I cannot say to anyone that I would *not* do my best to perform a *duty*."[34]

If Eisenhower was uncertain that duty obligated him to enter politics, he was sure that it required him to serve the nation when the United States entered the Korean War. In June 1950, Truman ordered General MacArthur to use American forces in Japan to halt a North Korean invasion of South Korea. Eisenhower endorsed the president's decision and rushed to Washington to offer his help to Pentagon officials who were planning the war effort. He told them that "in a fight we . . . can never be too strong," and so they should prepare "for whatever may happen, even if it finally came to the use of an A-bomb (which God forbid)."[35] Privately, however, he deplored the lack of readiness of United States armed forces. He blamed "the civilian authorities of our government" for failing to heed military recommendations for the creation of "a fine, properly balanced, effectively commanded and reasonably strong task force" that would be capable not only of rapidly meeting aggression but also deterring potential enemies.[36] Such criticism ignored the services' persistent inability during the late 1940s to agree about the proper allocation of military resources.

Because of his desire to help build the military strength that could prevent future aggression, Eisenhower accepted Truman's invitation to take command of the armed forces of NATO. In April 1949, the United States and eleven other nations had signed the North Atlantic Treaty, which obligated members through "self-help and mutual aid" to "develop their individual and collective capacity to resist armed attack."[37] For Truman and Eisenhower, the attack on Korea made imperative the strengthening of defenses in Western Europe, lest the concentration of American military strength in East Asia encourage the Soviets to test the vulnerability of NATO. Eisenhower was the ideal choice to take charge of NATO's military efforts, not just because of his experience but also because of his conviction that the alliance was "about the last remaining chance for the survival of Western civiliza-tion." Truman and his advisers were also counting on Eisenhower's reputation to help win acceptance at home and abroad of two controver-sial proposals: the rearmament of West Germany and its integration into NATO and the permanent stationing of American military units in Europe under NATO command. Taking a leave of absence from Colum-bia, Eisenhower went to Paris in January 1951 to begin what he thought was the most important "job in the world today."[38]

While Eisenhower was abroad, the war became unpopular at home. The draft, shortages of consumer goods, and inflation caused grumbling and discontent. But Truman's direction of the war effort produced anger, outrage, and partisan division. The president's most controver-sial action was the firing of General MacArthur in April 1951. To Truman, MacArthur was insubordinate, a danger to the fundamental principle of civilian supremacy over the military. To many Americans, the general was a martyr, brusquely dismissed because of his unwilling-ness to tolerate the president's policy of limited war that produced a stalemate. MacArthur returned home to a thunderous welcome, while Truman's approval rating in the Gallup Poll sank to a new low of 23 percent. During congressional hearings following MacArthur's return, Republicans excoriated Truman for his "no-win" policies of warfare. Eisenhower had no desire to become involved in such a contentious issue as MacArthur's dismissal. He carefully avoided commenting, as he explained to a friend, "in every language of which I have ever heard."[39]

Extremism flourished in those times of discontent and bitterness, and no demagogue exploited the fears and frustrations of the American people more relentlessly than Senator Joseph R. McCarthy (R., Wis.). McCarthy offered a simple, scary, and scandalous explanation for American difficulties in the Cold War and in the hot war of Korea: a conspiracy of Communist agents or sympathizers had penetrated the highest reaches of the federal government. McCarthy first grabbed headlines in February 1950 by charging that the State Department was infested with Communists, subversives who continued to hold sensitive positions because of the lethargy—or worse, sympathy—of high officials in the Truman administration. McCarthy was repeatedly unable to prove his accusations. A Senate subcommittee concluded in mid-July that his charges amounted to "a fraud and a hoax" and that McCarthy used "the totalitarian technique of the 'big lie' employed on a sustained basis."[40] Yet McCarthy maintained his popularity by crying smear and coverup and by pointing to the arrest, also in July 1950, of Julius and Ethel Rosenberg for allegedly passing atomic secrets to the Soviet Union. As the Korean War continued to grind up American infantry units without producing victory, McCarthy pointed his finger at the highest officials in the Truman administration. The most notorious traitor in Washington, he screamed, was none other than Secretary of State Dean Acheson. In a speech to the Senate, McCarthy asserted that wounded veterans ought to say to the secretary of state, "Dean, thousands of American boys have faced those twin killers [Communist China and North Korea] because you and your crimson crowd betrayed us."[41] After MacArthur's dismissal, McCarthy declared that Secretary of Defense George C. Marshall—Eisenhower's mentor and a paragon of loyalty to all who knew him—was part of the nefarious Communist conspiracy. McCarthy found that bigger lies produced bigger headlines and bigger influence in Republican party politics.

Eisenhower was contemptuous of those who peddled fear and hatred in the guise of patriotism. He called McCarthy and his followers "disciples of hate." Although he believed that there was "plenty for which to criticize the administration legitimately and decently and strongly," he also worried that McCarthy's relentless attacks on the Truman administration would "backfire" by arousing sympathy for the president as an "underdog."[42]

Eisenhower worried even more about the foreign policy views of Senator Robert A. Taft (R., Ohio). Taft was a powerful figure in the GOP and the leading candidate for his party's presidential nomination in 1951. A nationalist on questions of foreign affairs, Taft criticized the Truman administration's heavy spending on economic and military aid. He also worried that American treaty commitments might discourage allies from strengthening their own defenses and feared that executive action was eroding congressional prerogatives in foreign and military policy. During a visit to Washington in early 1951, Eisenhower discussed these issues with Taft in a secret meeting at the Pentagon. At the time, Taft and other Republicans were raising a furor in the Senate over Truman's plan to commit American troops to NATO. Eisenhower was ready to issue a strong statement removing his name from further political consideration if Taft expressed even a general commitment to collective security. Despite Eisenhower's pleas, Taft refused. "This aroused my fears that isolationism was stronger in the Congress than I had previously suspected," Eisenhower recollected. His disappointment over Taft's obstinacy eventually made him more willing to consider pleas to rescue the Republican party from such retrogressive leadership.[43]

Beginning in mid-1951, influential Republicans started to organize support for an Eisenhower candidacy. The leader of this movement was Dewey, who took himself out of the running for the nomination and made sure that the New York delegation to the national convention was pledged to Eisenhower. Dewey also helped arrange for Harold E. Stassen, the former governor of Minnesota, to enter the race in order to prevent Taft from developing an insurmountable lead. While Stassen insisted that he was not a "stalking horse" for another candidate, privately he assured the general that he would "not only become your lieutenant but shall deliver to you . . . all the strength that has been pledged to me" once Eisenhower announced his candidacy.[44] In November, Dewey also joined with Harry Darby, a GOP national committeeman from Kansas, Gen. Lucius D. Clay, a close friend of Eisenhower, and Senator James Duff of Pennsylvania, among others, to form an organization to direct the draft-Eisenhower movement. Their choice for campaign manager was Senator Henry Cabot Lodge, Jr., of Massachusetts, a leading Republican internationalist who had met Eisenhower while serving in the army during World War II.

Eisenhower paid close attention to these developments, but he refused to sanction them directly. The stumbling block was duty. As he explained repeatedly to those who beckoned him to run, any partisan activity was incompatible with his responsibilities as supreme commander of NATO. He thought that to express an interest in the presidency while in uniform, as historian H. W. Brands has written, "would smack of Caesarism, or at least MacArthurism, and it would betray, in a sense, the hundreds of thousands of ordinary soldiers who had fought and died to preserve freedom, not to put Dwight Eisenhower in the White House."[45] Eisenhower recognized the frustrations of those who so insistently urged him to make a clear statement of his intentions. "I know that you understand . . . that I am not trying to duck any difficult question, or to be evasive or coy," he told Clay. "My present duty is to help develop the defensive power of twelve countries. If I ever have to do any other, I shall have to be *very clear* that I know it to be *duty*."[46]

During the fall of 1951, Eisenhower gave his backers significant, albeit limited, encouragement, though he still did not cross the boundary he established between politics and military affairs. In September, he replied to Lodge's appeal for permission to enter his name in the presidential primaries by promising to "think the matter over." In retrospect, Eisenhower considered his remark "a turning point," since "for the first time I had allowed the smallest break in a regular practice of returning a flat refusal to any kind of proposal that I become an active participant."[47] Two months later, he wrote to his friend Clifford Roberts to suggest names for an advisory committee that Roberts was forming to counsel Eisenhower on political matters. Eisenhower emphasized that

19

the committee's existence had to be confidential, since he did not want anyone to think that he intended the advisory group to engage in anything other than mere "thinking."[48] Yet it was clear that Eisenhower had moved to the brink of entering the presidential race.

As the beginning of the election year approached, Eisenhower finally made a critical decision. In reply to Lodge, he pledged not to repudiate any effort made by the senator and his allies to secure the nomination for him. "I must be completely frank," Eisenhower wrote to Lodge on 12 December, "particularly in emphasizing again the limitations that propriety, ethics, and custom impose upon me. . . . But there is a vast difference between responding to a duty imposed by a National Convention and the seeking of a nomination." This was the statement that Lodge had been seeking for months. In early January 1952, the senator announced that he would enter Eisenhower's name in the Republican primary in New Hampshire. Eisenhower then issued a statement of his own in which he reiterated his duty to NATO, one that he would not leave unless called to a more important service, such as accepting the Republican nomination for president. He expected the call to come only from the GOP, since, as he finally revealed, he considered himself a Republican. Eisenhower thus satisfied his scruples about not seeking the nomination. Instead he would let others do so in his behalf.[49]

But the pressure mounted steadily on Eisenhower to reconsider his hands-off approach to the nomination. When the general saw a film of an Eisenhower-for-president rally at Madison Square Garden in early February, he told Clay that he was "deeply touched, not to say moved." "It's a real experience," he confided in his diary, "to realize that one could become a symbol for many thousands of the hope they have!!"[50] The results in New Hampshire were highly encouraging. A month later, Eisenhower won 50 percent of the vote and easily defeated both Taft and Stassen. Eisenhower was so astonished by his strong showing the following week as a write-in candidate in Stassen's home state of Minnesota that he announced he was reconsidering his decision not to campaign for the nomination. Truman's announcement at the end of March that he would not be a candidate for reelection eliminated whatever apprehension Eisenhower might have felt about having to run against the commander in chief. Finally, the importuning of friends and advisers such as Dewey, who warned that if Eisenhower stayed on the sidelines the GOP might turn to MacArthur, forced the general to act. On 12 April, he announced that he would resign his NATO command in June and return to the United States to campaign for the Republican nomination.

Long after he left the presidency, Eisenhower told an interviewer, "My hand was forced by Lodge."[51] It was not. He had already decided on a set of requirements that had to be met before he would venture into partisan politics; at the end of 1951 those circumstances were at hand. During the preceding years, domestic and international issues had caused Eisenhower to enlarge his concept of a soldier's duty to include a dimension beyond military responsibilities. As early as September 1948, he wrote to advise Forrestal that the time had arrived "when everyone must begin to think in terms of his possible future duty and be as fully prepared for its performance as is possible."[52] For Eisenhower, the NATO command was both that duty and a time of preparation. While in Paris, he wrote to his brother Milton about the possibility of a larger duty; and in December 1951 he admitted to Lodge that he hoped he would always be ready to accept any duty, including one "which would, by common consent in our country, take priority over the one I am now performing."[53] Eisenhower, in short, made sure that his entry into presidential politics occurred on his own timetable and accorded with his principles.

Having entered the political arena by waiting until circumstances caught up with his scruples, Eisenhower perhaps continued to hope that the nomination would seek him. If he clung to this naive belief, it was rudely shattered by the strength and aggressive tactics of the Taft Republicans. They scoffed at Eisenhower as a superficial candidate who stood for nothing more than "mother, home and heaven." "Draft Ike," they cried in a none too subtle allusion to the general's support of universal military training, "and he will draft you."[54] They whispered nefarious stories about a wartime affair with Kay Summersby and a letter to Marshall asking him to approve a divorce from Mamie so that he could marry his paramour. A delegation from one midwestern state even visited Eisenhower in Abilene to ask him if his wife was an alcoholic. "The truth of the matter," he reportedly replied, "is that I don't think Mamie has had a drink for something like eighteen months."[55]

Eisenhower was used to the customs and behavior of army life, but not to the political maneuvering that he found in July 1952 at the Republican National Convention in Chicago. While he watched the proceedings on television in his hotel suite, his campaign staff tried to cut into Taft's apparent lead. Heading the Eisenhower forces were Lodge and New Hampshire governor Sherman Adams. They concentrated on securing disputed delegates from Georgia and Texas, which, if awarded to Taft, might have locked up the nomination for the senator. Because Taft supporters controlled the credentials committee, Lodge

21

conceived of the stratagem of placing the decision in the hands of the convention under the terms of a Fair Play resolution. The Eisenhower camp insisted that they were leading the party to the moral high ground and protested that the party could not stand before the voters promising to end Democratic corruption if its own hands were dirty. Fair Play, however, was little more than a shrewd power play to win the nomination for Eisenhower. The critical votes to pass the resolution came from the California delegation through the timely intervention of Senator Richard M. Nixon, who thereby ensured himself the vice-presidential nomination. Because of the victory of Fair Play, the balloting for the presidential nomination was almost an anticlimax. At the end of the first roll call, Eisenhower went over the top when Minnesota switched its votes to him from favorite son Stassen.

In triumph, Eisenhower was generous and conciliatory. His first action was to visit Taft and ask for the senator's support. In the hotel lobby, diehard Taft supporters booed the victorious candidate until one of the senator's aides urged the crowd to desist. Eisenhower returned to his hotel somewhat shaken by the reception, but determined to do all he could to heal the wounds of the bruising contest for the nomination. He performed a far sadder duty when he drafted a letter resigning his five-star rank, thereby becoming a civilian for the first time in almost forty years. On the evening of 11 July, however, he appeared before the convention beaming and resolute and promised that he would lead another crusade, this one for freedom in the United States.

Eisenhower appointed Adams as his campaign chief of staff, but he retained final authority on all important matters. He supplemented the advice that he received from the political professionals on his staff by conferring with friends and business leaders who had previously counseled him on political matters. He considered their suggestions thoroughly, but many of the most important decisions were entirely his own. He insisted, for example, on campaigning in the South, even though party leaders had crossed off that region as irretrievably Democratic. He also decided to invite Taft to a meeting at his home in New York in which he formally received the senator's endorsement.

Campaigning was a new experience, but Eisenhower quickly mastered its techniques. He adopted much of the rhetoric that Republicans had honed to perfection during the past four years. Indeed many of his remarks aimed at assuring GOP conservatives—those who had backed Taft—that his positions on domestic affairs and even on some foreign matters conformed to their principles. While he focused on the main issues of Korea, communism, and corruption in Washington, he preferred to discuss, as he said, consequences rather than personalities. He thus refused to criticize Truman directly or to attack his Democratic opponent, Governor Adlai E. Stevenson of Illinois, by name. By adhering to these rules, Eisenhower persuaded himself, but not his Democratic adversaries, that he had risen above partisanship.

On the stump, Eisenhower concentrated on three themes: the dangers of power centralized in the federal government; the debilitating influence of government domination of the economy; and the inadequacy of the U.S. response to Communist threats to freedom around the world. In these matters he urged the restoration of initiative to the states and local communities; an equitable partnership between the federal government and private enterprise in the development of the economy; responsible federal funding of the nation's essential needs; and in foreign affairs, a reliable internationalism and a careful balancing of resources against commitments. To the disappointment of many conservative members of his party, Eisenhower did not advocate dismantling the complex of federal social welfare measures enacted during the New Deal and Fair Deal nor did he make what he considered a demagogic promise to cut taxes.

In mid-September a scandal involving Nixon threatened to destroy Eisenhower's chances for the White House. Newspaper reports charged that the vice-presidential nominee was the beneficiary of a secret slush fund raised by wealthy California industrialists. When the story broke, most of Eisenhower's top campaign aides suggested that the general jettison Nixon in order to preserve his own image and electoral chances. The reporters traveling with Eisenhower recommended by an overwhelming margin that the only possible course of action was to dispose of the tainted nominee. Some editorial writers and a few leading Republicans suggested that Nixon should save Eisenhower any further embarrassment by immediately resigning from the ticket.

Eisenhower, however, would not be stampeded by the press, his staff, or even Nixon. Weighing his options, he reasoned that if the senator was precipitously dropped from the ticket, party unity might be threatened since Nixon was extremely popular with GOP conservatives because of his pursuit of alleged subversives in high government positions. On the other hand, if Nixon was guilty of financial impropriety and not promptly dropped, the party's appeal to morality would be undermined. Because of these perils, Eisenhower avoided hasty action and tried to reserve final decision to himself. As Eisenhower deliberated, Nixon waited in vain for an unqualified statement of support from his running mate. When Eisenhower finally telephoned, Nixon could not contain his anger and resentment. "There comes a time in matters like this," he scolded the general, "when you've either got to shit or get off the pot."[56] Eisenhower was taken aback, not by the profanity, but by the impertinence of his running mate. After pausing to regain his composure, he told Nixon to go on national television to refute the charges. Based on the public reaction, which would take several days, Eisenhower would decide what to do.

While Nixon's political future hung in the balance, his relationship with Eisenhower deteriorated. The two had not been close even before the slush-fund crisis. They had first met in 1949, when Nixon, then a member of the House of Representatives, had briefed Eisenhower on the dangers of Communist subversion. Although he was only in his second term in Congress, Nixon had gained considerable attention for his role in the House Un-American Activities Committee's investigation of Alger Hiss, a former State Department official who was eventually convicted of perjury for denying that he had provided secret government documents to Soviet agents. The two talked only a few more times before the 1952 convention, but Nixon impressed Eisenhower's top campaign strategists as a desirable choice for the vice-presidency. Only thirty-nine, he brought youth to the ticket. He was an internationalist like Eisenhower, but he appealed to the conservative wing of the GOP as well because of his zeal for hunting Communists in government. With his hard-hitting, partisan style—Nixon had waged a viciously effective campaign for a Senate seat from California in 1950 against the "Pink Lady," Helen Gahagan Douglas—Nixon could rouse the GOP faithful with denunciations of Truman and Stevenson, while Eisenhower remained above the battle. Eisenhower strategists counted on Nixon to be a real asset in California, a state that was important for Eisenhower to carry in November. Eisenhower chose Nixon, then, for good political reasons, but not because of the strength of any personal ties. Indeed, after the convention Nixon did not enter Eisenhower's inner circle and played no significant role in shaping campaign strategy. Eisenhower tended to treat Nixon as something of a junior officer, someone who had important responsibilities yet a distinctly subordinate position. During the slush-fund scandal, this inequality and lack of intimacy only exacerbated tensions as both Nixon and Eisenhower maneuvered to gain control of their respective political fates.

As the hour of Nixon's speech approached, Eisenhower decided to try to force Nixon from the ticket. Distressed by the seriousness of the allegations of financial improprieties, Eisenhower told his advisers that he wanted Nixon to announce his resignation at the end of the speech. Choosing to act obliquely, he said that Dewey should deliver the bad news to Nixon. Dewey made the call, only to learn that Nixon was in his hotel room "crying his eyes out." Unwilling to hang up without delivering his message, Dewey held the phone until Nixon could compose himself. Stunned by the governor's message, Nixon finally stammered that it was too late to change his televised remarks. Then, summoning his courage, he defiantly declared that Dewey should tell the Eisenhower campaign staff that he had no idea of what he might do when he went on the air. "If they want to find out," he snapped, "they'd better listen to the broadcast."[57]

Nixon gave a brilliant performance that saved his place on the ticket, but he did not salvage his relationship with Eisenhower. To some listeners, the Checkers speech seemed maudlin and corny, memorable primarily for Nixon's bathetic promise that no matter what happened he would not return the cocker spaniel named Checkers that he had received as a gift and that his daughters adored. To many viewers, however, the speech was the direct, sincere, and heart-felt plea of a common man who was asking for public understanding to help over-come a scurrilous accusation. In an effort to control his own political destiny, Nixon urged his viewers to wire their preferences about whether he should stay on the ticket to the Republican National Committee, not to Eisenhower. The general resented Nixon's end run but nonetheless recognized that Nixon had won his case. He summoned Nixon to a meeting the next day at his campaign stop in Wheeling, West Virginia. After mounting the steps to Nixon's airplane, Eisenhower greeted his running mate by saying, "You're my boy." For both, the incident was over. But Nixon never could overcome his belief that Eisenhower had kept him hanging, and Eisenhower never forgot Nixon's disrespectful language and attempted insubordination.[58]

Even before the turmoil over the Nixon scandal had abated, a second controversy undermined the Eisenhower campaign. The difficul-ties were brought on by Eisenhower's dealings with Joseph McCarthy. Although Eisenhower thoroughly agreed with McCarthy's objective of expelling subversives from government jobs, he detested the senator's surly, vicious methods. And nothing McCarthy did infuriated Eisen-hower more than the senator's denunciation of General Marshall as a traitor who had abandoned China to communism. In reply to McCarthy, Eisenhower delivered a moderate but certain defense of Marshall in a speech in Denver. As the campaign train moved toward the senator's home grounds in Milwaukee, Eisenhower planned to repeat his defense of Marshall while McCarthy was on the platform. Enthusiastic campaign aides passed the word to reporters that McCarthy would get his comeuppance. Before the speech, Eisenhower met with McCarthy and gave him an angry and profane lecture that left the senator stunned.

Then Eisenhower changed his mind. Walter Kohler, the Republican governor of Wisconsin, urged him to remove the passage about Marshall from the speech. The candidate's feelings about Marshall were already on record, Kohler argued, and to raise the matter again would point to differences within the party and embarrass everyone else on the platform. Eisenhower accepted that counsel, and the reporters did not learn of the change until they heard the speech. Worse, since Eisenhower lambasted the Truman administration for sheltering traitors in Washington, it seemed that the candidate had fully embraced McCarthy's cause. He had not, but the incident was the low point of the campaign. It also raised serious questions about Eisenhower's willingness to confront controversial issues, even those about which he cared deeply.

Referring to the Nixon and Marshall episodes, the Democrats added timidity and indecision to their portrait of Eisenhower. Their caricature also showed him to be dim-witted and, compared to Stevenson, lacking in executive experience. These charges were predictable and largely ineffective. The repeated warnings that Eisenhower was a militarist also redounded against their advocates. No campaign issue better summed up the nation's disenchantment, doubt, and dislocation than the war in Korea. It had cost lives, money, and resources, yet after two years of fighting there was nothing better than stalemate. Many voters blamed this dismal situation on what they believed was the ineptitude and disloyalty of the decision makers in the Truman administration. Instead of making Americans distrust military leaders, the war made them view favorably the prospect of a soldier in the White House.

Because of his NATO assignment, Eisenhower had not evaluated the situation in Korea firsthand. Early in the campaign, therefore, he decided that he would go to the battle front once the people had elected him. He waited, however, until late in the campaign before announcing that he would make the trip. The overwhelmingly favorable response buoyed Republican hopes, but Democrats denounced the pledge as little more than demagoguery. In private, Eisenhower himself expressed doubts about the wisdom of the statement. Some citizens, he thought, might conclude that he could magically bring victory in Korea. Worse, he feared, they might assume that all other national security and foreign policy matters would be handled that same way. Political analysts, however, later found that the pledge to visit Korea was an important factor in Eisenhower's election.

On 4 November 1952, the newcomer to politics received 33.9 million votes, or 55.1 percent of the ballots. He won the electoral votes of every state except for one outside the South; three southern states went to the Republicans for only the second time since Reconstruction. The morning after the election, a banner was hung from the balcony of an old brownstone house in the Beacon Hill section of Boston; it read simply, "Thank God."[59] Across the nation in the Pacific Northwest, citizens believed that "the course of history" had been changed by an election that was "so very necessary."[60]

The victory was a stunning affirmation of Eisenhower's personal appeal. While a strong majority of Americans "liked Ike," they gave the Republicans a much smaller margin of victory in Congress. Although Eisenhower always resented the suggestion that Americans would cast their votes for president on such a superficial basis as the candidate's personality, there is no doubt that Eisenhower's campaign capitalized on his personal attributes. His genial manner and broad smile charmed millions of voters. His reputation as a hero in a war that produced a decisive Allied victory certainly influenced those who were upset by the deadlock in Korea. His image as a candidate who thought only of principle at a time when political scandals embarrassed the Truman administration appealed to those who had grown weary of government that seemed only to cater to partisan interests. Eisenhower, in short, managed to present himself as a hero whose most notable qualities were the perfect antidote for the nation's ills.

2

★ ★ ★ ★ ★

ORGANIZING THE PRESIDENCY

"My first day at the president's desk," Dwight D. Eisenhower wrote in his diary on 21 January 1953. "Plenty of worries and difficult problems. But . . . today [just seems] like a continuation of all I've been doing since July 1941—even before that."[1] For Eisenhower politics was new, but the demands of the presidency seemed familiar. As supreme Allied commander and army chief of staff, Eisenhower became highly experienced in managing large organizations, reconciling divergent factions, choosing subordinates who could act responsibly, and making decisions on the most vital issues. From his military career, Eisenhower derived a set of beliefs—the importance of teamwork, the need for clear lines of authority, an abhorrence of partisanship—that shaped his presidency. Contemporaries often misunderstood Eisenhower's style of leadership; they mistook, for example, his delegation of authority for his abdication of it. Despite these misapprehensions, Eisenhower was in control of his presidency from its inception. Indeed during the months between his election and inauguration, he carefully organized an administration that reflected his style of leadership and his assessment of the needs of the nation.

The transition from the Truman to the Eisenhower presidency was anything but smooth. Truman wanted "an orderly transfer of authority" and took the unprecedented step of inviting his successor to the White House. But bitterness between the president and the president-elect impeded cooperation. Truman resented Eisenhower's criticism of his foreign and military policy and considered the pledge to visit Korea the rankest form of demagoguery. Eisenhower, in turn, regarded Truman as an inveterate partisan who had besmirched the dignity of his office. When the two men met on 18 November, their conversation was brief and chilly. Truman thought the advice that he offered about how to organize the White House staff ''went into one ear and out the other.'' Eisenhower believed that Truman had little to say that was useful or informative. The two did not meet again until inauguration day, when they had an even nastier exchange. Eisenhower told Truman that he had declined to attend the last inaugural for fear of upstaging Truman. Truman curtly replied, ''Ike I didn't ask you to come—or you'd been here.'' Although neither remembered, Eisenhower did attend the inauguration and met privately with Truman later that day. The animosity between the two had grown so strong that it even distorted their memories.[2]

Eisenhower's differences with Truman were philosophical as well as personal. Eisenhower condemned the Fair Deal, the program of domestic reform that Truman presented to Congress at the beginning of his second term in 1949. Building on the foundation of Franklin D. Roosevelt's New Deal and his own proposals for domestic legislation during his first administration, Truman proposed a series of measures that aimed at providing ''every segment of our population and every individual'' with a fair deal from government. Central to the Fair Deal was a sweeping new civil rights bill, which, among other things, banned the levying of poll taxes and discrimination in interstate commerce and imposed federal criminal penalties for lynching. Truman also asked Congress to approve federal health insurance, aid to elementary and secondary schools, and subsidies to boost farmers' incomes. In addition, he urged modification of the Taft-Hartley Act of 1947, legislation that was anathema to organized labor because it outlawed the closed shop and empowered the federal courts to grant injunctions should a strike or lockout create a national emergency. Truman got none of these Fair Deal measures through Congress. The opposition of Republicans and conservative Democrats was too strong; liberal supporters of the Fair Deal were neither numerous enough nor sufficiently adept at legislative compromise. Among the few Fair Deal measures enacted was watered-down legislation for the construction of public housing and an increase in the minimum wage from forty cents to seventy-five cents per hour, but at the cost of reducing the number of eligible workers by 500,000.[3]

Despite this meager legislative record, Eisenhower still worried about the philosophy that underlay the Fair Deal. He considered the Fair

Deal little more than the opportunistic accommodation of various interest groups—unions, farmers, the elderly, blacks—each of which placed selfish needs ahead of the common good. Rather than mediating among special interests, Truman pandered to them, in Eisenhower's view. While Eisenhower acknowledged the necessity for social welfare measures that protected the poor or disadvantaged, he nevertheless feared that Truman had gone too far toward creating the impression that "only government can bring us happiness, security and opportunity."[4] However laudable Truman's intentions, his actions were dangerous. "A paternalistic government," Eisenhower warned, "can gradually destroy, by suffocation in the immediate advantage of subsidy, the will of a people to maintain a high degree of individual responsibility." The result would be a dangerous concentration of power in the federal government that could threaten private enterprise and, in turn, "every human right we possess."[5] So much did Eisenhower dislike Truman's conduct of office that he later explained his decision to run for the presidency as "offering myself as a political leader to unseat the New Deal-Fair Deal bureaucracy in Washington."[6]

Truman's leadership, Eisenhower believed, dangerously aggravated the fault lines of a modern, complex society, such as the United States. Industrialization produced great wealth but also created conflict between capital, labor, and management. These divisions were not fatal, Eisenhower assured the American Bar Association on Labor Day 1949. Because it produced such enormous material bounty—enough to raise labor into the middle class—capitalism would not collapse from its own contradictions, as Marx had predicted. Shortsightedness and selfishness, however, continued to threaten free enterprise and human freedom. "If we do not eliminate selfish abuse of power by any one group . . . ," he warned, "selfish retaliation by other groups will ensue."[7] The federal government thus should not yield, Eisenhower insisted, to the demands of corporate interests that wanted to repeal taxes and regulations supporting modest and necessary welfare programs, such as Social Security and unemployment insurance. Such measures, he argued, allayed class antagonisms and so served the common good. Nor, he asserted, should the federal government embrace, as it had during the Truman administration, the cause of special interests, since it could do so only by acquiring unwarranted power and interfering "more than is necessary in our daily lives."[8] Eisenhower considered this latter course a far greater danger because it imperiled individual freedom, politicized class conflicts, and threatened social stability.

Eisenhower believed that the president should instead lead the nation "down the middle of the road between the unfettered power of concentrated wealth . . . and the unbridled power of statism or partisan interests." In a modern, industrial nation, all groups were interdependent; none could prosper in the long run, Eisenhower asserted, unless the entire society did. Thus the president must avoid advocating policies that might provide temporary benefits, such as higher profits or increased wages, to particular constituencies but would jeopardize long-term goals, such as price stability and high productivity, that served the national interest. Ideally Eisenhower wanted "to blend, without coercion, the individual good and the common good." Should voluntarism fail, Eisenhower believed that the president should use his power with restraint to reconcile divergent interests. "I am convinced that leadership in the political as well as in other spheres consists largely in making progress through compromise," he wrote during the 1952 campaign.[9] By emphasizing consensus, by hewing to the center, Eisenhower hoped to lift the presidency above politics.[10]

Despite his denials of partisanship, Eisenhower expounded a conservative philosophy of governing. His ideas recalled those of Herbert Hoover, who during the 1920s extolled the virtues of a corporate economy and declared that the federal government should concentrate on promoting cooperation among private interests for the common good. Like Hoover, Eisenhower attracted the support of corporate leaders because of his emphasis on voluntarism and restraint in the use of federal power. While he did not agree with ultraconservatives who wanted to dismantle the New Deal, Eisenhower shared their fears about the dangers of federal paternalism. While he promised to favor no special interest, he tended to exclude business groups from that derogatory category. While he appealed for sacrifice, cooperation, and public spiritedness, he was reluctant to use the powers of the presidency should the American people fail to conform to his ideals. Eisenhower, in short, hoped for progress, but his philosophy of government tended to favor the status quo.

Despite Eisenhower's determination to break with the Fair Deal, his views on political economy in many ways coincided with Truman's. Both insisted government should try to promote economic growth, although Truman was more willing to use federal spending to stimulate a sluggish economy. Both disliked budget deficits because of their persistent concern about the dangers of inflation. Although Eisenhower railed against his predecessor's supposedly free-spending policies, Truman managed to balance the budget three times, even though the country was at war for three of his eight years in the White House. Indeed Truman's record of avoiding red ink might have been better had not Congress cut taxes over his veto in 1948 and rejected his proposal to increase taxes the following year. Eisenhower did tend to emphasize free enterprise, while Truman talked more about social welfare. Yet, as historian Donald R. McCoy has observed, "the fact of the matter was that the Truman administration could not do without capitalistic growth to finance its goals, any more than the Eisenhower administration could do away with earlier social reforms and still sustain stability."[11]

To achieve his goals, Eisenhower assembled a team of assistants who he believed could exercise disinterested leadership. The complexities of governing, just as the intricacies of waging war, demanded teamwork. "Now look," he told his cabinet, "this idea that all wisdom is in the President, in me, that's baloney."[12] "No one has a monopoly on the truth and on the facts that affect this country," he declared at a conference of state governors.[13] In selecting his top advisers, Eisenhower concentrated on an individual's qualifications, not political associations. He did not regularly consult some important Republican leaders, such as Dewey or Taft, on appointments. Patronage was at odds with his conception of the proper workings of government; indeed Eisenhower thought that "by itself it could well-nigh defeat democracy."[14] Thus he chose few professional politicians for staff or cabinet positions. Instead he selected many individuals with managerial experience in business or finance. Although these appointments revealed the president's bias toward corporate interests, Eisenhower thought they provided the federal government with people of broad vision who would do what was best for the nation.

Eisenhower's first choice for the cabinet was John Foster Dulles, a lawyer for the Wall Street firm of Sullivan and Cromwell who had represented many corporate clients with overseas interests. The grandson of one secretary of state, the nephew of another, Dulles had been the leading Republican expert on foreign policy since the end of World War II. Because of Truman's efforts to cultivate bipartisan support for his Cold War policies, Dulles had been a member of official delegations to meetings of the United Nations and the Council of Foreign Ministers in the late 1940s and a consultant to the State Department on the negotiation of the Japanese Peace Treaty from 1950 until 1952. Dewey's defeat in the election of 1948 was a great blow to him, since he expected to become secretary of state in a Republican administration. Dulles began to maneuver for the same position in 1952 by criticizing the Truman administration's foreign policies and helping to draft the plank in the Republican platform that condemned containment as "negative, futile and immoral."[15] Although some Republicans remained suspicious of Dulles because of his close association with Truman's State Department, Eisenhower liked Dulles when they first met in May 1952 and deeply respected his knowledge of international affairs. Within days of his election, Eisenhower decided to name Dulles as secretary of state.

Eisenhower also quickly decided to entrust the Justice Department to Herbert Brownell, Jr., and to ask him to help select the remaining members of the cabinet. Eisenhower considered Brownell a first-rate attorney. He also admired his unimpeachable integrity. Even though Brownell had managed Dewey's two campaigns for the presidency in 1944 and 1948 and had served as chair of the Republican National Committee between 1944 and 1946, he never abandoned his ethical principles, according to Eisenhower, to secure votes. "I am devoted to him," Eisenhower confided in his diary, "and am perfectly confident that he would make an outstanding president of the United States."[16] Because of his respect for Brownell, he asked his attorney general-designate and Gen. Lucius D. Clay, a longtime friend and associate, to suggest nominees for the other cabinet posts. Although Eisenhower made the final decisions, he simply concurred in the choices of Brownell and Clay.

For secretary of the Treasury, Brownell and Clay recommended George M. Humphrey. The chair of the M. A. Hanna Company of Ohio, Humphrey was one of several corporate executives who joined the Eisenhower cabinet. Humphrey knew little about economic theory— only enough to pronounce it useless. Instead he relied on his business experience, which sustained his faith in the old-time Republican ortho-doxy that what was good for business was good for the economy. Specifically he urged restraint in federal spending in order to balance the budget, curb inflation, and minimize corporate taxes. Despite Humphrey's staunchly conservative, probusiness outlook, Eisenhower nonetheless regarded his secretary of the Treasury as a guardian of "the welfare of the United States and all the people that compose it."[17] Such statements revealed how thoroughly Eisenhower himself equated busi-ness and national interests. It was to Humphrey that the president usually turned first for advice on economic matters. Eisenhower also rapidly developed a friendship with his secretary of Treasury and often spent holidays hunting on Humphrey's Georgia plantation.

For secretary of defense, Eisenhower chose Charles E. Wilson, the president of General Motors. Wilson lacked expertise in military affairs, but he had gained unique experience in budgeting and procurement as head of the world's largest corporation. An electrical engineer by training, Wilson proved his executive abilities as he rose in various managerial positions at General Motors until he reached the presidency of the corporation in 1941. Under his supervision, GM exceeded all expectations for rapid production of military equipment during World War II. Eisenhower wanted Wilson to apply his administrative skills so that the Pentagon would operate smoothly and efficiently. Wilson, however, failed to fulfill those expectations. Too often he brought to the White House matters that Eisenhower thought Wilson should have resolved by himself. "Charlie," Eisenhower eventually declared in exasperation, "you run defense. We both can't do it, and I won't do it. I was elected to worry about a lot of other things than the day-to-day operations of a department."[18] Wilson also annoyed the president by blurting out embarrassing personal opinions in public. During his confirmation hearings, for example, Wilson made the notorious statement that "What was good for the country was good for General Motors and vice versa."[19] In the midst of the 1954 campaign, which occurred while the economy was recovering from a recession, Wilson asserted that unemployed automobile workers had lost their jobs because they were lazy.

Although Wilson's gaffes made occasional headlines, Secretary of Agriculture Ezra Taft Benson aroused more controversy that any other member of the cabinet. A high official in the Mormon Church, he pursued his task of overhauling federal farm policy with unrelenting righteousness. During a quarter century of work as a specialist in agricultural marketing, Benson had developed strong convictions that the federal government ought sharply to reduce its role in the farm economy. Eisenhower agreed, but counseled Benson to do "a lot of zigging and zagging" because "that's the way you run a military campaign . . . that's also the way you run a political enterprise."[20] Benson ignored this advice and bluntly asserted from the time he took office that the only solution to the woes of the farmers was to end federal price supports and let the free market determine supply and demand. Repeatedly farmers called for his resignation, and once a group threw eggs at him during a speech in South Dakota. Privately Eisenhower deplored Benson's stubbornness but fervently defended the secretary in public against his detractors. Benson certainly was no politician or diplomat, but he did advocate policies, however unpopular, that Eisenhower supported.

The only mistake Eisenhower admitted in the selection of his cabinet was his choice of Martin P. Durkin as secretary of labor. Durkin's background set him apart. He was the lone regular Democrat and Catholic in the cabinet; as a leader of a plumbers' union, he stood in sharp contrast to his business-oriented colleagues. Taft threw a tantrum when he learned that Eisenhower had chosen a trade unionist to oversee labor matters. Eisenhower began to express his own reservations within weeks of the inauguration. He chided Durkin for acting as organized labor's special representative in the Eisenhower administration instead of "serving the entire people."[21] Durkin, for his part, charged that the president had reneged on his promise to support revisions in the Taft-Hartley Act, which was the preeminent legislative goal of the union movement. The dispute culminated in Durkin's resignation only eight months after taking office.

Determined to avoid another mistake, the president selected James P. Mitchell to succeed Durkin. Although not a union member, Mitchell had long experience in labor relations, first for the Army Service Forces during World War II and then for Bloomingdale's department store in New York. An effective administrator, Mitchell proved adept at explaining the interest of workers without provoking charges that he was engaged in special pleading. Mitchell also earned a reputation as a humanitarian by serving as chair of the President's Commission on Migratory Labor. His ability to persuade friends in the labor movement to vote Republican especially impressed Eisenhower.

Acting on the advice of Brownell and Clay, Eisenhower chose mediocrities to fill the top positions at Commerce and Interior. Sinclair Weeks, former finance chair of the Republican National Committee, held economic views that were even more conservative than Humphrey's. Although Eisenhower did not think of him as an advocate for special interests, Weeks perpetuated the Commerce Department's traditional role as defender of the nation's business. His colleague at the Interior Department, Douglas McKay, proposed public-private partnership in the development of natural resources. A folksy former automobile dealer and longtime governor of Oregon, McKay obtained his cabinet position because of his apparent familiarity with the resource problems of western states. In office, however, McKay was another Charles Wilson. He suffered from the same foot-in-mouth affliction, depended on his subordinates to run the department, and proved to be an ineffective defender of administration programs.

Eisenhower filled two other seats in the cabinet by following a long-standing political tradition and making a gesture toward change. Like many of his predecessors, he named the chair of his party's national committee, Arthur E. Summerfield, as postmaster general. For secretary of the new Department of Health, Education, and Welfare, Eisenhower designated Oveta Culp Hobby. He respected her administrative skills, which she demonstrated as head of the Women's Army Corps during World War II and as a newspaper publisher in Texas. Although a nominal Democrat, Hobby supported Dewey in 1948 and Eisenhower in 1952. Only the second woman ever to sit in a presidential cabinet, she was selected in part because she was a woman. The appointment, however, was little more than tokenism. Eisenhower did not support the equal rights amendment to the Constitution, which would have prohibited discrimination on account of sex, and he named few women to high federal office.

For the first time, Eisenhower accorded cabinet status to the director of the Bureau of the Budget, Joseph M. Dodge. Although he was president of the Detroit Bank for two decades beginning in 1933, Dodge accumulated long experience in government, particularly in international economics. After holding several positions in defense procurement during World War II, Dodge went to Germany where he worked with Eisenhower as a financial adviser to American occupation forces. In 1949, he held a similar post in Japan on the staff of Gen. Douglas MacArthur. Insisting on financial austerity, he was principal shaper of the first balanced budget in occupied Japan. Eisenhower wanted Dodge, as director of the Bureau of the Budget, to show the same zeal in holding down federal expenditures. Thus his role in the Eisenhower administration and that of his successors, Rowland R. Hughes, Percival F. Brundage, and Maurice H. Stans, was to scrutinize the spending proposals of executive departments and prune them sufficiently so that they did not exceed the president's budgetary limits.

The final member of the cabinet was elected, not appointed. In an effort to upgrade the traditionally insignificant role of the vice-president, Eisenhower asked Nixon to participate in meetings of the cabinet. He also entrusted the vice-president with a variety of assignments, including speeches to a variety of Republican groups, liaison with congressional leaders, and goodwill trips to East and South Asia in 1953, and to Mexico, Central America, and the Caribbean in 1955. In fulfilling these duties, Nixon impressed Eisenhower with his cooperation, energy, and loyalty. Although he occasionally deplored the partisan zeal of Nixon's rhetoric, Eisenhower recognized that the vice-president's excesses made him appear by contrast even more statesmanlike. Yet while Eisenhower accorded Nixon responsibility, he did not offer him friendship, much less intimacy. Despite Nixon's prominent public role, his influence within the White House was small.

Although he did not sit in the cabinet, Arthur F. Burns, the chair of the Council of Economic Advisers (CEA) had as much influence on economic policy as any member of the Eisenhower administration. An academic whose specialty was the business cycle, Burns impressed Eisenhower with the organization and thoughtfulness of the briefings he presented on economic issues. The CEA, which had sporadic influence in the Truman administration after its statutory creation in

1946, was a considerable force in the Eisenhower White House. Burns's preoccupation with the long-term effects of inflation reinforced Eisenhower's belief that price stability was absolutely essential to a healthy economy. The recommendations of the chair of the CEA often coincided with those of Humphrey and Dodge, since Burns was clearly on the right of the political spectrum. But Burns's ability to ground his views in economic theory often made them seem less partisan—and more persuasive—than those of Humphrey.

While Eisenhower sought people who shared his views about the relationship between government and society to serve in his cabinet, he desired those devoted to efficiency for his White House staff. Because of his long experience with military organization, Eisenhower believed that clear lines of authority radiating from the Oval Office would ensure the smooth workings of his presidency. He divided the responsibilities of his immediate staff into four areas: domestic affairs, foreign affairs, special projects, and routine scheduling and coordination. He appointed subordinates to handle specific tasks, not to compete with each other for power or presidential approbation. Among his most notable appointments to this inner circle were Gen. Wilton B. (Jerry) Persons to head a new office of congressional liaison and Maxwell Rabb to handle relations with minority groups. The former had worked on congressional relations for the army and had served on Eisenhower's staff at NATO headquarters. The latter was an attorney who had been an aide to Senator Henry Cabot Lodge. As special assistant for national security affairs, he named Robert Cutler, a Boston banker who had served in the War Department during World War II. Tom Stephens, an attorney who had worked for Dewey, became appointments secretary, and Gen. Paul T. Carroll, who had assisted Eisenhower both in Washington and Paris, held the position of staff secretary. After Carroll died of a heart attack in 1954, Gen. Andrew J. Goodpaster, who had also worked for Eisenhower at NATO headquarters, took over. The chief speechwriters were Emmet Hughes and C. D. Jackson, both from Time-Life Corporation. As his personal secretary, Eisenhower selected Ann C. Whitman, who had held that position during the campaign.

As his press secretary, Eisenhower chose James C. Hagerty, who had served Dewey in that same capacity. "You'll know everything I'm doing," he promised Hagerty, "and I'll keep you fully informed. If you get any questions, don't shoot off your mouth before you have the answers. If you have anything you don't know the answer to, come to me and I'll tell you."[22] In turn, Hagerty encouraged the president to expand the format of the news conferences by allowing direct quotation of presidential statements—something Truman had not permitted—and authorizing live television coverage beginning in 1955.

Supervising the White House staff was Sherman Adams, the former governor of New Hampshire and campaign adviser to Eisenhower. Adams held the unprepossessing title of assistant to the president, but he wielded the power of a chief of staff. Neither Franklin D. Roosevelt nor Truman had thought such a staff aide necessary, but Eisenhower, because of his military experience, considered the position essential. Adams made staff assignments and personnel changes and decided what subjects would appear on the president's daily agenda. He also gave and withheld permission to enter the Oval Office. He usually was present, but only infrequently participated, in cabinet meetings and monitored most of the president's conversations with advisers and visitors.

Observers who mistook propinquity for power thought that Adams was an assistant president, or worse, a master of intrigue, who determined most of Eisenhower's decisions. Adams made many enemies in Washington with his laconic, negative responses to requests for an appointment with the president. His critics repeated the joke that answered the question, "What if Eisenhower died and Nixon became president?" by asking, "What if Adams died and Eisenhower became president?" Yet Adams was no more than what Eisenhower required of him: a firm subordinate dedicated to protecting the president's interests. Adams handled procedural matters so that Eisenhower could devote his full attention to substantive decisions. He said no often so that Eisenhower would not have to. To be sure, Adams made mistakes as doorkeeper of the Oval Office and custodian of the president's agenda. But throughout his six years in the White House, he enjoyed Eisenhower's confidence.

Although he held no position in the administration, Milton S. Eisenhower served without portfolio as his brother's principal confidant. The younger Eisenhower had been an assistant to three secretaries of agriculture, and his counsel led to the appointment of Ezra Taft Benson. After service in government, he pursued a career as a college and university president, first at Kansas State, then at Pennsylvania State, and finally, beginning in 1956, at Johns Hopkins. He also developed considerable expertise on Latin American affairs, which the president tapped repeatedly. His liberal views often counterbalanced his brother's political and economic conservatism. The president turned to him on many occasions, confident that he would receive a thoughtful and disinterested reply to any question. Of his brother, the president wrote, "I have no hesitancy in saying I believe him to be the most knowledgeable and widely informed of all the people with whom I deal."[23]

Eisenhower's emphasis on teamwork in his administration convinced many contemporary observers that he was incapable of exercising strong individual leadership. The president depended so heavily on his associates, many critics believed, because he lacked the qualities of mind to understand complex issues and so was overwhelmed—or bored—by the duties of his office. This caricature is as false as it was popular. To be sure, Eisenhower was no intellectual, nor, for that matter, was he even well-read. As he once explained, a general has little time to read or reflect on matters other than those that require immediate attention. Instead Eisenhower became accustomed to getting essential information from summary sheets or briefings from his staff. As president, Eisenhower continued this practice to master the essentials of an issue quickly and prepare to make a decision. He also read portions of books or articles that his assistants brought to his attention. In weighing the evidence in those written or oral digests, Eisenhower usually showed a keen ability to cut to the heart of an issue. Someone could not make the momentous decisions that he had as a military commander without developing exceptional analytical skills. His extraordinary involvement in world affairs also provided him with a breadth of knowledge that awed many of his aides. "He had a quick mind and a very strong and vigorous personality," Goodpaster recollected. "When he was ready to take a position on an issue there was no doubt left in anybody's mind that the decision had been made." George F. Kennan, a specialist in Soviet affairs who did not suffer fools lightly, declared that Eisenhower "showed his intellectual ascendancy over every man in the room" during a sweeping review of national security policy in 1953.[24] Critics who denigrated Eisenhower simply did not recognize that intelligence can take many forms. They failed to appreciate the store of knowledge Eisenhower had amassed or the analytical skills he had honed during his military career.

The president's private papers confirm that Eisenhower had a logical and critical mind. The records of cabinet meetings and of the National Security Council reveal that Eisenhower could shrewdly dissect the arguments of his associates. His speech files show that while several writers usually contributed to his major public statements, Eisenhower frequently guided their efforts with lengthy and specific instructions and edited their drafts up until the final moment. The president dictated letters in a clear and simple style devoid of the verbiage or jargon so common in federal—and, particularly, military—

prose. For more than thirty years, from late 1935 almost until the end of his life, he kept diaries that documented the workings of a keen analytical thinker.

Yet to a great extent, Eisenhower's public remarks seemed to prove just the opposite. Eisenhower's awkward and confusing performances at news conferences contributed to much of the speculation about his intellectual capabilities. Throughout his presidency, he answered questions from representatives of the news media frequently, usually two or three times each month. Although he prepared for these encounters—Hagerty anticipated the questions that would arise and helped Eisenhower rehearse his answers—Eisenhower often seemed to be flummoxed at best, uninformed at worst. His worst fault was a tendency to meander into unknown linguistic territory. Sometimes Hagerty would have to issue a clarification so that reporters could discern the president's meaning. Eisenhower's garbled syntax only looked worse when compared to the effortless eloquence of Adlai E. Stevenson, the Democratic governor of Illinois who twice ran against Eisenhower for the presidency.

Yet sometimes Eisenhower's indirect or dense answers were the result of design rather than ineptness. For example, when reporters raised an issue that Eisenhower wished to avoid, he sometimes purposely mangled his reply. He also tried to parry some questions by declaring, "I'll have to look that up," or by urging correspondents to take their questions to the official directly in charge of the subject. To avoid disclosing secret information, the president sometimes talked in circles. On occasion, Eisenhower even shrewdly capitalized on his reputation for torturing the language. Once when Hagerty warned his boss to deal carefully with an issue that was sure to arise at a news conference, Eisenhower smiled and replied, "Don't worry Jim. . . . If that question comes up, I'll just confuse them."[25] Critics seized upon such responses as evidence that the president did not know what was going on in his own administration. Usually he did, but his spontaneous oral statements seemed to suggest otherwise.

Another major criticism of Eisenhower was that he was little more than a figurehead in his own government. White House assistants and cabinet officials, according to this view, exercised the real power in the Eisenhower White House. Journalist Marquis Childs gave this interpretation a conspiratorial twist in his 1958 best-seller, *Eisenhower: Captive Hero.* Other observers maintained that the extraordinary influence of Eisenhower's associates was less the product of intrigue than the president's inattention, insufficiencies, or indifference.

Again Eisenhower contributed to these unflattering interpretations, although not necessarily unwittingly. In accordance with his concept of teamwork, he did entrust his principal associates with considerable responsibility and expected them to make some decisions without consulting him. He had no desire, for example, to become involved in running the day-to-day affairs of the cabinet departments and resented the intrusion of such matters into the Oval Office. Yet Eisenhower sometimes created the impression that his cabinet secretaries or White House assistants were acting independently when they were actually carrying out his instructions. At times, the president also preferred to exercise his power quietly, behind the scenes, without issuing public declarations, indeed without doing anything to reveal his role. Political scientist Fred I. Greenstein has called this method of governing "hidden-hand leadership."[26] Eisenhower made the critical policy decisions, but he carefully muffled his responsibility.

Governing by indirection often accorded with Eisenhower's personal inclinations and political purposes. Because he disliked partisan controversy so much, Eisenhower hoped that working behind the scenes would insulate him from such strife. By deflecting any criticism toward his associates, he would remain above the battle, thus preserving his popularity and his freedom to maneuver. Divisions in the Republican party also encouraged him to operate behind the scenes. When Eisenhower took office, the GOP was divided into conservative and moderate factions. The former, commonly called the Old Guard, abhorred the "statism" of the New Deal and Fair Deal and supported a nationalist—or, in the view of critics—an isolationist foreign policy. The latter, often known as Eisenhower Republicans, accepted the necessity of some social-welfare programs and held an internationalist world view. To avoid exacerbating these divisions, Eisenhower sometimes tried to use indirection rather than confrontation to achieve his goals. Hidden-hand leadership was not necessarily wise or effective, and it created the appearance that Eisenhower was not in charge of his own administration. Yet despite popular perceptions, Eisenhower, at the very least, knew what was happening in his own administration. Indeed, his political skills were much greater than most contemporaries recognized.

In organizing the first Republican administration in two decades, Eisenhower encountered some difficulties with appointments. Although he was determined to put in office only qualified individuals, the GOP had been out of power for so long that many of his appointees had little or no federal experience. Some Republicans who had backgrounds in business or banking continued to think that profit was the ultimate goal even after they took federal positions. "Whether the thing pays or not," a presidential staff member impatiently explained to some new federal officials, "is not the primary thing. It's . . . a matter of service, and responsiveness to the public will.[27] If unfamiliarity with government was a problem for prospective Republican officeholders, so were low salaries. Eisenhower himself believed that "we can afford to have only those people in high political offices who cannot afford to take them."[28] Despite such admonitions, some of the choices of the president and his advisers found the price of sacrifice too high.

A few Republican appointees embarrassed the president because of their involvement in scandal. Secretary of Defense Wilson caused a furor by refusing to divest himself of his General Motors stock until forced to do so by the president. After only two months on the job, C. Wesley Roberts quit as chair of the Republican National Committee in March 1953 because of charges that he had profited by exerting improper influence as a lobbyist in his home state of Kansas. Sherman Adams resigned under fire in 1958 because of allegations that he had used his influence with federal regulatory agencies on behalf of a friend. Perhaps because of his own lack of interest in personal aggrandizement, Eisenhower paid little attention to possible conflicts of interest in evaluating the credentials of nominees for office. Yet these incidents created political difficulties, especially since the Republicans had excoriated the Truman administration for its corruption in the campaign of 1952.

However much Eisenhower was a familiar figure because of his official duties, he guarded his personal life from public scrutiny. At home, the president and his wife enjoyed a happy, if conventional, marriage. Occasionally gossips revived stories of the president's alleged wartime affair with Kay Summersby and sneered that the Eisenhowers had stayed together only for appearances. Family and friends knew otherwise. In the White House, the Eisenhowers shared a double bed—something that neither their immediate predecessors or successors did. Mamie was an ebullient, well-organized woman who never wanted to be anything more than Eisenhower's wife. Traditional in her outlook, she thought that her primary responsibility was to make the living quarters of the executive mansion a refuge for her husband from his work.

Despite her success at that task, neither of them ever liked Washington. On many weekends and holidays, they were delighted to escape to their farm adjacent to the Gettysburg battlefield in nearby Pennsylvania. Most of the friends they welcomed there were not connected with government. To entertain official guests, the president used Franklin Roosevelt's former retreat in the Catoctin Mountains of Maryland. But he changed the name from Shangri-La, which he said was "just a little fancy for a Kansas farm boy," to Camp David, after his only grandson.[29]

Although he was usually engaging and genial in public, Eisenhower could be moody and temperamental in private. He had a ferocious temper, which he had to work hard to control. Occasionally he might flash his anger at a press conference, but only members of his inner circle ever saw how mad he could become. To his son John, for example, he blurted out, "What the hell is this? Do you expect a President to sign a bunch of garbage like that?"[30] He usually expressed his rage by drawing on the profanity that had long been part of his soldier's vocabulary. Once, for example, when he reluctantly signed legislation that he thought provided undeserved benefits to an inventor, he exclaimed, "God damn it to hell! Jesus Christ, I hope the son of a bitch dies!"[31] Just as he could explode in rage, so could he sink into despair. Thoughts about his son Icky, who died in early childhood, could often make him morose.

To relax and unwind, Eisenhower enjoyed music, books, and films. His tastes were generally prosaic. He liked to listen to the recordings of Fred Waring and the Pennsylvanians, and he once told an aide that his favorite song was "Ragtime Cowboy Joe." Western themes particularly appealed to him, and he usually kept some light, escapist cowboy stories on his bedside reading table. He enjoyed the film *High Noon* so much that he whistled the theme song for months. To his secretary, Ann Whitman, he confessed that his preferences were not always so mundane. He also liked classical music but was "deathly afraid of being considered highbrow."[32]

Eisenhower enjoyed himself most thoroughly in the company of male friends and associates. Periodically he would invite about two dozen men, often from a variety of backgrounds and occupations, to a stag dinner in the White House. He relished the spirited discussion at the dinner table and afterwards. Even more invigorating were Eisenhower's holidays with the "gang," a group of wealthy friends who were mainly in business and finance. With them he indulged his passion for trout fishing in the mountain streams of Colorado and nonstop bridge playing. They also joined him in the recreation for which he became notorious—golf. So great was his interest in golf that he sometimes hit iron shots on the South Lawn of the White House during a break in his schedule. He managed to get out on the fairways frequently, and his favorite course was Augusta National, where he held a membership thanks to the generosity of gang member Clifford

Roberts. Whether the main activity was golf, fishing, or bridge, Eisenhower would often cap off the day's activities by cooking a barbecue dinner. Indeed he prided himself on being the best cook in his family.

Eisenhower, in short, was a complex man, far more so than most of his contemporaries recognized. He developed a conservative philosophy of government and a style of leadership through teamwork that fit his values, temperament, and experience. He chose assistants who he believed could rise above particularism and, if necessary, shield him from controversy. As much as he valued their counsel, he knew that ultimately he was responsible for all important decisions. He was, however, both modest and realistic when he realized that "because of the infinite variety of problems" that come to the president's attention and "the rapidity with which they are placed" before him, "the struggle is to apply common sense—to reach an average solution."[33] In 1953, the American people looked to him to apply that prosaic wisdom to the nation's foreign and domestic affairs.

No issue more urgently demanded a solution, average or otherwise, when Eisenhower became president than the Korean War. Truman had committed American armed forces in June 1950 to a war that he was unable to win or end. In only six months, American objectives changed from "police action" to liberation to containment, much to the perplexity and consternation of the American public. After the unexpected intervention of Chinese Communist troops in November 1950, the war soon sank into a stalemate, with both sides dug in near the 38th parallel, which divided North and South Korea. Popular frustrations exploded in April 1951, when Truman relieved the supreme commander, Gen. Douglas MacArthur, for publicly advocating what Truman had explicitly rejected, an expansion of the war that included attacks on Communist China. MacArthur promised to fade away, but few people forgot his ringing admonition, "There is no substitute for victory."

Echoing MacArthur, millions of Americans thought the real problem in Korea was not the difficulty of balancing a limited war in East Asia against global interests and nuclear perils, but simply that the Truman administration had decided not to win. Only adding to public frustration was the opening of armistice negotiations in July 1951 and their eventual deadlock over whether prisoners of war would be required to return to the countries for which they fought or whether repatriation, as the American negotiators insisted, would be voluntary. The war seemed to produce little more than mounting casualties—21,000 American dead, 91,000 wounded, and 13,000 missing in action by the time of Eisenhower's election.[34] Dissatisfaction with the war destroyed Truman's popularity and had much to do with Eisenhower's emphatic victory in the election of 1952.

Eisenhower inherited not only the shooting war in Korea, but the Cold War with the Soviet Union. Only a year after the end of the Second World War, Truman and his principal advisers had become convinced that the Soviets were implacably hostile. Although they doubted that the Russians would launch another major war, they were certain that Stalin would use subversion and intimidation to extend the Soviet sphere of influence. In March 1947, the president declared that "it must be the policy of the United States to support free peoples who are resisting attempted subjugation by armed minorities or by outside pressures."[35] Although more selective—at least at first—than the Truman Doctrine implied, American policy aimed at containing the spread of communism primarily by providing economic and military assistance to friendly nations.

In the late 1940s, the Truman administration concentrated on consolidating anticommunist strength in Western Europe through the Marshall Plan in 1948 and the formation of NATO in 1949. Far less assistance went to the Nationalist Chinese government of Chiang Kai-shek, which took refuge on Taiwan after losing a civil war to Communist forces under Mao Tse-tung. Angry and persistent Republican criticism that the United States had lost China persuaded the Truman administration to expand its containment efforts in East Asia. The Korean War vastly expanded the size of those programs as national security expenditures quadrupled in only a year to more than $50 billion annually. By the time Truman left the White House, containment had become a costly, global policy that aimed at preventing a "slave state" from carrying out its fundamental "design for world domination."[36]

If the Cold War dominated international affairs when Eisenhower assumed the presidency, McCarthyism strongly influenced domestic politics. The junior senator from Wisconsin, Republican Joseph R. McCarthy, gave his name to the hysteria over Communist subversion within the United States. Since the beginning of the Cold War, fear of spies, saboteurs, and security risks, had been growing progressively deeper with each investigation by the House Un-American Activities Committee or arrest by the Federal Bureau of Investigation. Recognizing a winning issue, McCarthy began to hunt Communists with such a vengeance that he eventually became the leading figure in the effort to expose alleged disloyalty at any price. He made headlines by crying that the Red conspiracy's agents, or worse, dupes, in Washington included none other than Secretary of State Dean Acheson and Secretary of

Defense George C. Marshall. It is a measure of how poisoned and paranoid public attitudes had become during the Korean War that these charges made McCarthy a political power rather than a crank.

In the Senate hearing room, McCarthy's methods were surly and truculent. Yet the senator was not alone in giving civil liberties minor consideration when the security of the nation was supposedly at stake. The Truman administration's own loyalty program showed little concern with the rights of the accused. While McCarthy pounded the table and threatened witnesses, the search for Communists turned into a national orgy of investigations and declarations of right thinking, as schools banned books, Hollywood blacklisted alleged "pinks," and states required loyalty oaths of public officials, teachers, and even professional wrestlers (in Indiana). Underlying these efforts was a pervasive fear that American freedom, openness, and material abundance created a kind of complacency, even decadence, that corrupted the nation's moral fiber and allowed the virus of subversion to flourish.

While McCarthyites worried about the corrupting influences of modern society, other Americans saw in 1953 an extraordinary national strength that rested on rapid population growth. The baby boom, which began at the end of World War II, reached its peak during the Eisenhower years. There were 181 million Americans when Eisenhower left office in 1961, 21 million more than when he began his presidency. This demographic explosion occurred because those Americans who came to maturity in the 1940s and 1950s were more likely to marry than any previous, or succeeding, generation. They did so early in life—at a median age of twenty for women, twenty-two for men—and usually had a family of two to four children.[37]

Rapid population growth helped fuel a strong expansion of the economy during the 1950s. Throughout the Eisenhower presidency, the gross national product increased at an annual rate of 2.4 percent, from $364.6 billion to $520.1 billion. Because of the growth in the number of families, many basic industries prospered, such as housing, automobiles, and steel. Contemporary observers declared that Americans were a people of plenty, and indeed they were, but hardly in equal measure. Nonwhites, who constituted 10.6 percent of the population when Eisenhower entered the White House, earned far less than whites. In 1953, the median income for a nonwhite family was $2,461, as opposed to $4,392 for a white family. In 1960, comparable figures were $3,233 and $5,835. Black family income thus remained constant during the Eisenhower years at 56 percent of white family income. The Eisenhower prosperity, in short, brought no relative improvement for blacks.[38]

In the 1950s, the baby boom and the Cold War were intimately connected. As historian Elaine Tyler May has observed, "The legendary family of the 1950s, complete with appliances, station wagons, backyard barbecues, and tricycles scattered on the sidewalks, . . . was not, as common wisdom tells us, the last gasp of 'traditional' family life." Rather it was "something new." It represented an effort to make home and family a refuge in a troubled and terrifying age of Cold War, nuclear weapons, and domestic subversion. In Eisenhower's United States, then, the quest for security, both international and domestic, dominated life.[39]

3

PRESIDENT, PARTY, AND CONGRESS

In his dealings with Congress, no less than in his direction of the executive branch, President Eisenhower was determined to exercise strong and effective, but ultimately quiet, leadership. Despite widespread popular belief to the contrary, Eisenhower took seriously his relationship with Congress. Indeed he thought that one of the most important duties of a president was to "devise a program that is in general conformity with the platform of his party, and do his best to get it enacted into law."[1] In discharging this responsibility, Eisenhower eschewed public confrontation in favor of shrewd lobbying, private negotiation, and, when necessary, behind-the-scenes pressure. Because he enjoyed only slender Republican majorities in both houses of Congress, Eisenhower worked assiduously to win the support of all factions of his party. When unable to do so, most notably in fights over the Bricker amendment and the McCarthy investigations into Communist subversion, Eisenhower used his power indirectly, and with decidedly mixed results, to disarm his opponents. Yet by the close of the Eighty-third Congress in 1954, Eisenhower succeeded in gaining enactment of much of his legislative program and in strengthening his leadership of the Republican party.

Like many Americans, Eisenhower viewed Congress in somewhat contradictory terms. He frequently lauded the constitutional system of separation of powers that allocated some responsibilities exclusively to

Congress. He insisted that his Democratic predecessors had upset the constitutional equilibrium between the White House and Capitol Hill and promised to exercise restraint in order to restore the balance. In addition, he praised the legislature in somewhat textbook-like fashion as a great unifier, the mechanism of democracy that forged consensus. Yet he also viewed Congress as a center of the partisanship he so thoroughly deplored. At times, he complained that legislators were interested in working for nothing more than their own reelection. By mid-1954, he concluded that a constitutional amendment was necessary to lengthen the term of House members to four years so they would not be constantly calculating the partisan advantages of their votes. "I am always upset," he confided to a friend, "when I know that a politician is putting selfish interests ahead of the interest of his country. So many of them do just that."[2] Thus he feared that Congress was all too vulnerable to the influence of pressure groups and special interests whose demands rarely promoted the common good.

To ensure that legislative action furthered the nation's and the administration's interest—the two, he believed, were identical—Eisenhower devoted considerable attention to congressional liaison. He established a White House office of congressional liaison, the first of its kind. Headed by Gen. Wilton B. (Jerry) Persons, a master of diplomacy and compromise, the staff proved adept at the delicate task of exerting influence without bruising egos on Capitol Hill. While assistants did much of the work, Eisenhower reserved critical tasks for himself. He held regular meetings with the Republican congressional leadership and made personal telephone calls to many legislators timed for maximum effect. At the same time, he eschewed public criticism of Congress, however much he doubted the wisdom of its action. Harry Truman's denunciation of the "do-nothing" Eightieth Congress, in his opinion, smacked of demagoguery. At times, his public statements seemed so deferential toward congressional prerogatives that the press and the public doubted that his influence reached to the other end of Pennsylvania Avenue. In reality, congressional liaison was one of the most professional, sophisticated, and effective operations of the Eisenhower White House.

Liaison activities were critical because of the Republicans' tenuous control of the Eighty-third Congress. The GOP margin in the House of Representatives was less than a dozen votes; in the Senate the majority was just one. Adding to the precariousness of the Republican position were factional differences that the recent victory had not diminished. Many moderate, often newly-elected Eisenhower Republicans were ready to follow the administration's lead. Like the president, they tended to be internationalist on foreign policy, somewhat to the right on domestic matters. The Old Guard, in contrast, doubted that the president was willing or able to take the lead in dismantling the welfare state erected by Roosevelt and Truman. Regarding themselves as the true keepers of the Republican covenant, these veterans introduced a sheaf of bills to force the withdrawal of federal responsibilities in many economic and social areas. In matters of foreign policy, they were vehement anticommunists, but strong nationalists who were suspicious of overseas commitments and reluctant to support programs of foreign aid. Eisenhower hoped to secure their cooperation, especially on domestic matters, but still girded himself for trouble.

Much to his delight, Eisenhower established a far better working relationship with the Republican congressional leadership than he had anticipated. The greatest surprise was the friendship that he developed with Senator Robert A. Taft, the dean of the Old Guard and the Senate majority leader. The amicability between the president and the senator, as Eisenhower noted, was "curious," since it did not ensure "compatibility of intellectual viewpoint, nor even . . . complete courtesy in the public discussion of political questions." The two battled, for example, over Eisenhower's failure to consult Taft on cabinet appointments. Taft resented his exclusion from such critical decisions, and Eisenhower detested Taft's preoccupation with patronage, a practice he considered "wicked" and dangerous to democracy. Although the two frequently agreed on domestic matters, their discussions of foreign policy often caused Taft to lose his temper.

Yet by early April, Eisenhower noted with astonishment and pleasure that he and the majority leader were becoming "right good friends." The two had developed a new mutual respect anchored in a "definite understanding as to the methods of handling common problems." Eisenhower learned to count on Taft's enormous influence, which could bring Republican senators into line even when they differed with the White House. Thus Taft's death from cancer on 31 July 1953 was a sharp blow to Eisenhower. Taft's successor as majority leader, William F. Knowland of California, was well-meaning, but "cumbersome," in Eisenhower's opinion, and unable to command great respect in the Senate. In the House, the Republican leadership was stronger and cooperation with the White House more effective. Speaker Joseph W. Martin, Jr., of Massachusetts was a "splendid" leader, according to the president. Charles A. Halleck of Indiana, the majority leader in the House, was "smart, capable, and courageous," "a real team player" with "no patience whatsoever" with those who would not conform on "a matter of Republican regularity."[3]

However strong the cooperation with the GOP leadership on Capitol Hill, the thinness of Republican majorities in both houses meant that Eisenhower had to work with the Democrats to ensure passage of most legislation. "It was impossible to do anything just by asking [for] the loyalty of your party," he recollected. Whatever was accomplished was done "by cajolery and argument and secret conferences with the opposition."[4] The leaders of the Democrats in Congress were Sen. Lyndon B. Johnson and Rep. Sam Rayburn, both from Texas. Because he had been born in Rayburn's district, the president thought that he might have some special influence with the House Democratic chief. More often, he sought the cooperation of the minority leaders by asserting that administration policies served the national interest and thus merited bipartisan support. Neither Johnson nor Rayburn was prepared to surrender partisan advantage, but both strongly backed Eisenhower's legislative proposals and often delivered critical Democratic votes to ensure the success of those measures. Even though Eisenhower occasionally deplored the Democrats' partisanship, he was grateful for the parliamentary skills of Rayburn and Johnson in support of his programs. Indeed, one of his most remarkable legislative achievements was a well-above-average record of legislation adopted and vetoes sustained by the three Democratically-controlled Congresses during the last six years of his presidency.

Eisenhower used his influence with Congress to secure passage of legislation that reflected several basic principles. First was federal restraint. Eisenhower thought the national government ought not to intrude into matters that properly belonged in the hands of local officials or private individuals. "If Federal authority should be extended throughout the country, . . ." he warned, "it would eventually stifle the individual freedom that our government was designed to protect." The second principle was cooperation between the public and private sectors. In a modern state that consisted of a welter of competing interests, government, he declared, must aim at "blend[ing], without coercion, the individual good and the common good." Skillful management that emphasized voluntary cooperation between business, labor, and government would promote social harmony and build consensus. The final principle was fiscal responsibility. The federal government, he asserted, had an inescapable role in stimulating economic growth and raising productivity. Yet it ought to use its powers cautiously and avoid providing favors that benefited special economic interests. Even more important, the federal government ought to avoid living beyond its means. An unbalanced budget promoted inflation, which exacerbated domestic problems and weakened national defense. Prosperity could not be attained by sacrificing wage and price stability.[5]

In accordance with these principles, the president's first order of business was to ask Congress to curb the growth of federal spending. The Korean War had shattered the restraints that Truman had previously imposed on government expenditures; during Truman's last three years in office, defense spending quadrupled, and the federal budget almost doubled. Despite the imposition of new income and excise taxes, Truman projected a deficit of almost $10 billion for fiscal year 1954. However much he wanted to balance the budget, Eisenhower knew that it would take time to solve the economic problems that he inherited. Relying on the advice of Secretary of the Treasury George M. Humphrey and Budget Director Joseph M. Dodge, he presented to Congress a new budget for fiscal year 1954, one that reduced Truman's proposed expenditures of $79 billion by $5 billion and slashed the projected deficit by almost half. In planning this budget, Eisenhower and his advisers gave priority to paring the deficit over lowering taxes. "Reduction of taxes," he told the Congress, "will be justified only as we show we can succeed in bringing the budget under control."[6]

Senator Taft vigorously disagreed. Determined to push for an immediate tax cut, Taft exploded when he heard Eisenhower's proposals at a meeting of congressional leaders in April 1953. He dismissed the cuts in Truman's budget as "puny," a characterization that so infuriated Eisenhower that a nasty confrontation might have occurred had not Humphrey and Dodge intervened until the president cooled down. After regaining his composure, Eisenhower declared that further reductions were impossible without jeopardizing the security of the United States or its allies. Deeper cuts in national expenditures would have to await the end of the Korean War.[7]

During the next year, Eisenhower fought several battles over budgets and taxes, occasionally against prominent members of his own party. One of the first occurred with the Republican chair of the House Ways and Means Committee, Daniel A. Reed of New York, who introduced legislation to hasten by six months the expiration of a wartime income tax surcharge scheduled to end on 1 January 1954. Unwilling to add to the deficit, Eisenhower used his influence to bottle up Reed's bill in committee. He also secured extension of a temporary excess profits tax, again over Reed's opposition. These successes culminated in congressional acceptance of the outlines of his budget for fiscal year 1954. Deficit limitation, as Eisenhower insisted, had triumphed over tax reduction.

By the end of 1953, the most critical economic problem that Eisenhower had confronted was a sluggish economy. The Korean armistice of July 1953 had produced sharp cutbacks in military expenditures. Steps by the Federal Reserve to tighten credit in anticipation of postwar inflation encouraged businesses to shift sharply from accumulating to liquidating their inventories. The result was a mild recession that reached its peak in January 1954 when unemployment exceeded 6 percent.

Eisenhower took important, but limited, steps to invigorate the economy. He told the cabinet that he gave higher priority to reducing unemployment than to cutting the deficit. Unlike those who thought the government ought simply to wait for the economy to bottom out, he believed that "the dangers of doing nothing are far greater than those of doing too much." Yet his actions did not accord with his rhetoric. Eisenhower authorized early implementation of federal public works projects scheduled for fiscal year 1955 as a way of creating jobs without burdening the government with additional expenses. The acceleration of these and other planned federal expenditures, though, was the only step he took in fiscal policy to combat the recession. Eisenhower, however, did not try to continue his efforts to cut the deficit at a time when such attempts could only have worsened the hard times. He also constantly tried to raise confidence that the economy would soon improve, without issuing Hooverian pronouncements that would only have destroyed his credibility. Overall, the administration policy was competent, and by the last half of 1954 the recession was over.[8]

Even before the recession had run its course, Eisenhower was prepared to consider tax reform. He strongly endorsed a bill written by Reed that conformed to his specifications. Designed mainly to eliminate what many Republicans considered inequities in the tax code, it lowered taxes on corporate dividends and facilitated the deduction of business depreciation costs. Democrats charged that these provisions favored the wealthy and fought to distribute the benefits of tax reform more broadly by raising personal exemptions by $100, to $700. Eisenhower considered this proposal too costly and exerted heavy pressure on Congress to defeat it. One Washington columnist described the White House congressional liaison staff as "the smoothest-working machine Capitol Hill has seen in years." In the end, the work sustained the president's position. Both the House and Senate defeated the proposal to change the personal exemption on almost straight party-line votes. Eisenhower considered the tax reform bill, which he signed into law in August 1954, a cornerstone of his economic program.[9] He saw it as a means of stimulating growth while maintaining price stability. And by the end of

1954, the economy was booming. By fiscal year 1956, the Treasury showed a small but impressive surplus. Perhaps most important to Eisenhower, inflation remained low, running at an annual rate of just 1 or 2 percent.

Eisenhower was also determined to encourage private initiative in agriculture by reducing the role of the federal government. The system of federal farm subsidies, adopted during the Great Depression and expanded in the postwar years, was, in his opinion, anachronistic, wasteful, and narrowly partisan. The worst feature of this system, he believed, was rigid price support of basic commodities, such as cotton, corn, and wheat, at 90 percent of parity, a standard used to ensure farmers a fair income and adequate purchasing power. The principal result of these rigid subsidies, he argued, was enormous surpluses— enough wheat and cotton in government warehouses to meet national needs for a year—and falling commodity prices. These deleterious results only strengthened his abhorrence of government management of the economy. Eisenhower realized, however, that political and economic realities dictated a policy of gradualism. Accordingly, he sent legislation to Congress in early 1954 to replace the rigid subsidies with a flexible scale ranging from 75 to 90 percent of parity. This reform, Eisenhower argued, would begin to restore market forces that would help increase consumption, dissipate the surplus, and enhance farmers' interests in the long run.

The administration's farm proposals distressed Republican legislators from agricultural states. They feared a loss of farm income that would follow the reduction of subsidies, but they worried even more about the political consequences. Secretary of Agriculture Ezra Taft Benson, a blunt and unyielding advocate of free market policies, only added to the administration's difficulties while the Congress deliberated by using his discretionary power to cut back federal price supports for dairy farmers. In "a long session" with Benson, Eisenhower emphasized "the necessity for a most astute handling" of farm legislation.[10] But the damage was already done. Representative Clifford Hope of Kansas, the chair of the House Agriculture Committee, broke with Eisenhower and reported a bill that provided for retention of the rigid system of subsidies. The White House relentlessly applied pressure on GOP legislators to secure the necessary votes to amend Hope's bill, and in August 1954 secured passage of legislation that established a system of flexible subsidies, one that ranged, however, only from 82.5 to 90 percent of parity. Although Eisenhower claimed a major victory, the legislative battle was a harbinger of even greater difficulties with subsequent congresses over farm policy.

Even though he resolved to rein in federal spending, Eisenhower endorsed expansion of some social-welfare programs. Social Security, he believed, was an absolute necessity in a modern, industrialized society. Members of the Old Guard might rail against the socialism of the New Deal, but Eisenhower warned that "should any political party attempt to abolish Social Security [or] unemployment insurance, . . . you would not hear of that party again in our political history."[11] Whether out of humanitarianism or expediency, large majorities in Congress approved Eisenhower's recommendations in 1954 to incorporate 10.5 million new workers into the Social Security system and to expand monthly benefits. Division rather than consensus, however, was the result of his proposal to extend health insurance coverage through federal underwriting of the policies of private carriers. The legislation became fatally snarled in conflict between liberals, who advocated even greater federal responsibility, and conservatives, who feared the onset of socialized medicine. On public housing, Congress authorized in 1954 part of what Eisenhower requested: federal construction of 35,000 units annually during the next four years, but with restrictions that made impossible the filling of each year's quota.

In the development of natural resources, Eisenhower advocated cooperation between government and private enterprise. The partnership he desired implied mutual benefits, but in actual practice it often granted business interests unique advantages. For example, Eisenhower signed legislation that ceded submerged coastal lands, potentially rich in oil, to the adjacent states, many of which were eager to open these areas to private development. When he approved the Atomic Energy Act of 1954, he asserted that the new law would "advance both public and private development of atomic energy." Yet the legislation barred the Atomic Energy Commission from producing nuclear power for commercial sale, while allowing private corporations to do so.[12]

Controversy erupted over Eisenhower's plans for the development of water resources and hydroelectric power. A lengthy dispute arose over the construction of dams and reservoirs along the Upper Colorado Basin. At issue was the cost of the project, $1 billion, and its supervision by the Bureau of Reclamation of the Interior Department. Many Republicans objected to such heavy federal expenditures and involvement, although the popularity of the project in the four basin states—Wyoming, Colorado, Utah, and Arizona—tended to moderate their criticism. Eisenhower considered these objections unwarranted, since he was advocating the use of government power to stimulate private enterprise through the development of farmlands. Greater opposition came from conservationists, who decried the use of a reservoir in Dinosaur National Monument and warned that several of the proposed dams would endanger other parts of the national park system. Although he declined to reply publicly to his environmentalist critics, Eisenhower privately believed that water for agriculture should take priority over the preservation of natural features. The president was unable, however, to persuade the Eighty-third Congress to accept his reasoning and enact the Upper Colorado Basin project.

Another brouhaha occurred over a water development project in Hells Canyon, Idaho. In May 1953, Secretary of the Interior Douglas McKay withdrew the objections of his Democratic predecessor to private construction of several dams along the Snake River in Hells Canyon. Democrats charged that under the guise of partnership, the administration had abandoned public interests to private benefit. Although Eisenhower endorsed McKay's action and praised local initiative and private enterprise, he had to wait until 1957 for final approval of the Hells Canyon project.

No resource development project aroused stronger emotions than the Tennessee Valley Authority. While few citizens were familiar with the Upper Colorado Basin or Hells Canyon, many knew that the TVA was the showpiece of federal resource management. For some critics, of course, it was the epitome of government paternalism. Eisenhower personally believed that the TVA discouraged private enterprise in the seven states served by its flood control and electric power programs. Furthermore, he noted, it provided benefits to only one region even though it was sustained by federal taxes. (Curiously, he did not apply the same reasoning to the Upper Colorado Basin, although some of the project's opponents did.)

Eisenhower raised grave doubts about the administration's intentions when he referred to the TVA at a press conference as an example of the "creeping socialism" Republicans meant to halt. The comment caused such a sensation that neither he nor his staff could erase the impression that the administration intended to dismantle the TVA. Eisenhower tried to clarify his remarks by describing the TVA as "a going historical concern . . . [that] served a useful purpose" and promising not to "wreck" it. In reality, Eisenhower was no friend of TVA and hoped to stop its growth and eventually force it to meet its own expenses without relying on federal subsidies. As he explained in private correspondence, "No one has worked harder than I have to stop the expansion of the area of TVA."[13]

In 1954, when the Democratic director of TVA resigned, Eisenhower appointed in his place a former army engineer opposed to the extension of the system's operations. About that same time, rather than allowing the expansion of TVA, he authorized a contract permitting a private firm, Dixon-Yates, to distribute power to the city of Memphis, Tennessee. Once again, critics accused the president of plotting the demise of TVA. The furor finally abated when Memphis opted to build its own power distribution system, thereby forcing the cancellation of the contract with Dixon-Yates. Only then did Eisenhower say that he favored the municipal alternative. The affair, he lamented, had obscured public recognition of private capital's distress in the TVA region—the point that he had been trying to make all along.

One project for power and resource development that caused little, if any, controversy was joint construction with Canada of a seaway linking the Atlantic Ocean and the Great Lakes through the St. Lawrence River. Truman supported the project but failed to persuade Congress to approve it because of the high cost of federal construction of hydroelectric facilities along the river. Eisenhower endorsed legislation that omitted this provision and called for greater federal, state, and private cooperation in developing the waterway. The new plan also provided for the recovery of some federal costs through user fees. Eisenhower further justified the seaway on the grounds of national security, since it would facilitate the transportation in wartime of iron ore from eastern Canada to steel mills along the shores of the Great Lakes. In 1959, five years after Congress gave its consent, Eisenhower helped dedicate the St. Lawrence International Seaway.

Eisenhower also had to wait several years for the achievement of statehood for Alaska and Hawaii. During the 1952 campaign, he endorsed the admission of both territories. But when he presented his recommendations to the Eighty-third Congress, he called for immediate approval of only Hawaii's statehood, while delaying Alaska's pending further arrangements for the administration of defense installations. Interior Department officials, some of whom were eager to open Alaska's reserves of land and resources to private development, adamantly supported the president's reservations in order to prolong federal jurisdiction over the territory. In Congress, statehood for Hawaii encountered subtle but persistent opposition from southern legislators because of the territory's substantial nonwhite population. Because of his concern about defense facilities, Eisenhower threatened to veto compromise legislation for simultaneous admission of both territories. As a result of the deadlock, Alaska and Hawaii did not enter the Union until 1959.

Even though he suffered such occasional setbacks, Eisenhower was extraordinarily successful at getting legislation through the Eighty-third Congress. Yet at times this achievement was overshadowed by two controversial issues that threatened his position as leader of the Republican party. The first was a constitutional amendment sponsored by Senator John W. Bricker (R., Ohio), a staunch conservative on domestic matters and an unyielding foe of the growth of presidential power in foreign affairs. First introduced in the Senate in September 1951, the Bricker amendment prohibited the negotiation of any treaty that abridged any individual right or freedom under the Constitution or affected "any other matters essentially within the domestic jurisdiction of the United States."[14] To ensure that a president would not bypass these restraints through unilateral action, the amendment expressly forbade the making of executive agreements, which did not require the consent of Congress, in place of treaties. Obviously, if ratified, the Bricker amendment would have severely curtailed the president's power to reach accords with foreign nations.

Supporters of the Bricker amendment deplored the circumvention of Congress brought on by the dramatic rise in importance of the executive agreement during World War II and the Cold War, from a device for handling minor international matters to a major instrument of presidential diplomacy. The Old Guard, which unanimously endorsed the amendment, and even some internationalist Republicans also associated the transformation of the executive agreement with alleged Democratic perfidy, such as Franklin Roosevelt's secret, personal, and duplicitous summit diplomacy and Harry Truman's no-win policy of containment. Senator H. Alexander Smith (R., N.J.), declared, for example, that he supported the Bricker amendment because of his distress over the "outrageous Yalta accords, entered into by President Roosevelt individually with Stalin and Churchill without even the knowledge of [the] Secretary of State . . . and certainly without conferring with our ally Chiang Kai-shek."[15]

Although Bricker was worried about presidential usurpation of congressional prerogatives in foreign affairs, he was even more fearful that international agreements might cause sweeping changes in domestic affairs. Like many strong nationalists, Bricker thought that such an insidious document would be most likely to originate in the United Nations, which, he believed, had become less an agency for safeguarding world peace than for promoting liberal causes under the guise of human rights. The Constitution, Bricker warned, left the back door open to UN liberal activists, since any treaty, when ratified, became "supreme law of the land." Thus, according to Bricker, high-minded or seemingly innocuous language in an international accord could actually deprive states and localities of their traditional power to regulate their own social or economic affairs.

In 1951, Bricker insisted that this danger was imminent. He pointed his finger at a draft International Covenant on Human Rights, which had been written by a UN committee that included such "global dreamers" and "international do-gooders" as Eleanor Roosevelt. While the International Covenant affirmed basic civil and political liberties, such as freedom of speech and assembly, it allowed governments to suspend these rights in the event of an emergency. Even worse, it also proclaimed a series of economic, social, and cultural rights, including social security, adequate housing, health care, education, membership in a trade union, and "an adequate standard of living and the continuous improvement of living conditions." Bricker thus concluded that a court might rule that the provisions of the International Covenant, if ratified, required vast new federal social-welfare programs, designed to ensure "the right of all human beings to satisfy all their material wants."[16] The result, he predicted, would be a drastic shift of power to Washington that would destroy the federal system and allow socialism to prevail.

Others echoed Bricker's dire prophecies. White supremacists backed the Bricker amendment to defend against international threats to racial segregation and states' rights; medical societies embraced it to prevent "socialized medicine" from being "foisted upon the American people through ratification by the Senate of treaty commitments made in the United Nations;" and the United States Chamber of Commerce endorsed it to forestall destruction of "vital parts of our free enterprise system."[17] At stake, then, to the proponents of the Bricker amendment was nothing less than the survival of constitutional liberty, capitalism, and the federal system of government.

Eisenhower did not share these fears, and his handling of the Bricker amendment controversy constitutes an instructive case study in his use of presidential power. Privately Eisenhower denounced the amendment because it would "cripple the Executive power to the point that we [would] become helpless in world affairs."[18] Publicly he avoided expressing his personal opposition to the amendment, while deftly using his influence to strangle it. After failing to persuade Bricker to postpone the introduction of a revised version of his amendment into the Eighty-third Congress, Eisenhower and his aides played for time by asking Bricker not to push for action in the Senate until the administration had studied the amendment thoroughly. During hearings before a subcommittee of the Senate Judiciary Committee in April 1953, Dulles and Attorney General Herbert Brownell, Jr., lavishly praised Bricker, while emphasizing, as Eisenhower had advised them, that the amendment went too far in restricting American initiative in international affairs. Dulles also tried to reassure Bricker and his allies that the Eisenhower administration would not sign the International Covenant on Human Rights or any accord that affected American domestic affairs.

Yet support for the Bricker amendment remained sufficiently strong that Eisenhower met several times with the senator in an effort to reach a compromise. The president was eager to avoid a rift with Bricker, especially since practically all of the Senate Republicans had endorsed the amendment. The meetings with Bricker were cordial, partly because Eisenhower had carefully crafted his public statements to insulate himself from the controversy over the amendment. The president, for example, announced at a press conference that his opposition rested on an understanding of the amendment's implications "as analyzed for me by the Secretary of State."[19] Bricker thus directed his wrath at John Foster Dulles, while conferring hopefully with Eisenhower. The negotiations foundered, however, over Bricker's unwillingness to yield on a clause that he thought essential to prevent treaties from encroaching on the powers of state governments and that the administration believed would cut "the treaty power back to what it was under the Articles of Confederation."[20]

Still hoping to avoid a complete break with Bricker, Eisenhower searched for a new basis for compromise. At a press conference on 1 July 1953, he stated that in order to quiet public fears he would now endorse an amendment that embodied the principle that an international agreement that conflicted with any provision of the Constitution would be null and void. He prevailed on Senate Majority Leader Knowland to introduce such an amendment and then immediately announced his "unqualified support" for it. Bricker, however, considered the Knowland substitute "woefully inadequate"—a judgment echoed by most Senate Republicans—and criticized "administration leaders," a thinly-disguised reference to Dulles, for providing the president with bad advice.[21] Bricker's misapprehension about presidential decision making, of course, was the product of Eisenhower's design. Dulles once again absorbed the blame, while Eisenhower determined the policy. With Congress in recess during autumn 1953, administration officials quietly offered assistance to a private group, the Committee for the Defense of the Constitution by Preserving the Treaty Power, as part of its efforts to mobilize public support for a compromise.

The denouement came when the Senate reconvened in early 1954. Because so many Republicans persisted in their support for Bricker's amendment, Eisenhower sought the help of Senate Democrats. With the president's behind-the-scenes encouragement, Senator Walter F. George (D., Ga.), ranking member of the Foreign Relations Committee, introduced a new compromise amendment. To prevent the Democrats from reaping political gains, both Knowland and Bricker offered revised versions of their earlier proposals, but both amendments went down to defeat in the Senate in February, the former for want of support from Bricker and the Old Guard, the latter for lack of backing from Republican moderates. The upper house then defeated the George substitute by the thinnest of margins—a single vote—the decisive vote cast by Harley Kilgore (D., W.V.), who allegedly tottered onto the Senate floor from a nearby saloon and muttered ''nay.'' The fate of the George resolution was determined not so much by the unexpected action of an inebriated legislator as by the resolute efforts of administration lobbyists, who emphasized that the president now believed that the passage of any amendment would unduly weaken the United States in world affairs.

Eisenhower's complex maneuvering ultimately frustrated the Brickerites and staved off the most serious challenge by the Old Guard to his control of foreign affairs. Eisenhower was unwavering in his opposition to the Bricker amendment, but he preferred indirection to confrontation so as to avoid inflicting wounds upon his Old Guard opponents that would not heal. As a result, Eisenhower defeated Bricker without alienating him—but without securing his surrender. For the next three years, Bricker continued to offer new versions of his amendment (they never came to a vote), consult periodically about them with the president, and hope for the replacement of Dulles and Brownell, whom he considered his real foes within the administration. Eisenhower also mollified Bricker and many of his allies by consulting legislative leaders on Indochina in 1954, or securing congressional resolutions, on Formosa in 1955 and the Middle East in 1957, before deciding whether to use American military power during an international crisis. Eisenhower thus gained his objective and did so largely on his own terms, but at the cost of considerable effort and exasperation. As he explained to his press secretary, ''If it's true that when you die the things that bothered you most are engraved on your skull, I'm sure I'll have there the mud and dirt of France during invasion and the name of Senator Bricker.''[22]

If Bricker troubled Eisenhower and tried his patience, Senator Joseph R. McCarthy of Wisconsin infuriated him and offended his most basic standards of decency. Eisenhower detested ''that goddamn McCarthy'' so much that he once blurted out to an aide, ''I don't understand how you can come into this office altogether clean after shaking hands with that fellow."[23] Yet despite his disgust, Eisenhower reserved his condemnations of McCarthy for private listeners, not public audiences. Instead he attempted to disarm McCarthy through a combination of masterly inactivity and backstage maneuvering, much as he had dealt with Bricker. Yet while Bricker was unable to stir much public interest in his campaign to save the Constitution, McCarthy excited popular passions and garnered headlines. As a result, Eisenhower endured extensive criticism even from some friends and advisers for failing to use his moral authority to confront a dangerous demagogue and his sordid crusade against domestic subversives.

For three years, McCarthy had been a powerful and destructive force in national politics by making outlandish charges of Communist subversion in Washington. McCarthy's accusations produced front-page stories but no confessions, indictments, or convictions. Yet McCarthy's reputation, popularity, and power grew with frightening speed as he preyed on the fears and discontent of those who wanted a simple explanation for American difficulties in the Cold War with the Soviet Union and the hot war in Korea. In his efforts to unmask treason, McCarthy showed no interest in due process or even simple decency. His wild accusations often destroyed reputations, even if subsequent investigations or hearings proved the accusations baseless. Many Republican leaders were suspicious of McCarthy's pugnacious, shoot-from-the-hip style. Still, they recognized the political advantages of keeping the heat on the Truman administration. "Keep talking and if one case doesn't work . . . ," Taft told his junior colleague, "proceed with another."[24] GOP leaders eventually regretted that advice. McCarthy became so enthralled with his own power that he was unwilling to moderate—much less abandon—his furious search for Communists, even with a Republican in the White House.

McCarthy caused problems for the new administration almost from Eisenhower's first day in the White House. Eisenhower learned on 22 January that McCarthy was trying to block confirmation of Gen. Walter Bedell Smith, Ike's former chief of staff during World War II, current director of Central Intelligence, and the president's choice for under secretary of state. Smith's offense was his commendation of a State Department official whom McCarthy accused of being a Communist. A few days later, McCarthy also made trouble over Eisenhower's choice for American High Commissioner of Germany, James B. Conant, the president of Harvard University, and Ike's selection for ambassador to the Soviet Union, career foreign service officer Charles E. Bohlen. The former irked McCarthy by insisting that no Harvard faculty member was a Communist, a statement so incredible to McCarthy that he took it as conclusive proof that Conant was a party member. The latter incurred McCarthy's wrath by failing to repudiate the Yalta agreements. Eisenhower stood by his nominees and through intermediaries persuaded McCarthy to desist on Smith and Conant and to tone down his criticism of Bohlen. He dispatched Vice-President Richard M. Nixon—whose methods resembled "McCarthyism in a white collar," in Adlai Stevenson's telling phrase—to get the senator to play ball. Yet while McCarthy told Nixon that he would cooperate with the administration and use his chairmanship of the Senate Committee on Government Operations only to root out "graft and corruption," he actually had no intention of giving up his hunt for Communists in government—the issue that had made him a national sensation—now that the Republicans had taken power. McCarthy had always been a rogue elephant and had no desire to become part of the herd. Eisenhower, for his part, did not believe the senator's assurances and dismissed Nixon's advice that the best way to deal with McCarthy was to make him "part of the team."[25]

Eisenhower, however, had no quarrel with McCarthy about the need to keep Communists out of government. In April 1953, Eisenhower signed an executive order that drastically revised the federal government's internal security program by authorizing the heads of all federal departments and agencies to fire any employee if there was reasonable doubt not only about his or her loyalty, but also reliability, or "good conduct and character." This executive order and two others issued during the next fifteen months stripped away most of the protection that an accused employee had enjoyed against summary dismissal, including a hearing to determine the accuracy of any charges, an appeal before dismissal, and an opportunity to exercise the Fifth Amendment right to avoid self-incrimination.[26]

Eisenhower told Dulles that such drastic restriction of due process was necessary because the top ranks of the State Department were filled with subversives. Blurring the distinction between New Dealers and Communists, the president asserted that the department's senior officials were loyal to Truman and Roosevelt, and worse, devoted to "the socialistic doctrine . . . practiced over the past two decades." Dulles, who had raised the suspicions of the McCarthyites because of a recommendation that he had written in 1946 for Alger Hiss, needed little prodding from the president to purge the State Department. His internal security officials boasted of removing almost five hundred employees in less than a year. Dulles himself made the final decision in the case of foreign service officer John Carter Vincent, an expert in Chinese affairs who had presciently warned of the collapse of the Nationalist government of Chiang Kai-shek. Though Vincent had been commended and promoted during his twenty-eight year diplomatic career and though Dulles concluded that Vincent was neither disloyal nor a security risk, the secretary of state nevertheless forced Vincent to resign in early 1953 because of "failure to meet the standard which is demanded of a Foreign Service Officer . . . at this critical time." Although McCarthy was still not satisfied—he was outraged that Vincent remained eligible for a pension—this forced retirement and other dismissals seemed to confirm that McCarthy's wild charges had been true all along.[27]

Eisenhower's handling of the Rosenberg case may also have deepened the climate of fear that sustained McCarthy. Julius and Ethel Rosenberg had been sentenced to death in 1951 for providing atomic secrets to agents of Communist countries. The case raised a storm of controversy because of doubts about the Rosenbergs' guilt and widespread fear that they had been the victims of McCarthyite hysteria. When their lawyers asked the new president for clemency, Eisenhower relied mainly on the counsel of Herbert Brownell. The attorney general argued that every legal, judicial, and procedural facility had been made available to the Rosenbergs during the course of their trial. The jury, moreover, had expressed no doubts about their guilt. Impressed by the weight of these arguments, Eisenhower announced on 11 February that he would not commute the sentences of the Rosenbergs. Their crime, he declared, "far exceeded that of the taking of the life of another citizen; it involves the deliberate betrayal of the entire nation and could very well result in the death of many, many thousands of innocent citizens. By their act these two individuals have in fact betrayed the cause of freedom for which free men are fighting and dying [in Korea] at this very hour." When the Rosenbergs were executed four months later, Eisenhower pursued this logic to a frightening conclusion. He accused the Rosenbergs of "immeasurably increasing the chances of atomic war" and so, perhaps, condemning "to death tens of millions of innocent people all over the world."[28]

Such inflammatory rhetoric, albeit contrary to Eisenhower's intentions, seemed to justify McCarthy's efforts to uncover treason in government. Despite his earlier assurances that he would desist in his hunt for Communists, McCarthy turned his Subcommittee on Investigations of the Government Operations Committee on the International Information Agency. After hearings on the Voice of America produced few results, McCarthy shifted his attention to another part of the IIA, the Overseas Library Program. McCarthy's assistants, Roy Cohn and G. David Schine, made a whirlwind inspection tour of overseas libraries in Europe during April 1953. Even though Dulles had already ordered the removal of books written not just by "Communists" and "fellow travellers" but also "controversial persons," Cohn and Schine still found objectionable material on the shelves. They also turned their junket into a tawdry media event. During a stop in Munich, for example, they resorted to sleazy humor about the sexual orientation of foreign service officers when they trumpeted their request for separate accommodations and then told the press, "We don't work for the State Department." McCarthy's subsequent hearings produced noisy allegations of Communist and "anti-anti-Communist" books on the shelves of official American libraries. Among the results of McCarthy's investigations and Dulles's new regulations concerning the holdings of overseas libraries was the burning of books, including some by none other than the eminent historian Foster Rhea Dulles, the secretary's cousin.[29]

Eisenhower was outraged. He could not stand the partisanship and the sensationalism of McCarthy's search for subversives; instead these matters should be handled, he thought, through the administrative procedures of the executive branch or, in the event of an alleged violation of law, by the courts. Furthermore, McCarthy offended some of the president's fundamental values, and Eisenhower publicly expressed his consternation. "Don't join the book burners," he implored the graduates of Dartmouth College in June 1953. "Don't be afraid to go in your library and read every book as long as that document does not offend our own ideas of decency. . . . How will we defeat communism unless we know what it is?" The people's right to read any book, he declared, is unquestioned, "or it isn't America."[30] Although he named no names in this commencement address, Eisenhower at last seemed to be ready "to crack down on McCarthy." The prospect of such strong action elated some of the president's aides, such as C. D. Jackson, who had long insisted that there was no other way to neutralize the senator.

Yet Eisenhower quickly disappointed the advocates of confrontation. At a press conference only a few days after his Dartmouth speech, he refused again to criticize McCarthy by name. The reason, as he confided in a letter to his friend Swede Hazlett, was that he completely disagreed "with the 'crack down' theory." McCarthy thrived on publicity, he explained. Recalling the career of another demagogue, Huey Long of Louisiana, Eisenhower decided that anything he might do to McCarthy would serve only to increase the senator's notoriety and make him a hero to those who admired the underdog. Because of "the special significance" of the office of president, any public criticism would immediately increase "the headline value" of McCarthy. Even worse, "an outburst intended to excoriate some individual, his motives and his methods, could do far more to destroy the position and authority of the attacker than it would do to damage the attacked."[31] Eisenhower refused to sully the dignity of the presidency with such an outburst. He expressed contempt for columnists and editorial writers who demanded that he get tough with McCarthy. "I was rather resentful," he wrote to a friend in July 1953, "that the very agencies who had made McCarthy were . . . loudest in their demands that I be the one to cut him down to size." Or, as he had said earlier, "I just won't get into a pissing contest with that skunk."[32]

While Eisenhower's analysis of McCarthy's popularity was shrewd, his strategy for lessening that appeal was flawed. Many people mistook Eisenhower's unwillingness to denounce McCarthy for timidity or quiet approval. Neither, of course, was the case; the president even went so far in private conversation as to liken McCarthy to Hitler—a man drunk with power, demanding unquestioning loyalty no matter how he acted. But the misapprehension about Eisenhower's attitude persisted and served to inflate McCarthy's reputation as a man too powerful for even the president to take on. Eisenhower was not craven, but simply convinced that he could effectively combat McCarthy by indirection, without sullying his office or exacerbating his differences with the senator's Old Guard supporters. Trying to put McCarthy's significance in perspective, Eisenhower dismissed the senator as "a pimple on [the] path of progress."[33] Yet such an assessment sadly underestimated the senator's malicious influence. Eisenhower preached decency and justice in defense of those McCarthy unfairly attacked. Yet such methods often could not repair the damage done by the senator's accusations, no matter how unjust. Eisenhower's main weapon against McCarthy, however, continued to be self-restraint. McCarthy would eventually hang himself, the president said, if given enough rope—but not before he had lynched many others, something Eisenhower apparently failed to consider.

Despite Eisenhower's endorsement of decency and fair play, his administration did not always live up to those standards. In November, Brownell told a meeting of business leaders that President Truman had allowed a Communist spy among his top advisers. The alleged subversive was Harry Dexter White, an assistant secretary of the Treasury, who had been investigated by the FBI. A grand jury did not think the evidence warranted an indictment, and Truman appointed White executive director of the International Monetary Fund, a position he held until his death in 1948. Because of Brownell's accusations, the chair of the House Un-American Activities Committee subpoenaed former President Truman. The whole affair quickly took on the appearance of a partisan effort to discredit the previous administration and raised embarrassing questions, which the president could not answer satisfactorily when he met the press. Eisenhower admitted that he had authorized the attorney general's speech. He implied that he thought Brownell had evidence to substantiate his charges, but he did not offer any explanation for the attorney general's failure to present his case to the proper judicial authorities. The frailty of the president's remarks further aroused public doubts. And Truman deepened them by going on national television to blast Brownell—whom he pointedly referred to as the former chair of the Republican National Committee—and assert that the Eisenhower administration had "fully embraced, for political advantage, McCarthyism."[34]

McCarthy himself now entered the fray. In a nationally televised reply to Truman's speech, McCarthy not only denounced the former president, but criticized the shortcomings of Eisenhower's policies. Enraged by this attack, C. D. Jackson insisted that the president could no longer continue his "Three Little Monkeys act" and tried to rally support within the White House for an end to "appeasing McCarthy." Eisenhower, however, reiterated that he would "not get into the gutter with that guy." He did agree, though, to issue a statement that left out the senator's name but declared emphatically that Communist subversion would not be an issue in the 1954 elections because the administration's own policies were eliminating the problem. Under pressure from Republican leaders, McCarthy publicly replied that he was not "challenging President Eisenhower's party leadership" but refused to concede that the Communists in government issue would fade away. Gallup Polls at the end of 1953 revealed that almost two-thirds of the public agreed with McCarthy and that his approval rating had climbed significantly since the previous summer. During his first year in the White House, then, Eisenhower had done little to rein in McCarthy and nothing to lessen his popularity.[35]

Indeed fear of McCarthy's power shaped the administration's handling of a controversy over the security clearance of J. Robert Oppenheimer, the scientist who had headed the Los Alamos National Laboratory where the first atomic bomb was built. In early December 1953, Secretary of Defense Charles Wilson informed Eisenhower that the FBI had submitted a report that carried "the gravest implications" about Oppenheimer's loyalty. Eisenhower, however, quickly discovered that the FBI had uncovered no new information but had simply recapitulated the well-known fact that Oppenheimer had friends and family members who were Communists. Many previous investigations of this evidence, Eisenhower noted, had invariably concluded that there was no proof of Oppenheimer's disloyalty.[36]

Nonetheless, Eisenhower still worried that Oppenheimer might be "a security risk" and that if McCarthy got wind of the charges, the Oppenheimer affair would be "our scandal." Thus Eisenhower took swift and secret action. He ordered the erection of a "blank wall" between Oppenheimer, who was a consultant to the Atomic Energy Commission, and all classified information pending a thorough administrative review. The AEC made that temporary order permanent several months later after the review revealed that Oppenheimer had tried to delay the development of the hydrogen bomb by discouraging fellow scientists from working on the project. Even though the AEC made its decision on the basis of its assessment of Oppenheimer's character rather than his loyalty, Eisenhower still thought that justice had been done because the investigation had followed "orderly procedure" and stuck to the facts. Moreover, he was relieved that he had kept McCarthy out of the Oppenheimer affair and so prevented reckless allegations that made out "all our scientists . . . to be Reds."[37]

Although Eisenhower prevented McCarthy from exploiting the Oppenheimer case, he could not stop the senator from launching an investigation into Communist penetration of the army. In early 1954, McCarthy decided that he could demonstrate that the army was unable to weed out subversives by concentrating on a single case, that of Maj. Irving Peress. A dentist who was drafted into the army, Peress was deemed a security risk because of past associations and was recommended for discharge. Through bureaucratic bungling he was instead promoted. In public hearings, McCarthy first grilled Peress and then his post commander, Gen. Ralph W. Zwicker, whom he pronounced unfit to wear a soldier's uniform. Appalled by the virulence of McCarthy's attack, Secretary of the Army Robert T. Stevens announced that he would not permit Zwicker or any other officer to appear at the hearings. Stevens relented after making a private deal with McCarthy but then erred by failing to secure the senator's public declaration that he would not mistreat army witnesses. Newspaper headlines screamed that the army had surrendered to McCarthy.

Eisenhower was "very mad and getting fed up," and his public reaction, although still measured, was more effective at undercutting McCarthy than ever before. McCarthy was now attacking "his Army" and a general—Zwicker—whom he had commended for heroism in battle following the D-Day landings. Moreover, Eisenhower believed that it was one thing to expose the failings of his Democratic predecessors, but quite another to criticize Republican officials and, by implication, the president himself. Eisenhower thought that McCarthy was now trying to embarrass his administration in order to prepare the way for a run for presidency. "He's the last guy in the world who'll ever get there," Eisenhower vowed, "if I have anything to say." The president would still not utter McCarthy's name in public, but he commended Zwicker's patriotism and insisted that members of his administration be given "the same respect and courtesy that I require that they show to the members of the legislative body."[38]

After McCarthy made a patronizing reply that alienated many Republican leaders, Eisenhower took additional steps. He intervened to ensure that Nixon, not McCarthy, would deliver the GOP reply over national television to Adlai Stevenson's accusation that the Republican party "was half Eisenhower, half McCarthy." Then he allowed Secretary of Defense Wilson to release a report charging that McCarthy and Cohn had repeatedly pressured the army to give favorable treatment to their associate, G. David Schine, who had been drafted in late 1953. Adding to the senator's distress was a highly critical report by Edward R. Murrow on his influential television program, "See It Now," and a mocking speech on the Senate floor by moderate Republican Ralph Flanders of Vermont, who ridiculed McCarthy for going forth to battle communism and proudly returning "with the scalp of a pink dentist."[39]

Eisenhower soon dealt McCarthy an even more stunning blow by invoking executive privilege to prevent congressional interrogation of members of the executive branch. Eisenhower took this step—his only direct action to disarm the senator—on 17 May, shortly after the beginning of nationally televised Army-McCarthy hearings. The proceedings quickly degenerated into a rowdy tussle over whether McCarthy and his staff had sought to exert improper influence with the army on behalf of Private Schine. When the committee threatened to subpoena members of the White House staff, Eisenhower objected for constitutional and political reasons. A strong believer in the separation of powers, he asserted that he had the right to withhold information from Congress about conversations between members of the executive branch to ensure that they would "be completely candid in advising with each other on official matters."[40] Eisenhower also wanted to avoid the political embarrassment that would result from the disclosure that the White House had sought to use the Schine matter to derail McCarthy's investigation of the army.

Accordingly, Eisenhower directed members of the executive branch not to testify on confidential matters and justified his action with the boldest assertion of executive privilege in the history of the republic. Although the president cited precedents that reached back to the administration of George Washington, a recent authority on constitutional law, Raoul Berger, has dismissed Eisenhower's claim as "altogether without historical foundation."[41] Taken aback, McCarthy urged members of the executive branch to defy the president's injunction, an appeal that Eisenhower considered "the most disloyal act we have ever had by anyone in the government of the United States." Without administration witnesses, the hearings finally collapsed in June, but not before McCarthy had put on a performance that Eisenhower found "disgusting," sad, and shameful.[42] Most people agreed. Public opinion turned against McCarthy, and many people now shared the contempt of army counsel Joseph N. Welch, who asked, "Have you no sense of decency, sir, at long last?"[43]

Because of the widespread belief that the Army-McCarthy hearings were a degrading spectacle, a handful of apprehensive Republican senators was finally prepared to act. Concerned about the approaching congressional elections, they resolved not merely to halt McCarthy's hearings, but to break his power. In late July, Flanders introduced a resolution of censure. While McCarthy stood by muttering obscenities, Arthur Watkins (R., Utah), conducted the hearings on the resolution with dignity and fairness. Five months later—and after the elections—about half the Republicans joined with the Democrats to censure McCarthy for "obstructing the constitutional processes of the Senate" and acting in a manner that "tended to bring the Senate into dishonor and disrepute."[44] Eisenhower played no role in the Senate's action, but he made clear his reaction to the vote by inviting Watkins to the White House and releasing a letter of congratulations to the senator. McCarthy's power was broken, just as Eisenhower had long predicted. Yet in retrospect one can only wonder whether Eisenhower's earlier and sustained intervention could have hastened McCarthy's downfall and spared many of his innocent victims.

McCarthy got his last headline by bitterly attacking Eisenhower. Rather than expressing regret to the Senate over his conduct, McCarthy instead declared that he owed the American people an apology for campaigning for Eisenhower. By supporting Ike in 1952, McCarthy said that he had unintentionally perpetrated a hoax on the public; he had promised a new administration that would make "a vigorous, forceful drive against Communists in government," but actually had helped elect a president who "urges that we be patient with the Communist hoodlums."[45] Eisenhower, who fully expected this parting shot, thought that McCarthy had only disgraced himself one last time. Despite prodding at a press conference, Eisenhower as ever refused to quarrel with McCarthy personally. In response to a reporter's question, he expressed no fear that McCarthy would bolt the GOP and run for president on a third-party ticket in 1956. The only hope for the GOP, he predicted, lay with the mainstream group that he was leading, the "progressive moderates."[46]

Eisenhower had repeatedly offered such advice to party leaders throughout the Bricker and McCarthy controversies. The Republican image needed an overhaul, he argued. The party should take to the middle ground, the only terrain for building consensus and reaching the vast majority of voters. While the Democrats clung to the rhetoric of the depression years and offered paternalistic security, the Republicans could inspire hope in the future by stressing growth and individual opportunity. Eisenhower believed that such thinking would appeal to young Americans and provide the GOP with a decisive advantage in the contest for voters under thirty-five.

The president encouraged Republican candidates to carry this moderate message to the voters, but he was reluctant to join in the campaign of 1954. His hesitancy was not for lack of concern. He urged members of his cabinet, for example, to do all they could to elect Republican candidates, and that included using federal money on authorized projects for maximum political advantage. It was his desire to remain above partisanship that kept him from direct participation in the campaign. He confessed to Dewey that nothing had so offended his sense of propriety as Truman's barnstorming campaign in 1948. Quite apart from his scruples about proper presidential conduct, Eisenhower wanted to retain bipartisan support for his programs; that support would be seriously jeopardized if he publicly attacked the opposition.

Only when polls indicated that the Democrats might win a sweeping victory did Eisenhower reconsider his stand. In the month preceding the election, he traveled some ten thousand miles and made almost forty speeches. He concentrated his public remarks on the notable improvement in national affairs after two years of his administration. Under Republican stewardship, the anguish and disruption of the Korean War had ended; the national budget had been reduced, the deficit slashed, and taxes lowered. If Democrats won control of Congress, there would be a kind of Cold War stalemate in Washington, he predicted. The prospect of running the government under such circumstances, he said, would be most frustrating.

Yet the election produced precisely those circumstances he dreaded. The Democrats picked up some twenty seats in the House for a thirty vote majority and added two in the Senate for a majority of one.

The Republican reverses actually were smaller than the usual losses by the party in power in midterm elections. Many observers thought Eisenhower had minimized the defeat and "prevented what might have been a great disaster."[47] Still, the recession that had reached its peak earlier in the year may have prevented Eisenhower, despite his personal appeal, from persuading the voters to put the Republicans back in control of Congress. Some polls indicated that many people thought that a Democratic Congress would result in a stronger economy.[48]

Yet bickering and recriminations among Republicans followed the defeat. Bitter members of the Old Guard blamed the GOP losses on Eisenhower. His administration had not sustained traditional Republican principles, they said, nor had it successfully sold its own policies to the nation. In private remarks, the president turned their criticism back on them. Republicans would have to realize, he argued, that they could not survive unless they became a party of "progressive moderates" and proved to people that they were not controlled by proselytizers of the extreme right. Too many of the accomplishments of his administration, he complained, had "been overshadowed by the headline value of the McCarthy argument . . . and the Bricker Amendment debates."[49] Eisenhower had no desire to purge these right-wing elements from the GOP or to form a new party of his own. Yet if the Old Guard tried to reclaim the GOP by nominating one of their own for the presidency, "they've got another thought coming," he vowed to his press secretary James C. Hagerty. "I'll go up and down this country, campaigning against them. I'll fight them right down the line."[50] Thus, for Eisenhower the election raised fundamental questions about the future of the Republican party. These concerns remained at the back of his mind, but his most immediate task in the aftermath of the election was to determine how to govern now that the Democrats controlled Congress.

4

★ ★ ★ ★ ★

WAGING COLD WAR

"Our country has come through a painful period of trial and disillusionment since the victory of 1945," President Eisenhower told the American people on 2 February 1953 in his first state of the union message. Instead of "a world of peace and cooperation," Americans inhabited "a world of turmoil" created by "the calculated pressures of aggressive communism." The "one clear lesson" of the previous troubled eight years, Eisenhower declared, was that the United States needed "a new, positive foreign policy," one that seized the initiative from Communist aggressors, made "the free world secure," and rested upon military strength that did not overburden the economy.[1]

Soon after taking office, Eisenhower began the enormous task of reshaping national security policy to conform to these standards. In doing so, the president and his aides struggled with developments that were revolutionary—the advent of thermonuclear weapons—or baffling—the emergence of powerful Third World nationalist movements. Not surprisingly, the results of Eisenhower's reformulation of foreign and defense policy during the first two years of his presidency were decidedly mixed. Despite the New Look, as Eisenhower's basic national security policy was commonly known, the president and his advisers were better at assessing the shortcomings of past policies than at devising new ones to alleviate these problems. Despite their desire to take the initiative, they faced repeated crises in the Middle East, Latin America, and East Asia. Despite their longing for peace, Eisenhower and his associates had to settle for new—and in some cases far more dubious, dangerous, or destructive—methods of waging Cold War.

One of the new administration's first orders of business was to reduce the budget for national security expenditures for fiscal year 1954 proposed by the departing Truman administration. During Truman's last three years in office, defense spending skyrocketed from $13.5 billion to more than $50 billion. The Korean War, of course, provided the impetus for this astounding increase. Yet even before the North Korean attack, the Truman administration had been inclined toward such a build-up, owing to a sweeping reassessment of national security policy known as NSC 68. Presented to the president by the National Security Council in April 1950, NSC 68 concluded that the Soviet Union aspired to "world domination" and would attain such powerful military capabilities by 1954 that it might risk war to carry out its totalitarian design. To meet this extraordinary danger, NSC 68 called for a rapid increase of "political, economic, and military strength in the free world."[2] Unwilling at first to approve this frightening analysis, Truman endorsed it barely three months after the outbreak of the Korean War. In early 1953, Eisenhower inherited Truman's three-year-old basic statement of national security policy as well as his predecessor's vastly expanded defense budget.

Eisenhower considered the analysis of NSC 68 unsound and Truman's national security expenditures fundamentally dangerous. The president agreed that the Soviet Union gravely imperiled U.S. security, but he rejected the idea that the threat would reach a peak in any given year. The situation in the 1950s was nothing like 1944, when the Allies invaded Nazi-occupied France, he told reporters. In planning Operation OVERLORD, he explained, "We picked the day. We knew when we wanted our maximum force. We knew the buildup we wanted. We knew exactly what we were up against." A decade later, the United States faced not "a moment of danger," but "an age of danger."[3] The nation had to prepare for the long haul and make sure that national security expenditures did not progressively weaken the health of the economy. Eisenhower feared that Truman's proposed budget for fiscal 1954 would do so because of its projected deficit of $9.9 billion. Continued in successive years, such spending, Eisenhower warned, would lead to "a permanent state of mobilization" in which "our whole democratic way of life would be destroyed."[4] Thus in April, he approved a revised request for new appropriations in fiscal 1954 of $63.2 billion, an amount that was almost $10 billion less than Truman's proposal, with the largest reduction—$5.2 billion—in national security programs.[5]

Eisenhower approved this measure despite heated criticism from within and outside his administration by those who thought he was wielding a budgetary meat ax and others who complained that he had not cut deeply enough. The Joint Chiefs of Staff vehemently protested that any reductions in defense spending would harm national security, but Eisenhower had little patience with their warnings. "Perhaps the [National Security] Council should have a report as to whether national bankruptcy or national destruction would get us first," he shot back in reply to the Joint Chiefs' dire predictions. To those such as Secretary of the Treasury George M. Humphrey who wanted greater reductions than Eisenhower had approved in the Mutual Security Program, the president replied that foreign aid was no "giveaway" program.[6] The most vociferous demand for further cuts came from Senator Robert A. Taft of Ohio, the Republican majority leader, who dismissed Eisenhower's savings as "puny" and predicted that the budget would doom the Republicans in the 1954 elections because it precluded tax reductions. Eisenhower was so infuriated by Taft's outburst that associates steered the conversation in a different direction until the president had "cooled down somewhat."[7] Taft's objections, however, reflected the thinking of many of the GOP Old Guard, a faction that often struck a very different balance than the president between domestic economy and national security.

However significant, the reduction in fiscal 1954 spending was only a beginning. Before Congress acted, Eisenhower's associates had time to make only incremental adjustments, not to reshape military and foreign policy programs or reevaluate the premises on which they rested. In early May, as soon as the administration settled its position on the immediate question of next fiscal year's expenditures, Eisenhower established Project Solarium to undertake a comprehensive reappraisal of national security policy.

Project Solarium came under the supervision of the National Security Council, an organization on which Eisenhower relied heavily to formulate Cold War policy. Established in 1947, the NSC, Eisenhower believed, was only a "shadow agency" with limited effectiveness during the Truman years. At the beginning of his presidency, Eisenhower implemented changes based on the recommendations of Robert Cutler, a banker with organizational expertise who began a study of the NSC during the presidential transition. Among Eisenhower's innovations was the creation of a Planning Board and an Operations Coordinating Board to help prepare and monitor the implementation of policy.

Eisenhower also established the office of special assistant to the president for national security affairs, a position to which he appointed Cutler. These reforms reflected Eisenhower's penchant for orderly staff procedures and effective teamwork. Because of his deep concern about the economic implications of national security programs, Eisenhower also expanded the team to include the secretary of the Treasury and director of the Bureau of the Budget in addition to the statutory members—the president, vice-president, secretaries of state and defense, and the director of the office of defense mobilization. Even more important was Eisenhower's active participation in the NSC debates. In sharp contrast to Truman, who usually absented himself from council deliberations, Eisenhower attended more than 90 percent of the 366 NSC meetings during his presidency. Although the president sometimes reserved his opinions, he often guided the exchange by asking pointed questions or clearly enunciating his own position.[8]

The president and the National Security Council heard the reports of three task forces established under Project Solarium, each proposing very different basic policies. The first group, headed by Soviet specialist George F. Kennan, recommended that Eisenhower adopt the essentials of Truman's containment policies. No one was better equipped than Kennan to argue the case for continuity, since he had been one of the architects of Truman's containment policies during the late 1940s. Envisioning a long-term political threat to Western interests, Kennan counseled in his famous article in *Foreign Affairs*, written under the pseudonym X, "the adroit and vigilant application of counter-force at a series of constantly shifting geographical and political points, corresponding to the shifts and maneuvers of Soviet policy."[9] To some critical observers, notably the prominent columnist Walter Lippmann, the X article appeared to be a prescription for endless military involvement on the periphery of Soviet power that would drain American resources. Kennan, however, never advocated such dispersion. In policy papers, he urged that the administration concentrate on protecting vital areas of economic and military power, such as Western Europe and Japan, from Communist expansionism. Ultimately, he envisioned the mellowing of the Soviet regime and negotiations that would lead to a détente in Russian-American relations.

As implemented, containment ultimately diverged from Kennan's ideas. At first, major administration initiatives, such as the Marshall Plan and the consolidation of the western powers' occupation zones into West Germany, generally conformed to Kennan's version of containment. But the creation of the North Atlantic Treaty Organization in 1949, in Kennan's view, rested on an exaggerated fear of the possibility of

Soviet attack. By the time the Truman administration began to implement NSC 68, Kennan had left the government convinced that containment had become excessively militarized and unduly rigid. Conservatives, including many Republicans, attacked containment from a different angle. They charged that it was a strategy that yielded the initiative to the Soviets and that forswore the liberation of peoples who lived under Communist rule. The Korean War, from this perspective, epitomized the failings of containment. It produced nothing more than deadlock, largely because of self-imposed limits on the use of military power, and did so at enormous human and material expense. The Republican party platform reflected this outlook when it condemned containment as "negative, futile and immoral." Containment—or at least the Truman administration's version of it in the early 1950s—was anything, then, but a popular policy.

In his report for Project Solarium, Kennan recommended that the Eisenhower administration accept the containment principles that he had advanced in the late 1940s but support them with national security expenditures equal to those of the early 1950s. The United States had to prepare not for imminent war, but for a long-term political and psychological threat, Kennan's task force concluded. Although containing the growth of Communist power would necessitate the continuation of defense spending at current levels, "there is no question," Kennan's panel insisted, "that our country has the *economic capacity*" to do so. The strength and persistence of the United States and its allies would eventually contribute to the deterioration of Soviet power "to a point which no longer constitutes a threat . . . to world peace."

The other two Solarium study groups proposed that Eisenhower break sharply with the approach of his predecessor. The second task force, headed by Air Force General James McCormack, recommended that the president put the Soviets on notice that he would respond to any effort to expand the Communist bloc by waging nuclear war. Creating such "a military seal around the Soviet Union," McCormack pointed out, had the advantage of limiting defense expenditures, since the United States had to be ready only to launch a long-range atomic offensive. The third group, directed by Adm. Richard L. Conolly, called for winning the Cold War by pushing back Soviet influence and fomenting division and disruption within the Communist bloc. Conolly's panel urged heavy reliance on propaganda and covert operations as well as military, diplomatic, and economic instruments. Such a comprehensive effort was necessary, they insisted, because Soviet strength would only continue to grow until "reversed by positive action."[10]

Although the three reports had many similarities, as Eisenhower noted, they precipitated an extended debate among the president and his national security advisers. The Planning Board attempted to write a new basic statement of national security policy that drew on the reports from Project Solarium but could not agree at first about how to balance economy and security. The budget and Treasury representatives stressed that deficits or high taxes "over a sustained period" could "dangerously weaken" the American economy, destroy incentives for long-term economic growth, and undermine free institutions. State and defense representatives insisted that current defense costs could be maintained indefinitely without serious damage to the economy, provided taxes were increased. The real difference between these two views, Budget Director Joseph M. Dodge told the NSC on 7 October, was their assessment of the Soviet threat. Diplomatic and military officials failed to recognize, he charged, that the Soviets intended "to destroy our capitalist economy by means of economic warfare." It would do the country no good to succumb to the internal threat because it had tried to do too much to meet the external threat, added Humphrey. Dulles shot back that the United States could not throw its "defense system out the window because we had to balance the budget." In support of Dulles's position, Secretary of Defense Charles E. Wilson declared, "If we ever go to the American people and tell them that we are putting a balanced budget ahead of defense it would be a terrible day."[11]

Those who advocated economy prevailed. They did so because Eisenhower shared their views. During the NSC debate on 7 October, the president insisted that the real issue "was the long-term capacity of the United States to survive." The economy could endure anything for a year or two, but "in the long run this country must have a sound dollar," he stated firmly. "Moreover, this sound dollar lies at the very basis of a sound capability for defense." NSC 162/2, "Basic National Security Policy," which Eisenhower approved on 30 October, affirmed this philosophy. "A strong, healthy and expanding economy is essential to the security and stability of the free world," concluded NSC 162/2.[12]

To meet the Soviet threat without endangering the health of the economy, the Eisenhower administration relied heavily on nuclear weapons. NSC 162/2 called for "a strong military posture, with emphasis on the capability of inflicting massive retaliatory damage by offensive striking power." The Eisenhower administration hoped that fear of an atomic strike would prevent the Soviets from resorting to military action. But should war erupt, nuclear weapons, despite their devastating effect, would be "as available for use as other munitions."[13]

Eisenhower's basic national security policy, known as the New Look, reduced defense spending and drastically changed allocations among the services. Eisenhower's defense budget in fiscal 1955 was almost $5 billion less than his request for funds for the previous year. The end of the Korean War obviously contributed to some of the savings, but so too did the New Look. Because of the emphasis on nuclear retaliation, Eisenhower allocated proportionately more money to the service that would carry out an atomic strike on the Soviet Union, the air force, and less to the army and navy. The strength of the army shrank by 500,000 in the eighteen months after the approval of the New Look, and that service's share of the defense budget sank from 33 percent to 25 percent. The air force, conversely, actually increased modestly in size and enlarged its share of the services' financial pie from 39 percent to a whopping 47 percent.[14] Clearly these changes arose from Eisenhower's fundamental reshaping of national security policy.

Not so new was the Eisenhower administration's assessment of the Soviet threat that the armed forces prepared to meet. The death of Soviet Premier Josef V. Stalin on 5 March 1953 seemed to create a new opportunity for the easing of Cold War tensions. A Soviet peace offensive—a flurry of statements that the new Russian leadership genuinely desired to resolve East-West problems—nurtured those hopes. Eisenhower responded on 16 April by delivering a speech entitled "The Chance for Peace," in which he demanded "concrete evidence" of Soviet sincerity, such as the willingness to sign an Austrian peace treaty or contribute to a settlement of the Korean War. Movingly Eisenhower equated "every gun that is made, every warship launched, every rocket fired" with "a theft from those who hunger and are not fed, those who are cold and not clothed." The United States was ready to commit its strength "to serving the *needs*, rather than the *fears*, of the world. . . . What is the Soviet Union ready to do?" he inquired.[15] Nothing constructive, was the answer of NSC 162/2. The peace offensive was only propaganda aimed at dividing the West "by raising false hopes" and making the United States appear to be intransigent, according to Eisenhower's basic national security document. In short, "the basic Soviet objectives continue to be consolidation and expansion of their own sphere of power and the eventual domination of the non-communist world," asserted NSC 162/2.[16]

The New Look also did not significantly alter the importance of collective security in American defense policy. NSC 68 had called for the mobilization of the political, economic, and military strength of the free world in order to prevent the Soviet Union from winning the Cold War. NSC 162/2 reiterated that the United States could not "meet its defense needs, even at exorbitant cost, without the support of allies." NATO was absolutely critical, and Eisenhower and Dulles tirelessly—albeit unsuccessfully—urged their allies to approve the European Defense Community, a plan for the integration of West German military forces into a European army under NATO command. Because of the New Look's emphasis on atomic retaliatory power, the United States also had to win or retain allies and friends in the Middle East and East Asia to ensure that the free world had sufficient manpower for local defense. In contrast, however, to NSC 68's emphasis on expanding military and economic aid, NSC 162/2 advocated reforms in international trade and tariff policies that would progressively lessen foreign dependence on American assistance and so reduce the burden on the American economy.[17]

On the emotional issue of the liberation of Communist bloc nations, the New Look also did not represent a significant departure from Truman's containment policies. During the campaign of 1952, the Republicans adopted a platform that condemned containment as "negative, futile and immoral" because it abandoned "countless human beings to a despotism and Godless terrorism." Dulles specifically promised that if Eisenhower entered the White House, he would use "all means to secure the liberation of Eastern Europe." Eisenhower insisted on adding the qualifying adjective "peaceful" to Dulles's pledge, and NSC 162/2 made clear that this restriction made liberation nothing more than hollow rhetoric.[18] The Soviet Union, the paper concluded, would not yield control except by force in any European satellite. Greater possibilities existed, however, for driving a wedge between Russia and the People's Republic of China, since "basic differences" might eventually "strain or break the alliance" between the two nations. Like its predecessor, then, the Eisenhower administration did not view communism as solidly monolithic, but neither did it realistically expect to do anything to break up the Soviet bloc.[19]

Doubts also arose about whether Eisenhower's New Look would be more successful than Truman's policies at avoiding limited war on the periphery of Soviet power. Eisenhower hoped retaliatory atomic power would prevent another Korea, an indecisive conflict that drained American resources. The problem with atomic retaliation was the credibility of the threat. Growing Soviet atomic capabilities, as NSC 162/2 pointed out, might tend to weaken American deterrence. "As general war becomes more devastating for both sides," the document explained, "the threat to resort to it becomes less available as a sanction against local aggression." "What if they [the Soviets] call our bluff and do move," asked one of the Project Solarium participants of General

McCormack. "How do you convince the American people and the U.S. Congress to declare war?" "This is a problem," McCormack replied.[20] Indeed persuading the public that local aggression perhaps in an area not critical to American security required a nuclear response was the fundamental difficulty with the New Look.[21]

The advent of new weapons only compounded the dilemma. During the early years of Eisenhower's presidency, tactical nuclear weapons became an important part of air, naval, and ground forces. Smaller and more versatile, these new atomic devices could be fired by artillery pieces, incorporated into depth charges, mounted on surface-to-surface guided missiles, or carried in most fighter aircraft. Even more frightening was the development of the hydrogen or thermonuclear bomb, a weapon with destructive capacity hundreds of times greater than an atomic bomb. First tested by the United States in November 1952 and by the Soviet Union in August 1953, the H-bomb threatened to make war so devastating "as to threaten the survival of Western civilization."[22] Indeed Eisenhower predicted that at the end of a nuclear war, every nation, even if victorious, would emerge as a dictatorship. Because of this catastrophic potential, Eisenhower reasoned, the United States would become involved in a never-ending race to maintain the effectiveness of its deterrent, a contest that might lead to a garrison state and the extinction of cherished values. "In such circumstances," he wrote to Dulles, "we would be forced to consider whether or not our duty to future generations did not require us to *initiate* war at the most propitious moment that we could designate."[23] The startling result of Eisenhower's reflection was that preventive thermonuclear war might be the nation's best option.

Fearful that the world was "racing toward catastrophe," Eisenhower made an innovative proposal to "put a brake on this movement."[24] The president's action was the product of Operation Candor, a proposal advanced by physicist J. Robert Oppenheimer to inform the public about "the grim situation" arising from the nuclear arms race. Speaking to the National Security Council on 27 May 1953, Oppenheimer insisted that it was imperative that the American people understood that atomic arsenals were rapidly expanding and now included hydrogen bombs and that there was no sure defense against surprise attack. Although worried about disclosing classified information, Eisenhower agreed in principle with Oppenheimer's suggestion for Operation Candor, since free government could only work with an informed citizenry. After months of debate and planning, Eisenhower addressed the United Nations General Assembly on 8 December. He warned of "two atomic colossi" eying each other malevolently "across a trembling world" and threatening "the annihilation of the irreplaceable heritage of mankind." The time had come, he asserted, to get the atomic bomb out of the hands of soldiers and into "the hands of those who will know how to strip its military casing and adapt it to the arts of peace." Accordingly he called on the Soviet Union and Great Britain to join with the United States in contributing small amounts of fissionable material to an International Atomic Energy Authority, which would use it for constructive purposes. Under Eisenhower's Atoms for Peace plan, "the miraculous inventiveness of man shall not be dedicated to his death, but consecrated to his life."[25]

Despite an overwhelming ovation from the General Assembly, Atoms for Peace failed to brake the race toward catastrophe. Eisenhower hoped for "the tiniest of starts" toward cooperation with the Soviet Union that "might expand into something broader."[26] Stockpiles of fissionable material were small enough in 1953 that even modest contributions to an international agency would slow the nuclear build-up. The Soviets, however, protested that Atoms for Peace would encourage nuclear proliferation, among its many shortcomings. Reaction at home was often critical as well. Many members of Congress worried that Eisenhower would give away atomic secrets. Some commentators derisively referred to his plan as "Watts for Hottentots." Eisenhower, in short, took a small, symbolic first step toward arms control, but others did not follow in his footsteps.[27]

The results of the New Look, then, were uncertain. Eisenhower elevated economic considerations to a central place in national security policy, and he shaped a defense policy that was less expensive over the long haul. Yet it was doubtful that the New Look provided "more basic security at less cost," as Dulles boasted.[28] The heavy reliance on nuclear weapons created problems of credibility that the administration had not resolved. Negotiations for arms control also went nowhere. Eisenhower had fundamentally revised defense policy, but it was by no means clear that the country was more secure.

Eisenhower distinguished between national security policy and diplomacy—the daily management of foreign relations—and entrusted principal responsibility for the latter task to Secretary of State John Foster Dulles. Eisenhower also relied heavily on Dulles in shaping the administration's basic foreign and military policies. This close collaboration aroused strong and persistent controversy. Critics often wondered who was in charge of foreign policy and usually suspected that the secretary of state was the senior partner, if not the sole proprietor.

Eisenhower, they maintained, had delegated—or abdicated—to Dulles responsibilities that should have been the president's alone.

Misunderstandings sometimes arise from appearances. The secretary of state looked like an effigy on a medieval tomb. His countenance was dour and his demeanor austere. He seemed to lack elementary human warmth. He spoke with an excruciating slowness and solemnity. He had an unfortunate penchant for apocalyptic phrases, such as "agonizing reappraisal" and "brink of war." His personality seemed to be a deadly mixture of Presbyterian moralist and prosecuting attorney. If it was easy to like Ike, it was even easier to dislike Dulles.

Dulles was far more complex than this stereotype, and Eisenhower appreciated the secretary of state's strengths and shortcomings. According to the president, Dulles had the best training of anyone he knew for the senior cabinet post. "There is probably no one in the world who has the technical competence of Foster Dulles in the diplomatic field," Eisenhower exclaimed. "He has spent his life in this work in one form or another and is a man of great intellectual capacity and moral courage." Yet Eisenhower also frankly acknowledged Dulles's insufficiencies. The secretary of state seemed to lack, the president speculated, any "understanding as to how his words and manner may affect another personality." Eisenhower also decried Dulles's tendency to act as "a sort of international prosecuting attorney." But he made clear that Dulles's deficiencies lay "in the general field of personality, not in his capacity as a student of foreign affairs."[29]

Eisenhower more than held his own with Dulles. Indeed the two forged an extraordinary partnership in the making of foreign affairs. Both had strong personalities, subtle and fertile minds, and wide experience in international relations. Neither was capable of dominating the other, and their relationship probably could not have been so close if one had exercised predominant influence. To be sure, Eisenhower recognized that he had final authority, and Dulles never forgot that he was acting in the president's name. Yet as Richard H. Immerman, one of the closest students of the Eisenhower-Dulles relationship, has concluded, "They were in a real sense a team."[30]

One of the first and most pressing issues in foreign policy that they faced together was Korea; so urgent was it that Eisenhower had begun to look for a solution to this stalemated war even before he took office. Fulfilling his campaign pledge, Eisenhower left New York in secrecy in late November 1952 and flew across the Pacific to South Korea. There, he interviewed officers and enlisted men—including his own son John, who was serving in a frontline infantry division—and examined the blasted terrain of the battle front. The visit provided him with "a

renewed appreciation of the efficiency, durability, and fighting qualities" of American troops and a determination not to allow these soldiers
to "stand forever on a static front and continue to accept casualties
without any visible results."[31]

After returning from Korea, he visited Gen. Douglas MacArthur,
whose outspoken criticism of Truman's limited war policies had by no
means faded away. MacArthur proposed that Eisenhower hold a summit conference with Stalin to negotiate an agreement for the neutraliza-
tion not only of Korea, but also Germany, Austria, and Japan. Should
Stalin refuse to cooperate, MacArthur urged an all-out effort to win in
Korea, which might include atomic bombing, amphibious landings on
North Korean coasts, or the spreading of radioactive materials along
enemy lines of communication. Chary of actions that could alienate
allies and turn world opinion against the United States, Eisenhower
simply thanked MacArthur and promised to study the general's recommendations. Despite MacArthur's counsel and his own reconnaissance
of the battlefield, Eisenhower remained uncertain about how to extricate
the United States from the Korean deadlock.[32]

During his first several months in office, Eisenhower searched for a
plan to end the war. Peace talks had broken down over the issue of the
repatriation of prisoners of war, and Eisenhower looked for a way to
move the negotiations off dead center. The president discussed a wide
range of political and military options in a series of meetings of the
National Security Council that included not only top military and
political officials, but also, on one occasion, civilian consultants—mainly
prominent Republican internationalists. The discussions were often
rambling and indeterminate, but they covered a wide range of possibilities. Dulles advocated an offensive that would carry up to the waist
of the peninsula—around the 39th parallel. Eisenhower, however,
retorted that Communist opposition to such an escalation might force
the United States to undertake a general mobilization. The president
raised the possibility of using tactical atomic weapons, but Gen. Omar
N. Bradley, the chair of the Joint Chiefs of Staff, pointed out that there
were few targets. The upshot of these discussions was an agreement
that if the United States did expand the war, the escalation would
include the use of atomic weapons against targets in Manchuria and
China. Yet this agreement, which took three months to hammer out, did
not constitute a plan to settle the war, only one that would be
implemented if all hope of a negotiated settlement failed.

To secure such an agreement, Dulles applied international pressure
on the Chinese and Soviets. In conversation with Indian Prime Minister
Jawaharlal Nehru, Dulles made clear that if negotiations failed to yield

results, the United States would probably step up its military efforts and "might well extend the area of conflict." Several days later, American ambassador Charles E. Bohlen told the Soviet foreign minister that the breakdown of peace talks would "create a situation which the U.S. Government is seeking most earnestly to avoid." Dulles later claimed that these statements constituted an "unmistakable warning" to Communist China that the United States would use its atomic arsenal if there was not a prompt settlement of the Korean War. Yet the signals were so indirect and obtuse that it seems unlikely that they conveyed the message that Dulles later said he intended. The North Koreans and the Chinese, however, did accept a compromise on the prisoner of war issue that allowed an armistice to take effect on 27 July. More influential with the enemy than Dulles's alleged nuclear diplomacy was war weariness and pressure from the post-Stalinist leadership of the Soviet Union. The Eisenhower administration nevertheless could rightly celebrate a major achievement.[33]

While Korea preoccupied Eisenhower during his first months in office, the complexities of Third World nationalism demanded his attention throughout the eight years of his presidency. "Nationalism is on the march," Eisenhower observed in his diary just two weeks before his inauguration. British Prime Minister Winston Churchill was then visiting Washington, and Eisenhower observed how sadly out of touch Churchill was with "present international complexities." The prime minister did not recognize the profound international consequences of the emergence of previously dependent Asian, African, and Latin American nations. Instead he was "trying to relive the days of World War II," when the British and Americans, at least to some extent, had been able to direct world affairs from "some rather Olympian platform."[34] Churchill dwelt, Eisenhower believed, in a world that had ceased to exist.

Yet as much as Eisenhower recognized the importance of Third World nationalism, he found it profoundly unsettling. Eisenhower accepted the legitimacy of nationalist aspirations but worried that "the confusion resulting from the destruction of existing relationships" created new opportunities for Communists "to further the aims of world revolution." His fears of Communist inroads in the Third World made him suspicious of nationalist leaders who rejected the "slower and more orderly" processes of development that he favored and who rallied support with anti-Western rhetoric.[35] Throughout his presidency, Eisenhower struggled to come to terms with nationalist reformers but too often jumped to the conclusion that they had already embraced communism.

One of the first times he did so was in dealing with Mohammed Mossadegh, the prime minister of Iran. Mossadegh came to power in May 1951, at the same time that the Iranian parliament nationalized the Anglo-Iranian Oil Company, a symbol of British domination of Iranian affairs. The British, in turn, did everything they could to close down the oil industry in Iran and prevent other countries from purchasing Iranian crude. Mossadegh rallied nationalist support by severing diplomatic relations with Britain, but his country's finances were in shambles because of the lack of oil money. Just before his inauguration, Eisenhower received a message from Mossadegh, who pleaded for help "in removing the obstacles" that were preventing the Iranian people "from realizing their aspirations" for political and economic independence. The president-elect replied that he was personally impartial in the British-Iranian dispute.[36]

Yet Eisenhower was anything but indifferent to the actions of Mossadegh and his nationalist regime. Friends in the oil industry told him that the example of Iranian nationalization might endanger western corporate interests in other Third World nations.[37] Even more critical were Eisenhower's concerns about Communist penetration of Iran. Since 1946, the United States had provided military assistance to Iran to strengthen it against Communist subversion. Both Truman and Eisenhower considered Shah Mohammad Reza Pahlavi a staunch, if somewhat overzealous, anti-Communist ally. Mossadegh's cooperation with the Tudeh or Iranian Communist party jeopardized both the shah's rule and the American investment in containing communism. Ambassador Loy W. Henderson reported to the president that if Mossadegh managed to force the shah from power, "chaos would develop in Iran, a chaos that would be overcome only by a bloody dictatorship working under orders from Moscow." Based on such reporting, Eisenhower soon decided that Mossadegh was either a Communist himself or Moscow's stooge.[38] In late June, Eisenhower rejected Mossadegh's appeal for urgent financial assistance.

By then, Eisenhower had already given the word to the Central Intelligence Agency to overthrow Mossadegh. Planning for a coup had been going on since November 1952, when the British Secret Service had approached CIA agent Kermit Roosevelt, the grandson of the first President Roosevelt and the cousin of the second. Partly because of his experience with wartime intelligence, partly because of his desire for efficient and inexpensive means to achieve American Cold War goals, Eisenhower decided to place far more emphasis than had Truman on covert operations. Operation AJAX in Iran was the CIA's first major test during the Eisenhower presidency. Under Roosevelt's direction, CIA operatives distributed in Iranian currency the equivalent of $100,000 to recruit street demonstrators who demanded Mossadegh's removal. The coup succeeded in mid-August, and the shah, who had fled the country only a few days earlier, returned from his brief exile.

Eisenhower was pleased with the results of Operation AJAX. Iran established an international consortium for the development of its oil in which both Britain and the United States had 40 percent control. Eisenhower, in turn, provided economic and military aid to the Iranian government. In 1955, Iran joined with Britain, Iraq, Turkey, and Pakistan in an anti-Communist alliance known as the Baghdad Pact, which the United States encouraged but did not sign. Iranian nationalism may have been dealt a severe blow, but Eisenhower really did not notice. Instead he emphasized that U.S. intervention had repulsed a Communist advance in the Middle East.

The CIA intervention in Iran may have had the most deleterious consequences—at least, immediately—half a world away, in Latin America. The ease with which the CIA brought down Mossadegh made Eisenhower all too willing to use covert intervention to deal with another objectionable regime, the government of Jacobo Arbenz Guzmán in Guatemala. In mid-1954 covert intervention swiftly rid the Americas of its only supposedly Communist ruler. Yet Operation PBSUCCESS was a hollow victory, since it created lasting problems for the United States in Latin America. It also revealed once more the Eisenhower administration's penchant for mistaking nationalism for communism.

Fighting communism was the administration's top priority in Latin America. Only two months after taking office, Eisenhower approved NSC 144/1, a hastily-prepared but comprehensive statement of United States objectives in Latin America. While recognizing the imperative of raising living standards in the other American nations, the NSC worried about the drift "toward radical and nationalistic regimes" within the hemisphere because of their vulnerability to Communist exploitation. Yet to satisfy the demand for economic development, the Eisenhower administration thought that the Latin Americans should rely not on foreign aid but mainly on trade and private investment, a formula that could do little more than perpetuate the existing state of economic dependency. NSC 144/1 said nothing at all about promoting democracy or encouraging respect for human rights within the hemisphere. Instead it emphasized that the United States should concentrate on developing hemispheric support for its Cold War policies, securing Latin American cooperation in collective defense "against external aggression," and eliminating "internal Communist or other anti-U.S. subversion."[39]

These objectives shaped the administration's diplomatic, cultural, and military initiatives in Latin America. Drawing on the help of labor leaders such as George Meany, the president of the American Federation of Labor, the State Department tried to strengthen anti-Communist unions in the other American nations. The United States Information Agency disseminated anti-Communist cartoons, comic books, and radio show scripts in many neighboring countries. The administration also stepped up the supply of military aid to Latin America, although appropriations were modest and deliveries lagged because of more urgent needs in Europe and East Asia. Much like their predecessors in the Truman administration, Eisenhower's advisers privately acknowledged that these arms deliveries had far greater political than military significance. Military aid did little to further collective defense but earned good will in Latin American ruling circles and secured cooperation in the form of base rights, access to strategic raw materials, and participation in measures to suppress Communist influence within the hemisphere.[40]

Eisenhower and his top advisers believed that the principal Communist threat to the hemisphere was the Guatemalan government of Arbenz. After winning a fair and free presidential election in November 1950, Arbenz ruled Guatemala with minor cooperation from the Communist party. Communists accounted for only four of the fifty-one votes in his majority coalition in the Guatemalan Congress; they held none of the ministries in his cabinet, and they were barred entirely from the army, police, and foreign ministry. By mid-1954, the Guatemalan Communist party had a membership of only 5,000, "not as many as [in] San Francisco," as one of Eisenhower's friends reminded him.[41] Still, United States intelligence authorities maintained that the Communists exercised influence far out of proportion to their numbers, owing to their "coordinated activity . . . within . . . leftist political parties and labor unions" and their "personal influence" with Arbenz.[42] Eisenhower told the departing Guatemalan ambassador in January 1954 that he thought the Arbenz government was "infiltrated with communists, and we couldn't cooperate with a Government which openly favored communists."[43] Just three weeks earlier, Ambassador John E. Peurifoy reported that after a lengthy private dinner with Arbenz, "I came away definitely convinced that if [the] President is not a Communist he will certainly do until one comes along."[44]

As the last remark suggests, the administration's assessment of Arbenz was mainly the product of inference, extrapolation, and guesswork. Eisenhower and his top advisers reached their speculative conclusions primarily because of their suspicions of Arbenz's program of social and economic reform. Building on the innovations of his predecessor, Juan José Arévalo, Arbenz promised economic modernization of his underdeveloped, predominantly agricultural country. The key to his program was land reform, which provided for expropriation of uncultivated portions of large estates and their redistribution among the impoverished rural population. Guatemala's largest employer and wealthiest corporation, U.S.-owned United Fruit, lost 400,000 of its 550,000 acres under Arbenz's land reform. The company also shrilly complained about the inadequacy of government compensation of $3 per acre, even though United Fruit had itself determined that figure for tax purposes.

Arbenz did not attempt to nationalize United Fruit or establish rural collectives, but his land redistribution program still struck Washington officials as a radical attack on private property and a clear indication of the regime's anti-U.S. orientation. Intelligence authorities also argued that the Communists had been the driving force in the enactment of land reform and that they were administering the program so as ''to mobilize the hitherto politically inert peasantry in support of the regime.''[45] The president and his top aides apparently never noticed the circularity of their argument—Arbenz enacted land reform because of his Communist inclinations, expropriation proved that Arbenz was in league with the Communists—but simply fit into a Cold War outlook events that should have been evaluated in a local or regional context.[46]

Eisenhower and his advisers thought they had incontrovertible evidence of Arbenz's Communist ties when a ship carrying Czechoslovakian armaments arrived in Guatemala in mid-May. Although the manifest listed optical supplies as the vessel's cargo, CIA operatives discovered long before it made port that the Swedish freighter *Alfhem* actually carried small arms and light artillery. As a result, Peurifoy met the ship at the dock in Puerto Barrios, and the State Department immediately announced that Arbenz intended to use the arms to foment Communist revolution in Central America. Whatever its propaganda value, the State Department press release did not accurately reflect Arbenz's intentions. Arbenz turned to Czechoslovakia because the United States had refused since 1950 to provide Guatemala with military equipment, and Eisenhower had used his influence to get friendly European nations to join the embargo. At the same time, Eisenhower provided military aid to neighboring Honduras and Nicaragua. Fearful of an uprising against his regime, Arbenz secured armaments from one of the few available sources.[47]

Eisenhower swiftly authorized unilateral and patently illegal action. On 21 May, four days after the *Alfhem* docked in Guatemala, Eisenhower announced that the navy would patrol the waters off Guatemala and search vessels suspected of carrying armaments. The State Department concluded that such surveillance had no justification under international law, but Eisenhower and his aides could find no other way to cut off the supply of munitions to Arbenz. The British angrily objected to Eisenhower's interference with legitimate commerce on the high seas. These complaints greatly annoyed the president, and he impatiently growled that the British had "no right to stick their nose into matters which concern this hemisphere entirely." Press Secretary James C. Hagerty, however, thought that the blockade was "a very bad mistake." Recalling the willingness of the United States to fight for neutral rights in the War of 1812, Hagerty lamented the abandonment of "our traditional opposition to . . . search and seizure" and thought the British were entirely justified in "getting pretty rough" in their protests.[48]

On 18 June 1954, the United States took far more drastic unilateral action by launching a coup against the Arbenz regime. Almost a year earlier, Eisenhower had authorized the CIA to begin preparations for Operation PBSUCCESS. At a base in Honduras, CIA operatives assembled a mercenary army under the command of Col. Carlos Castillo Armas, a counterrevolutionary who had participated in a failed revolt against Arévalo in 1950 and who had miraculously escaped from prison the following year. Castillo Armas's motley force of 150 men actually did little fighting once the invasion began. Instead the planners of PBSUCCESS hoped to use psychological warfare to immobilize the Guatemalan army and depose Arbenz. Broadcasting from Honduran territory, the CIA's Voice of Liberation persuaded listeners that the invasion force was large and invincible. Air raids on Guatemala City flown by U.S. pilots recruited by the CIA seemed to confirm the exaggerated claims of the Voice of Liberation. The psychological offensive worked. On 27 June, Arbenz fled the country, and five days later Castillo Armas became president of a military junta.

The Eisenhower administration jubilantly celebrated the overthrow of Arbenz, but without acknowledging United States complicity. "In Guatemala," the president explained, "the people of that region rose up and rejected the Communist doctrine." Dulles praised the "loyal citizens of Guatemala, who, in the face of terrorism and violence and against what seemed insuperable odds, had the courage and the will to eliminate the traitorous tools of foreign despots." When Castillo Armas visited the White House in autumn 1955, Vice-President Richard M. Nixon toasted his guest's courageous leadership of the Guatemalan people, who "revolted against Communist rule, which in collapsing, bore graphic witness to its inherent shallowness, falsity and corruption." These official explanations aimed at concealing United States involvement. They also recklessly suggested to peoples living under Communist rule that popular discontent could lead to the heroic overthrow of oppressive governments.[49]

The legacy of PBSUCCESS was far more complicated. By installing and subsequently supporting Castillo Armas, the Eisenhower administration nurtured a regime that ruled by repression. Castillo Armas restricted the franchise, suspended habeas corpus, eliminated collective bargaining rights, and ended land reform before he was assassinated in 1957. His successor, Miguel Ydígoras Fuentes, was even more reactionary, but stoutly anti-Communist. Eisenhower hoped for more enlightened rule but did nothing to pressure Castillo Armas or Ydígoras to implement reforms. Eager to eliminate radicalism and anti-U.S. sentiment, the Eisenhower administration backed a government that created conditions that were certain to generate discontent and extremism. And the administration did so at the price of alienating Latin American public opinion that valued democracy, national self-determination, international law, and human rights. "We ha[ve] won a round against the Communists," the State Department rightly concluded, "but [have] paid a price in terms of prestige and good-will."[50]

The cost of containing communism in Southeast Asia in 1954/55 ultimately was far greater. In those years, Eisenhower faced a crisis in Vietnam the roots of which reached back to the Truman administration. In May 1950, Truman authorized the extension of military assistance to the French, who were fighting to suppress a Communist-led insurgency against their colonial rule. Following Mao Tse-tung's victory in China in October 1949, Truman and his advisers decided to draw the line in Southeast Asia. The National Security Council advised the president in February 1950 that Communist domination of French Indochina—Vietnam, Cambodia, and Laos—would cause Thailand and Burma to topple like a row of falling dominoes and place the remainder of Southeast Asia "in grave hazard."[51] Eisenhower shared this logic, increased American military aid, and considered armed intervention in spring 1954 as the French war effort collapsed. Although he avoided war, Eisenhower's subsequent decisions made it difficult for his successors to resist military intervention.

The Indochina crisis began in March 1954, when Vietminh forces surrounded a garrison of 12,000 French troops in a remote outpost at Dien Bien Phu. In the previous months, Gen. Henri Navarre had attempted to invigorate the French war effort, and Eisenhower had authorized $385 million in arms aid to support his offensive operations. At the same time, the French government promised to "perfect" the independence of the Indochinese states, a concession that American officials had long urged upon the French in order to undercut the nationalist support of the Vietminh.[52] The optimism of late 1953 vanished quickly as Navarre allowed his troops to be tied down at Dien Bien Phu, their airstrips rendered inoperable by Vietminh artillery on nearby hills.

Urgently the French pleaded for American help. Before the Vietminh assaulted Dien Bien Phu, Eisenhower had approved with alacrity Navarre's request for twenty B-26 bombers and 200 American technicians to service them. He told congressional leaders on 8 February that he did not like putting Americans in dangerous situations, "but we can't get anywhere in Asia by just sitting here in Washington and doing nothing. My God, we must not lose Asia."[53] In March the French asked for far more than weapons or technicians; they wanted an American air strike to rescue the besieged Dien Bien Phu garrison. The Joint Chiefs of Staff considered Operation VULTURE, a plan devised by American and French officers for a massive B-29 assault on the Vietminh positions at Dien Bien Phu, as well as several army and air force studies, which examined the possible use of both conventional and atomic bombs. Each of these proposals encountered strong opposition from the service chiefs. Only Adm. Arthur W. Radford, who succeeded Bradley as chair of the Joint Chiefs, favored the use of American air power.[54]

Eisenhower had a divided mind about American military intervention. He certainly had doubts about whether air strikes could be effective at Dien Bien Phu and feared that they might be only the prelude to the commitment of American ground troops. Eisenhower clearly appreciated the perils of land warfare in Vietnam. "I'm convinced that no military victory is possible in that kind of theater," he confided in his diary while he was supreme commander of NATO.[55] When composing his memoirs in the early 1960s, he wrote all too presciently, "The jungles of Indochina would have swallowed up division after division of U.S. troops."[56] Yet despite these reservations, Eisenhower worried about the consequences of a French withdrawal from Indochina. "Indochina," he reminded the NSC on 6 April 1954, "was the first in a row of dominoes. If it fell its neighbors would shortly thereafter fall with it, and where did the process end?" When Secretary Humphrey countered that the United States could become endlessly involved in trying to prevent the spread of communism, Eisenhower replied, "in certain areas at least we cannot afford to let Moscow gain another bit of territory." Dien Bien Phu could be "just such a critical point."[57]

Rather than unilateral intervention, Eisenhower and Dulles proposed United Action in order to keep the Southeast Asian dominoes from falling. They reasoned that United Action—a coalition including Great Britain, France, Australia, New Zealand, the Philippines, and Thailand as well as the United States—would be a powerful and versatile means of defending Indochina. Its formation, they hoped, would bolster French morale and deter Chinese Communists from entering the war, thereby obviating the need for American military action. Yet if the worst occurred and the French required armed assistance, United Action would enable the United States to concentrate on air, naval, and logistic support while leaving the bulk of the ground fighting to the other members of the coalition.[58] United Action would also conform to the stipulations of congressional leaders, who informed Eisenhower at a critical meeting on 3 April that they would authorize intervention in Indochina only if the administration could secure the participation of other nations.

Although Eisenhower and especially Dulles tried mightily, they could not enlist the required international support. The secretary of state flew to London and Paris but returned to Washington empty-handed. Churchill and Foreign Secretary Anthony Eden considered the Indochinese war unwinnable and worried that it might escalate into a global conflagration if United Action provoked Chinese or Soviet intervention. The French flatly rejected Dulles's proposals. They did not want to promise to carry on the war indefinitely, share responsibility for planning and directing military operations, or grant the Indochinese states complete independence, conditions that Dulles and Eisenhower required as prerequisites to United Action. The failure to secure agreement sealed the fate of the French garrison at Dien Bien Phu, which surrendered on 7 May.

What made the fall of Dien Bien Phu so critical was the opening only a day later of an international conference on East Asian problems at Geneva. For Eisenhower and Dulles, the Geneva Conference was fraught with peril. The president and secretary of state worried that the French would abjectly surrender Indochina to international communism and that they would suffer blistering criticism for participating in an East

Asian Munich. Dulles, who attended the conference, thus comported himself with the "pinched distaste of a puritan in a house of ill repute," in the words of one of his biographers.[59] He found so distasteful the participation of delegates from the People's Republic of China that he ostentatiously refused to shake the hand of Premier Chou En-lai. Although he was aware of differences between the Chinese and the Soviets, Dulles showed little patience or persistence in trying to exploit them. Instead he took pains to adopt a belligerent attitude by promoting new versions of United Action in the hope that they would moderate the demands of the Soviets, Chinese Communists, or Vietminh. Eisenhower and Dulles actually would have preferred the collapse of the Geneva Conference, provided the French continued to fight. By late June, however, they recognized that the French were determined to secure a negotiated settlement, and they prepared to accept such a compromise, even though it would probably make them "gag."[60]

The Geneva accords of 21 July actually were not so unpalatable. Cambodia and Laos obtained their independence, and Vietnam was temporarily divided at the 17th parallel—the Vietminh withdrawing to the north, the French to the south—pending national elections within two years. In order to preserve a free hand in Southeast Asia as well as dampen criticism of Old Guard Republicans, the administration refused to sign the Geneva accords but did promise not to use force to upset them.

In the aftermath of Geneva, Eisenhower and Dulles devised new ways of holding the line against communism in Southeast Asia. The most important innovation was the establishment of United Action in the form of the Southeast Asia Treaty Organization. Signed at Manila in September, this collective security treaty obligated the member nations—the United States, France, Great Britain, Australia, New Zealand, Pakistan, and the Philippines—to consult in the event of common danger. Because the Geneva settlement prevented the former Indochinese states from joining such an alliance, Dulles formulated a separate protocol that extended the protection of SEATO to the territory of Laos, Cambodia, and southern Vietnam. The president and the secretary of state viewed the alliance as a means of deterring Communist aggression and of protecting the "free areas" of Vietnam against absorption into a unified state under Vietminh rule.[61]

The creation of SEATO was a major step toward establishing South Vietnam as an independent non-Communist state in defiance of the Geneva accords. The Eisenhower administration did not resort to force to violate Geneva, but it did utilize economic and military aid, technical assistance, and covert operations. The beneficiary of such help was Ngo Dinh Diem, who became prime minister of South Vietnam in June 1954. A Catholic in a predominantly Buddhist land, an authoritarian who made practically no effort to win the confidence of other Vietnamese nationalists, Diem had critical liabilities for a leader who was trying to forge a nation out of the chaos of South Vietnam. Many American officials argued against making a commitment to support Diem or his ramshackle government. The prime minister "is a messiah without a message," cabled chargé Robert McClintock, whose "only formulated policy is to ask [for] immediate American assistance in every form." Radford told the NSC that the Joint Chiefs thought that it would be extremely difficult to create reliable armed forces in South Vietnam "in the absence of a stable government."[62] Yet whatever the risks, Dulles insisted that it was essential to make "a good stout effort even though it is by no means certain that we will succeed."[63] On 20 August, Eisenhower endorsed the conclusion of the NSC that the United States must "restore its prestige in the Far East" and "prevent further losses to Communism" in Southeast Asia.[64]

The debate over whether to back Diem culminated in April 1955. Based on the counsel of Eisenhower's personal representative to South Vietnam, Gen. J. Lawton Collins, the administration prepared to withdraw its support from Diem in the hope that a more capable leader would emerge. Eisenhower reluctantly acquiesced in Collins's recommendation because the United States had "bet pretty heavily" on Diem.[65] Yet at precisely that moment, Diem, perhaps alerted by a sympathetic CIA operative, moved swiftly and effectively with military force against challengers to his rule. In the wake of Diem's surprising action, Dulles and Eisenhower brushed aside Collins's warnings about the prime minister's insufficiencies. Instead the administration lavished support on Diem out of conviction that there was no reasonable alternative to him. "Sink or swim with Ngo Dinh Diem" aptly summarized Eisenhower's policy.

In 1954/55, Eisenhower won a short-term victory in Vietnam. The president properly deserves credit for eschewing armed action in Indochina during the siege of Dien Bien Phu. Neither he nor Dulles was eager to undertake a risky military intervention on the Asian mainland so soon after the end of the Korean War. Eisenhower, however, must share the credit for not going to war in Southeast Asia in 1954. The hesitations of congressional leaders and the reluctance of potential allies also stayed his hand. Eisenhower did not craftily create these obstacles in order to shield his administration from the criticism of anticommunist zealots.[66] Along with Dulles, he seemed genuinely prepared to use military force provided that he could secure the necessary political support. He was unable to do so.

Eisenhower's decision to fasten American prestige to Ngo Dinh Diem and a non-Communist South Vietnam was, at the very least, unwise. Because of their overweening desire for a triumph to offset the loss of northern Vietnam, Eisenhower and Dulles plunged the United States into a political vacuum that it was ultimately unable to fill. "The United States became," as historian David L. Anderson has written, "the guarantor not only of an independent South Vietnam but also of a particular Vietnamese leader."[67] In retrospect, that commitment seems by far the more significant action than the temporary avoidance of war.

The Eisenhower administration came even closer to the brink of war in East Asia in 1954/55 when the People's Republic of China (PRC) started bombarding the Nationalist Chinese islands of Quemoy and Matsu in the Taiwan (Formosa) Strait. Although they were mere specks of territory with negligible strategic value, these islands became such important symbols of American credibility that the president prepared to wage nuclear war in order to defend them. Eisenhower protected American interests in the Taiwan Strait without crossing the nuclear threshold, but the peaceful resolution of the crisis arose more from good fortune that shrewd diplomacy.[68]

Eisenhower recognized from the beginning of the bombardment in September 1954 that Quemoy and Matsu were charged with psychological significance for the Chinese. Nationalist forces had occupied these and other offshore islands in 1949 as they retreated from the Chinese mainland to Taiwan. Nationalist President Chiang Kai-shek had stationed more than 50,000 troops on Quemoy and had used that island primarily to launch guerrilla raids against the mainland. Yet Nationalist abandonment of Quemoy and Matsu to the Chinese Communists would have had practically no military consequences, since the raids on the mainland had not been "very profitable," and the islands were not essential to the defense of Taiwan.[69] The fate of Quemoy and Matsu, however, could significantly alter the perceptions of Chinese power. At risk for Chiang was the credibility of his promise to invade the mainland, a pledge that would inevitably seem fatuous and chimerical after a retreat on Quemoy and Matsu. At stake for the Chinese Communists was the believability of their oft-repeated resolve to bring the offshore islands, including Taiwan, under their control, by force, if necessary.

For the United States, the Quemoy-Matsu crisis created an opportunity to increase national prestige, but only at the risk of grave military danger. By forcing them to desist, the United States could make the Chinese Communists suffer a "loss of 'face' " that would increase the morale of anti-Communist governments around the world and especially in East Asia, Admiral Radford argued. At a meeting of the National Security Council on 12 September 1954, Eisenhower replied that his advisers "must get one thing clear in their heads, and that is that they are talking about war," since that was the only way to defend Quemoy and Matsu against an attack by the PRC. Eisenhower worried, on the one hand, about getting tied down in another limited and indecisive military action in East Asia and, on the other, about becoming involved in a general war with China, rather than the Soviet Union, the latter of which he considered "the head of the snake." The president sternly reminded the NSC that he could not order American military action without congressional authorization unless he wanted to risk impeachment. He warned that it would "be a big job" to convince the public of the importance of Quemoy and Matsu to national security, and he ruled out asking the American people to support a war "at this time." Dulles added that while a strong stand on Quemoy and Matsu would have an invigorating effect on the governments of Korea, Japan, and the Philippines, the rest of the world would condemn American resort to nuclear weapons to defend those islands. In short, Dulles concluded the administration faced "a horrible dilemma."[70]

Eisenhower and Dulles devised a two-pronged strategy to extricate the United States from this difficult situation. First, the secretary of state prepared to refer the conflict over Quemoy and Matsu to the United Nations. Dulles reasoned that a cease-fire resolution might cause real difficulties for the Soviets, since the Russians would harm their peace offensive if they vetoed such a measure and strain their relationship with the PRC if they did not. By turning to the UN, Eisenhower and Dulles also hoped to win greater international support for their policies or, at the very least, to buy time. The second part of the strategy was to provide reassurance to Chiang through the negotiation of a mutual defense treaty. Dulles and Nationalist Foreign Minister George Yeh signed such an agreement in mid-December, one, however, that explicitly committed the United States only to the defense of Taiwan and the Pescadore Islands. Yet Eisenhower and Dulles avoided making clear public statements about what they might do to protect the other offshore islands. "Let's keep the Reds guessing," Dulles argued, out of conviction that American ambiguity would make the Chinese Communists wary of escalating the Quemoy-Matsu crisis.[71]

He was wrong. In late 1954, the PRC revealed that thirteen American flyers who had been captured during the Korean War after their planes went down in China had been convicted of espionage. Then in January 1955, Chinese Communist troops seized Ichiang Island from Nationalist defenders, while their aircraft attacked the Tachen Islands. The Nationalists retaliated with raids on PRC ports and ships. Eisenhower and Dulles worried that the two Chinas and perhaps the United States were drifting toward war.

As the tensions mounted in the Taiwan Strait, the pressure increased in Washington for Eisenhower to take strong action in support of Chiang Kai-shek. Right-wing Republicans had excoriated Truman for lavishing foreign aid on Europe, while neglecting Asia and supposedly allowing China to fall to Communist control. The leaders of these Asia-Firsters, such as Senator William F. Knowland of California and Representative Walter Judd of Minnesota, considered Chiang the only legitimate leader of China. They also warmly supported military and economic aid to the Nationalists, which by the end of 1954 had amounted to $1.6 billion since the end of the Chinese civil war.[72] Eisenhower and Dulles recognized the importance of appeasing this China bloc, and so domestic politics undoubtedly influenced them to take a strong stand once the crisis began. At the beginning of 1955, Knowland, who was commonly known as "the senator from Formosa," stepped up the pressure by calling for a blockade of the mainland in reprisal for the conviction of the American flyers and by equating UN mediation with appeasement. Eisenhower and Dulles privately tried to discourage such calls for drastic action, yet at the same time they knew that it was essential for political reasons to maintain the support of the China bloc.

As the Quemoy-Matsu crisis deepened in early 1955, Dulles advocated a clarification of American policy. Ambiguity had only persuaded the Communists that the United States would not defend any of the islands in the Taiwan Strait. Despite the strenuous opposition of Humphrey, Wilson, and Cutler, Eisenhower agreed with Dulles and declared that it was now "necessary to draw the line." American policy had long been to promise air and naval support to indigenous ground forces that would defend against Communist aggression. The president stated that the United States now faced "a concrete test of this policy, and we must be concerned with the morale of those soldiers who might well be called upon to defend Formosa if the Chinese Communists attacked it."[73]

Eisenhower and Dulles thus formulated a new two-part strategy. On 24 January 1955, Eisenhower sent to Capitol Hill a resolution granting him broad powers to use American military power in the Taiwan Strait. Four days later and with few dissenting votes, Congress gave the president discretionary authority to commit the armed forces to the defense of Taiwan, the Pescadores, and "such related positions and territories of that area now in friendly hands."[74] Despite their insistence on drawing the line, Dulles and Eisenhower decided "not to nail the flag to the mast by a detailed statement respecting our plans and intentions on evacuating or holding certain of these islands."[75] Thus the second part of their strategy aimed at informing Chiang precisely what the United States would do. In return for Nationalist withdrawal from the Tachens, islands that Eisenhower considered difficult to hold, the president privately assured Chiang that the United States would not yield Quemoy and Matsu for the duration of the crisis. Chiang reluctantly agreed but felt betrayed when the Eisenhower administration refused to make this commitment public.

Once again these actions did not prevent the worsening of the crisis. Dulles returned in early March from a trip to East Asia with the conviction that there was "at least an even chance" that the United States would have to fight in the Taiwan Strait. He told the National Security Council that the Chinese Communists were determined not only to take the offshore islands, but Taiwan itself. Dulles worried about the reliability of Nationalist troops, since he found morale on Taiwan "not too good" and remembered that China had a long history of generals susceptible to bribery. Even more troubling to the secretary of state was the lack of public support for American use of atomic weapons in East Asia. Only by using tactical nuclear weapons, Dulles reminded the NSC, could the United States effectively attack Chinese Communist airfields, gun emplacements, and railroad lines. If American forces intended to use these devices, "perhaps within the next month or two," the administration needed to undertake an urgent public relations campaign. The time had come, he continued, to confront the fundamental question of whether the administration's basic national security policy approved in NSC 162/2 "was or was not in fact designed to permit the use of atomic weapons."[76]

Neither Eisenhower nor Dulles had any doubt about the answer to that last question. The two agreed on 6 March that the defense of Quemoy and Matsu "would require the use of atomic missiles."[77] Eisenhower instructed Dulles to make sure to explain in his nationally televised report on his Asian trip that the United States was prepared to use both nuclear and conventional weapons as necessary. A few days later, Vice-President Richard M. Nixon announced in a speech that "tactical atomic weapons are now conventional and will be used against the targets of an aggressive force."[78] At his news conference on 16 March, Eisenhower emphatically endorsed such thinking. "Now, in any combat where these things [tactical nuclear weapons] can be used on strictly military targets and for strictly military purposes," he asserted, "I see no reason why they shouldn't be used just exactly as you would use a bullet."[79] Eisenhower was furious, however, when the news media carried sensational stories about imminent nuclear war based on the indiscretions of Adm. Robert B. Carney, the chief of naval operations. During what he thought was an off-the-record briefing, Carney told reporters that the United States was making plans for all-out war with Communist China and that such a conflict might erupt by 15 April. Eisenhower threw a tantrum over Carney's loose talk, since it seemed only to frighten, rather than educate, the public.

Despite his readiness to wage nuclear war, Eisenhower was still determined to avoid such a conflict. Once more he tried to find a way to reduce the significance of Quemoy and Matsu—to persuade Chiang to consider them outposts rather than citadels—so that the United States could focus its efforts on the defense of Taiwan and the Pescadores. Together with Dulles, he devised an extraordinary plan in mid-April to encourage the Nationalists to withdraw from Quemoy and Matsu in return for an American blockade of the coast of the PRC along the Taiwan Strait, about five hundred miles, until the Chinese Communists renounced their goal of forcibly seizing Taiwan. Whatever its merits, this proposal seemed certain to escalate rather than ease tensions, since a blockade was an act of war. Chiang, however, prevented Eisenhower and Dulles from ever finding out how the PRC would react; he summarily rejected the plan. After evacuating the Tachen Islands, Chiang obstinately refused to yield additional territory. He also implied that he doubted American credibility, since only three months earlier Eisenhower had secretly promised to help the Nationalists defend Quemoy and Matsu.

Despite the collapse of Eisenhower's initiative, the crisis ended almost immediately afterward because of a Chinese Communist démarche. While attending the Bandung (Indonesia) conference of non-aligned nations in late April, Premier Chou En-lai stated that "the Chinese people are friendly to the American people."[80] Dulles quickly replied that the United States was willing to negotiate an end to the conflict over Quemoy and Matsu. During the next few months, the bombardment of the islands ended, direct talks began between American and PRC diplomats, and the Chinese Communists freed the American flyers whom they had convicted of espionage.

Eisenhower claimed that the United States had triumphed. "For nine months the administration moved through treacherous cross-currents," he recollected in his memoirs, "with one channel leading to peace with honor and a hundred channels leading to war or dishonor."[81] Indeed Eisenhower deserves credit for avoiding war, especially since some of his advisers in the Pentagon, such as Radford, were advocating policies that probably would have precipitated nuclear conflict. The president also thought his policies had been successful because Quemoy and Matsu remained in Nationalist hands, and the security of Taiwan was unimpaired.

Some recent historians have lauded Eisenhower's handling of the crisis. "The beauty of Eisenhower's policy," Robert A. Divine argued, "is that to this day no one can be sure whether or not he would have responded militarily to an invasion of the offshore islands, and whether he would have used nuclear weapons."[82] Historian Stephen E. Ambrose took Divine's logic a step further. The beauty of Eisenhower's ambiguity, according to Ambrose, was that "Eisenhower himself did not know" whether he would use nuclear weapons. Eisenhower's crisis management, Ambrose concluded, was "a *tour de force*, one of the great triumphs of his long career."[83]

These assessments give Eisenhower too much credit for keeping his options open and controlling the course of events. Eisenhower limited his flexibility during the crisis by secretly promising to defend Quemoy and Matsu and, over the long term, by agreeing to a mutual defense treaty with Nationalist China. Despite Ambrose's claim, Eisenhower knew that he would use nuclear weapons in the event of war with Communist China, and his public statements and those of other top administration officials aimed at preparing the public for such an eventuality. Throughout the crisis, Eisenhower's principal problem was the inability to dissociate American credibility from the defense of Quemoy and Matsu, islands that he stated repeatedly lacked strategic significance. As much as he disliked it, a Communist threat determined American interests throughout the crisis in the Taiwan Strait. Furthermore, Eisenhower realized how much influence Chiang exerted over American policy. Wryly, but with all too much accuracy, the president reminded the NSC that "we were in the hands of 'a fellow who hasn't anything to lose.'"[84] While Eisenhower ultimately achieved some of his goals, Chinese Communist motives for ending the crisis remain a matter of speculation. It is by no means clear that Eisenhower forced the PRC to back down. The lack of Soviet support or a desire to cultivate the support of Third World nations may have been far more important in Peking's decision to call for negotiations.

The Quemoy-Matsu crisis also illustrated some of the limitations and perils of the administration's basic national security policy. Eisenhower and his top advisers emphasized that the crisis in the Taiwan Strait was a test of "our whole military structure." If public opinion precluded the use of nuclear weapons or adversaries refused to believe the credibility of the threat, "our entire military program would have to be drastically revised" to include conventional as well as nuclear options.[85] What made the crisis so dangerous was the administration's simultaneous penchant for escalation and inability to control events.[86] Beauty may be in the eye of the beholder, but it is hard to be dazzled by policies that bring the world to the brink of nuclear war over territory whose value to American—or for that matter Taiwanese—security was close to nil. Yet in many ways, such a frightening situation was the logical outcome of the New Look and Eisenhower's whole approach to waging Cold War.

5

★ ★ ★ ★ ★

PERSONAL VICTORIES

"This is a solemn moment," Dwight D. Eisenhower told the American people as he claimed victory on election night in 1956. Eisenhower overwhelmingly defeated his Democratic challenger, Adlai E. Stevenson, by winning 57.6 percent of the ballots and 457 electoral votes, totals that surpassed his decisive majorities of four years earlier. "Such a vote . . . cannot be merely for an individual," he told his supporters, "it is for principles and ideals for which that individual and his associates have stood and have tried to exemplify."[1] Yet despite Eisenhower's assertion, the voters liked Ike far more than they did the Republicans. Indeed for the first time in more than a century, the party of the victorious presidential candidate failed to gain a majority in either house of Congress. Eisenhower ran so far ahead of his party because of a string of individual triumphs in 1955/56—a dramatic performance at the first Soviet-American summit conference since the end of World War II, a booming economy popularly known as the Eisenhower prosperity, restraint in handling the Suez crisis in the days preceding the election, and recovery from two major illnesses. Like these achievements, Eisenhower's reelection in 1956 was a personal victory.

In January 1955, when the Eighty-fourth Congress convened, Eisenhower hoped for the best but expected difficulty. With Democrats in control of both houses, Eisenhower realized that the Republicans would often have to work closely with Senate Majority Leader Lyndon

B. Johnson and Speaker of the House Sam Rayburn in order to secure passage of important legislation. Characteristically he tried to neutralize the opposition by claiming that he stood above politics and that his programs were "in the best interest of all Americans." Still he knew that the Democrats would try to compile a legislative record that they could use to regain the White House in 1956. Eisenhower foresaw the greatest problems in the House, where the opposition held a thirty seat advantage. In the Senate, where the Democratic margin was a single vote, he expected that conservative southern Democrats would often side with the administration. Because the Republicans were in the minority, Eisenhower demanded more than ever before that GOP legislators support the administration and, on occasion, imposed political sanctions on those who did not. When five House Republicans voted with the Democratic majority on a crucial tax measure that the administration opposed, Eisenhower told his press secretary, James C. Hagerty, "if . . . anyone in the White House wants me to see any one of them, you bring it to my attention and I'll stop it."[2]

During the congressional session of 1955, partisan controversy ensnared most of Eisenhower's major legislative proposals, such as his plan for federal aid for the construction of new schools. Because of the baby boom that began during World War II, schools in many states were woefully overcrowded. The deficit in 1955 was 300,000 classrooms at a time when the annual construction rate was 60,000 classrooms, just enough to meet the increase in the student population each year.[3] Eisenhower proposed a $7 billion federal subsidy, which would go to those states least able to pay for school construction. Many Democrats, however, wanted an even larger program, one that would help to defray other education costs, such as teachers' salaries. Led by Representative Adam Clayton Powell of New York, liberal Democrats tried to amend the legislation to ensure that aid would go only to those school districts that complied with the Supreme Court's May 1954 decision in *Brown* v. *Board of Education,*which barred racial segregation in the classroom. To Eisenhower's dismay, these disagreements prevented the enactment of any bill for the building of new schools.

So great were the divisions within the Congress that inaction was often the result. Once again, as in the previous congress, partisan disputes stalled action on Eisenhower's plan for federal subsidizing of private health insurance policies. Congress also could not agree on a bill for highway construction, even though Eisenhower insisted that the need for new roads was urgent. On resource development, the disputes did not always follow party lines. An alliance of economizers and conservationists blocked approval of a series of federal dams on the

Upper Colorado River, which Eisenhower strongly supported. A combination of westerners and federal waterpower advocates tried unsuccessfully to authorize construction of the enormous, multipurpose federal dam in Hells Canyon, which the administration had rejected two years earlier. Few major bills escaped these paralyzing divisions.

Eisenhower believed that the main problem was the Democrats' eagerness to play politics, and he thought no issue more flagrantly demonstrated their partisanship than their bill to cut taxes. Sponsored principally by Rayburn, the legislation proposed to give each taxpayer a $20 tax exemption for himself or herself and for each dependent. Eisenhower considered such an idea reckless and dangerous at a time when he was trying to narrow the deficit in the federal budget. He urged Republican leaders to "denounce the Democrats every step of the way." If they succeeded, the tax cut would "bring back inflation and . . . cause the cost of living to skyrocket." Following his own advice, he condemned the tax exemption at a press conference on 23 February as "some kind of heights in fiscal irresponsibility."[4] Although unable to persuade the House, Eisenhower won in the Senate, thereby stopping what he considered a sordid Democratic effort "to buy votes with the public's money."[5]

The Democrats also tried to capitalize on the unpopularity, ineptitude, or impropriety of several high administration officials. They excoriated the secretary of the interior as "Giveaway McKay" and called for the resignation of Secretary of Agriculture Ezra Taft Benson. They reaped a political windfall when Secretary of Health, Education, and Welfare Oveta Culp Hobby seemed responsible for the slow distribution of the Salk polio vaccine. Even her departure from the cabinet and replacement by Marion B. Folsom did not silence Democratic cries that the Eisenhower administration could not meet pressing human needs. The Democratic leadership also held hearings to investigate Air Force Secretary Harold Talbott, who resigned because of a conflict of interest.

The Democrats found a much larger scandal in the administration's handling of the Dixon-Yates contract. At issue was the role of Adolphe H. Wenzell, who simultaneously served as a consultant to the Bureau of the Budget and an adviser to Dixon and Yates. Under the chairmanship of Estes Kefauver (D., Tenn.), a special panel of the Senate Judiciary Committee investigated the negotiation of the contract. The inquiry made front-page news not only because of the sensational allegations about Wenzell's role, but also because of an apparent administration cover-up. At first, Eisenhower mistakenly denied that Wenzell had ever worked for the Bureau of the Budget. When Hagerty promptly issued a clarification that corrected the record, some critics wondered about the effectiveness of Eisenhower's staff system. Eisenhower also raised eyebrows by invoking executive privilege when the Kefauver panel asked for files from the Bureau of the Budget. The files, Eisenhower said, included staff memoranda that represented conflicting points of view that were debated before the decision was made to sign a contract with Dixon-Yates. "If any commander is going to get the free, unprejudiced opinions of his subordinates," the general-turned-president indirectly lectured the senators, "he had better protect what they have to say to him on a confidential basis."[6] Fortunately for Eisenhower, the city of Memphis decided to construct its own power plant, which allowed the president to cancel the contract with Dixon-Yates in July 1955, just as the scandal reached a high point.

Dixon-Yates in no way detracted from what appeared to be Eisenhower's greatest domestic achievement of his first administration—a booming economy. By mid-1955, the country had pulled out of the recession of the previous year, and the gross national product was growing at the highest annual rate of the Eisenhower presidency, 7.6 percent. So great was the economic boom that an anticipated budget deficit became a surplus of $4.1 billion in fiscal year 1956. The expansion in the economy occurred without inflation. During 1955/56, the cost of living index rose at an annual rate of just 1 percent. The boom put people back to work, and unemployment dropped from 5.5 percent in 1954 to 4.1 percent two years later.[7] The Eisenhower prosperity simply was one of the greatest periods of peacetime growth in the American economy during the twentieth century.

The prosperity of the mid-1950s, of course, was part of a much larger expansion of the American economy in the two decades after World War II. During the baby boom, middle-class families tried to achieve the American dream by moving to the suburbs and spending their money on household and family goods. The construction, appliance, automobile, and recreation industries, among others, made huge profits from these patterns of consumer spending. While Eisenhower's policies certainly helped to lift the country out of the 1954 recession, he simply had the good fortune to benefit from one of the high points in a long-term pattern of growth. A measure of the widespread satisfaction with the economy was the popular description of these good times as the Eisenhower prosperity.

In mid-1955, Eisenhower also enjoyed a major triumph in international affairs by holding the first summit conference with the Soviets in a decade. So impenetrable were the divisions of the Cold War, so skeptical were Truman and Stalin of diplomacy as a means of resolving East-West tensions, that the two leaders did not meet after their triumph over common foes in World War II. Eisenhower too was reluctant to confer with the Soviets, even after the death of Stalin. He did not want to incur the wrath of the Old Guard, who equated summitry with Yalta, which for them was a symbol of Roosevelt's capitulation to Soviet interests. He also had his own doubts about whether the Soviets were serious about negotiations or simply wanted a forum to unleash a barrage of propaganda. In late 1954, he established a test of sincerity that the Soviets would have to pass if they wanted a summit: signature of an Austrian peace treaty, a document that the Soviets had been unwilling to endorse throughout nine years of negotiations. Six months later, the Soviets did so. Soon afterward, the United States, the Soviet Union, Great Britain, and France announced that their leaders would hold a Big Four meeting in Geneva in July 1955.

Rather than being encouraged by the arrangement of the summit conference, Secretary of State John Foster Dulles was "terribly worried." He thought that there were no quick solutions to the problems of the Cold War, and he feared that the British and French might too easily yield to Soviet demands. But Dulles was even more concerned about what Eisenhower might do. In a remarkable confession to former presidential assistant C. D. Jackson on the eve of the Geneva Conference, Dulles revealed that he was afraid that Eisenhower might mistake Soviet congeniality for sincerity and then agree to something that would "upset the apple cart. . . . We have come such a long way by being firm, occasionally disagreeably firm," he reminded Jackson, "that I would hate to see the whole edifice undermined in response to a smile."[8]

Dulles thus tried carefully to limit Eisenhower's role in the conference. He did not think that the president should make new proposals at the summit, but simply try to create an atmosphere that would augur well for further negotiations. When discussing major issues, such as the reunification of Germany or Soviet influence in Eastern Europe, the president, Dulles advised, should be unyielding. He suggested instead that Eisenhower recommend that the Big Four foreign ministers should take up these issues, along with a Soviet proposal for the establishment of international inspection stations at Russian and American airports, rail stations, and ports to assure both sides that neither nation was mobilizing its armed forces for war. Finally, Dulles lectured the president about the dangers of smiles. He admonished Eisenhower to maintain "an austere countenance" on those occasions when he would be photographed with Soviet leaders in order to diminish the propaganda value of the pictures for the Communists.[9]

Another presidential adviser, Special Assistant Nelson A. Rockefeller, challenged Dulles's suggestions. Rockefeller believed, as he later recollected, that the president "was going to have to take the initiative [at the summit] . . . and it had to be something that immediately electrified everybody." The issue he chose was arms control, and he recognized that the key to any agreement was an adequate system of verification. Acting on the recommendations of a panel of academic and government experts on national security that he had assembled in early June, Rockefeller urged the president to propose that the Soviets and Americans have the right to unlimited inspection through aerial reconnaissance of each other's military installations and armaments as the way of guaranteeing compliance with a disarmament accord. Eisenhower considered the Rockefeller plan "an idea that might open a tiny gate in the disarmament fence."[10]

Dulles, however, was unenthusiastic. He regarded Rockefeller warily as a competitor for power who operated outside State Department channels, and he urged the president to leave Rockefeller and his staff in Washington during the Geneva summit. As so often happened when he was faced with a conflict in personalities, Eisenhower put off making a choice. He did not decide whether to present the Rockefeller inspection plan at Geneva. And he tried to satisfy both his secretary of state and special assistant by not inviting Rockefeller to Geneva, but instructing him to stand by in Paris.

Eisenhower also attempted to reassure Congress and the public before departing for Europe. On 12 July, he emphasized to legislative leaders that he would make no agreements that did not require congressional approval. He also assured the Old Guard that Geneva would not be a repetition of Yalta. Three days later, Eisenhower addressed the nation on television. He candidly admitted that the Big Four could not solve the problems of the arms race in a single meeting. But he promised that the talks would occur in an atmosphere of conciliation, toleration, and understanding. "I say to you, if we can change the spirit in which these conferences are conducted we will have taken the greatest step toward peace, toward future prosperity and tranquility that has ever been taken in the history of mankind."[11] After making this sincere, but inflated pledge, Eisenhower asked all Americans to pray for peace that Sunday. Minutes later, he boarded an airplane.

Upon arriving in Geneva, Eisenhower made clear that he intended to take an active role in the conference. At the airport, he declared that on this trip he brought something much more powerful than the armed force that liberated Europe eleven years earlier: "the good will of America—the great hopes of America—the aspirations of America for peace."[12] Abandoning Dulles's suggestion that he remain socially aloof, he mingled with the Russians, hoping to determine who really held the power in the Soviet collective leadership. He sought out his wartime associate Marshal Georgi Zhukov, who had become the Soviet minister of defense. Zhukov was cordial but seemed tense and acted as if he had been coached to make certain points about Soviet intentions. Eisenhower concluded that Zhukov was not a major figure in the Soviet leadership.

Although Eisenhower rejected Dulles's advice about social deportment, he followed the State Department's recommendations to make no concessions to communism. In his opening statement on 18 July, he condemned the Soviet Union for exporting revolution, preventing free elections in Eastern Europe, and restricting contact between Soviets and Americans. "It is time," he said pointedly, "that all curtains whether of guns or laws or regulations should begin to come down." He also decried the continued division of Germany ten years after the end of World War II. He implied that the Soviets were mainly responsible for this "grievous wrong." Yet only two months before the Geneva summit, a rearmed West Germany had become a member of NATO, a step that the Eisenhower administration considered essential to the effectiveness of the western alliance. A reunified Germany, Eisenhower insisted, must remain a member of NATO, a proposal that the Soviets would not accept. Only on arms control did Eisenhower leave the door open to real progress at the summit, but he offered no specific suggestions on the first day of the conference.[13]

A series of critical meetings determined exactly what Eisenhower would propose to the Soviets on disarmament. In Paris, Rockefeller secured the endorsement of Adm. Arthur W. Radford, chair of the Joint Chiefs of Staff, for his plan for mutual Soviet-American aerial inspection. After Radford and Rockefeller sent messages to Geneva, Eisenhower invited them to join his party. At a meeting of his top assistants on the evening of 20 July, Eisenhower announced his support for the Rockefeller inspection plan. He did so in part because of the counsel of his top military advisers, Radford and Gen. Alfred M. Gruenther, the supreme commander of NATO. In addition, the idea also appealed to Eisenhower because it would breach the Iron Curtain and "benefit us more than the Russians because we knew very little about their installations."[14] Eisenhower also may have thought that the inspection system would avoid the risks of secret overflights by the U-2 spy plane, which was under development and would be ready for use a year later. Finally, he thought an aerial inspection proposal would be a dramatic gesture that would give the United States the initiative in the negotiations and provide a foundation for a workable disarmament agreement.

At the Big Four session the next afternoon, Eisenhower unveiled the plan that journalists soon called Open Skies. Speaking in what appeared to be a spontaneous manner, he said, "I have been searching my heart and mind for something that I could say here that could convince everyone of the great sincerity of the United States in approaching this problem of disarmament."[15] Turning to the Soviet delegation, he then suggested that the two nations should open their skies to aerial inspection, exchange charts of all military facilities, and agree on rules for conducting surveillance flights. As if to emphasize his words, a clap of thunder boomed outside the hall, and the lights went out momentarily. Some members of the Soviet delegation suspected that the Americans had somehow arranged this spectacular event.

The Soviet response was discouraging. Nikolai A. Bulganin, chair of the Council of Ministers and nominal head of the Soviet delegation, assured Eisenhower that Open Skies would receive the most serious consideration, since it built on Soviet proposals for on-site inspection. But after the Big Four session adjourned, Nikita S. Khrushchev, the first secretary of the Communist party, came up to the president, shaking his head. "That is a very bad idea," he said.[16] "In our eyes, this is a very transparent espionage device. . . . You could hardly expect us to take this seriously."[17] It was then, Eisenhower later remarked, that he realized who was boss in the Kremlin.

When he returned to the United States, the president proclaimed that the meeting at Geneva had fulfilled his expectations. It had produced few concrete achievements, he conceded, except for a general agreement that there should be greater cultural exchange between East and West. Proposals such as Open Skies would be discussed at a gathering of foreign ministers in October. Eisenhower nevertheless emphasized "a new spirit of conciliation and cooperation" among the Big Four.[18] However intangible, the spirit of Geneva was a real achievement, since it was an essential prerequisite to successful negotiations. It did not, of course, ensure the success of those talks, which failed to produce an accord on Open Skies or slow the arms race. The spirit of Geneva also established Eisenhower's reputation as a champion of peace. In the wake of the summit, his approval rating in the Gallup poll rose to 79 percent, the highest level of his entire presidency.[19]

Buoyed by his achievements in foreign and domestic affairs, Eisenhower went to Colorado at the end of August to vacation. After three weeks of relaxation for the president, his personal secretary, Ann Whitman, wrote, "I have never seen him look or act better."[20] He attended to business at an office at Lowry Air Force Base in Denver. He spent far more time, however, fishing in mountain streams and giving outdoor barbecue parties for friends and reporters.

Friday, 23 September, was not much different from other vacation days. After a few hours of work, Eisenhower shot a round of golf, lunched on a hamburger heaped with onions, declined an evening cocktail, and then dined with his family and close friends. At 1:30 the next morning, his restlessness woke his wife, and he complained of indigestion pains. Eisenhower actually suspected something far worse. "It hurt like hell . . . ," he later told Vice-President Richard M. Nixon, "[but] I never let Mamie know how much it hurt."[21] She called Dr. Howard Snyder, the president's personal physician, who gave Eisenhower a shot of morphine for the pain that allowed him to sleep until noon. After administering an electrocardiogram that revealed a coronary thrombosis, Snyder ordered the president taken to Fitzsimons Army Hospital in Denver. He placed Eisenhower in an oxygen tent and then summoned the noted cardiologist, Paul Dudley White, from Boston. White confirmed the diagnosis and determined that Eisenhower had suffered "a slightly more than moderate attack."[22]

How much information about Eisenhower's condition did the public have a right to know? Nothing at all, Snyder thought at first. While Eisenhower was still asleep on the morning of 24 September, Snyder telephoned the president's personal secretary and informed her that Eisenhower had experienced a digestive upset and would not go to his office. This report appeared in many afternoon newspapers. Snyder later explained that he had put out this inaccurate story to buy time until he could confirm his diagnosis and inform Eisenhower's relatives. When Hagerty arrived in Denver from Washington late that night, he adopted a policy of full disclosure. Hagerty did so at the request of Eisenhower, who did not want a repetition of the confusion and uncertainty that arose from the concealing of information after Woodrow Wilson suffered a stroke in 1919. Hagerty carried out Eisenhower's instruction with a zeal that later made the president grimace. (Eisenhower found out that Hagerty had reported the details of bowel movements.) Although Hagerty's briefings seemed graphic by the standards of the day, they were informative, educational, and reassuring. Anxious citizens learned that Eisenhower had weathered the attack, retained full control of his faculties, and daily made progress toward recovery.

The heart attack stunned Eisenhower's top aides and caused some tension among them. After the shock had worn off, several top officials began maneuvering for position. Eisenhower mitigated the competition by ordering that regular meetings of the cabinet and the National Security Council should continue, with Nixon presiding. Nixon had no desire to appear to be grasping for power for fear such intemperance would only harm his long-term political prospects. Yet Sherman Adams, the president's chief of staff, and Secretary of State John Foster Dulles, among others, remained suspicious of Nixon and his Old Guard connections. They did not want to see him exploit the opportunity, created by Eisenhower's incapacity, to alter administration policy or secure his hold on the Republican nomination, should a disabled Eisenhower have to retire at the end of his term. Thus Dulles insisted that Adams, not Nixon, go to Denver to serve as liaison between the president and the rest of the Eisenhower team. After doing so, Adams guarded access to the president more jealously than ever.

Eisenhower's steady convalescence also helped ease the competition for influence. After a month, the doctors finally allowed him to walk. About the same time, he also met reporters for the first time. He flashed his famous grin and showed off the pajamas that he had gotten from the press corps. Stitched above the breast pocket were the words, "much better, thanks." At first, Adams and Hagerty filtered out any news that they thought might upset Eisenhower, and his family confined their conversation to amiable topics. This screening arrangement was not needed for very long. Two weeks after his heart attack, Eisenhower began holding individual meetings with each member of his cabinet. Although by that time Eisenhower was fully capable of making decisions on important issues, Congress was not in session, and no urgent foreign policy matters required action.

Eisenhower returned to Washington on Veterans Day. He told the large welcoming crowd at the airport that his doctors had given him "a parole if not a pardon." He explained that he would have to ease himself back into his duties, not "bulldoze" his way into them.[23] He then went on to his Gettysburg farm to continue his convalescence. He experienced the usual postcoronary depression but generally kept busy with official business. Although he went to Camp David for a meeting with the cabinet on 22 November, he did not try to resume a normal work schedule until the beginning of 1956.

In late 1955, at the end of his convalescence, Eisenhower began to decide whether to seek reelection. To friends and associates, Eisenhower had repeatedly intimated that he might leave the presidency after one term. As early as December 1953, he wrote to his boyhood friend,

Swede Hazlett, that among his "secret intentions" was "never again to be a candidate for anything," unless some unforeseen international cataclysm made impossible his retirement from the presidency after four years. Following the midterm elections of 1954, he dismissed Lucius Clay's argument that he alone could revitalize the Republican party and lead it to victory. Instead he recorded in his diary several reasons that he ought not to try for a second term, including his age and the need to yield to younger leaders who symbolized the vigor of the Republican party. In addition, he often complained that if reelected, he would immediately become a lame duck who would command little influence because of the ratification of the Twenty-second Amendment in 1951, which barred a president from serving a third term.[24]

He summarized the case against his running again in mid-1955 when he explained to Hazlett that he had already accomplished much of what he had set out to do at the beginning of his administration. There had been "tremendous improvement" in the international situation, great progress in securing essential legislation concerning domestic affairs, and "renewed confidence in personal initiative and responsibility as the indispensable foundation of free government." Advisers and friends could not again prevail upon him, as they had four years earlier, to set aside his reservations against running because he had an obligation to serve the nation in its hour of need. Eisenhower believed that his "special duty" to his country had been "largely fulfilled."[25]

Yet however strongly Eisenhower felt that he had done his duty, he could not abide the possibility of turning over power to the Democrats when he actually confronted the decision of whether to run. As the election year was about to begin, it seemed that the Democratic nomination would once again go to Adlai Stevenson or to either Senator Estes Kefauver or Governor W. Averell Harriman of New York. Eisenhower privately scorned each of these "crackpot Democrats" who "did not have the competency to run the office of President." Both Stevenson and Kefauver, he maintained, advocated the liberal paternalism that would jeopardize free enterprise and individual freedom. Harriman, a railroad magnate who had served the previous two presidents as ambassador to the Soviet Union and director of Mutual Security, was, if anything, even worse than his rivals. "You know," Eisenhower told Hagerty as they discussed the coming election at Gettysburg in late 1955, "he's nothing but a Park Avenue Truman."[26] Eisenhower feared that if any of these three candidates won the presidency, many of the accomplishments of his administration would be jeopardized, if not destroyed.

For Eisenhower, the real problem was that no other Republican seemed capable of stopping Stevenson, Kefauver, or Harriman. "We have developed no one on our side within our political ranks who can be elected or run this country," Eisenhower complained to Hagerty. Although he expected that he could "delicately" but firmly control the 1956 Republican National Convention so that it would nominate his candidate, who would that be? He continued to have reservations about Nixon's character and maturity. Senator William F. Knowland of California, who expressed interest in running if Eisenhower retired, was too partisan. Thinking out loud, Eisenhower raised the unlikely possibility of a third nomination for Thomas E. Dewey, but Hagerty persuaded him that such a candidacy would badly divide the Republicans. The president toyed with the idea of a George Humphrey-Milton Eisenhower ticket but conceded to Hagerty that neither one had a popular following. Eisenhower thought highly of Attorney General Herbert Brownell, former Deputy Secretary of Defense Robert B. Anderson, and Sherman Adams, but he knew that none of them had the stature to secure the nomination. In reply to Hagerty's suggestion, Eisenhower ruled out Earl Warren because he "is very happy right where he is . . . and wants to go down in history as a Great Chief Justice." Furthermore, Warren's deliberative style of making decisions was more suited to the judiciary than the presidency.[27]

After several days of such musings with his press secretary, Eisenhower was not yet ready to make a decision about his candidacy. Yet he seemed far more inclined toward running than at any previous time. In his conversations with Hagerty, Eisenhower focused not on why he should not seek reelection, but on the reasons that others could not win. Clearly there was no successor to whom Eisenhower was prepared to entrust his legacy. Probably for this reason, Eisenhower laughingly responded to Hagerty's comments by saying, "Listen, Jim, I haven't said I'm not going to be a candidate." Hagerty then revealed his own choice for 1956—Eisenhower-Nixon.[28]

After Eisenhower returned to Washington in early January 1956, his closest advisers strengthened his nascent conviction to stand for a second term. Attending a dinner meeting on Friday the thirteenth called by the president were Dulles, Humphrey, Brownell, Lodge, Hagerty, Adams, and Milton Eisenhower. The president's inner circle easily reached the conclusions that Eisenhower must have expected to hear. Eisenhower alone, they declared, could lead the Republican party to victory in 1956. His retirement would endanger prosperity at home and the chances for peace abroad. The group conceded, however, that only Eisenhower himself could determine whether he could withstand the rigors of four more years in the Oval Office. In summarizing the arguments of the inner circle, Milton Eisenhower expressed his own fears that a second term would endanger his brother's health. Milton also maintained that the president could act as an elder statesman who could continue to influence the course of world events even after leaving office. Yet this argument actually reinforced the case for running, since other members of the group pointed out that a Democratic president would be unlikely to turn to Eisenhower for advice. When the discussion ended, the president thanked his guests but expressed no opinion. Once again he had used a meeting to build a consensus for a course of action he was almost certain to follow.

The only remaining obstacle was his health. Even before his heart attack, Eisenhower was well aware that his age would raise questions about his ability to serve a second term. "No man has ever reached his 70th year in the White House," he wrote Hazlett in June 1955. "This may not mean much in itself, but it does remind us that every Presidential term is for four years and no one has the faintest right to consider acceptance of a nomination unless he honestly believes that his physical and mental reserves will stand the strain of four years of intensive work." Following his heart attack, Eisenhower returned to a full schedule in January 1956, but with restrictions imposed by his physicians. Among them were resting before and after lunch, exercising daily, and taking a ten-minute break each hour during every long meeting. The doctors also admonished him to avoid situations that caused anxiety, irritation, or anger, which prompted Eisenhower to inquire, "Just what do you think the Presidency is?"[29] After further tests in mid-February, the physicians publicly declared that Eisenhower should be able to maintain his current active life for another five to ten years. Dr. Paul Dudley White even told reporters he would vote for Eisenhower, if the president chose to run again.

After receiving medical clearance, Eisenhower made his final decision while golfing and quail hunting on George Humphrey's Georgia plantation. "It's your decision, not mine," Mamie told him. "I'm not going to have anything to do with it." "Well, I've made up my mind," he replied, "I am going to run again."[30]

Eisenhower returned to Washington and declared his candidacy in a fumbling, roundabout, and amusing manner. At his regular news conference on 29 February, Eisenhower greeted reporters with a poker face and a series of routine announcements—about the current Red Cross drive, the impending visit of the president of Italy, and the need for congressional approval of farm legislation and the Upper Colorado Basin project. Then, in what was surely one of the most notable examples of "Eisenhower syntax," he revealed his decision:

Now, my next announcement involves something more personal, but I think it will be of interest to you. . . . I have promised this body that when I reached a decision as to my own attitude toward my own personal future, I would let you know. . . . Now, I have reached a decision . . . , but . . . there were so many factors and considerations involved, that I saw the answer could not be expressed just in the simple terms of yes or no. . . . Moreover, I would not allow my name to go before the Republican Convention unless they, all the Republicans, understood, so that they would not be nominating some other individual than they thought they were nominating. . . . And my answer within the limits I have so sketchily observed, but which I will explain in detail tonight so as to get the story out in one continuous narrative, my answer will be positive, that is, affirmative.[31]

In other words, Eisenhower was running for reelection.

In a televised address that evening, Eisenhower asserted that he had made his decision only after assuring himself that he had fully recovered from his heart attack. He offered a detailed summary of his physicians' assessment of his health and their recommendations that he curtail his ceremonial duties and limit his travel. Because of these restrictions and his own distaste for "barn-storming," he stated that he would not campaign "in the customary manner" and would rely instead on television and radio to carry his message to the people. "But let me make one thing clear," he declared emphatically. "As of this moment, there is not the slightest doubt that I can perform as well as I ever have, all of the important duties of the Presidency. This I say because I am actually doing so."[32]

The heart attack and its consequences were central to Eisenhower's decision in other ways. A proud and competitive individual, Eisenhower could not retire from the presidency after an illness because, as Sherman Adams explained, "it would seem like accepting personal defeat." At the same time, Eisenhower thought that no one else could equal his qualifications for the nation's highest office. He believed that "no man of our times has had the standing throughout the world that seems to be mine." If his successor would necessarily have "less experience, lesser prestige," and less familiarity with world leaders, "then the question arises," Eisenhower wrote, " 'What will happen?' "[33] He did not want to find out, and he could not accept the idea that his work was finished. The challenge of continuing his work after his illness reinforced his ambition and renewed his sense of duty. As Eisenhower explained to Adams, "You know, if it hadn't been for that heart attack, I doubt if I would have been a candidate again."[34]

Eisenhower had far more difficulty settling the question of his running mate. For months Eisenhower tried to ease Nixon off the ticket but refrained from telling the vice-president directly that he wanted another running mate. The result was a lengthy period of indecision that only widened the distance between the two men.

Even before he had made up his mind about running again, Eisenhower met with Nixon to discuss the coming election. On 26 December 1955, the president told Nixon that he ought to consider taking a cabinet post in the next administration. While heading defense or health, education, and welfare, Nixon could build up his administrative experience, something he sorely lacked. Furthermore, Eisenhower suggested, Nixon as cabinet secretary would emerge as his own person, rather than second fiddle to the president. Eisenhower reminded Nixon that as secretary of commerce, Herbert Hoover had gained the national attention that enabled him to secure the presidency.

Nixon was "taken aback." He thought that the public would consider his moving to the cabinet not as a promotion designed to improve his chances for the 1960 nomination, but as an indication of Eisenhower's lack of confidence in him as a successor. Furthermore, Nixon knew that the vice-presidential nomination would be even more important in 1956 than it had been four years earlier, especially if Eisenhower's diseased heart did not allow him to finish out a second term. Nixon, however, recognized that his fate was in Eisenhower's hands. He told the president, "If you believe your own candidacy and your administration would be better served with me off the ticket, you tell me what you want me to do and I'll do it. I want to do what is best for you."[35]

Although he professed only concern for Nixon's political future, Eisenhower had significant reservations about his vice-president. Eisenhower simply did not like Nixon, despite the latter's loyalty and his willingness to do the partisan dirty work that Eisenhower detested. Eisenhower's lamentations about the failure of the Republican party to groom a successor indicated that he did not think Nixon was ready for the presidency. He told speechwriter Emmet Hughes, "Well, the fact is, of course, I've watched Dick a long time, and he just hasn't grown. So I just haven't been able to believe that he *is* presidential timber."[36] Eisenhower also feared that Nixon would cost him votes if they ran together again. During their conversation on the day after Christmas 1955, Eisenhower mentioned some unfavorable Gallup polls and bemoaned Nixon's failure to increase his popularity during the previous three years. For his own reasons, then, Eisenhower wanted to rid himself of Nixon.

Yet there were problems. One was the difficulty of finding an alternative to Nixon. One candidate whom Eisenhower seriously considered was Frank Lausche, the Democratic governor of Ohio. Eisenhower told Hagerty in late 1955 that Lausche was "a natural" for the Democratic nomination as president. He considered Lausche a sensible alternative to Stevenson, Kefauver, or Harriman, one who would appeal to young voters, especially if Eisenhower chose not to run again.[37] Several weeks later, when Eisenhower had almost made up his mind to try for a second term, the president tried out the idea of an Eisenhower-Lausche combination on Leonard Hall, the chair of the Republican National Committee. Eisenhower insisted that Lausche, a Catholic, would bring considerable strength to the ticket. Furthermore, his running with a Democrat "would just knock the props out of the [opposition]." Hall professed interest in Eisenhower's unrealistic suggestion, but the president never approached Lausche about the vice-presidency.[38]

Eisenhower, however, did offer the second spot on the ticket to his first choice, Robert B. Anderson. A Texas lawyer and business leader, Anderson had served Eisenhower as secretary of the navy and deputy secretary of defense. In early 1956, he undertook a secret mission as the president's personal representative to try to arrange a peace between Egypt and Israel. Although both Egyptian President Gamal Abdel Nasser and Israeli Prime Minister David Ben-Gurion were eager to secure the lavish aid Anderson offered to induce a settlement, neither was willing to make concessions to his adversary. The failure of this diplomatic mission in no way diminished Anderson's standing in the president's eyes. Before Anderson left for the Middle East, Eisenhower wrote, "Nothing could give me greater satisfaction than to believe that next January 20, I could turn over this office to his hands."[39] In April, shortly after Anderson returned from his secret mission, Eisenhower asked Anderson to be his running mate in 1956. Anderson declined. A life-long Democrat, he doubted that he could secure the Republican nomination to succeed Eisenhower in 1960. In addition, he simply lacked an overwhelming desire to become president.[40]

Eisenhower might have had less trouble finding another running mate if Nixon had removed his name from consideration. Eisenhower tried to get Nixon to do so by authorizing Hall to have a talk with Nixon but admonishing his emissary to "be very, very gentle."[41] When Hall spoke to the vice-president in mid-February, Nixon refused to step aside unless Eisenhower made the request directly. Yet Eisenhower would not do so. Instead he repeatedly counseled Nixon to improve his political prospects by moving to the cabinet, but he left the decision to the vice-president. Nixon, for his part, replied that he only wanted to help the administration and would do whatever Eisenhower wanted. Milton Eisenhower later remarked that "a more sensitive man" would have taken the president's hint and withdrawn from the ticket. "But he [Nixon] wanted to be there," the president's brother sneered. "He thought this was his chance to be president."[42]

Eisenhower's preference for dealing with Nixon by indirection arose from both political and personal considerations. Eisenhower appreciated Nixon's popularity with regular Republicans. Three years of making speeches and campaigning had earned him hundreds of allies among state and local GOP officials. Nixon also had the strong support of the Old Guard because of his zealous pursuit of Communists in government. Dumping Nixon, Eisenhower realized, might divide the Republican party. At the same time, Eisenhower had no stomach for dismissing a subordinate who had faithfully performed his duties. He did not like confrontations, personal or political, and apparently hoped that hints, signals, and rumors would persuade Nixon to step aside. Years later he insisted that if he had not wanted him as a running mate, "I would have said 'Dick, I just don't want you this time.' You see, that would be the soldier's way."[43] On controversial matters, however, the soldier's way was not always Eisenhower's.

In public, Eisenhower effusively praised Nixon but refused to endorse him. Following his own announcement that he was running again, Eisenhower repeatedly faced questions about his preference for a running mate. He responded by expressing his "unbounded" respect and admiration for Nixon, "a loyal and dedicated associate," who "should be one of the comers in the Republican Party." "If anyone ever has the effrontery to come in and urge me to dump somebody that I respect as I do Vice President Nixon, there will be more commotion around my office than you have noticed yet," he promised reporters. Yet he also maintained that he would not presume to dictate either to the Republican convention or Nixon. Instead the vice-president should "chart out his own course."[44] Such remarks caused Nixon "absolutely indescribable anguish."[45] He did not see how a vice-president could possibly determine his own fate.

Nixon twisted slowly, slowly in the wind until the end of April. When Eisenhower once again reminded reporters that Nixon had still failed to chart out his course, the vice-president took the initiative. The next day he informed Eisenhower that he "would be honored to continue as Vice President." He had failed to express a preference earlier, he explained to Eisenhower, only for fear that the president might think that he was trying to force himself onto the ticket.

Eisenhower told Nixon and Hagerty to make the announcement. While he authorized them to tell reporters that he was delighted, Eisenhower still did not issue an endorsement.[46]

The vice-presidential nomination seemed settled—until Eisenhower once again became ill. On 7 June, the president suffered an attack of ileitis, a painful condition arising from the inflammation of the small intestine. Although he had previously experienced milder distress, his physicians had not diagnosed the cause. Once they did, they performed an emergency operation to relieve his ailment. Eisenhower came through the operation in fine shape and recovered quickly. Yet his second major illness within a year raised new fears about the fragility of his health and the qualifications of his constitutional successor. A final effort was made to find an alternative to Nixon.

The instigator of this effort was Harold Stassen, the president's special assistant for disarmament. Stassen privately informed Eisenhower that he intended to announce his support for Governor Christian A. Herter of Massachusetts for vice-president. He also made clear that his decision arose from recent public opinion polls, which showed that Nixon might cut into Eisenhower's margin in the election. Eisenhower apparently did not try to stop Stassen. He may even have hoped that Stassen might be able to start a contest for the nomination—one in which an acceptable alternative to Nixon would emerge. If that was Eisenhower's wish, he was disappointed. With his dull personality and stuffy manner, Herter generated no enthusiasm. Quietly Eisenhower informed the governor that he could expect a job in the state department if he withdrew his name from consideration for the vice-presidency, something Herter did promptly. Yet on 1 August, in reply to reporters' questions, Eisenhower still refused to express a preference for vice-president, although Nixon was a "perfectly acceptable" running mate.[47] Three weeks later, the Republican National Convention did what Eisenhower could not do: it chose a vice-presidential candidate. With only one dissenting vote, it nominated Richard Nixon.

Following his own unanimous renomination, Eisenhower kicked off his campaign by declaring that he was running on his record. He told the delegates at the Republican National Convention in San Francisco that his policies had created a sound and sustained prosperity and military strength that was unsurpassed in peacetime. Referring indirectly to the Geneva summit, he reminded the convention that an even greater achievement was progress toward peace, "little by little," through "international understanding based on truth" replacing "mistrust based on falsehoods." These achievements, he asserted, pointed to the even larger conclusion, that "the Republican Party is the Party of the Future."[48]

Eisenhower thought that the legislative achievement that most clearly demonstrated the Republicans' ability to handle the issues of today and tomorrow was the Federal Aid Highway Act. The president's signing of this legislation on 29 June 1956 brought to an end a lengthy struggle over the modernization of the nation's roads. When Eisenhower entered office, a variety of powerful interest groups supported a new federal highway program but could not agree on its major provisions. Farmers desired roads that speeded travel in rural areas; truckers wanted more superhighways but opposed tolls, taxes, or fees on users; state officials eagerly sought federal aid, but without restrictions on their power to select routes. Even Eisenhower's own advisers were divided. Some, such as John H. Bragdon of the Council of Economic Advisers, wanted a centralized program so that highway construction could be timed to prevent the economy from falling into a recession. Others, such as Sherman Adams, advocated a plan that would give a federal agency responsibility for financing roads but leave construction and operations mainly to state and local officials.

Eisenhower considered a new highway bill imperative. When he returned to the United States in 1945, he thought American roads were in "shocking condition," especially when compared to the modern German autobahns.[49] During the next decade, the number of automobiles on the roads doubled as Americans moved to the suburbs and drove to work, school, and shopping. Eisenhower believed more cars meant "greater convenience, . . . greater happiness, and greater standards of living."[50] Yet he reminded legislative leaders in February 1955 that new expressways were essential to handle this increased traffic. An improved interstate highway system, Eisenhower reasoned, would provide many economic benefits by encouraging the development of new residential and commercial areas and helping major industries, such as automobiles and construction. Furthermore, better highways were essential to national defense, since they could facilitate the evacuation of urban centers in the event of atomic attack and speed the movement of troops in time of war. To devise a plan for new highway construction, Eisenhower appointed a blue-ribbon advisory committee headed by Gen. Lucius D. Clay, a trusted friend, an engineer, and a member of the board of directors of General Motors.

Based on the recommendations of the Clay commission, Eisenhower sent legislation to Congress in February 1955. Much to his chagrin, the bill encountered fierce opposition. Some critics wanted to finance the construction through the collection of tolls rather than the issuance of bonds, as Clay had proposed. Rural interests cried that the administration plan concentrated on expressways between urban areas to the neglect of farm-to-market roads. Mired in controversy, the administration bill languished in Congress for more than a year.

In the spring of 1956, Eisenhower threw his support behind compromise legislation that provided something for almost every major interest group and that avoided some of the most divisive issues. As passed, the Federal Aid Highway Act created a forty-one thousand-mile National System of Defense and Interstate Highways. A federal Highway Trust Fund, financed through taxes on gasoline, tires, and trucks, would pay 90 percent of the costs of construction. About the only group that objected to this highway program was urban planners, who predicted that it would accelerate suburban sprawl and the decay of central cities and retard the development of urban mass transportation. Eisenhower had no such reservations. He thought instead about solving the immediate problems of inadequate, clogged, or dangerous roads. The new interstate highway system, he told voters, would be a great monument to his administration and a measure of its vision.

During the 1956 campaign, the president endorsed all Republican candidates, even though many of them held views that could hardly be described as forward-looking. He personally did little campaigning, however, on their behalf. But his assistants were active behind the scenes in trying to help the GOP regain control of Congress. Sherman Adams, Hall, and, ultimately, Eisenhower persuaded John Sherman Cooper of Kentucky to resign as ambassador to India and run once again for the Senate seat he had given up to take his diplomatic post. Cooper triumphed in November. Not so Douglas McKay, the secretary of the interior and former governor of Oregon. Prodded by Adams, McKay reluctantly agreed to run for the Senate in his home state against the incumbent, Wayne Morse. Eisenhower and his aides were eager to unseat Morse, who had left the GOP during the 1952 campaign because of his distress over "reactionaries running a captive general for President."[51] McKay agreed to challenge Morse, who had recently declared himself a Democrat, provided the other Republican contenders withdrew from the race. Adams assured McKay that he would not face any competition for the nomination but became greatly embarrassed when McKay had to defeat an opponent in the primary. McKay, however, lost in November. He was one of many Republican disappointments in the congressional races.

As much as he tried to campaign on his own record, Eisenhower could not avoid criticizing the Democrats. The Democratic Congress, he repeatedly charged, had frivolously played politics with his proposals. This campaign rhetoric distorted the record. Partisan advantage certainly influenced some Democratic votes, but Eisenhower was actually quite successful in winning bipartisan support on the House and Senate floors. The Democratic Eighty-fourth Congress supported the administration on 72 percent of roll-call votes, compared to 83 percent success in the Republican Eighty-third Congress. On those votes in which the administration position prevailed, a majority of the Democrats voted with the president 69 percent of the time.

Yet Eisenhower hammered away at Democratic partisanship by concentrating on certain specific issues, such as the Agricultural Act of 1956. The legislation arose from the administration's determination to diminish the surplus in farm products, which was holding down prices and farmers' income. In early 1956, Eisenhower submitted a bill to create a Soil Bank, a plan that would allow farmers to take land out of cultivation in return for federal subsidy. The Soil Bank offended Secretary of Agriculture Ezra Taft Benson, who explained that "the idea of paying farmers for not producing—even as a one-shot emergency measure—outraged my sensibilities."[52] Eisenhower, however, thought the Soil Bank would provide short-term price relief and long-term conservation benefits. Congress passed legislation creating the Soil Bank but also added a provision that required rigid price supports for staple crops at 90 percent of parity. On 16 April, Eisenhower vetoed what he later called "a jumbled-up, election-year monstrosity," and explained his action in a televised address.[53] Six weeks later he signed a bill that he considered more palatable. In accepting the presidential nomination, he told the San Francisco convention that on the farm issue, he had rejected "expediency in favor of principle."[54]

Eisenhower saved his harshest rebukes for his Democratic challenger, Adlai Stevenson. As always, Eisenhower refused to criticize his opponent directly, but he could hardly conceal his contempt for Stevenson as the campaign wore on. The reason for Eisenhower's consternation was Stevenson's call for a ban on the testing of nuclear weapons. Hoping to cut into Eisenhower's reputation as an advocate of peace, Stevenson stepped up his attacks on the administration for failing to respond to Soviet proposals for a test ban. He said that such a moratorium would move disarmament negotiations off dead center and halt "the danger of poisoning the atmosphere." Eisenhower was enraged. He thought that such a complex issue ought not to be turned into a campaign issue. Eisenhower found an opportunity to deprive Stevenson of his issue in mid-October when Soviet Premier Bulganin called for a test ban and praised "certain prominent public figures in the

United States" for taking a similar position. Eisenhower castigated Bulganin for meddling in American politics, while Nixon denounced Stevenson as a naive appeaser.[55] In private, Eisenhower fully revealed the extent of his dislike for his opponent. On the eve of the election, he wrote to Swede Hazlett that "the Stevenson-Kefauver combination is, in some ways, about the sorriest and weakest we have ever run for the two top offices in the land."[56]

As the campaign moved into its final weeks, Eisenhower was less concerned about Stevenson than he was tensions in the Middle East. He had no doubts that he would defeat Stevenson. "This fellow's licked and what's more he knows it," Eisenhower exclaimed to his son John in early October.[57] He could not be so confident about the outcome of the crisis that was building over the Suez Canal.

The real source of trouble in the Middle East, Eisenhower believed, was Gamal Abdel Nasser, the president of Egypt. Nasser was part of a military junta that forced the abdication of King Farouk in 1952. Two years later Nasser took over as head of the Egyptian government. A fervent nationalist, Nasser signed an agreement for the withdrawal of British troops from Egypt by mid-1956. At the Bandung (Indonesia) Conference of nonaligned nations in April 1955, Nasser emerged as a leading champion of Arab interests by condemning the vestiges of British and French colonialism in the Middle East and denouncing Israel. The Eisenhower administration attempted to persuade Nasser that he could fulfill his nationalist goals through cooperation with the United States. Ambassador Henry A. Byroade sedulously tried to cultivate Nasser's friendship, and the Central Intelligence Agency's Kermit Roosevelt secretly offered the Egyptian leader $3 million.[58] What Nasser wanted was not a bribe, but arms, especially after Israel launched a raid on 28 February 1955 on an Egyptian army camp in the Gaza strip. But Eisenhower was not willing to provide them, for fear of setting off a deadly arms race between Egypt and Israel. As a result, Nasser struck a deal with Czechoslovakia to supply Egypt with weapons. While Eisenhower recognized Third World nationalism was a powerful and legitimate force, he feared that Nasser was using it to encourage Communist penetration of the Middle East.

Eisenhower became deeply pessimistic about Nasser's willingness to cooperate after the failure of the Anderson mission in early 1956. After weeks of shuttling between Cairo and Tel Aviv, Robert Anderson informed Eisenhower that he had made no progress in bringing Egypt or Israel any closer to peace. Based on Anderson's report, Eisenhower described Nasser as "a complete stumbling block." The Egyptian leader was determined "to be the most popular man in all the Arab world" and so made speeches that "breathe[d] defiance of Israel" and that ruled out any concessions that might lead to peace. Nasser's inflammatory posturing, the president believed, was simply the most notorious example of the Arabs "daily growing more arrogant and disregarding the interests of Western Europe and of the United States in the Middle East." Such a trend was alarming because of the importance of Middle Eastern oil to Europe. For difficulties such as these, Eisenhower concluded, "there is, of course, no easy answer."[59]

Eisenhower did propose a solution, although by no means a simple one. He wanted to isolate Nasser. Eisenhower hoped to use American economic aid to win Libyan cooperation. He also wanted to try to build up King Saud of Saudi Arabia as a champion of Arab nationalism and a rival to Nasser. If this plan worked, "Egypt could scarcely continue intimate association with the Soviets and certainly . . . would no longer be regarded as leader of the Arab world." At the end of March, Eisenhower approved a program to put pressure on Egypt that included delay or denial of shipments of food, medical supplies and other economic assistance; a continued moratorium on the export of armaments; and increased support for Libya, Saudi Arabia, Lebanon, and Ethiopia. These actions, Dulles asserted, would "let Colonel Nasser realize that he cannot cooperate as he is doing with the Soviet Union and at the same time enjoy most-favored nation treatment from the United States."[60]

The Eisenhower administration's efforts to use its leverage against Egypt caused a dispute over the financing of construction of the Aswan High Dam. Nasser envisioned the dam as a monument to his rule, since it would provide water for the irrigation of more than one million acres of farmland and electricity for over half of Egypt's power requirements.[61] To counter the Communist influence from the Czech arms deal, American officials offered Nasser in late 1955 loans and grants that would defray a large portion of the costs of building the dam. But a few months later, Eisenhower ordered a delay in the negotiations to arrange this financial aid as part of his program of applying pressure against Nasser. Nasser responded with pressure of his own. He extended diplomatic recognition to the People's Republic of China, apparently in the hope of securing Chinese arms. He also threatened to accept Soviet financial aid if the Americans kept dragging their feet in discussions over construction of the dam. Finally, he made new demands for a change in the terms of the proposed American assistance. Eisenhower later remarked that Nasser "gave the impression of a man who was convinced that he could play off East against West by blackmailing both.''[62]

Eisenhower and Dulles thought the Egyptian leader had gone too far, and they agreed that they should do something more to "weaken Nasser."[63] At the same time, Congress also tried to force the administration to withdraw its offer to help in the construction of the Aswan High Dam. Members of the Old Guard objected to the cost of the project, especially since it would benefit a leader whom they considered a Communist masquerading as a neutralist. Southerners complained that the Eisenhower administration would hurt American agriculture by indirectly subsidizing Egyptian cotton. In mid-July, Knowland told Dulles that Congress was ready to prohibit the use of American foreign aid to pay for the dam. Rather than risking congressional termination of the project, Dulles acted first. He halted negotiations on 19 July. Ambassador Ahmed Hussein was taken aback, since he had opened the meeting with Dulles by announcing that Egypt had withdrawn its demand for a change in terms and was prepared to accept the original American offer.

In this game of diplomatic one-upmanship, Nasser responded with a stunning move: he nationalized the Suez Canal. Before 26 July, when Nasser took possession of the canal, the British government owned 44 percent of the stock in the canal, and private French investors held most of the other shares. Nasser said he would use the revenue from the canal to pay for the construction of the Aswan High Dam. The attempt of Eisenhower and Dulles to weaken Nasser had backfired.

Although he was determined not to let Nasser get away with the nationalization of the canal, Eisenhower thought that the United States and its allies should simply step up the pressure on Egypt. In a meeting with the leaders of Congress in mid-August, Eisenhower pointed out that Nasser's control of the canal jeopardized the security of Western Europe "and the heavy investment that the United States has made in strengthening" that region. By closing the canal, Dulles added, Nasser could bring Britain and France to their knees, since two-thirds of the oil for Western Europe passed through the Egyptian waterway.[64] To avert these dangers, Eisenhower supported international action. Gathering in London, representatives of almost two dozen maritime nations approved American resolutions first for an international authority to run the canal and then for a users' association to take over the work of piloting vessels through the waterway. Nasser brusquely rejected both schemes. Still determined to make Nasser back down, Eisenhower hoped instead to reroute oil shipments and build new pipelines, while continuing the program of economic and political pressures against Egypt that he had approved last spring.

The British and French proposed sterner measures. In the eyes of Prime Minister Anthony Eden, the nationalization of the canal was an affront to British honor, an attack on British imperial interests, and a "theft" of British resources. Nasser, Eden asserted, could not be permitted "to have his thumb on our windpipe."[65] The French, irate over Nasser's support of a rebellion in their colony of Algeria, considered nationalization of the canal the last straw. Both the French and British made contingency plans for military action against Egypt, although the British chiefs of staff informed Eden that they would not be ready to strike against Nasser for several weeks. On 27 July, Eden cabled Eisenhower that the British were ready to use force, albeit as a last resort, to "bring Nasser to his senses."[66]

Beginning in late July—and continuing for the next three months—Eisenhower warned Eden that he could not endorse armed intervention in Egypt. Even though he was prepared to "respond affirmatively" to British and French requests for military equipment, the president sent Dulles to London to dissuade Eden from taking any drastic action without first trying to find a diplomatic solution to the Suez crisis. Dulles went out of his way to express his sympathy for the British situation and his contempt for Egyptian arrogance. He also asserted that "a way had to be found to make Nasser disgorge what he was attempting to swallow."[67] At the same time, Dulles emphasized to the prime minister that nationalization of the canal was not a sufficiently provocative act to rally American public opinion in support of armed action against Egypt. In a message to Eden on 31 July, Eisenhower reiterated these conclusions and revealed that he thought it unwise even to consider the possibility of military intervention at that time.

In early September, Eisenhower once more urged Eden to give diplomacy a chance. Again he stressed that British and American differences over Suez concerned means, not ends. Like Eden, Eisenhower wanted to curb Nasser's anti-Western excesses and ensure international access to the Suez Canal. Yet the president made clear that unlike Eden, he thought the use of force was out of the question, barring a drastic change in circumstances. Armed intervention, he predicted, would disrupt the supply of oil and cause havoc in the economies of Western Europe. Furthermore, it would turn Middle Eastern opinion so strongly against the West that the damage would not be undone for a generation or even a century, if the Soviets took advantage of the situation. Diplomacy, on the other hand, could make Nasser retreat and so destroy his standing as the leader of the Arab world. Negotiations and economic pressures might take time, Eisenhower conceded, but they would deprive Nasser of the thing on which he thrived, drama. "If we . . . concentrate upon the task of deflating him through slower but sure processes . . . , we could isolate Nasser and gain a victory which would not only be bloodless, but would be more far-reaching in its ultimate consequences than could be anything brought about by force of arms."[68] Eisenhower, in short, wanted to deal with Nasser as he had Joseph McCarthy, by strangling rather than cracking down on him.

Although Britain and France took the Suez dispute to the United Nations, Eisenhower discovered that the two nations were secretly making ominous military moves. In mid-October, the president found out that the French had transferred sixty Mystère jet aircraft to Israel. The information came from high-altitude reconnaissance flights by the U-2, which had flown its first spy missions several months earlier. The French had reported the provision to Israel of only twenty-four Mystères under the terms of the Tripartite Declaration of 1950, an agreement between Great Britain, France, and the United States to regulate the supply of armaments to the Middle East. Thus France had not only breached the Tripartite Declaration, but also deceived the United States about its actions. Subsequent U-2 missions in late October revealed the shipment of military equipment from French ports on the Mediterranean and the concentration of British ships at Malta and Cyprus.

Based on this intelligence, Eisenhower concluded that Israel was preparing to go to war against Jordan. The president believed that Israeli Prime Minister David Ben-Gurion coveted territory on the west bank of the Jordan River, and a number of Israeli raids across the Jordanian border convinced him of Ben-Gurion's "obviously aggressive attitude." The prime minister, Eisenhower reasoned, was counting on the Suez imbroglio to keep Egypt or Great Britain, the latter of which had an alliance with Jordan, from interfering with an Israeli attack. Eisenhower also believed that the Israelis thought that his hands would be tied because of the impending election and the importance of the Jewish vote. Eisenhower, however, made clear that he would not let domestic political considerations determine his foreign policy, especially since he thought an Israeli-Arab war would provide an opportunity for the Soviet Union to extend its influence throughout the Middle East. Eisenhower told Dulles to inform the Israeli ambassador that the United States wanted the cessation of military action against Jordan.[69]

The Israelis were indeed planning to attack in late October, but to the west into the Sinai and then on toward the Suez Canal. They had conspired with the French and British, who intended to use the Israeli invasion as a pretext for intervention to protect the canal. The French had taken the lead in devising this scheme, and the British had joined the cabal somewhat reluctantly in mid-October. Eden hesitated because of his fears that military action would irreparably harm Britain's reputation in the Arab nations. Yet by mid-October he doubted that diplomacy would produce a satisfactory resolution of the Suez dispute, and he faced pressure from members of his own Conservative party, who equated negotiations with appeasement. After a series of highly secret meetings and messages, Eden, Ben-Gurion, and French Premier Guy Mollet agreed on 25 October to commence action four days later.

At that moment, the world's attention shifted from the Middle East to Eastern Europe. In Poland, popular uprisings brought to power Wladyslaw Gomulka, who immediately proclaimed, "There is more than one road to Socialism."[70] Despite his determination to liberalize Poland's Communist government, Gomulka declared that "any attempt to sow distrust of the Soviet Union will find no fertile soil among the Polish people."[71] In Hungary, Imre Nagy was not so prudent. Only days after street demonstrations forced the Communist party to appoint him premier, Nagy announced that Hungary was withdrawing from the Warsaw Pact, the military alliance between the Soviet Union and its Eastern European satellites. The Soviets responded on 4 November by sending 200,000 troops and 4,000 tanks into Budapest to depose Nagy and crush the demonstrations.

The Hungarian revolutionaries expected American help. The liberation of "captive" nations had long been a staple of the Cold War rhetoric of the Republican party and a prominent theme in the public statements of Dulles, Nixon, and other officials high in the Eisenhower administration. For years, broadcasts from Radio Free Europe had proclaimed that the United States was trying mightily to emancipate Eastern Europeans from Communist enslavement. After Khrushchev delivered his famous secret speech to the Twentieth Party Congress in Moscow in February 1956, the Central Intelligence Agency obtained a copy, and Eisenhower authorized its release. The text contributed to the onset of disturbances in Poland and Hungary, since Khrushchev had denounced Stalin as a barbaric tyrant and indicated that he wanted a moderation of internal conditions in the Soviet Union and Eastern Europe. Eisenhower had also approved a covert CIA program known as RED SOX/RED CAP to train East European emigrés to undertake secret paramilitary missions.[72] These agents helped organize the demonstrations that rocked Hungary in the last week of October. As Soviet tanks rolled into Budapest, the

CIA was eager to parachute weapons and other supplies to the Hungarians in order to sustain their insurgency.

Eisenhower ordered the CIA not to furnish such assistance. Despite his sympathy for the Hungarians, Eisenhower concluded that the risks of intervention were far too great. He recognized that the RED SOX/RED CAP agents, however well equipped, were no match for Soviet armor. Covert air drops to the freedom fighters ultimately would only prolong the insurrection and increase Hungarian casualties. Direct American military action was out of the question. For all practical purposes, Eisenhower noted, Hungary was ''as inaccessible to us as Tibet.''[73] Even more important, American armed intervention would have precipitated a general war with the possibility of a nuclear exchange. Instead Eisenhower did only what he realistically could: denounce Soviet aggression and assist the Hungarian refugees. These actions unmasked liberation as a sham policy that the Eisenhower administration had recklessly encouraged to score propaganda points and win the support of voters of East European ancestry.

If Eisenhower was distressed over the Soviet invasion of Hungary, he was infuriated over Franco-British-Israeli intervention in Egypt. On 29 October, according to plan, Israeli forces thrust into the Sinai, and the British and French then promptly issued an ultimatum giving both sides twelve hours to pull their forces back from the Suez Canal. Dulles considered the Anglo-French declaration ''about as crude and brutal as anything I have ever seen.''[74] Following the inevitable rejection of the ultimatum, British and French bombers began hitting Egyptian airfields, while an invasion force sailed toward Port Said.

''I just can't believe it,'' Eisenhower exclaimed as the Franco-British-Israeli plot unfolded. ''I can't believe that they [the British and French] would be so stupid as to invite on *themselves* all the Arab hostility to Israel.'' Because the British had all but ceased formal communication for two weeks before the attack, Eisenhower knew nothing of the conspiracy to strike at Egypt, except for intelligence reports from U-2 flights that revealed the plotters' military preparations. Eisenhower was outraged at the brazenness and stupidity of the Suez intervention. Because the Egyptians continued to operate the canal effectively, public opinion would not support the intervention, Eisenhower correctly predicted. Moreover, the attack was certain to rally Arab opinion behind Nasser. ''What are they [the British and French] going to do,'' Eisenhower contemptuously asked his staff, ''fight the whole Moslem world?''[75] Britain was using gunboat diplomacy ''in the manner of the Victorian period," an instrument that was hopelessly out of date and patently offensive. "I don't see the point in getting into a fight," he wrote to a friend, "to which there can be no satisfactory end, and in which the whole world believes you are playing the part of the bully."[76]

Eisenhower also felt betrayed and exploited, and he was determined not to let the actions of friends and allies sully the reputation of the United States. In 1950, the United States, Britain, and France had agreed to take immediate action to restore peace and stability should force be used to violate the borders between Israel and the Arab nations. "Are they going to *dare* us—dare *us*—to defend the Tripartite declaration," Eisenhower wondered of the British and French.[77] Eisenhower resented the apparent assumption of Eden, Mollet, and Ben-Gurion that the importance of the Jewish vote in the approaching election would constrain his action. He resolved to shape policy "as though we didn't have a Jew in America," he confided in a letter to Hazlett. "The welfare and best interests of our own country were to be the sole criteria on which we operated."[78] In one of his last campaign speeches, Eisenhower explained that American policy rested on a fundamental principle. "We cannot . . . subscribe to one law for the weak, another law for the strong; one law for those opposing us, another for those allied with us. There can be only one law—or there shall be no peace."[79]

Probably the most important reason Eisenhower so firmly opposed the Suez intervention was that he feared the Soviets would capitalize on the crisis to extend their influence into the Middle East. Hours after learning of the Israeli attack, Eisenhower telephoned the British ambassador and informed him that the United States would put the Suez issue before the United Nations "first thing in the morning—when the doors open, before the U.S.S.R. gets there."[80] After the British and French vetoed the resolution in the Security Council, Eisenhower told Dulles to take it to the General Assembly. He explained that the United States had to take the initiative at the UN in order to prevent the Soviets "from seizing a mantle of world leadership through a false but convincing exhibition of concern for smaller nations. Since Africa and Asia almost unanimously hate one of the three nations, Britain, France and Israel, the Soviets need only to propose severe and immediate punishment of these three to have the whole of two continents on their side."[81] The General Assembly's adoption of the American-sponsored resolution had the desired effect. Henry Cabot Lodge, the United States ambassador, reported to Eisenhower from the UN that "never has there been such a tremendous acclaim for your policy. Absolutely spectacular."[82]

Although Eisenhower's actions during the Suez crisis were consciously anti-Soviet, he did not intend them to be anti-British or anti-

French. However much he was flabbergasted or outraged by the behavior of his allies, he still tried to be conciliatory. On 30 October, he wrote to Eden, addressing him as "my long-time friend who has, with me, believed in and worked for real Anglo-American understanding." He implored Eden to join him in laying out their "present views and intentions," so that misunderstanding would not interfere with concerted action in the crisis.[83] Even though Eden continued to keep Eisenhower in the dark about British military plans, Eisenhower still tried to moderate international reaction to Anglo-French actions. One of the reasons that he ordered Dulles and Lodge to take the initiative at the UN was to prevent approval of a resolution more harshly critical of France and Britain. In a televised address on 31 October, Eisenhower assured a national audience that his condemnation of the use of force in no way diminished his determination to maintain the friendship of the United States with those two nations. Several days later, he described western differences over the Suez intervention as a "family fight."[84]

The tensions in Washington reached a high point on the day before the election, 5 November. By that time, the Egyptians had blocked the Suez Canal by scuttling some fifty vessels, while Arab saboteurs had blown up a pipeline of the Iraq Petroleum Company that carried vital oil supplies to Western Europe. British and French paratroopers landed in Egypt, a few hours before the invasion fleet arrived. As the British and French started to go ashore, Soviet president Bulganin warned Washington, Paris, and London that his country was prepared to use force, if necessary, to stop the invasion. Eisenhower replied that the United States would fight, if necessary, to halt Soviet military intervention in Egypt, and the next day he authorized a phased mobilization of the armed forces. Yet despite the gravity of the situation, Eisenhower maintained his sense of humor. When the CIA informed him that Nasser feared that he might be deposed, Eisenhower wryly remarked, "Tell Nasser we'll be glad to put him on St. Helena and give him a million dollars."[85]

On election day, the crisis broke. The British and French announced that they would accept the UN cease-fire resolution, even though they controlled only a small portion of the canal. The decision to halt the military operations was Eden's, one he made unilaterally and then imposed on the French. Eden did so because of divisions within his own government and resignations from his cabinet. He also worried about Britain's rapidly diminishing gold reserves and the falling value of the pound, a decline which the Eisenhower administration refused to try to halt unless the British agreed to a cease-fire. Weary of these problems and plagued by continuing doubts about the intervention, Eden gave in.

Although pleased with Eden's decision, Eisenhower actually stepped up the pressure on the British. He wanted to make sure that the British would speedily and unconditionally withdraw their forces. He also worried about the stability of the Eden government, which had faced two votes of confidence during the crisis and was in disarray, in no small measure because of the exhaustion and ineffectiveness of the prime minister. The economic privations of the war—the British had to institute gas rationing, for example—added to the precariousness of the government's position. Eisenhower and his top aides did not want Eden to try to hang on only to lose a vote of confidence that would bring to power the Labour party, those "socialists," in the contemptuous view of Secretary of the Treasury George M. Humphrey.[86]

Accordingly, American officials, with Eisenhower's approval, began dealing secretly with members of Eden's cabinet who might succeed to the prime ministership. Eisenhower told the American ambassador in London to relay the message that "as soon as things happen that we anticipate, we can furnish 'a lot of fig leaves.'"[87] The terms of this deal are still not entirely clear and may never have been specified at the time. Nonetheless, once the British revealed that they were about to withdraw their troops, Eisenhower authorized on 30 November the implementation of a plan to ease European petroleum shortages. Only a few weeks later, on 9 January 1957, Eden resigned, and Harold Macmillan, a wartime associate of Eisenhower and one of the cabinet members who held the secret conversations with American officials in the aftermath of Suez, formed a new government. The calamity of Suez brought Eden's government to the precipice; American pressure gave it a small, but not inconsequential, nudge.

As the Suez and Hungarian crises reached their culminations, Eisenhower did little campaigning. The lack of time for political rallies caused him no remorse, however. For weeks, he had been certain that he would defeat Stevenson. And if foreign policy occupied most of his time in the first week of November, Eisenhower was still as determined as ever to win a smashing victory. He wrote to Hazlett on 2 November that he sought victory by "a comfortable majority (one that could not be significantly increased or decreased in the next few days by any amount of speaking on either side)." The size of his victory would determine his ability to influence members of his own party as well as the opposition. If Republicans wanted his help in the next election—and they would if he remained popular with the voters—they would be more willing to support his policies. If Democrats were inclined to oppose him in Congress, they might think twice "if it is generally believed that I am in a position to go to the people over the[ir] heads."[88]

Eisenhower got the mandate he desired. The voters gave him a plurality of 9.5 million votes, three million more than he received in 1952. He also added fifteen electoral votes to his earlier total by taking forty-one states—two more than last time—including Louisiana, a feat so incredible that he jokingly likened it to winning in Ethiopia. By all measures, it was a landslide victory.

Eisenhower's personal triumph, however, did not mean a Republican victory. The Democrats maintained their control of Congress and added one seat in the Senate and two in the House to their majorities. Nonetheless, Eisenhower still believed that the size of his victory would enable him to secure much of the legislation that he proposed. At a postelection news conference, he told reporters that he considered the election "a mandate to . . . push forward with what I have been trying to tell the United States is my policy, my beliefs, my convictions, and . . . program. . . . If they [the voters] don't approve what I stand for, I would not understand why they voted for me."[89]

Eisenhower was right; the election was a vote of confidence in him, and an overwhelming one at that. It reflected satisfaction with an expanding economy, hope in the spirit of Geneva, and certainty in Eisenhower's ability to handle grave international crises. Suez and Hungary, if anything, probably increased Eisenhower's margin of victory. The president was often at his best in tense situations where coolness and restraint were essential, and the voters registered their approval of his leadership during those tense days in early November 1956. The events of the next year, however, revealed that this high point of his presidency was a pinnacle rather than a plateau.

6

THE HAZARDS
OF DELIBERATE SPEED

"No one is more anxious than I am to see Negroes receive first-class citizenship in this country," President Dwight D. Eisenhower told a group of black leaders in May 1958, "but you must be patient."[1] This contradictory statement summarized Eisenhower's approach to the issue of black civil rights throughout his presidency. Despite his endorsement of "first-class citizenship," Eisenhower was unwilling to use his powers as president to end discriminatory practices except in those few instances in which the federal government had clear constitutional jurisdiction. Sympathetic to the fears of white southerners, he branded as extremists black leaders who wanted to topple the system of racial segregation. Because of his insistence on gradualism, Eisenhower left a divided legacy in civil rights. For the first time since Reconstruction, the president ordered federal troops into the South to maintain public order and secured legislation from Congress to protect voting rights. Yet these actions were more symbolic than substantive, since they did little to ensure black access to the ballot box or to integrated public schools. Civil rights, in short, revealed more dramatically than any other issue the shortcomings of Eisenhower's philosophy of governmental restraint.

Eisenhower entered politics at a time when civil rights had recently become a pressing national concern. World War II and the Cold War had focused attention on the disparity between democratic ideals and the discrimination that was an ugly fact of the daily existence of black

Americans. The barbarism of Nazi Germany created new pressures throughout the world to eliminate all forms of racism. Even those who felt no moral imperative to end racial discrimination worried about the practical problems of enlisting foreign allies in a worldwide struggle against communism when bigotry sullied the international reputation of the United States. With new determination, African Americans insisted on sharing in the benefits of the freedom they were asked to defend. Under pressure from a black coalition headed by A. Philip Randolph, the head of the Brotherhood of Sleeping Car Porters, President Franklin D. Roosevelt established a temporary Fair Employment Practices Commission (FEPC) during World War II that took modest steps to prevent discrimination in defense employment. After the war, black veterans braved violence in many southern states to challenge Jim Crow restrictions on voting, while the National Association for the Advancement of Colored People, fortified by a sevenfold wartime increase in membership, filed a series of lawsuits to invalidate forced segregation in public schools. Acting upon the recommendations of his special Committee on Civil Rights, Truman asked Congress in early 1948 to take action to close the "serious gap between our ideals and some of our practices."[2]

Civil rights, however, split the Democrats so badly at their national convention that Dixiecrats bolted the party and ran their own candidate for president, Governor J. Strom Thurmond of South Carolina. During Truman's second term, a coalition of Republicans and southern Democrats prevented approval of civil rights legislation. The only significant progress against discrimination occurred through judicial and executive action, such as Truman's order in 1948 to desegregate the armed forces. Yet despite these limited advances, Truman was the first president since Reconstruction to proclaim that the federal government had a duty to protect black rights. Civil rights was now an issue that no aspirant for the presidency could avoid.

During the 1952 campaign, Eisenhower declared that he hoped for a United States that provided "a true equality of opportunity" for all its citizens but cautioned that the president could do little to hasten the creation of such a society. Even the laudable objective of eradicating racism, he reiterated, did not justify policies that could lead to statism or stultifying paternalism. Thus Eisenhower opposed the reestablishment of a Fair Employment Practices Commission out of conviction that compulsory federal intervention ought not to replace state, local, or private responsibility for preventing job discrimination. Such positions, of course, appealed to white southerners, and Eisenhower vigorously campaigned for their votes. His efforts paid off when several Democratic governors of southern states, including James F. Byrnes of South Carolina and Allan Shivers of Texas, broke party solidarity and endorsed him for president. On election day, Eisenhower took Florida, Texas, and Virginia, only the second time a Republican had carried those states since Reconstruction. On the other hand, he won only 25 percent of the black vote.

Eisenhower's conservative views on civil rights arose not just from principle or political expediency, but from long experience with segregation. Eisenhower often reminded friends that he had been born in the South and had spent much of his life in areas such as Kansas, Texas, Maryland, and Washington, D.C., where Jim Crow laws separated blacks and whites. Until the very end of his four decades of active duty, the army had confined blacks to segregated units and often relegated them to unskilled and undesirable duties. Eisenhower did not question these discriminatory practices and occasionally expressed common prejudices against blacks. While serving as supreme Allied commander, he reportedly chuckled over a propaganda film that showed African American soldiers carrying rifles in combat, something he said that he had never seen in real life. During his presidency, he repeated to family members stories about "darkies" that he heard during his golfing vacations in Augusta, Georgia.[3]

Yet by the end of his military career, Eisenhower hoped "that the human race may finally grow up to the point where it [relations between blacks and whites] will not be a problem." Expediency rather than toleration led to his first experiment with integration, when he temporarily ordered black laborers to fill vacancies in all-white units during the Battle of the Bulge in December 1944. After the war, Eisenhower thought that the army should move only very slowly to phase out segregation. He professed concern for the best interests of black soldiers, but his views sounded patronizing at best. Because they were generally "less well educated," blacks would find the competition for promotion in integrated units "too tough" and so their morale would suffer. Eisenhower also declared that government action could not eradicate individual prejudice. He warned that "if we attempt merely by passing a lot of laws to force someone to like someone else, we are just going to get into trouble."[4] The elimination of racial injustice, he concluded, ultimately depended on long-term change in public attitudes.

After entering the White House, Eisenhower periodically proclaimed his commitment to equal opportunity for blacks but carefully restricted his actions in support of that principle. In his first state of the union address in February 1953, he described racial discrimination as a national problem, which could be alleviated through the power "of fact, fully publicized; of persuasion, honestly pressed; and of conscience, justly aroused."[5] Several months later, he reiterated his commitment to racial justice "so that no man of any color or creed will *ever* be able to cry 'This is not a free land.'"[6] Eisenhower made these statements in speeches that dealt broadly with public policy and only briefly with civil rights. He did not intend to use his moral authority as president to take the lead in changing racial attitudes. Nor did he want his administration to act against discrimination except when the federal government possessed clear authority and could use it without arousing controversy.

Consequently, these executive actions produced mixed results. With much fanfare, Eisenhower reaffirmed Truman's commitment to eradicate Jim Crow in the military. In 1954, the armed forces abolished the last segregated unit, but blacks still complained that they did not enjoy equal treatment in duty assignments or promotion. Eisenhower took strong action to bar discrimination in federal facilities in the District of Columbia and to persuade the owners of local hotels and movie houses to end discrimination against blacks. The president also demanded equal opportunity in federal hiring, but did nothing to combat the latent bigotry that kept blacks concentrated in the lowest-paying jobs. In private employment, Eisenhower favored persuasion rather than coercion. All the President's Committee on Government Contracts (PCGC) could do about a complaint of employment discrimination against a private firm with a government contract was to appeal to the company to work out the problem or pass along the complaint to the federal agency that had signed the contract. The PCGC—Eisenhower's alternative to a reestablished FEPC—thus proved ineffective because it lacked power to force compliance with its rulings. Eisenhower nevertheless emphasized his administration's progress in combatting racial injustice in order to enhance the international reputation of the United States and to quiet demands for stronger federal protection of black rights.[7]

At the same time, Eisenhower tried to reassure southern segregationists that he believed in gradualism in race relations. When he lunched with Governor Byrnes in July 1953, he reiterated his doubts that "prejudices, even palpably unjustified prejudices, will succumb to compulsion." When Byrnes expressed fears that the Supreme Court would strike down segregation in the public schools, Eisenhower replied that "race relations is one of those things that will be healthy and sound only if it starts locally." Like Byrnes, he worried that "federal law imposed upon our states in such a way as to bring about a conflict of the police powers of the states and of the nation, would set back the cause of freedom in race relations for a long, long time."[8]

On 17 May 1954, the Supreme Court handed down the ruling that Eisenhower and Byrnes had dreaded. In the case of *Brown* v. *Board of Education of Topeka*, the court unanimously overturned the decision in *Plessy* v. *Ferguson* that for almost sixty years had permitted racial segregation in public schools. The justices concluded "that in the field of public education the doctrine of 'separate but equal' has no place. Separate educational facilities are inherently unequal."[9] The architect of this momentous decision was Earl Warren, whom Eisenhower had nominated eight months earlier as chief justice.

Years later Eisenhower considered Warren's appointment "the biggest damfool mistake I ever made," a judgment based largely on the Warren court's decisions in the 1960s on the rights of those accused in criminal cases.[10] But at the time of the *Brown* ruling, Eisenhower had only the deepest respect for the chief justice. Warren had impressed Eisenhower at the time they first met in 1948, while he was running for vice-president on the Republican ticket with Thomas E. Dewey. As Eisenhower became more involved in politics, he praised Warren's progressive record as governor of California. Even though Warren was concerned primarily with advancing his favorite-son candidacy at the Republican National Convention in 1952, he helped Eisenhower by preventing California's delegates from voting for Taft. In return for this assistance, Lucius D. Clay, one of Eisenhower's convention managers, promised Warren a position in the Eisenhower administration. After Warren declined Clay's offer to head the Interior Department, Eisenhower told Warren that he would nominate him to fill the first vacancy on the Supreme Court. As it turned out, the initial opening occurred on 8 September 1953, when Chief Justice Fred M. Vinson died of a heart attack.

Eisenhower hesitated. He did not think that his pledge to Warren covered the chief justiceship, so he considered other candidates. Secretary of State John Foster Dulles declined because he did not want to leave the office that represented the culmination of his life-long interest in foreign affairs. After eliminating several other possibilities, Eisenhower then turned to Warren. The president had no reservations about his choice. Warren, Eisenhower believed, shared his philosophy of government and at age sixty-two was likely to remain on the court long enough to make a lasting impression. In reply to conservative objections to the nomination, Eisenhower described Warren as a judicial statesman who would be able to overcome the factionalism that had frequently produced single-vote margins in the decisions of the Vinson court. He also sent words of admiration for Warren to his own older brother Edgar, who criticized the appointment, and to his younger brother Milton, who praised it. To the latter he swore that if the Republican-controlled Senate did not confirm Warren, he would form an independent party. Old Guard senators threatened to test his resolve by delaying the confirmation several weeks.

Eisenhower knew ahead of time that the Warren court would probably sustain the black plaintiff in the *Brown* case. At the request of the court, the Justice Department had submitted an *amicus curiae*, or friend of the court, brief while the case was being argued. Eisenhower, however, tried to divorce himself from the Justice Department's conclusion that segregation in the public schools was unconstitutional. On one embarrassing occasion in early 1954, he attempted to influence Warren's thinking in behalf of the defendants. At a White House stag dinner, he told Warren that the proponents of Jim Crow schools simply wanted to avoid seating their "sweet little white girls next to those big sexually advanced black boys."[11] Such reasoning, however offensive, accorded with Eisenhower's views on race relations. As he told his speechwriter, Arthur Larson, equality of opportunity did not necessarily mean that blacks and whites had "to mingle socially—or that a Negro should court my daughter."[12]

When the Warren court announced the *Brown* decision in May 1954, Eisenhower declined to endorse it. Asked by a reporter if he had any advice for southerners about what they should do, he replied tersely, "not in the slightest." Repeatedly he refused to say the court's decision was right or just or fair. Instead he insisted that his own opinion was irrelevant. Eisenhower usually withheld public comment on Supreme Court decisions out of respect for the constitutional separation of powers. Yet his silence on a matter of such enormous importance implied disagreement with the court's position and encouraged many of the opponents of the *Brown* decision. However destructive his silence on the merits of the decision, Eisenhower also firmly declared that his duty as president and citizen was compliance with the high court's ruling. "The Supreme Court has spoken and I am sworn to uphold the constitutional processes in this country; and I will obey."[13] Indeed only a day after the decision, Eisenhower asked the Board of Commissioners of the District of Columbia to set an example of peaceful desegregation.

In private, Eisenhower explained the reservations that he would not discuss in public. He denounced the court for assuming an impossibly vast responsibility and improperly intruding the federal government into the lives of millions of American families. Rather than integrate, some states might close down their public school system, a step, he emphasized, that would have a devastating effect on blacks and poor whites. "It's all very well to talk about school integration," he told his staff, but "you may also be talking about social *dis*integration. . . . We can't demand *perfection* in these moral questions. All we can do is keep working toward a goal and keep it high. And the fellow who tries to tell me that you can do these things by *force* is just plain *nuts*."[14] He even predicted that the decision would arouse so much animosity that it would actually set back progress in integration by fifteen years. Eisenhower, in short, viewed the *Brown* case not as a great victory over a moral evil, but as a tragic and destructive mistake.

Eager to avoid confrontations that might lead to violence or the closing of public schools, Eisenhower tried to persuade the court to implement its decision slowly. He asked Attorney General Herbert Brownell, Jr., to direct Justice Department lawyers to argue before the Supreme Court for minimum federal intervention and maximum local discretion in carrying out school desegregation. When the court issued guidelines on 31 May 1955 for compliance with the *Brown* decision "with all deliberate speed," Eisenhower expressed relief. Since the court also refused to set a timetable for the completion of this work, Eisenhower hoped that gradualism would ensure calm and public order.

For the remainder of the year, Eisenhower adopted a hands-off policy toward civil rights. Much of Eisenhower's inaction was because of his heart attack in late September and three-month convalescence. Yet even when he was healthy, the president kept his distance from the issue of school desegregation. He granted appointments to neither proponents of resistance to the *Brown* decision nor advocates of immediate compliance with it. His action suggested that he considered as extremists both those who wanted to defy the Supreme Court and those who wanted vigorous enforcement of its decisions. Acting in accordance with the president's wishes, Brownell ordered the Justice Department to keep out of disputes over school integration unless asked to intervene by a federal court. Eisenhower thought that his policy of restraint at least would avoid exacerbating divisions between blacks and whites, northerners and southerners over the *Brown* decision. His concern about the volatility of public attitudes was understandable; certainly misunderstanding, hatred, and violence could only further the interests of fanatics. Yet however much restraint seemed prudent, it was not necessarily fair, since it tended to favor the status quo. Eisenhower, in short, professed impartiality on an issue in which neutrality was impossible.

The hands-off attitude of the Eisenhower administration also reflected an uneasiness in dealing with blacks and civil rights organizations. According to one of his speechwriters, Eisenhower seemed uncomfortable during discussions of racial matters. He avoided talking to black leaders, such as Representative Adam Clayton Powell, Jr. (D., N.Y.), who attached desegregation riders to school construction bills. Powell, the president said, was nothing more than a demagogue. Like their chief, many of Eisenhower's subordinates distrusted pressure groups in general and black organizations in particular. The latter, they believed, tended to overdramatize incidents of racial injustice and to demand a disproportionate amount of attention and assistance. Some White House staffers also complained that African Americans seemed insufficiently grateful for the efforts of the Eisenhower administration in their behalf. Even Maxwell Rabb, the president's assistant for minority affairs, denounced the aggressiveness of black demands and the "ugliness and surliness" of the manner in which they were made.[15]

The experiences of E. Frederic Morrow, the only black on the president's staff, illustrated the unsympathetic and suspicious predispositions of administration officials. Morrow got his position on the White House staff in 1955 largely because the president's political advisers were trying to strengthen their appeal to black voters in the next election. Morrow's appointment was symbolic; at first his responsibilities involved arranging office and parking space for White House staffers. Eventually he took over the job of answering correspondence from blacks. Morrow endured humiliating treatment from White House clerks and stenographers who refused to do his filing or type his letters. During discussions of race relations, he was appalled by his colleagues' ignorance of such basic realities as the high unemployment rate among African Americans. As civil rights became an explosive topic, Morrow's associates regarded him ever more warily as a representative of black pressure groups. Gen. Wilton B. (Jerry) Persons, one of Eisenhower's top assistants and a southerner, ultimately refused to discuss race relations with Morrow. "Fred," he asked, "I would appreciate it if you would never approach me or come to me with anything involving civil rights. This thing has almost split my family in two, because of my relationships with the administration and its stand on civil rights. It would save both of us a lot of heartache if you would always discuss any matters in this area with somebody else, including the President himself, rather than with me." Yet Eisenhower kept Morrow at arm's length and refused to consult him on significant issues in civil rights. During one of his infrequent meetings in the Oval Office, Morrow tried to explain why blacks were increasingly sensitive to such phrases as "you people," a phrase Eisenhower commonly used. Morrow concluded that the president and his associates never understood "how deeply aggrieved black Americans felt."[16]

Eisenhower held to his policy of restraint despite frightening indications that southern officials were determined not to comply with the *Brown* decision. Early in 1956, the University of Alabama suspended its first black student, Autherine Lucy, after mob protests against her enrollment. When Lucy won reinstatement in federal court, the university expelled her, an action the court refused to overturn for lack of proof that it was racially motivated. Eisenhower refused to interfere. He also tried to put the best face on the Southern Manifesto, a declaration issued in March 1956 by well over one hundred southern representatives and senators calling for a reversal of the *Brown* decision. Eisenhower emphasized that the signers did not advocate violent resistance or state nullification of federal law. He then refused to endorse the court's ruling or criticize the manifesto and reiterated to reporters that it would simply take a long time to change people's hearts and minds on such a sensitive issue as racial integration.

Perhaps the most alarming manifestation of southern defiance was the growth of white citizens councils. Founded in the aftermath of the *Brown* decision, these local groups spread throughout the Deep South until they claimed about 250,000 members at the height of their influence in 1956/57. They aimed at coordinating state and local resistance to desegregation, particularly in the schools. The councils had a veneer of public respectability that distinguished them from the Ku Klux Klan, but their appeals to prejudice and hatred hardly seemed different. Local councils sponsored white supremacy rallies and promised harsh social and economic retaliation against anyone who dared breach the color line. In some states, the councils were a potent political force, instrumental in the passage of new laws or ordinances to frustrate integration.[17]

Eisenhower hoped to silence demands for strong action against white southern intransigence by sending a civil rights bill to Congress in 1956. The heart of the measure was greater federal protection of voting rights. The Constitution clearly provided for federal responsibility on this matter, and blacks clearly needed federal assistance in order to have equal access to this most basic right of citizenship. In most southern states, impediments such as poll taxes, literacy tests, or outright intimidation kept 80 percent of the blacks who were eligible to vote from registering.[18] In a few counties in Mississippi, no African American could cast a ballot. Eisenhower reasoned that if more blacks were enfranchised, they would be better able to protect their own interests without calling for help from Washington. Black political power, in short, would allow the Eisenhower administration to hold to its policy of restraint in civil rights.

Eisenhower included the voting rights provision in a larger package, one that he hoped would appeal to moderates of all persuasions. He warned Brownell, who supervised the drafting of the civil rights bill, not to act as if he were "another [Charles] Sumner."[19] Eisenhower issued this instruction after J. Edgar Hoover, the director of the Federal Bureau of Investigation, reported to the cabinet that Communists were capitalizing on the turmoil in the South by infiltrating civil rights organizations. While some advisers, such as Dulles, thought that any civil rights legislation would create political difficulties for the administration and further polarize southern opinion, Eisenhower thought that Brownell's moderate proposals would help restore calm and preserve order. The Justice Department bill provided the federal district courts with more power to ensure individual access to the polls and gave the attorney general new authority to file suit in cases of violations of civil rights. In addition, the legislation proposed the creation of a civil rights division within the Justice Department and the establishment of a bipartisan civil rights commission that would issue a report within two years on black-white relations. Eisenhower vigorously supported this last recommendation, since he thought that it would provide the administration a respite from dealing with an increasingly acrimonious problem.

Submitted to Congress near the end of the session in an election year, the civil rights bill had no chance of passage in 1956. Eisenhower blamed the Democratic majority for the demise of the legislation. Democrats, in turn, accused Eisenhower of sending the bill to Capitol Hill for no other reason than to win black votes. During the campaign of 1956, Eisenhower tried to avoid the appearance of partisanship by holding to a minimum his discussion of race relations. He even refused to comment on the civil rights plank in the Republican platform since it concerned a subject "charged with emotionalism." Informed that blacks were registering as Republicans in greater numbers than ever before, he merely replied that he was working for the interests of all Americans and that he welcomed the support of any citizen. When reporters asked how the executive branch would enforce the Supreme Court's desegregation order in the face of growing white southern resistance, he said that he preferred hard work, especially that kind that "is done privately and behind the scenes rather than charging up on the platform and hammering desks. . . . We are not going to settle this thing," he warned once more, "by a great show of force and arbitrary action."[20]

A few days after Eisenhower made that statement, the governor of Texas tested the president's resolve. Allan Shivers was a Democrat who had broken ranks to support the Republican ticket in 1952. At the beginning of the school year in September 1956, he asserted that the preservation of public order in two Texas cities required a halt to school desegregation. Ostentatiously he dispatched Texas Rangers to Texarkana and Mansfield to prevent black students from attending previously all-white schools. If Eisenhower was angered by this clear disobedience of federal law by someone he liked personally and respected as a state executive, he concealed his feelings behind bland and evasive replies to reporters. Eisenhower also pointed out that the federal government could intervene in such situations only when a state could not maintain public order. Even though attorneys for the black students asked for federal help, "the Texas authorities had moved in and order was restored, so the question became unimportant."[21] Eisenhower professed to know nothing about Shivers's public boast about defying federal authority.

Encouraged by the results of the 1956 election, Eisenhower resubmitted the civil rights bill to Congress at the beginning of his second term. The president increased his margin of victory over Stevenson by winning about 5 percent more of the black vote as well as a larger share of southern white votes as compared to 1952. Eisenhower considered his gains in these constituencies an endorsement of moderation, which, in his view, the civil rights bill epitomized. At the same time, a spate of violent incidents in the South underlined the need for the legislation. With these developments in mind, Eisenhower told Congress that his recommendations aimed at furthering justice and preserving law and order.

The civil rights bill set off a protracted and, at times, bitter debate in Congress. Eisenhower got his way in the House, which passed the measure in June by a large majority and without significant change. In the Senate, Majority Leader Lyndon B. Johnson at first promised a fight. Soon afterward, Johnson realized that he could raise his national stature and advance his presidential aspirations by guiding a compromise bill through the upper house. For Johnson and for Eisenhower, though, the real problem was securing the cooperation of southern Democrats, who charged that the legislation was a nefarious device for securing the necessary authority to use federal troops to enforce integration in the South.

As the wrangling in the Senate continued into the summer, Eisenhower complained to Brownell that the bill was slowly being destroyed, amendment by amendment. Yet Eisenhower contributed to the problem he decried through his own inept performance on 3 July at a news conference. In response to a question about one section of the legislation, Eisenhower declined comment until he could talk to Brownell. "I was reading part of that bill this morning," he blurted out, "and there were certain phrases I didn't completely understand."[22] Critics now gleefully used the president's foolish statement to justify their efforts to rewrite the legislation. The most important fight occurred over an amendment that allowed a jury trial in cases involving voting rights violations. The provision sounded democratic, but in the segregated courts of the South, all-white juries would not sustain black plaintiffs. Eisenhower sternly announced his opposition, but to no avail, as the Senate incorporated the amendment into the final version of the bill.

In early September, Congress sent Eisenhower a much weakened version of legislation that he had proposed seven months earlier. Not only did it contain the jury trial stipulation, but it did not give the attorney general the power Eisenhower had requested to deal with violations of civil rights. Southern segregationists were pleased with the measure. Senator Richard B. Russell (D., Ga.), a proponent of the jury trial provision, considered the bill "the sweetest victory in my twenty-five years as a Senator."[23] Some black leaders urged Eisenhower not to sign such an emasculated piece of legislation. But Martin Luther King, Jr., the president of the Southern Christian Leadership Conference, disagreed, as did Roy Wilkins of the NAACP. "If you are digging a ditch with a teaspoon and a man comes along and offers you a spade," Wilkens reasoned, "there is something wrong with your head if you don't take it because he didn't offer you a bulldozer."[24] Despite his disappointment over some of its provisions, Eisenhower was nevertheless pleased when he signed the Civil Rights Act of 1957, the first since the end of Reconstruction. The legislation conformed to his philosophy of government, since it established a disinterested fact-finding commission to report on civil rights and established enforcement procedures that relied on judicial process rather than executive compulsion. Eisenhower thus hoped that most Americans would accept these methods of dealing with racial injustice as moderate and fair. After Eisenhower signed the legislation, Deputy Attorney Gen. William P. Rogers called for a cooling-off period in the national debate over civil rights.

In some ways, Eisenhower simply hoped that the issue of civil rights would vanish. No question made him more uncomfortable or caused him more anguish. Eisenhower rarely wished to avoid responsibility, but civil rights was different. Because of his southern affiliations and lack of familiarity with blacks, Eisenhower did not like to deal with any matter of race relations. Because of his distrust of popular passions, he could not understand the moral urgency that drove the leaders of the civil rights movement. Because of his concern about the habits and traditions of white southerners, he found it painful to use his authority to enforce compliance with federal law. Because of his reluctance to take sides in partisan conflicts, he did not know how to provide the moral leadership that would hasten popular acceptance of desegregation. Thus he searched for a way to confine issues of civil rights to the courtroom, statehouse, or school board so he would not have to deal with them.

Because of his personal dubiety, Eisenhower's public statements often raised doubts about his commitment to the protection of civil rights. Even as he urged Congress to enact his civil rights bill, Eisenhower reassured a conference of governors in Williamsburg, Virginia, that he venerated states' rights. He made the remark as he warned of the dangers of a bloated national government and urged states not to surrender their authority to Washington. Although he was not referring specifically to civil rights, his comments were interpreted that way, especially in the South. His message thus tended to create the impression that the civil rights bill was little more than a gesture and that it would leave unimpaired the jurisdiction of states in matters of race relations.

In private correspondence, Eisenhower stated far more clearly his determination to uphold federal authority. Writing to his boyhood friend, Swede Hazlett, Eisenhower began with his usual admonition about government's limited power to affect public attitudes on sensitive social issues. The failure of Prohibition, he asserted, was a good example of the way "local opinion [could] openly and successfully defy Federal authority." He warned that "when emotions are deeply stirred, logic and reason must operate gradually and with consideration for human feelings or we will have a resultant disaster rather than human advancement." Precisely because of that cause-and-effect relationship, federal authority was essential. "There must be respect for the Constitution—which means the Supreme Court's interpretation of the Constitution—or we shall have chaos," he proclaimed. "We cannot possibly imagine a successful form of government in which every individual citizen would have the right to interpret the Constitution according to his own convictions, beliefs, and prejudices. . . . This I believe with all my heart—and shall always act accordingly."[25]

Yet southern officials who stubbornly held personal interpretations of the Constitution could have easily reached different conclusions about Eisenhower's intentions. Only a week before he wrote to Hazlett, Eisenhower told a news conference on 17 July not about his determination to enforce federal supremacy, but of his doubts that he would ever have to do so. "I can't imagine any set of circumstances that would ever induce me to send Federal troops . . . into any area to enforce the orders of a Federal court, because I believe that [the] common sense of America will never require it."[26] Designed to allay southern fears during the debate on the civil rights bill, this declaration may have emboldened diehard defenders of states' rights. Through his tortuous and confusing public statements, Eisenhower, then, may have contributed to the making of the greatest crisis over civil rights during his presidency, one that brought him into unavoidable conflict with the unscrupulous governor of Arkansas, Orval Faubus.

A populist Democrat, Faubus appeared to be a moderate among southern governors on race relations. Actually he was an opportunist. During his first gubernatorial campaign in 1954, he declared that Arkansas was "not ready for a complete and sudden mixing of the races in the public schools," but later pledged to use his powers as governor to carry out the decisions of local school boards.[27] Two years later, the local authorities in Little Rock, the state capital, devised a plan for the voluntary, phased integration of their schools over seven years. The federal district court approved the plan and ordered that it begin in September 1957 at all-white Central High School. Despite his earlier promise, Faubus tried to block the desegregation of Little Rock classrooms. Even though he praised the Little Rock plan in private conversation, he publicly sided with rabid segregationists who warned that the integration of Central High School would precipitate violence. Faubus reckoned that if he did not go along with the defenders of Jim Crow, he would destroy his chances for reelection in 1958. Thus he appealed to the court to postpone the admission of blacks to Central High School in the interest of preserving public order. When federal judge Ronald Davies rejected the governor's plea, Faubus called the national guard to active duty and ordered it to prevent blacks from entering Central High School.

Having defied federal authority, Faubus took the remarkable step of seeking presidential sanction. He sent a panicked telegram to Eisenhower at the vacation White House in Newport, Rhode Island, asking for the president's help because, he alleged, the Justice Department had tapped his telephone and was preparing to arrest him. Eisenhower brusquely dismissed those charges. He advised Faubus, however, that the attorney general was looking into the crisis in Little Rock and that he would defend the Constitution "by every legal means at my command."[28] Eisenhower certainly was upset with Faubus for causing a showdown between state and federal authority. Yet he apparently held Davies accountable as well, since he blamed the problems in Little Rock on those "people who believe you are going to reform the human heart by law."[29]

Against this backdrop of mutual suspicion, Eisenhower and Faubus arranged a meeting to defuse the crisis. Acting as the governor's emissary, Arkansas Representative Brooks Hays stated that Faubus had gotten into a more complicated situation than he had expected and wanted to find some way to extricate himself. Brownell advised Eisenhower that Faubus had caused his own problems and that the federal court ought to hold the governor accountable for his actions. Eisenhower, however, still hoped for a negotiated solution. At the same time, he did not want to appear to be interfering in the proper exercise of a governor's responsibilities. To resolve these difficulties, Sherman Adams, Eisenhower's chief of staff, and Hays drafted a message for Faubus to send to Eisenhower requesting a meeting. Adams insisted that Faubus declare that he intended to obey the court's order. Faubus apparently acceded to this precondition but then dispatched a telegram that contained qualifying language that Adams had not cleared. Nonetheless, Eisenhower agreed to talk to Faubus at Newport.

On 14 September, Eisenhower and Faubus seemed to settle their differences. While meeting alone with the president for fifteen minutes, Faubus repeatedly stressed that he deeply respected the rule of law and acknowledged the supremacy of federal authority. Eisenhower sympathetically assured Faubus that he did not want to see him humiliated and suggested an honorable way out of his predicament. Rather than go home and withdraw the national guard, which might make the governor appear to be backing down under pressure, Faubus should simply change the troops' orders so that they were instructed to maintain peace while the black students attended Central High School. Such action would avoid a test of strength in which "there could be only one outcome."[30] Hays and Adams then joined the conversation followed by Brownell and Press Secretary James C. Hagerty. When the meeting adjourned after two hours, Eisenhower definitely thought Faubus had agreed to his terms.

Both of the principals issued statements, which in retrospect indicate that the deal Eisenhower thought he had made was by no means solid. Faubus described the meeting as friendly and worthwhile and indicated his "*desire* to cooperate" with Eisenhower "in carrying out the duties resting upon both of us under the Federal Constitution." He added somewhat ominously that in meeting these obligations, "the complexities of integration [must] be patiently understood by all those in federal authority."[31] Eisenhower, for his part, said Faubus "stated his *intention* to respect the decisions of the . . . District Court and to give his full cooperation in carrying out his responsibilities in respect to these decisions." Eisenhower also stressed "the inescapable responsibility resting upon the Governor to preserve law and order in his state."[32]

After returning to Little Rock, Faubus temporized. He did not change the orders of the national guard, and he demanded a delay in the admission of the black students. After Judge Davies issued an injunction on 20 September that prohibited Faubus from doing anything more to stop the integration of Central High School, the governor announced the withdrawal of the national guard. He then departed for the Southern Governors' Conference in Georgia. Eisenhower prematurely breathed a sigh of relief.

Eisenhower's aides were not so sanguine. Gen. Andrew J. Goodpaster, the president's staff secretary, informed his chief that the federal government had an obligation to make Faubus obey the court "by whatever means may be necessary."[33] Brownell also worried that federal intervention might be necessary, especially since Faubus washed his hands of further responsibility for maintaining law and order in Little Rock when he left for Georgia. But the attorney general knew that neither federal marshals nor local police would be able to handle a civil disturbance in Little Rock. Eisenhower remarked that he was loath to send in troops because their very presence might cause violence to spread. He spent an impatient weekend wondering what would happen and uncertain about what he would do.

On Monday morning, 23 September, Little Rock erupted, much to Eisenhower's disgust. A frenzied mob of more than a thousand people, many from outside Little Rock, gathered outside Central High School to prevent its integration. "Niggers, keep away from our school," the crowd clamored. "Go back to the jungle." Just before the start of classes, some of the demonstrators attacked four black journalists, whom they apparently mistook for the parents of the students. One of the reporters, Alex Wilson, was hit in the head with a brick and "went down like a tree," according to one observer. The nine black students managed to enter unmolested through a side door. "Oh, my God, they're in the school," someone shrieked. Because the mob was so persistent and menacing, the nine black students were sent home at noontime for their own safety.[34] Eisenhower denounced the "disgraceful" behavior of a "mob of extremists" and warned that he would use "whatever force may be necessary . . . to carry out the orders of the Federal Court." He concluded, "It will be a sad day for this country—both at home and abroad—if school children can safely attend their classes only under the protection of armed guards."[35]

That sad day arrived only a few hours later. Once again a threatening crowd assembled near Central High School on 24 September. "People are converging on the scene from all directions," Mayor Woodrow Wilson Mann telegraphed Eisenhower. "Situation [is] out of control and police cannot disperse the mob. I am pleading with you as President of the United States . . . to provide the necessary troops within several hours."[36] Eisenhower responded quickly. He authorized Gen. Maxwell D. Taylor, the army chief of staff, to dispatch 1,000 paratroopers from the 101st Airborne Division to Little Rock. Eisenhower wanted such a display of force that no demonstrators would dare to challenge the troops. He also federalized the Arkansas National Guard but did not want them deployed near the high school because, as he later explained, "I didn't want to have brothers fighting up against brothers and families divided."[37] By nightfall, the troops had begun to police Little Rock. The next morning, newspapers carried shocking pictures of the troops patrolling with fixed bayonets. A few editors provided acid commentary by juxtaposing these photographs with pictures of Eisenhower playing golf at Newport.

After returning to Washington from Newport, Eisenhower sadly told a nationwide radio and television audience that he had sent the army into Little Rock only because of his "inescapable" responsibility to enforce the law. He laid the blame for the strife on "disorderly mobs" led by "demagogic extremists." As usual, he avoided discussion of personalities and did not even make reference to Faubus. He tried hard to make clear that the soldiers were in Little Rock not to promote integration, but to guarantee obedience to the law. Again he refused to endorse the *Brown* ruling. "Our personal opinions about the decision have no bearing on the matter of enforcement," he reminded his audience. The Supreme Court alone had the authority to interpret the Constitution, and disobedience of its rulings could lead to "anarchy." Eisenhower lamented the way in which the disorder in Arkansas had damaged the nation's image in the eyes of the world and had bolstered Communist propaganda efforts. "Our enemies are gloating over this incident and using it everywhere to misrepresent our whole nation," he reminded the American people. "We are portrayed as a violator of those standards of conduct which the peoples of the world united to proclaim in the Charter of the United Nations." He coupled appeals to patriotism with conciliatory gestures toward white southerners. From personal experience, he knew "that the overwhelming majority of the people in the South . . . are of good will, united in their efforts to preserve and respect the law even when they disagree with it." Thus he pleaded with the people of Arkansas to return to their "normal habits of peace and order" so that the troops could be speedily withdrawn.[38]

Eisenhower's handling of the Little Rock crisis was exceptional, but understandable. Absolutely central to his decision was the sense of personal betrayal he felt over Faubus's conduct. The governor had given his word and then reneged on it. Eisenhower was outraged, but far more important was his conviction that he could not trust Faubus to step in and restore order once the mobs gathered outside Central High School. Also critical was the sense of duty he felt to protect the Constitution and uphold federal law. Despite his own reservations about the *Brown* ruling, he could not turn his back on a mob that tried to substitute its will for that of a federal judge. "If the day comes when we can obey the orders of our Courts only when we personally approve of them," he reminded Swede Hazlett, "the end of the American system, as we know it, will not be far off." Finally, Eisenhower had exhausted all other alternatives short of armed intervention. His negotiations with Faubus had fallen through; his public appeal to the rioters to cease and desist had been ignored. Local officials appealed to him to act. Eisenhower had to heed their call. As historian Stephen E. Ambrose has written, "He could not have done otherwise and still been President."[39]

Yet white southern leaders had every reason to be surprised. Repeatedly Eisenhower said that coercion could not solve the problems of race relations. His admonitions about his responsibility to uphold the law at times sounded more ritualistic than resolute.[40] After all, he had done nothing when Governor Shivers flouted federal authority a year earlier. Furthermore, no president since Ulysses S. Grant had sent troops to the South to protect black rights.

Because Eisenhower's action was so unexpected, his adversaries reacted with unusual bitterness. Faubus claimed Arkansas was an "occupied territory."[41] Senator Russell compared the intervention at Little Rock to Hitler's use of storm troopers. In answer to the first charge, Eisenhower made clear that federal troops were not taking over the running of state or local institutions, but only assuming temporary responsibility for maintaining public order in the absence of effective action by Arkansas authorities. In reply to the second allegation, he said there was no similarity between Nazi tyranny and the fulfillment of the constitutional duty to carry out the decisions of a federal court. The courts, he told a news conference, were the people's shield against autocratic government.

Years later, Brownell asserted that Eisenhower's actions at Little Rock proved for all time that the federal government would guarantee blacks equal opportunity to enroll in public schools. Eisenhower's actions in the aftermath of the Little Rock intervention by no means justified that conclusion. The president went out of his way to explain that the dispatch of troops was an isolated event, not an indication of a new policy of firmness or coercion in dealing with recalcitrant southern officials. ''The very core of my political thinking is that it has got to be the sentiment, the good will, the good sense of a whole citizenry that enforces the law,'' he declared at a news conference in early October.[42] The president personally intervened to reduce the number of paratroopers and then to remove them altogether in early November. National guard troops remained on duty under federal control for the remainder of the school year, however. They guaranteed the integration of Central High, yet Eisenhower expressed no satisfaction about that achievement. Instead he told Arthur Larson, his speechwriter, ''I personally think the [Brown] decision was wrong.''[43]

Integration did not last beyond the demobilization of the national guard at the end of the school year. Faubus once again challenged the federal court order requiring integration. This time the Supreme Court affirmed the constitutionality of Judge Davies's order in September 1958. Faubus responded by closing the public schools and approving a plan that would transform them into segregated, private institutions. The president did not intervene, however, in that instance or in similarly defiant closings of public schools in several other states even though the ruling of the Supreme Court had been evaded. Privately, he was angered by officials who were undermining the concept of state responsibility; publicly, he said only that they should consider the damage their policy of closing schools inflicted on their own citizens. In effect, Eisenhower reaffirmed what he had said all along: he would act forcefully only to preserve public order, not to speed integration.

The administration's version of deliberate speed lagged significantly during Eisenhower's last years in office. Eisenhower called for business leaders, clergy, and civil rights activists to exhort their fellow citizens to solve the problems of desegregation through understanding, good will, and local action. But he did not engage in exhortation of his own. Instead he called on blacks to exercise patience and forbearance in their quest for equal rights and integrated schools.

Only with great reluctance did Eisenhower finally consent to a meeting with black leaders, the first and only one of his presidency. The conversation with King, Wilkins, Randolph, and Lester Granger, executive director of the Urban League, on 23 June 1958 was brief and unproductive. Granger stressed that unless the administration responded more sympathetically to the appeals of his fellow moderates, radicals would take over the civil rights movement. Randolph presented a nine-point plan for greater presidential leadership in civil rights that described the administration's cure for segregation as ''an occasional tablet of aspirin and a goblet of goodwill.'' King tried unsuccessfully to interest the president in using his moral authority to persuade his fellow Americans that integration was right and just. In reply, William P. Rogers, who had succeeded Brownell as attorney general, defended the administration's record in civil rights. Eisenhower petulantly added that if blacks were displeased after all he had done for them, he wondered if he should try to accomplish more.[44] After it was over, Eisenhower told reporters that he was satisfied with the meeting because nothing extreme had been proposed. Many black commentators described the meeting as a surrender to the government's policy of inertia.

Although unwilling to take action to speed integration, the administration remained determined to halt racial violence. Concerned about terrorist bombings of black schools and churches, Eisenhower asked his aides in late 1958 for recommendations for new civil rights legislation. In conference with Republican congressional leaders, Rogers presented a detailed package that included extension of the Justice Department's jurisdiction in cases of bombing or the use of force to prevent the implementation of federal court orders. Vice-President Nixon joined Rogers in defending these proposals against the objections of House Minority Leader Charles A. Halleck, who thought that civil rights could only cause Republicans political difficulty. Eisenhower also considered them moderate in purpose and in no way divisive. But during the first session of the Eighty-sixth Congress, southern Democrats prevented any action on the administration's proposals in the Senate.

The administration revised and resubmitted its civil rights proposals to Congress in early 1960. The key addition was a plan for the appointment of referees by federal courts to investigate situations in which discrimination prevented blacks from exercising their right to vote. Because both parties expected political benefits from the legislation in an election year, Congress acted promptly on Eisenhower's proposals but reported a diluted version of them. In its final form, the Civil Rights Act of 1960, which Eisenhower signed into law on 6 May, authorized the use of referees and established new criminal penalties for interfering with the exercise of voting rights and transporting explosives across state lines. The administration claimed a significant victory, but the signing ceremony, attended only by Rogers and his deputy, indicated otherwise.[45]

Eisenhower left the presidency justifiably convinced that he had contributed significantly to the cause of civil rights. The two civil rights acts, however compromised or weakened their provisions, were real achievements of the Eisenhower presidency. They acknowledged federal responsibilities that had lain dormant since the 1870s. They encouraged civil rights activists to work for even greater legislative protection of constitutional rights. The dispatch of troops to Little Rock, however uncharacteristic of the president's policy of implementing the *Brown* decision, also served notice that riotous obstruction of federal court orders might provoke the armed intervention of the national government, a possibility that had been unthinkable for eighty years.

Despite the symbolic value of these actions, their practical benefits were small. The two civil rights acts added only an additional 3 percent of black voters to the franchise rolls during the Eisenhower presidency.[46] The Justice Department secured during 1960 only one conviction for violation of voting rights. At the end of the 1959/60 school year, just 6.4 percent of southern black students went to integrated schools; in the Deep South, the figure was a scant 0.2 percent.[47]

Certainly Eisenhower was not solely or perhaps even principally to blame for this meager progress. Intransigent southern officials often were beyond his control. So were residential patterns or educational policies. Individual and community prejudices frequently could not be altered.

Yet Eisenhower still must bear significant responsibility. His sympathies clearly lay with southern whites, who he patiently said needed time to adjust, not with southern blacks, whom he impatiently criticized for wanting basic rights too soon. His philosophy of government emphasized local responsibility but failed to take account of the fundamental unwillingness or inability of communities and states to deal fairly with civil rights issues. Although Eisenhower clearly understood the need for education and moral leadership, he provided neither. "From all this there emerges the inescapable conclusion," as Arthur Larson has written, "that President Eisenhower . . . was neither emotionally nor intellectually in favor of combatting segregation."[48]

7

$$\bigstar \bigstar \bigstar \bigstar \bigstar$$

THE EROSION OF CONSENSUS

"We meet again, as upon a like moment four years ago, and again you have witnessed my solemn oath of service to you." With these words, Dwight D. Eisenhower began his inaugural address in 1957 and commenced his second term as president at the zenith of popularity and achievement. "In our nation work and wealth abound," Eisenhower exulted. "The air rings with the song of our industry . . . , the chorus of America the bountiful." Despite the stirring of "new forces and new nations," the president assured his fellow citizens that "the American experiment" inspired "the passion and courage of millions elsewhere seeking freedom, equality, [and] opportunity." While it was no time for rest or ease, neither was it a moment to doubt the vitality of the economy of the United States or the effectiveness of its global leadership.[1]

Yet during the next year, the assurance and optimism of the beginning of the second term crumbled because of a series of economic, international, and political shocks. The Eisenhower prosperity dissolved into the worst recession since the Great Depression. The Soviet launching of Sputnik, the world's first artificial satellite, shattered confidence in American technological superiority and raised troubling questions about American security. Allegations of influence-peddling against Sherman Adams compromised the integrity of the president's inner circle. Fractious disputes over the budget, farm subsidies, foreign aid, and space policy strained Eisenhower's relations with Congress and created doubts about the effectiveness of his leadership. Assailed by both the left and right, Eisenhower found the middle of the road a rocky and lonely route.

Eisenhower began 1957 as he had ended the previous year—trying to calm the turmoil in the Middle East. On New Year's Day, he summoned to the White House congressional leaders from both parties to gain their support for a new American initiative, a resolution that the United States would use military and economic aid and armed force to stop Communist aggression in the Middle East. Such a declaration was necessary, Eisenhower told the legislators, to thwart Soviet efforts to fill the void created by the disintegration of British and French influence in the Arab world in the aftermath of the Suez debacle. Eisenhower soon obtained the congressional approval he desired, but his approach to Middle East problems revealed the limitations of his Cold War outlook.

A day after the White House meeting, Secretary of State John Foster Dulles met in closed session with the Senate Foreign Relations Committee to explain in greater detail why the president thought the situation in the Middle East was so dangerous. For more than a century, Dulles reminded the committee, British power had checked Russian ambitions in the Middle East. But "that bulwark has [now] been swept away" because of "the very improvident and unwise action of the British in the attack upon Egypt." The result, Dulles concluded, was a perilous new situation in which "the free nations of the area . . . will almost certainly be taken over by Soviet communism" unless the United States acted. The power of the United States' strategic deterrent would not provide security in the Middle East. Nations in vulnerable positions, Dulles insisted, needed not only a declaration that the United States would come to their aid in the event of an attack, but also American assistance to build up their own armed forces and stabilize their economy. "It is human nature," he asserted, "that these people with exposed positions . . . have got to have in addition to an invisible protection outside of their own border which they cannot see, something within their border which they can see."[2]

Eisenhower also emphasized that American help was imperative when he appeared before a joint session of Congress on 5 January and asked for approval of the Middle East Resolution. "The Middle East has abruptly reached a new and critical stage in its long and important history," Eisenhower advised Congress. The critical danger, he warned, came from international communism, which aimed at world domination. "Expressions of good will" and "superficially attractive offers" of assistance were the insidious means that Communists used to achieve their goal of subjugating independent nations. "Remember Estonia, Latvia and Lithuania!" Eisenhower exclaimed in uncharacteristically inflammatory rhetoric. Soviet satellites on the eastern Mediterranean or the Persian Gulf would threaten strategic sea lanes and disrupt the supply of oil vital to the West. Most Middle Eastern nations, however, recognized the danger of international communism, Eisenhower declared, and so would "welcome closer cooperation with the United States." Accordingly he invited the Congress to join with him to protect the security of the Middle East. Specifically he requested authority to allocate at his discretion to Middle Eastern countries $200 million in economic and military aid during each of the next two fiscal years. He also sought the power to use the armed forces in the general area of the Middle East to meet any "overt armed aggression from any nation controlled by International Communism." This program, which soon became known as the Eisenhower Doctrine, would "give courage and confidence to those who are dedicated to freedom and thus prevent a chain of events which would gravely endanger all of the free world."[3]

Debate on Capitol Hill focused on Eisenhower's request for prior congressional authorization to commit American troops. Senator Hubert H. Humphrey (D., Minn.), complained to Dulles that the administration was asking "for a predated declaration of war." Senator Wayne Morse (D., Oreg.), warned that Congress, if it approved the Eisenhower Doctrine, would vote away its constitutional check on the warmaking power of the executive. Other senators, such as John Stennis, (D., Miss.), replied that the Eisenhower Doctrine would only make explicit the authority implied in the chief executive's constitutional role as commander in chief of the armed forces. Dulles informed the Senate Foreign Relations Committee that Eisenhower took a conservative view of the constitutional powers of the president and because of his military background was unwilling to use the armed forces "in ways which Congress has not indicated it wants."[4]

Because of the controversy over what Senator Richard B. Russell (D., Ga.), called the constitutional "shadowland between the President's authority to use Armed Forces and the necessity for a declaration of war," the Congress revised Eisenhower's proposed resolution.[5] The amended resolution proclaimed that "if the President determines the necessity thereof, the United States is prepared to use armed forces" to assist any Middle Eastern nation repel Communist aggression. This wording settled the divisive constitutional issue by simply avoiding it. At the same time, it served notice that the United States would commit its military power, if necessary, to the Middle East. The new language won praise from legislators with extremely different points of view.

Mike Mansfield (D., Mont.), who preferred greater American cooperation with UN peacekeeping efforts, described the Eisenhower Doctrine as an example of "responsible cooperation in foreign policy." John W. Bricker (R., Ohio), whose proposed constitutional amendment aimed at limiting the influence of international organizations on American policy, hailed it as a salutary example of executive-congressional action in conformity with the Constitution.[6]

Almost no one in Congress criticized Eisenhower's preoccupation with communism in a region in which nationalism seemed by far the more powerful force. In his address to the joint session of Congress on 5 January, Eisenhower did not even mention the rising tide of nationalism in Middle Eastern nations nor the unrest created by poverty, hunger, and unconscionably low standards of living. Instead he maintained that any unrest in the Middle East arose from Communist exploitation of indigenous demands for economic and political reform. The Middle East Resolution did give the president discretionary power to furnish economic aid, but such help aimed at fortifying efforts to resist Communist expansion. Legislators did not complain about the narrow purpose of economic assistance; instead, they worried that the president's authority to provide such aid might lead to costly new foreign commitments. In the Senate, only J. William Fulbright (D., Ark.), and John F. Kennedy (D., Mass.) seriously questioned whether Eisenhower's Cold War outlook could be properly applied to the Middle East. Both took issue with the conclusion of Adm. Arthur W. Radford, chair of the Joint Chiefs of Staff, that Egypt and Syria were Communist-dominated countries because they had accepted Soviet weapons. Neither Fulbright nor Kennedy—nor any of their colleagues—wondered, however, whether the United States would dissipate the prestige it had gained in the Arab world during the Suez crisis by threatening to use its military power to preserve Middle Eastern stability.

The target of Eisenhower's anticommunism was Egyptian President Gamal Abdel Nasser. Eisenhower and Dulles held to their belief that Nasserism was a Middle Eastern variety of international communism. They had objected not to the goal of deposing Nasser during the Suez invasion, but to British and French methods. Eisenhower continued to denounce the Egyptian president as "an evil influence" and to build up his rivals in the Arab world.[7] Even before Congress approved the Middle East Resolution, Eisenhower welcomed King Saud of Saudi Arabia to Washington and hailed him as a great leader of the Arab world and, by implication, an alternative to Nasser. Saud reluctantly endorsed the Eisenhower Doctrine, but more enthusiastic statements came from the leaders of Iraq, Libya, and Lebanon, all of whom received visits from

Eisenhower's special emissary, Ambassador James P. Richards. The Eisenhower Doctrine, in short, was a new expression of the continuing policy of discrediting and isolating Nasser.

Despite his preoccupation with communism, the most difficult problem in the Middle East Eisenhower faced before winning passage of the congressional resolution was Israeli reluctance to evacuate Egyptian territory. Britain and France had removed their armed forces, but the Israelis balked in early 1957 until they obtained assurances of navigation rights in the Gulf of Aqaba. In retaliation, Nasser halted operations to clear the Suez Canal. As long as the canal remained blocked, Western Europe would suffer from shortages of oil, one of the dangers that the Eisenhower Doctrine aimed at averting. Eisenhower and Dulles also worried that acquiescence in Israeli intransigence would lead to Arab charges that American policy was "controlled by Jewish influence in the United States."[8] To persuade Israel to yield, the president announced his support for proposed United Nations sanctions aimed at halting government and private assistance to Israel. The latter restriction was particularly significant, since American private gifts and purchases of bonds produced $100 million for Israel each year.[9]

Faced with such pressure, Israel backed down on 1 March. Several days later, the Senate consented to the Middle East Resolution, and Eisenhower signed it into law on 9 March. At the end of the month, the Suez Canal resumed operations. One dispute in the Middle East was resolved, and Eisenhower had secured a new mechanism for combatting unrest in that vital area. Yet the maneuvering over the withdrawal of troops from Egypt suggested a serious limitation of the Eisenhower Doctrine. The Arab-Israeli dispute, not international communism, posed the greatest danger to regional stability in the Middle East.

Although the Eisenhower Doctrine did nothing to resolve Arab-Israeli tensions, it did help restore harmony in Anglo-American relations. British Prime Minister Harold Macmillan took wry satisfaction in the enunciation of the Eisenhower Doctrine. "This gallant effort to shut the stable door after the horse had bolted was welcome to us," Macmillan wrote in a none-too-subtle allusion to American policy during the Suez crisis, "for it at least marked a return to the world of reality."[10] Also pleasing to the prime minister was Eisenhower's request for a summit meeting, which took place in Bermuda in March 1957. Macmillan and Eisenhower renewed their old wartime friendship as well as the closeness between their two nations. "The meeting was by far the most successful international conference that I had attended since the close of World War II," Eisenhower recollected.[11]

The Eisenhower Doctrine did produce another apparent success, during a governmental crisis in Jordan in April 1957. Problems arose when elections yielded a sweeping victory for the pro-Nasserist National Socialist party. The new government promptly terminated an alliance with Great Britain and strengthened its relations with the Soviet Union. Charging that Jordan was the victim of "international Communist subversion," King Hussein dismissed the pro-Nasserist prime minister, established a conservative government, and declared martial law.[12] Hussein's move triggered street demonstrations, clashes between rival factions of the army, and Syrian troop movements along Jordan's northern border. In reply to the king's appeal for help, Eisenhower ordered the Sixth Fleet into the eastern Mediterranean and provided Hussein with a grant of $20 million in aid. In the ensuing weeks, the king's forces reestablished domestic order.[13] The Jordanian crisis really was primarily a domestic affair, but Eisenhower could also claim that he had thwarted the growth of Communist influence.

Calamity was the result of the use of the Eisenhower Doctrine during problems in Syria several months later. For more than a year, American officials had fretted over Nasserite and Soviet influence in Syria. The appointment of a leftist chief of staff of the Syrian army in August 1957 and a purge of conservative officers deepened fears in Washington. The leaders of neighboring countries—Iraq, Lebanon, and Jordan—charged that Syria was trying to topple their governments. In early September, Eisenhower promised to take steps to protect these nations against "pro-Soviet" Syrian aggression. Again, he sent the Sixth Fleet into the eastern Mediterranean and emergency deliveries of armaments to Jordan, Lebanon, and Iraq. The administration, however, made a critical error in also relying on Turkey, a non-Arab nation, to help contain Syrian subversion. When Turkish troops began massing on Syria's border, the rifts in the Arab world quickly healed. Much to the president's dismay, Saudi Arabia joined Egypt in promising support for Syria should aggression occur; Jordan, Iraq, and Lebanon set aside their grievances in the interest of Arab unity. The Soviets took advantage of the tensions to extend military and economic aid and deepen their influence in Damascus. Yet most Arab nations drew together in opposition to American policy. Nasser shrewdly assumed the role of Syria's special protector against American aggression, and thereby strengthened his claim to leadership of Arab nationalism.[14] The Eisenhower Doctrine had clearly backfired.

Far more constructive was Eisenhower's effort to reform the Mutual Security Program to meet the needs of Third World nations. The main purpose of the grants of military and economic aid provided through MSP was to stop the spread of communism, but because of increasing Soviet efforts in the Third World, the program needed revision. Following the death of Stalin, the Soviets vastly expanded their economic assistance, particularly in the form of long-term, low-interest loans to India, Afghanistan, Egypt, Indonesia, and other developing nations. By 1956, this "Soviet economic offensive" worried the president and his advisers, especially since many nonaligned nations preferred Soviet loans, which seemed to carry fewer obligations, to American grants. Furthermore, the principal goal of the MSP since its inception in 1951 had been to meet Communist military threats, and the preponderance of assistance was for fighting aggression rather than hunger or poverty.[15]

Congressional complaints also encouraged Eisenhower to overhaul Mutual Security. Discontent with the foreign aid program was widespread on Capitol Hill. Old Guard Republicans grumbled about extensive and unwarranted involvement in overseas affairs. Fiscal conservatives denounced Mutual Security as an expensive foreign giveaway program. Liberal internationalists such as Mansfield protested that the foreign aid program lacked "specific objectives [and] specific yardsticks against which to measure cost in any rational fashion."[16] Staunch anticommunists objected to aiding neutralist nations, such as India or Yugoslavia. For a variety of reasons, then, Congress annually cut Eisenhower's request for Mutual Security funds. For at least one representative, Otto Passman (D., La.), parsimonious chair of a House appropriations subcommittee, such budget cutting provided perverse satisfaction. "Son, I don't smoke and I don't drink," Passman once told a State Department official. "My only pleasure in life is kicking the shit out of the foreign aid program of the United States of America."[17]

On 21 May 1957, Eisenhower asked Congress to make major changes in the MSP. That evening in a nationally-televised address, he explained that his recommendations were based on sweeping reassessments of the foreign aid program by special committees of Congress and a blue-ribbon panel appointed by the president. Foreign aid was neither charity nor extravagance, Eisenhower declared, but prudent investment in the nation's own defense. The United States, he explained, had to help Third World nations maintain not only the military strength to preserve their independence, but also the hope of improved standards of living to maintain their legitimacy. Should a moderate government fail at the latter task, "Communist extremists" would seize the opportunity to "extend their brand of despotic imperialism." Accordingly he proposed the creation of a Developmental Loan Fund that would receive $500 million in capital during fiscal year 1958 and $750 million more during each of the next two years. He also asked for permanent authority to provide technical assistance to other nations and for the creation of a $300 million emergency fund that he could use at his discretion. Finally, he urged a clear separation between economic and military aid by putting the latter in the defense budget. The total cost of these programs would be $3.87 billion, "a minimum figure," he insisted, "considering the issues at stake."[18]

Eisenhower's proposals got a chilly reception, even from his own secretary of the Treasury, George M. Humphrey. Committed to ultra-conservative principles, Humphrey urged Eisenhower to rely more on trade, rather than loans that he thought would never be repaid, to foster development. Furthermore, he thought Eisenhower's emphasis on foreign aid was encouraging statism at the expense of private initiative. Humphrey even went so far as to suggest that the United States ought to encourage colonialism rather than nationalism because European administration would raise living standards more rapidly in the Third World. Eisenhower patiently but decisively rejected Humphrey's antediluvian views. "It is my personal conviction," the president replied, "that almost any one of the newborn states of the world would far rather embrace Communism . . . than to acknowledge the political domination of another government even though that brought to each citizen a far higher standard of living." The time had come "to face up to the critical phase through which the world is passing and do our duty like men."[19]

On Capitol Hill Eisenhower encountered even more criticism of his foreign aid proposals and was not very effective at disarming it. Most legislators did not accept the president's logic that loans to developing countries would save the United States money in the long run. Instead they worried about short-term expenses and slashed the president's foreign aid budget. As finally passed by Congress, the Mutual Security Act of 1957 authorized $500 million less than Eisenhower had requested and a two- rather than three-year Developmental Loan Fund. The appropriations bill was an even worse setback for the administration. Passman, who headed the House appropriations subcommittee that dealt with foreign aid, charged that the president's advisers had been "purposely losing sleep working up figures that cannot be justified." Congress gave Eisenhower only $2.8 billion for Mutual Security—a cut of $1.1 billion in the administration's original request—and only $300 million for the first year of the Developmental Loan Fund. In a letter to his boyhood friend, Swede Hazlett, Eisenhower exploded: "I am repeatedly astonished, even astounded, by the apparent ignorance of members of Congress in the general subject of our foreign affairs."[20] Yet despite his exasperation, Eisenhower had succeeded in establishing an important instrument for American participation in overseas development projects.[21] Even though his principal goal was still containing communism, Eisenhower's foreign aid policy was progressive and innovative.

The clash over Mutual Security was part of an even larger conflict, the so-called Battle of the Budget that Eisenhower and Congress fought during the first session of the Eighty-fifth Congress. Like the struggle over Mutual Security, the Battle of the Budget severely strained relations between Eisenhower and members of Congress—and not just the Democrats, but many Republicans as well. The result was a major defeat for Eisenhower and searing public criticism of the quality of his leadership.

At the center of the dispute was Eisenhower's budget of $73.3 billion for fiscal year 1958. The budget was balanced—indeed Eisenhower's economic advisers predicted a slight surplus—but the level of expenditures was $2.8 billion more than in fiscal 1957 and a record in peacetime. For the president and his budget director, Percival Brundage, it had been difficult to keep the budget from growing even larger. Pressure had come from the Defense Department for $40 billion in military spending, but Eisenhower had insisted on a ceiling of $38.5 billion. "They don't know much about fighting inflation," Eisenhower said of the service leaders. "This country can choke itself to death piling up military expenditures just as surely as it can defeat itself by not spending enough for protection."[22]

Yet Eisenhower presented the budget to Congress and the public in such an inept manner that it seemed as if he had not won the approval of his own secretary of the Treasury. Humphrey was worried that the economy could not continue to support such a high level of federal spending. He expressed his concerns in a letter to the president, which he proposed to make public. Despite the objections of Brundage, Eisenhower decided at a cabinet meeting to authorize the release of the letter in the hope that its admonitions would discourage Congress from exceeding the president's budget. The decision produced disastrous results. At a press conference, Humphrey warned that if spending continued at current levels for a long period, "you will have a depression that will curl your hair."[23] Humphrey's colorful phrase made headlines, and his forecast seemed to be a repudiation of the administration's own budget.

Eisenhower did his best to limit the damage. At his news conference a week later, on 23 January, Eisenhower emphasized that he and Humphrey saw eye-to-eye on the budget. He had read every word of Humphrey's letter, he said, and thoroughly agreed with it. Furthermore, he took pains to indicate that Humphrey had predicted a hair-curling recession only if spending remained high for several years. But then Eisenhower got himself into further trouble. He encouraged the members of Congress—indeed he said it was their duty—to cut the budget if they could find some way to economize.

Old Guard Republicans heartily agreed. Senator Styles Bridges of New Hampshire and even Minority Leader William F. Knowland of California, among others, thought that Eisenhower had abandoned the Republican commitment to fiscal responsibility and embraced New Deal profligacy. Eisenhower dismissed such criticism as nonsense. The president explained to reporters that his budget provided for social programs that had ''now become accepted in our civilization as normal, that is the provision of social security, unemployment insurance, health research by the Government, assistance where States and individuals are unable to do things for themselves.''[24] Such expenditures accorded with Eisenhower's conception of Modern Republicanism, an approach, he thought, that both recognized the essential social responsibilities of the federal government and would forestall efforts of liberal Democrats to enact more ambitious and expensive programs. Yet conservative Republicans paid no heed to Eisenhower's pleas for social responsibility and political pragmatism. Instead they concentrated on Humphrey's letter, which asserted that despite administration efforts to limit spending, ''the overall net results are not sufficient.''[25]

The Democrats also joined in the criticism of the president's budget. At the beginning of the session, Eisenhower had hoped for a cooperative relationship with the Democrats. After a New Year's Day 1957 meeting on the budget, he told the majority leaders, ''If you come to the point where you think higher expenditures have to be made, let's confer together before your decision is finally made.'' Rather than pushing for increased spending, though, the Democrats quickly saw the opportunity to make partisan gains by paring the budget. Administration bungling gave the Democrats a chance to seize the leadership on the budget issue from the president as well as to deprive the GOP of their traditional role as guardians of the nation's fiscal integrity.[26]

As the budget battle dragged on through the spring, Eisenhower decided to outflank his opponents by taking his case to the American people. He began a televised address on 14 May with a backhand swipe at Congress. ''The yardstick of national interest,'' he reminded his fellow citizens, not the parochial needs of district, state, or region, had determined his budget decisions. Since entering the White House, his administration had eliminated nearly 250,000 federal jobs and had cut taxes. Still, the amount of federal spending was large, but he recalled Lincoln's folksy aphorism that a person's legs ought to be long enough to reach the ground. In the same way, a budget had to reach the ground of essential national interest, and the administration's proposal did so. "No great reductions in it are possible," he warned, "unless Congress eliminates or curtails existing Federal programs, or unless all of us demand less service from the government, or unless we are willing to gamble with the safety of our country." With an unusual show of emotion, he declared that it would be reckless to make unwarranted cuts in defense that might later require the sacrifice "of our sons, our families, our homes and our cities to our own shortsightedness."[27]

The speech had little effect on Capitol Hill. Congress slashed Mutual Security by $1 billion and cut $2.4 billion from the president's defense request. By the time it had finished its work, Congress had provided Eisenhower $4 billion less than he requested for fiscal 1958. As the session adjourned, Majority Leader Lyndon B. Johnson telephoned Eisenhower and declared, "Mr. President, I'll bet you're just as happy to see us go as we are to go."[28] Eisenhower, however, did regret the departure of Humphrey from the cabinet in midyear. Humphrey left voluntarily and for personal reasons, but many political observers considered him a casualty of the Battle of the Budget.

The budget struggle revealed how little progress Eisenhower had made in moving the GOP toward Modern Republicanism. Knowland had led the fight against many of the administration's spending proposals and had enlisted many allies from the Old Guard. The president was stung by criticism that somehow he had deserted Republican traditions by proposing a budget that he thought met only essential national requirements. In reply to a reporter's question, he dismissed any talk that he had drifted toward the left since his entering the White House. "If anything," he insisted, "I think I have grown more conservative." But Eisenhower also warned that any viable political group had to respond to the needs of people today, "not of 1860." The federal government could not shut its eyes or leave to the states the problems of the aged, unemployed, or disabled. "I believe that unless a modern political group does look these problems in the face and finds some reasonable solution, . . . then in the long run we are sunk."[29] For the remainder of Eisenhower's presidency, such admonitions produced few, if any, results.

The controversy with Congress over federal spending was only a prelude to a trying and, ultimately, disastrous autumn. No sooner had Eisenhower wearily bid farewell to the first session of the Eighty-fifth Congress than he was embroiled in conflict with Governor Orval Faubus over the latter's defiance of a federal court order to desegregate the Little Rock public schools. The governor's pandering to extremists and rioters disgusted Eisenhower and contributed significantly to his decision to dispatch federal troops to restore order. Eisenhower's action, of course, aroused thunderous opposition, especially among southern whites. Eisenhower rode out the storm, but he was not so fortunate during the next deluge.

The most jarring crisis of the Eisenhower presidency began on 4 October when a Soviet intercontinental ballistic missile lifted off from central Asia and placed in orbit the world's first artificial satellite, Sputnik. A few leading administration officials reacted with absurd nonchalance. The departing secretary of defense, Charles E. Wilson, called Sputnik "a neat scientific trick."[30] Sherman Adams, Eisenhower's chief of staff, cavalierly dismissed the Soviet "outer space basketball game."[31] Such foolish disdain persuaded no one. Scientists unanimously agreed that the orbiting of the 184-pound Sputnik was a momentous technological achievement. Throughout the nation, people worried that the United States had suffered a devastating blow to national security. Democratic leaders—and many others—cried that the nation had suffered a scientific Pearl Harbor. While Americans went routinely and unsuspectingly about their business, Russia had inaugurated the space age—or so it seemed.

Sputnik created such a pervasive sense of alarm because it shook public confidence in a fundamental basis of national security—the superiority of American science and technology. Since the beginning of the Cold War, many Americans had believed that the Soviet Union was so technologically backward that it had to employ spies to copy American plans and subvert or kidnap scientists from other countries. The United States, after all, had exploded the first atomic bomb, and only because of the stealing of American secrets—so popular reasoning went—had the Soviets managed to build their own bomb so quickly. Few citizens understood the intricacies of defense policy, but most thought that American military strength rested on the unsurpassed sophistication of the nation's weaponry. The apparent Soviet advantage in space-age technology, then, created fears of vulnerability that turned into panic. This sudden and ominous shift in the perceptions of power in the aftermath of Sputnik inevitably led to a frenzy of charges that

Eisenhower's lethargy had frittered away a previously unassailable advantage in the Cold War.[32]

Eisenhower was neither unaware of the Soviet satellite program nor lethargic in organizing an American counterpart, but he did not give first priority to beating the Russians into space. The U-2 spy plane, which began overflights of the Soviet Union in mid-1956, brought back photographs of the ICBM base at Tyuratum in Kazakhstan, the site from which Sputnik was launched. American scientists and intelligence authorities knew by late summer 1957 that the Soviets were on the verge of putting a satellite into space. More than two years earlier on 28 July 1955, Press Secretary James C. Hagerty had announced that Eisenhower had approved plans for the launching of an American satellite during International Geophysical Year, from July 1957 through December 1958. The Defense Department entrusted this mission to the navy's Project Vanguard. The association of the satellite program with IGY, an international scientific endeavor, and the choice of Project Vanguard, which would use a missile that was developed for scientific purposes, represented a calculated effort to emphasize the peaceful character of the American space effort.

Privately Eisenhower and his top national security advisers recognized that satellites would become revolutionary instruments of reconnaissance with enormous consequences for the arms race. But they also worried about Soviet reaction and so hoped to use the cloak of peaceful scientific inquiry to deflect any Russian objections, especially those based on international law. In choosing Vanguard, the Defense Department bypassed the army's Project Orbiter, which seemed the best bet to produce the fastest results. "But speed was *not* the primary consideration," as historian Walter A. McDougall has written. "In the end, assuring the strongest civilian flavor in the project was more important."[33] This decision turned out to be a grave miscalculation.

Eisenhower, however, betrayed no personal agitation or dismay as he endured a stern cross-examination at his first news conference after the launching of Sputnik. The presence of "one small ball in the air," he asserted, did not raise his apprehensions—"not one iota." There never had been a contest with the Soviets to orbit a satellite, he told clearly disbelieving reporters, and there was now no race to catch up. Apparently still failing to grasp the impact of Sputnik, he emphasized that the Russians had scored only a psychological victory, but not a scientific or military triumph. Nor was there much reason for concern about Soviet ICBMs. They were powerful, but not necessarily accurate. Eisenhower dismissed the suggestions of skeptical correspondents that Soviet missiles made the bombers in the Strategic Air Command obsolete or that they posed any immediate danger to American security. There was also no need for a crash program or other extraordinary measures in the American missile and satellite programs.[34] Eisenhower thus clearly implied that the hysteria and soul-searching of the past few days were completely unjustified.

But because the anxiety over Sputnik simply would not go away, Eisenhower soon presented the American people with a program of measured, prudent, and necessary action to protect national security. The launching on 3 November of Sputnik II, an 1,121-pound satellite that contained a live dog, only exacerbated public fears. Speaking on national television four days later, Eisenhower began by reassuring the nation that even though the Soviets were ahead in the development of some types of missiles, "the over-all military strength of the free world is distinctly greater than that of the communist countries." To maintain this edge, Eisenhower announced a series of steps that he was taking. To ensure that he had the best information on which to base his decisions, he established the office of special assistant to the president for science and technology, to which he appointed James R. Killian, the president of the Massachusetts Institute of Technology. To prevent service rivalry from impairing national security, he also promised that any new missile program would be administered by a single manager in the Pentagon.[35] In another major address six days later, Eisenhower added a final recommendation—a major national effort to train more scientists and engineers. Although such actions were needed to maintain national security, Eisenhower reminded his fellow citizens that the real strength of American democracy came from "the quality of our life, and the vigor of our ideals." American education, then, had to produce "not only Einsteins and Steinmetzes, but Washingtons, and Emersons" as well.[36]

Yet Eisenhower's reassuring words were contradicted by the apocalyptic rhetoric of the Gaither Report. This document was a top secret assessment of security in the nuclear age prepared by a blue-ribbon panel appointed by the president and headed by H. Rowan Gaither, Jr., chair of the board of the Ford Foundation. Presented to the president in early November, the Gaither Report concluded that the United States stood at the edge of doom. In the event of a surprise Soviet ICBM strike, the United States would be devastated, the panel warned, because of the inadequacy of American defenses. Gaither recommended to Eisenhower an immediate increase in the defense budget of $10 billion for bombers, missiles, submarines, nuclear weapons, and conventional forces. The panel also urged the president to approve a sweeping, five-year program for the construction of fallout shelters at an annual cost of about $5 billion.

Eisenhower had all sorts of objections to the assumptions and conclusions of the panel, but the most immediate problem with the Gaither Report was that summaries of it leaked to the news media. Doomsday stories shocked the nation. "The still-top-secret Gaither Report," the *Washington Post* informed its readers, "portrays a United States in the gravest danger in its history . . . [and] exposed to an almost immediate threat from the missile-bristling Soviet Union."[37] Democrats were eager to get their hands on the Gaither Report, since it seemed to confirm that Eisenhower's defense policies had been dangerously shortsighted. But when Senate majority leader Lyndon B. Johnson called for release of the document, Eisenhower firmly refused. Claiming executive privilege, he warned that disclosure would make it impossible in the future to assemble advisers or to retain their trust.

Eisenhower staunchly resisted the recommendations of the Gaither Report and a bevy of critics for crash programs to catch up with the Soviets. Because of his access to intelligence information, he knew that the nation did not stand on the brink of nuclear destruction. The United States held the lead in the number and design of nuclear weapons and in the technology for the solid-fueling of long-range missiles and guiding them to target. While the Soviets were ahead in overall ICBM development, they did not yet have the capacity to launch a nuclear missile attack on the United States. By the time the Russians developed this capability, the American missile force would be larger and far more reliable. The United States, in short, did not need to make up lost ground, Eisenhower concluded.

Nor should the country risk becoming a garrison state through frantic spending that would create deficits, threaten social programs, and erode cherished values. More than a year earlier, in a letter to his friend Swede Hazlett, Eisenhower explained the dangers of devoting too much national wealth to defense. Excessively high taxes for military equipment, he reasoned, would "tend to dry up the accumulations of capital that are necessary to provide jobs for the million or more new workers that we must absorb each year. . . . If taxes become so burdensome that investment loses its attractiveness for capital, there will finally be nobody but government to build the facilities." The result would be socialism, he concluded. Eisenhower worried about not only the economic, but also the social consequences of unduly large defense spending. Repeatedly he stressed that "American strength is a combination of its economic, moral and military force. . . . Let us not forget," he reminded Hazlett, "that the Armed Services are to defend a 'way of life,' not merely land, property or lives."[38]

Yet Eisenhower's prescription for calm and steadiness did not relieve the acute public anxiety. Sputnik had altered perceptions of power; neither Eisenhower's words nor his actions reshaped them. The ignominious explosion of the Vanguard missile on 6 December 1957 four feet above its launch pad seemed only to belie Eisenhower's assurances that there was no reason to panic. During a special Senate inquiry into satellite and missile programs that began in late November, Lyndon Johnson, the committee chair, flailed Eisenhower's policies and urged a determined national effort to repair the damage to American security. Democrats also derided Eisenhower for allowing the development of a missile gap. In reality there was no such gulf in Soviet and American ICBM capabilities, but the president did not want to reply too specifically to the charge for fear of compromising the secrecy of the U-2 program. So the Democrats continued to hammer away at the issue with considerable success through the campaign of 1960. On the fundamental issue of defense—ironically the area in which the president had his greatest expertise—Eisenhower remained vulnerable until the end of his presidency, and his critics relentlessly exploited that opportunity.

After all the tribulations of Sputnik, Little Rock, and the Battle of the Budget, Eisenhower endured a final, personal crisis in 1957 when he suffered a stroke. The attack occurred while he sat at his desk on the afternoon of 25 November and signed papers. Dizziness, disorientation, and dysfunction followed in rapid succession. "I found that the words . . . seemed literally to run off the top of the page," Eisenhower recollected. After frantically summoning his secretary, Ann C. Whitman, he found that he could only speak nonsense as he tried to explain his plight. Aides helped him to bed, and his personal physician, Howard Snyder, and neurological specialists quickly arrived to diagnose his condition. They concluded that a minor spasm had occurred in one of the capillaries of the brain. The result, Eisenhower later explained, was "a temporary interruption in communication between my mental 'dictionary' and the thought I wished to express."[39]

Eisenhower reacted to the stroke successively with denial, despair, and defiance. Only hours after the attack, Eisenhower horrified his wife by announcing that he intended to go to a state dinner that evening. Feeling neither pain nor impairment of physical skills, he thought that he should attend to his official duties. But after being forced to retire at least for the evening, Eisenhower brooded about his ability to serve out his term. "This is the end," he declared morosely. "Mamie and I are farmers from now on."[40] Yet within a few days he had recovered so fully that his physicians could detect no permanent damage from the stroke. Eisenhower found that he sometimes reversed syllables in a long word, but he alone noticed the difficulty. To satisfy himself that he could truly handle the demands of the presidency, he established a test. Over the objections of family and physicians, he stubbornly decided to go through with plans made before his stroke to attend a NATO meeting in Paris in mid-December. The trip restored his confidence and freed him of further worries about his capacity to serve out his term.

Three serious illnesses in three years, however, persuaded Eisenhower to arrange for a smooth transfer of power should he become incapacitated once again. The Constitution authorized the vice-president to assume the duties of the chief executive in the event of presidential disability but did not specify the procedures. In a letter to Nixon, Eisenhower set out those he wished followed for the remainder of his term. In case of temporary incapacity, Eisenhower would surrender his powers to the vice-president and determine when to reclaim them. But should Eisenhower not be able to recognize his own disability, then it was up to Nixon alone to do so and declare himself acting president. Whatever his reservations about Nixon, Eisenhower entrusted him with an extraordinary responsibility. Later, the Twenty-fifth Amendment, which was ratified in 1967, would require the certification of the vice-president and a majority of the cabinet to declare the president unable to discharge his duties.

Eisenhower began 1958 with waxing vigor but declining popularity. During the previous year, his approval rating had fallen from a high of 79 percent in February to a low of 57 percent at the end of the year. The decline of his standing in the Gallup Poll no doubt was the cumulative result of the Battle of the Budget, Little Rock, and Sputnik. In the first weeks of 1958, his popularity continued to slump, reaching a nadir—for his entire presidency—in March, when only 52 percent of the public approved of his conduct of office. For the remainder of the year, his rating climbed only slightly and then slid back to its previous low.[41]

Eisenhower's poor showing in the polls was also a measure of public dissatisfaction over the recession that gripped the nation. The economy had turned sharply downward in summer 1957 and reached its low point in spring 1958. The hard times were severe. Industrial production declined 14 percent, corporate profits fell 25 percent, and unemployment reached a high of 7.5 percent. Federal actions aggravated the recession. Restrictions on credit drove up interest rates and cut into consumption of durable goods, particularly automobiles. Cutbacks in defense procurement, implemented so that the federal government would not exceed the current ceiling on the national debt, also helped slow the economy. While most people were not aware of how these specific actions worsened the hard times, they still tended to blame the president for the nation's economic woes. "Eisenhower is my shepherd," ran a popular bit of doggerel, "I am in want. . . . He leadeth me through still factories. He restoreth my doubt in the Republican Party."[42] The Eisenhower prosperity had now become, in the eyes of the president's critics, the Eisenhower recession.

The administration's tepid and, at times, fumbling response to the recession only intensified public dissatisfaction. The president did not appreciate the seriousness of the downturn until midautumn 1957. Even then, he was convinced that the economy would recover quickly, as it had in 1954, and so issued a series of optimistic public statements the principal effect of which was to create the impression that he did not care about workers who had lost their jobs. Although Eisenhower presented Congress in early 1958 with a balanced budget of $73.9 billion for the coming fiscal year that was designed to provide a modest stimulus, the chair of the president's Council of Economic Advisors, Raymond J. Saulnier, thought that federal spending would still be insufficient to speed recovery.[43] The president was unwilling to do more to stimulate the economy because he was convinced that inflation—not unemployment—was the greater danger. Eisenhower candidly revealed his approach when he wrote in his diary, "We are basically conservative. . . . We believe in private enterprise rather than a 'government' campaign to provide the main strength of recovery forces. . . . We want to avoid a succession of budgetary deficits because of the inflationary effect."[44] Judging by the polls, more people thought Eisenhower's restraint arose from indifference to the plight of the unemployed rather than concern about the adverse inflationary effects of federal spending.

The economic slump provided the Democrats with a golden political opportunity, and Johnson effectively rallied his party behind a series of measures to boost the economy and embarrass the Republicans. Unlike 1957, when they tried to prove that they were thriftier than the president, the Democrats attempted to show in 1958 that they were more willing to spend public funds to alleviate economic hardship. Among the legislation that they introduced were measures to increase the construction of highways and housing and expand unemployment insurance benefits. Johnson did not weigh the economic effects of these measures so much as their political advantage. They aimed at making the Democrats appear sympathetic to the needs of common Americans, in contrast to the supposed indifference of the Eisenhower administration. "The important thing," Johnson declared, "is to get the show on the road."[45] Many of the show's acts triggered acrimonious disputes. Johnson, for example, pushed through Congress a rivers and harbors bill to stimulate the economy and increase employment. The president vetoed this "stupid" measure on 15 April, in part because some of the projects it authorized "made no economic sense whatever."[46] Yet even in defeat, the Democrats prospered, as Eisenhower's ratings in the Gallup Poll sank.

The nastiest confrontation over how to combat the recession concerned farm policy. In January 1958, Eisenhower asked Congress to enact legislation that would ease controls on acreage and lower price supports. These recommendations, which Secretary of Agriculture Ezra Taft Benson vigorously supported, encountered blistering criticism on Capitol Hill. Representative Harold Cooley (D., N.C.) charged that Benson was determined to aggravate the woes of farmers suffering from recession by continuing his efforts "to bring down prices and to lower farm income."[47] Republicans from agricultural states joined with Democrats to produce a farm "freeze" bill, which would prohibit the lowering of price supports for a year. One midwestern Republican urged Eisenhower to throw his support behind the measure. "It's high time," he declared, "the Republicans gave better evidence they're in the farmer's corner."[48] Other members of the GOP warned Eisenhower that only Benson's resignation could avert Republican losses in many congressional races in the Midwest. Privately the president chided Benson for taking inflexible positions that could not be adjusted to meet the objections of even the administration's friends in Congress. Publicly he stood solidly behind Benson. "If there ever was an issue that called for intelligence instead of prejudice, conviction instead of expediency . . ." he told a national conference of Republican women, "that issue is the farm program." On 31 March, Eisenhower vetoed the farm freeze bill. "With regard to government controls," Eisenhower lectured the Congress, "what the farm economy needs is a thaw rather than a freeze."[49] Congress did not heed his advice, but just before adjourning in August it did pass a bill with enough flexibility on price supports and acreage for Eisenhower to accept. By that time, the economy had begun to climb out of the recession.

At the same time that they grappled with the budget and the recession, Eisenhower and Congress confronted momentous issues of national security. In the aftermath of Sputnik, Eisenhower's attempts to ease national anxieties had produced disappointing results. Now, in his state of the union message in 1958, he proposed an ambitious program of action that went beyond the steps he had taken in November. Eisenhower stressed that the Soviet threat was not just in the skies or the heavens, but was all-inclusive and so required a comprehensive response. Conceding that he had not anticipated the psychological impact of the launching of Sputnik, Eisenhower recommended an accelerated defense effort—including the stepped-up development of ICBMs and bombers and increased dispersal and readiness of retaliatory forces—and administrative reorganization of the Pentagon. But it would be a tragic mistake, he warned, to concentrate solely on military matters, since the Soviet economic offensive in the Third World posed a grave peril to the Free World. Accordingly, he urged Congress not to cut foreign aid and trade programs to pay for new military measures. Finally, because of the importance of science and technology to national security, he proposed a series of measures to improve education and basic research. Yet Eisenhower emphasized that he was not calling for national mobilization or fundamental alterations in the relationship of government and society. Because it was essential to maintain economic health, he rejected a tax hike, an overall increase in federal spending, and deficit financing. Only by remaining faithful to ''the ideas and principles by which we live,'' could Americans preserve their fundamental strength.[50]

Congress heeded Eisenhower's admonitions when it passed the National Defense Education Act. Shortly after the state of the union address, Eisenhower proposed a program of scholarships, fellowships, and grants to the states to improve secondary school and university education, mainly in science, mathematics, engineering, and foreign languages. Because of his abhorrence of statism, he promised that federal assistance would not undermine or supplant local control of schools. Congress gave Eisenhower most of what he wanted, although Democrats added $60 million for vocational education in the interest of equity. The legislators also substituted low-interest loans for federal scholarships, a change that Eisenhower heartily endorsed, and authorized $1 billion to carry out the program for seven years.

Despite strong resistance, Congress also approved most of the president's recommendations for the reorganization of the Department of Defense. The new weaponry of modern warfare, he pointed out in a special message on his plan, had altered the nature of combat; ''separate ground, sea, and air warfare is gone forever.'' It was essential, therefore, to establish truly unified commands controlled by the president through the secretary of defense and Joint Chiefs of Staff, but not the individual service secretaries. Eisenhower also wanted money for the armed forces appropriated directly to the secretary of defense, rather than to the individual service departments. Strong protests came from defenders of service interests and from some legislators, such as Carl Vinson (D., Ga.), chair of the House Armed Services Committee, who feared that the president's reorganization would weaken congressional influence over military affairs. Others invoked the specter of a Prussian general staff, military czar, or a single service uniform to rally opposition. Eisenhower, however, effectively lobbied Congress and mobilized public opinion. The Defense Reorganization Act, which he signed into law on 6 August, contained only a few unwelcome features. Congress refused to shift defense appropriations from the service departments to the secretary of defense and reserved the right to veto any change in a major combatant function. The legislators also authorized the uniformed and civilian service chiefs to take their own recommendations on defense matters directly to Capitol Hill. Eisenhower called the latter provision "legalized insubordination," but nonetheless thought it "a small hole in the doughnut."[51]

Eisenhower was not nearly as satisfied with the annual Mutual Security legislation. Mindful of the perennially stubborn resistance on Capitol Hill, Eisenhower skillfully orchestrated bipartisan public support for foreign assistance. At a White House conference timed to coincide with the presentation of the Mutual Security bill to Congress, Eisenhower enlisted the support of such diverse figures as Stan Musial, Archbishop Fulton J. Sheen, and Harry S. Truman. In his testimony before the House Foreign Affairs Committee, Dulles emphasized that foreign aid was no giveaway, but actually a subsidy for the American economy, since it provided foreign countries with the means to buy American goods. As always, Congress provided less than Eisenhower requested, but the cuts were not nearly as deep as the previous year. The $3.3 billion appropriation—the president had asked for $600 million more—also provided more money for economic assistance than for military aid for the first time during the Eisenhower presidency. Yet even this amount fell far short of the needs of Third World nations for developmental aid. Eisenhower complained to Speaker of the House Sam Rayburn that "he could not understand what the members of Congress were doing—to vote extra money for war—and to deny the money that was needed for peaceful purposes."[52]

Eisenhower got more than he wanted with the creation of the National Aeronautics and Space Administration. Sputnik had aroused a clamor on Capitol Hill for an agency that could coordinate American efforts to overtake the Russians in the race for space. The launching of the first American satellite, Explorer I, on 31 January 1958 by no means eased the pressure. Lyndon Johnson again seized the initiative by making himself chair of the Senate Special Committee on Science and Astronautics and using his highly visible position to urge the creation of a space agency. Eisenhower opposed transfer of the space program from the Pentagon for fear that American resources would be dissipated in spectacular but ultimately "useless" projects, such as a rocket to the moon. But eventually he yielded and signed the NASA legislation, which did contain a provision excluding military space activities from NASA control.[53] Yet despite the creation of NASA, Eisenhower largely succeeded in holding the line against crash programs or drastic increases in spending in the aftermath of Sputnik.

Even while clashing over space and defense, the president and Congress did cooperate on statehood legislation for Alaska. Eisenhower dropped his objections that arose from his concern about maintaining federal control of defense installations on Alaskan soil. The bill that he sent to Congress simply reserved large sections of Alaskan territory for military purposes. The discovery of oil on the Kenai Peninsula persuaded some members of Congress that those resources would be developed more rapidly under state control. With bipartisan support, Congress passed the necessary legislation in mid-1958. Admission of the forty-ninth state on 3 January 1959 helped create sufficient pressure for the approval of Hawaiian statehood two months later.

No political controversy during 1958 distressed Eisenhower more than the brouhaha over the improprieties of Sherman Adams. In June 1958, the Subcommittee on Legislative Oversight of the House Interstate and Foreign Commerce Committee made public allegations that Bernard Goldfine, a New England textile manufacturer, had provided gifts to Adams in return for the latter's help in resolving problems with the Federal Trade Commission and Securities and Exchange Commission. The scandal deepened when newspapers reported that Goldfine had not only paid hotel bills for Adams and his wife, but had provided the president's chief of staff with a vicuña coat, a present that sounded far more expensive than its $69 wholesale cost. Appearing voluntarily before the subcommittee, Adams admitted receiving the gifts but insisted that they were tokens of a friendship of many years' duration. Categorically he denied using his influence with federal regulatory agencies to obtain preferential treatment for Goldfine. Adams, however, did admit to imprudence in making inquiries to the FTC and SEC in response to Goldfine's requests for information. "I did not stop to consider," Adams recollected, "that in making a personal call . . . concerning a matter in which he was involved I might be giving the officials in the federal agency the erroneous impression that I had a personal interest in their ruling or decision on the case."[54]

At first Eisenhower stood loyally behind his chief of staff. Shortly after Adams's testimony before the House subcommittee, Eisenhower expressed unqualified support for his aide. Eisenhower conceded that Adams had shown bad judgment, but not any lack of integrity in his dealings with Goldfine. "A gift is not necessarily a bribe," Eisenhower reminded those who he thought were rushing to unwarranted conclusions. "I believe with my whole heart that he [Adams] is an invaluable public servant doing a difficult job efficiently, honestly, and tirelessly," the president continued. "I need him."[55]

Aside from Eisenhower, Adams had few friends in Washington and many enemies in both political parties. In an election year, Democrats viewed the Adams scandal as a major campaign issue, one that would particularly embarrass an administration that had repeatedly proclaimed its fidelity to the highest principles of integrity in government. Many Democrats particularly relished the opportunity to attack Adams, since they had not forgiven him for a ferociously partisan speech earlier in the year in which he blamed their party, among other things, for the attack on Pearl Harbor. Many Republicans had their own scores to settle with Adams. Some GOP legislators had long resented the brusque manner in which he had handled their requests for access to the president. Conservative Republicans particularly disliked Adams, because they considered him a liberal *éminence grise* who was responsible for Eisenhower's failure to support many of their policies or programs. The president's vote of confidence in Adams did little, if anything, to neutralize this bipartisan opposition.

Adams's difficulties worsened during the summer, when the House subcommittee released new information that suggested that Goldfine had provided his gifts as a way to obtain political influence. According to the subcommittee, Goldfine had sent presents to dozens of governors, senators, and other federal officials and had deducted as a business expense part of the cost of his gifts to Adams. Adams's friendship with someone so eager to use his wealth to curry favor became an even greater political liability in the estimation of some leading Republicans. GOP chair Meade Alcorn confidentially reported to Eisenhower that an informal poll of state campaign officials revealed overwhelming support for Adams's resignation or dismissal. In part because of their concern about the impending campaign, conservative GOP senators Knowland and Barry Goldwater of Arizona publicly called for Adams to step down.

By late summer Eisenhower agreed that Adams had to go, but he was unwilling to tell his chief of staff the bad news. Eisenhower worried that Adams's continued presence on the White House staff would badly hurt the Republican campaign and even tarnish his own reputation for integrity. Yet even though Eisenhower was determined to get rid of Adams, he was unwilling to do so himself or to appear to accept responsibility for his decision. In late August, Eisenhower instructed Nixon to have a frank talk with Adams about the political realities of the situation. But the chief of staff stubbornly refused to resign, even when Nixon bluntly announced that he was sure that was Eisenhower's preference. "Sherm won't take any of the responsibility," Eisenhower complained after hearing Nixon's account of the conversation. "He leaves it all to me."[56] Eisenhower in turn delegated the responsibility to Alcorn, who persuaded Adams to step aside during a long and grueling conversation. On 22 September, Adams formally submitted his resignation to the president and then announced his decision on national television that evening. He was leaving, he told the public, so as not to harm the efforts of the Republicans to gain control of Congress or impede the efforts of the administration to achieve its political goals.

After Adams's resignation, Eisenhower reorganized his White House staff. Succeeding Adams as chief of staff was Gen. Wilton B. (Jerry) Persons. Informal, light-hearted, and always accessible, Persons was a noticeable contrast to the dour Adams. Three deputies assisted Persons. Bryce Harlow supervised legislative liaison, and Robert E. Merriam oversaw domestic issues. Staff Secretary Andrew J. Goodpaster handled national security issues, assisted in turn by the president's son, John. Gordon Gray, a former secretary of the army, succeeded Robert Cutler as special assistant for national security affairs, and Don Paarlberg replaced Gabriel Hauge as special assistant for economic affairs.

The cabinet also had a new look as Eisenhower approached the middle of his second term. Fred A. Seaton, owner of a chain of midwestern radio and television stations and newspapers, had succeeded Douglas McKay as secretary of the interior in June 1956. Before moving to interior, Seaton had held a succession of administrative posts, including assistant secretary of defense and White House assistant for congressional liaison. Seaton shrewdly used his knowledge of Capitol Hill to avoid the brouhahas over water and resource development that regularly engulfed his embattled predecessor. He managed, for example, to quiet the controversy that had lasted for years over McKay's decision to allow private construction of three dams in Hells Canyon, Idaho. He also succeeded in mollifying both resource developers and wilderness preservationists. In the president's eyes, Seaton's effective management and moderate politics epitomized Modern Republicanism.

Several other departments got new secretaries in 1957/58. Replacing Humphrey at the Treasury in mid-1957 was Robert B. Anderson, whom Eisenhower had courted for the vice-presidency in 1956. Taking over as secretary of defense in October 1957 was Neil H. McElroy. Like his predecessor, Charles E. Wilson, McElroy had headed one of the country's largest corporations, Procter & Gamble. Unlike Wilson, who could not control bickering among the services or his own propensity toward embarrassing public statements, McElroy used his background in advertising to build support within the Pentagon and among the public for the president's policies. Succeeding Marion B. Folsom at Health, Education, and Welfare in August 1958 was Arthur S. Flemming, the president of Ohio Wesleyan University.

The administration's new faces did little to ease Republican woes as the fall elections approached. Adams had departed, but his improprieties became a staple of Democratic campaign rhetoric. In the Midwest, Secretary of Agriculture Benson was an inviting target for Democratic stump speakers, and in the South the issue was the president's dispatch of troops to Little Rock. Throughout the country, the opposition attacked Eisenhower's defense policies that had supposedly allowed the Soviets to take the lead in the missile age and the space race. Encouraged by the drop in unemployment in August, Eisenhower urged the party faithful to "lead the defeatists away from the wailing wall. Time has proved right this Administration's confidence in the American economy. We are on the upward road."[57] Yet the improvement was too small and too late to deprive the Democrats of probably their most powerful national issue—Republican responsibility for hard times.

Eisenhower's role in the campaign was limited, his rhetoric shabby, and his influence with the voters meager. He appeared in only six states. A few "people-ask-the-president" telecasts, presentations that were contrived and uninteresting, did little to make up for Eisenhower's restricted schedule of personal appearances. Eisenhower made a major effort only in California where Knowland was seeking the governorship, while the incumbent, Governor Goodwin J. Knight, was trying to win the Senate seat Knowland was surrendering. Despite past differences, the president thought that Knowland's election was essential to save California from extremism. One wing of the Democratic party, he told a television audience in California, was dominated by "political radicals," who were reckless spenders of government money. "Long ago," he recalled, "I found out that, to a political radical, a sound program for America is an invitation for demagogic excess." The president said that he had watched his own proposals "mangled and mushroomed" by Democratic congresses led by extremists who were "pursuing economic and political goals at odds with American tradition."[58] Such rhetoric was a notorious example of the extreme partisanship—even demagoguery—that Eisenhower so frequently ascribed to his opponents. On this occasion Eisenhower sounded very much like the McCarthyites whose tactics he professed to abhor.

The defeat of both Knowland and Knight was a good measure of the magnitude of the Republican disaster in the election. In the biggest congressional sweep since the New Deal, the Democrats increased their control of the Senate by thirteen seats and of the House by forty-six. They also held governorships in thirty-five states. One of the very few Democratic candidates who lost was Congressman Brooks Hays from Arkansas, who was burdened by his connections with administration officials during the Little Rock crisis. The only major Republican victory was the election of Nelson A. Rockefeller as governor of New York. Nine incumbent GOP senators went down to defeat, including John W. Bricker of Ohio and Arthur V. Watkins of Utah. In the wake of the Democratic landslide, some members of the Old Guard charged that Eisenhower had not only merely betrayed GOP principles, but also had almost destroyed the Republican party.

The president walked into the Oval Office the morning after the election, looked at the gloomy faces around him, and said, "Pretty bad, wasn't it?" When Hagerty reminded him that the reporters would certainly have questions about the disaster, the president growled, "You don't have to bring that up. I know what I'm going to say on that. Just skip it." Then he angrily blurted out, "I'm going to go on the attack . . . [and] relate every bit of legislation from now on to the pocketbook of the individual Americans. I'm going to put a price tag on everything."[59] But, as usual, Eisenhower had calmed down considerably by the time he met with the press corps. First, he stressed that he had not meant that all Democrats were fiscally irresponsible. Then he reminded the reporters that he had considerable experience in working with Democratic legislators. Indeed he was right; his experience actually was unique. Never before had a president faced three consecutive congresses controlled by the opposition.

Despite his guarded optimism about executive-congressional relations, Eisenhower thought that the election showed that the Republicans needed to make fundamental changes. The Democratic landslide arose from more than the recession, Sputnik, or the Sherman Adams scandal. Instead Eisenhower thought that the election proved the need for the formation of a special committee that could analyze Republican failures and suggest new ways of rejuvenating party organization. The emphasis, he said, should be on "youth, vigor, and progress," so that on the grassroots level the GOP would have "the finest young leaders." The committee also ought to study the victorious races of Mark O. Hatfield, the governor-elect of Oregon, and John V. Lindsay, representative-elect from New York, both of whom were moderates and models of what Eisenhower meant by Modern Republicanism. One of the major problems that he thought should be corrected was the lack of party discipline. Many members of Congress—he really meant the Old Guard—followed their own line, irrespective of the president's wishes, but still received campaign funds from the Republican National Committee.[60] In effect, Eisenhower was renewing his call for Modern Republicanism and perhaps even suggesting a purge of the Old Guard. The latter suggestion, of course, was both unworkable and unrealistic. It was a measure, though, of the frustration and despair Eisenhower felt at the nadir of his presidency.

8

INTERVENTION
AND DIPLOMACY

"Maybe I should be digging out my uniforms," President Eisenhower suggested to his wife in May 1958, "to see if they still fit."[1] Eisenhower made his remark at a time when American forces readied for intervention in Venezuela, where a mob had threatened the life of Vice-President Richard M. Nixon, and in Lebanon, where rioters attacked an American library. The president, of course, did not don his uniform, but he did ultimately send marines ashore in Lebanon. He also intervened in strife in Indonesia and the Taiwan Strait and ordered American troops to be prepared to fight in Berlin. During 1958, the succession of Cold War crises revealed the weaknesses of Eisenhower's rigid anticommunism and cut into his popularity. During the following year, Eisenhower handled the challenge in Berlin more deftly and engaged in personal diplomacy, including a summit conference with Nikita S. Khrushchev, that allayed public anxieties even if it produced few concrete results. By the end of 1959, Eisenhower seemed to be searching for a way to ease Cold War tensions, yet détente remained only a fragile—albeit stronger—hope.

One of the first of many foreign policy tribulations in 1958 concerned an embarrassing revelation about American intervention in Indonesia. Eisenhower and Secretary of State John Foster Dulles had long been upset by Indonesian President Achmed Sukarno's neutralism. With Eisenhower's knowledge, the CIA provided advice and aid to Indonesian plotters, who intended to overthrow Sukarno. When a rebellion erupted in 1958, the CIA furnished military assistance to the insurgents and recruited civilian pilots to fly B-26 bombers in combat. Eisenhower proclaimed that the United States was adhering to "careful neutrality and proper deportment all the way through so as not to be taking sides where it is none of our business." If there were Americans involved in the conflict, he assured reporters, they were "soldiers of fortune," men who always found adventure in small wars.[2] Three weeks after he gave that assurance, one of the B-26s crashed, and the American pilot was captured by Sukarno's forces.[3]

While the Indonesian intervention was an embarrassment, Eisenhower's first foreign policy crisis of 1958 occurred in Latin America, during the goodwill visit of Vice-President Nixon. Because of his involvement in Republican preparations for the fall campaign, Nixon had resisted State Department suggestions that he travel to Latin America until Eisenhower and Dulles insisted that he go. The trip caused Nixon enormous problems, but for very different reasons than the vice-president had anticipated. In Lima, students pelted him with rocks. On May 13, a frenzied mob in Caracas surrounded his limousine and threatened his life. "The crowd was rocking the car back and forth— slower and higher each time . . . ," Nixon recalled. "I believe that at that moment, for the first time, each of us in the car realized we might actually be killed."[4] After twelve harrowing minutes, the Nixon motorcade broke free and found sanctuary on the grounds of the American embassy. At the height of the crisis, Eisenhower dispatched 1,000 soldiers and marines to Caribbean bases, where they awaited the order to rescue the Nixon party. Venezuelan authorities, however, managed to get the vice-president and his entourage safely to the airport. Eisenhower headed the dignitaries who gave Nixon a hero's welcome when the vice-president's plane landed in Washington.

Nixon's frightening brush with death came at a time when Eisenhower and his top advisers generally believed that hemispheric relations were "close and friendly." The National Security Council reached this conclusion in September 1956, when it reviewed U.S. policy toward Latin America. The overthrow of the Arbenz regime in Guatemala had eliminated the only immediate Communist threat to the hemisphere, according to the NSC. In a progress report completed in September 1957, the Operations Coordinating Board found that Latin American Communists, "though vocal and still having a potential for making trouble, generally have been held in check." Many Latin Americans, the OCB noted, complained about the lack of United States economic assistance, particularly the paucity of long-term, low-interest loans. Yet the OCB recommended clearer explanations of policy, rather than more developmental aid, to help overcome these feelings of resentment and discrimination. The Eisenhower administration continued to rely most heavily on military assistance to solidify relations with Latin American leaders, many of whom used the armaments they received to strengthen repressive regimes. Although aware of protests against U.S. support of dictatorial rule, administration officials continued to praise the tough anticommunism of Latin American strongmen. Thus in the months before the Nixon trip, Eisenhower and his top aides thought they were making "reasonable progress" toward achieving their "basic policy objectives" in Latin America.[5]

Jolted by the attack on Nixon, the president and most of his aides blamed Communists for the disturbances. While still in Caracas, Nixon told reporters that the demonstrators were part of "the international Communist conspiracy," a theme he reiterated in speeches after his return to the United States.[6] While refraining from a "direct accusation" against the Communists, Eisenhower nonetheless insinuated that "where there is a lot of smoke . . . there is probably some fire." Economic difficulties had contributed to Latin American discontent, but it was Communist agitators, he speculated, who had used these grievances to instigate violence in Lima and Caracas.[7] The CIA, however, failed to produce any evidence to sustain these charges. Indeed CIA Director Allen W. Dulles asserted that "there would be trouble in Latin America if there were no Communists."[8]

As Dulles's remark suggested, the Nixon trip made Eisenhower and his top advisers suddenly aware that hemispheric relations were not as placid as they had imagined and that the administration needed to modify some of its Latin American policies. To recoup lost prestige, the president and other top administration officials quickly backed away from displays of public support for repressive rulers. Nixon pithily summed up the new guidelines as "a formal handshake for dictators; an *embraso* for leaders in freedom." The administration also altered its foreign economic policies to meet some of the criticisms of Latin American leaders. Soon after Nixon's return, Eisenhower authorized the relaxation of U.S. opposition to commodity agreements—international accords to stabilize the prices of certain products or raw materials. The president also endorsed the creation of the Inter-American Development Bank, which was established in October 1960 with $1 billion capital.[9]

Despite their importance, these new departures did not drastically change the administration's approach to Latin America. The Inter-American Development Bank, the most important of the new initiatives, fell far short of the recommendation of the influential president of Brazil,

Juscelino Kubitschek, that the United States promise Latin America $40 billion in economic aid during the next two decades. The administration also continued to provide substantial grants of military assistance and even hoped to become the sole provider of armaments to the other Latin American nations in order to increase its political influence over its neighbors. Eisenhower recognized that Latin America was an "area in ferment," as his brother Milton advised him after touring Central America in mid-1958.[10] Yet despite the explosions during Nixon's trip, the president still did not think that communism posed any grave or immediate danger in Latin America. Eisenhower believed that policy adjustments, not an overhaul, could once again stabilize United States-Latin American relations.[11]

At the same time that he faced difficulties in Latin America, Eisenhower confronted an even more dangerous situation in the Middle East. Arab nationalists, inspired by Egypt's Gamal Abdel Nasser, caused political turmoil in Iraq and Lebanon and threatened western interests. Once again Eisenhower feared that Nasserism was little more than communism by another name. Once more, as during the Suez crisis, Eisenhower forcefully directed American policy. But rather than restricting the use of military power, Eisenhower ordered American troops into Lebanon in mid-July, almost without considering other options. The results of the Lebanon landings—the only overt military intervention that Eisenhower ordered during his presidency—fully exposed the weaknesses of the Eisenhower Doctrine.

In April 1958, political strife threatened Lebanon's fragile internal unity and the government of pro-Western President Camille Chamoun. A Maronite Christian, Chamoun headed a regime whose major offices were apportioned among Lebanon's Muslim and Christian sects. This confessional system created a precarious political unity, which became even more uncertain after Chamoun's enthusiastic endorsement of the Eisenhower Doctrine. Muslim leaders denounced Chamoun not only because they were attracted to Nasser's Arab nationalism, but also because they suspected that he intended to circumvent Lebanon's constitutional prohibition against a president serving consecutive terms. Violence between pro- and anti-Chamoun forces that began during the parliamentary election campaign in 1957 intensified after the announcement on 1 February 1958 that Egypt and Syria had formed the United Arab Republic. According to the State Department, Syrian arms and terrorists contributed to the disturbances in Lebanon. Egypt also exacerbated the Lebanese difficulties by unleashing a barrage of propaganda that Robert McClintock, the American ambassador in Beirut, described rather fantastically as "audio-visual aggression."[12]

By early May, Lebanon seemed to be on the verge of civil war. Tensions rose after a member of the Chamber of Deputies revealed that he would introduce a constitutional amendment to enable Chamoun to succeed himself at the end of his six-year term in September. An explosion of riots and strikes followed the assassination of a prominent anti-Chamoun journalist. One of the targets of a mob in Beirut was the U.S. Information Service Library, whose holdings were ransacked and then burned in the streets. Chamoun feared that the army would not restore order, since it was commanded by Fuad Chehab, a Maronite who opposed the president's efforts to secure a second consecutive term. As the turmoil worsened, Chamoun informed McClintock that he might request American troops.

Eisenhower was prepared to send in the marines. After meeting with the Dulleses and Gen. Nathan F. Twining, the chair of the Joint Chiefs of Staff, Eisenhower took the preliminary steps of directing the Sixth Fleet to move into the eastern Mediterranean and expediting deliveries of internal security equipment to Lebanon. Eisenhower discounted reports that Chamoun's political aspirations had brought about the crisis. Instead he insisted that "the Communists were principally responsible for the trouble."[13] Eisenhower believed that Chamoun did not covet another term as president but simply wanted to make sure that the government remained under the control of a strong, pro-Western leader. Neither of the Dulles brothers, however, interpreted Chamoun's actions as charitably as Eisenhower, who remembered the Lebanese leader's generous expressions of concern after his heart attack in 1955. They worried about a hostile Arab reaction to an American intervention whose purpose would appear to be to sustain Chamoun's political ambitions. Because of the Dulleses' reservations, Eisenhower refrained from taking stronger action. Within days, government forces managed to calm the turbulence in the streets.

Two months later, trouble flared up again in Lebanon, and this time Eisenhower swiftly ordered the marines to go ashore. The precipitating event was a coup in Iraq that deposed the pro-Western monarch and brought to power Gen. Abdel Karim Kassem, who appeared to be pro-Nasser. Chamoun worried that Lebanon would be the next Middle Eastern domino to fall and issued an urgent appeal for American help. Eisenhower and his top advisers shared Chamoun's reasoning and feared "a chain reaction which will doom the pro-West governments of Lebanon and Jordan and Saudi Arabia and raise grave problems for Turkey and Iran." Such discussion only confirmed Eisenhower's inclination to use force, a decision he had made even before meeting the secretary of state, the CIA director, and military officials. All agreed that the Soviets would do little more than denounce the American action. "The Russians aren't going to jump us," Twining assured the president in colorful but unanalytical language, ". . . because we've got them over the whing whang and they know it."[14]

Two battalions of marines had already gone ashore near Beirut when Eisenhower announced the intervention in a televised address on 15 July. Lebanon was a small country, he explained, but its future would have the most profound effect on the security of the entire world. The president declared that Lebanon was "the victim of indirect aggression from without," "the same pattern of conquest" by which "Communists attempted to take over" Greece, Czechoslovakia, China, Korea, and Indochina between 1945 and 1950. Even though American intelligence could find no hard evidence that Nasser was involved in the Iraqi coup, much less that those who seized power in Baghdad were Communists in any meaningful sense, Eisenhower's strained logic created the frightening impression that the entire Middle East was in danger of falling to Communist control. Eisenhower warned that failure to act would have even graver consequences, since the world had learned two decades earlier that indifference to aggression encouraged the forces of conquest "that made World War II inevitable." The president thus invoked the Eisenhower Doctrine to protect Lebanon and the Middle East and prevent World War III. "The United States," he solemnly promised, "is determined that . . . history shall not now be repeated."[15]

Just as important to Eisenhower was putting Nasser and other Arab nationalists on notice that the United States would act vigorously to protect important interests in the Middle East. Eisenhower keenly understood the strategic importance of the Middle East and its oil, an appreciation he had developed during World War II. "Since 1945, we have been trying to maintain the opportunity to reach vitally needed petroleum supplies peaceably," he explained to Nixon before his decision to send in the marines. The turmoil in Lebanon arose from Nasser's efforts "to get control of these supplies—to get the income and the power to destroy the Western world."[16] Nasser was emboldened to do so because he had mistakenly concluded during the Suez crisis "that the United States government was scarcely able, by reason of the nation's democratic system, to use our recognized strength to protect our vital interests."[17] Eisenhower wanted to teach Nasser—and any others who doubted American resolve—a lesson that they would not forget. Conversely he also wanted to reassure the leaders of friendly nations in Southwest Asia, such as Iran, Pakistan, and Turkey, that their faith in the United States was not misplaced.[18]

Fortunately American troops did not have to prove these points by going into combat. The marines went ashore near Beirut without opposition and were greeted with "wild acclaim," according to McClintock.[19] The most difficult moment of the intervention occurred on the second day when Lebanese forces attempted to block the movement of the marines into the city. General Chehab and McClintock quickly stepped in and prevented any bloodshed. During the three months that American troops remained in Lebanon, they encountered no further opposition from the Lebanese army and only sporadic fire from the militants in the streets. Nor did they have to put down any new uprising against the Chamoun government. Instead their principal task was to secure the airport, port facilities, embassies, and other critical installations. Only one of the 14,000 American soldiers and marines who served in Lebanon died from hostile fire.

Negotiations, rather than military operations, ended the crisis in Lebanon. At the same time that he dispatched troops, Eisenhower sent Deputy Undersecretary of State Robert Murphy to Beirut to try to arrange a political settlement. Murphy had worked closely with Eisenhower on political affairs during World War II, first in North Africa, then in Italy and Germany. Eisenhower had grown to admire Murphy's diplomatic acumen and thought him ideal for the difficult assignment of trying to reconcile Lebanon's warring factions. Upon his arrival, Murphy made clear that the United States would not support Chamoun's bid for a second term, thereby defusing much of the opposition to the American landings. After many meetings with Chamoun and opposition leaders, Murphy helped work out an agreement that called for Chamoun to step down at the end of his term and Chehab to succeed him. Ironically the terms of this settlement were almost identical to a proposal that Nasser had made in June, but which the Eisenhower administration had refused to support for fear of becoming an "accomplice" of the Egyptian leader.[20]

Although he was pleased with the results of the intervention, Eisenhower endured some bitter criticism for his action. To no one's surprise, Nikita S. Khrushchev released a vituperative letter in which he condemned the American intervention and called for a great-power summit meeting to resolve Middle Eastern problems. Eisenhower rejected the Soviet leader's proposal—he wanted to avoid "being jockeyed into the position of having to attack Nasser publicly"—and declared that the UN was the appropriate forum.[21] Congressional Democrats excoriated the president for resorting to the same gunboat diplomacy that he had vehemently opposed when the British had used it two years earlier. Indeed the parallels between Lebanon and Suez seemed uncomfortably close. While American troops occupied Lebanon, British forces went into Jordan to protect King Hussein from a Nasserite coup. Prime Minister Harold Macmillan wanted American forces to join the Jordanian operation. But Eisenhower, who feared that the British wanted an American "blank check," limited the U.S. role to logistical assistance. Nonetheless, Macmillan's facetious description of American action seemed all too accurate to Eisenhower's detractors. "You are doing a Suez on me," the prime minister told Eisenhower by transatlantic telephone.[22]

In reality, Eisenhower was not repeating British mistakes in the Middle East, but his own. By equating Nasserism with communism, Eisenhower continued to misunderstand the power of Arab nationalism. By viewing Middle Eastern events through a Cold War lens, Eisenhower saw Communist causes behind events that arose from local or regional origins. The strife in Lebanon was the product of that country's tangled religious politics and Chamoun's personal ambitions, not the agitation of Communist subversives. In Iraq, General Kassem was no pawn of Nasser, but a new rival for leadership of the pan-Arab movement. Even though Kassem strengthened his ties to Moscow, he increased the flow of Iraqi oil to the West. The realities of the Middle East were far more complex than Eisenhower's rigid Cold War framework allowed. The dispatch of troops to Lebanon—and the Eisenhower Doctrine that justified that action—aimed at meeting a threat that was certainly not immediate and perhaps nonexistent.[23]

The intervention in Lebanon persuaded the Eisenhower administration to alter its course in the Middle East. The National Security Council still found in November 1958 that Western interests faced "a grave challenge" in that region. Yet the Eisenhower administration had learned from its experience with Lebanon that it should no longer try to cope with the "flood" of Arab nationalism by "put[ting] sand bags around positions we must protect." Instead the NSC recommended a new effort to "work more closely with Arab nationalism." Challenging Nasser earned the United States the enmity of the Arab masses and played into the hands of the Soviets. "To be cast in the role of Nasser's opponent would be to leave the Soviets as his champion," the NSC explained.[24] In late 1958, Eisenhower agreed with Ambassador Mustapha Kamel that Egypt and the United States should "freeze" their differences and cooperate on matters of mutual interest. Accepting this "icebox approach," the president improved relations with Egypt by authorizing $153 million in food aid in 1959/60.[25] Also consigned to the icebox was the Eisenhower Doctrine.

American troops were still in Lebanon when a new, but familiar, Cold War crisis erupted in the Taiwan Strait. On 23 August 1958 artillery of the People's Republic of China began bombarding the Nationalist Chinese islands of Quemoy and Matsu. Despite the president's exaggerated rhetoric about the significance of Lebanon, the confrontation over the offshore islands was far more dangerous. The shelling threatened to trigger a war between the Communists and the Nationalists that could involve the United States and force Eisenhower to decide whether to use nuclear weapons. Yet despite these potentially grave consequences, Eisenhower's ability to control events was limited. Often the initiative was in the hands of an adversary whose intentions were uncertain or an ally, Chiang Kai-shek, whose actions were provocative. Just as during the offshore island crisis four years earlier, the American public wondered whether dots of territory half a world away would precipitate nuclear war.

When the bombardment began, Eisenhower and Chiang still differed in their assessment of the military significance of the islands. Eisenhower thought Quemoy and Matsu were important to the defense of Taiwan. Chiang maintained that they were essential. Since the last confrontation in the Taiwan Strait, Chiang had increased his forces on Quemoy and Matsu to 100,000 troops, one-third of the strength of the Nationalist army. This build-up irritated Eisenhower, since it directly contravened American advice that the Nationalists should garrison the islands with only a token force.

Yet Eisenhower agreed with Chiang that Quemoy and Matsu ought not to be yielded under pressure. The president believed far more strongly than he had four years earlier that the islands should be defended, albeit for symbolic reasons. The shelling of Quemoy and Matsu, the president concluded, was a critical test of "Western unity and resolve," an attempt by Khrushchev to divert attention from American success in Lebanon and demonstrate that the Communists were "still on the offensive." After those tiny dominoes fell, so would Taiwan, and perhaps "the anti-Communist barrier . . . in the Western Pacific," including South Korea, Japan, the Philippines, and Southeast Asia. The effects on the American position in East Asia "would be even more far-reaching and catastrophic than those which followed when the United States allowed the Chinese mainland to be taken over by the

Chinese Communists.'' Such a drastic shift in the configuration of power, which might take several years, would be the result of a psychological collapse, as pro-Western governments buckled under Communist pressure. Needless to say, the political consequences in the United States as those Asian dominoes fell would be nothing short of calamitous. Eisenhower, then, considered the Quemoy-Matsu crisis a symbolic contest that the United States could not afford to lose.[26]

Such concatenated reasoning inflated the significance of the off-shore islands and misconstrued the origins of the Communist bombardment. Although Khrushchev visited Peking in early August, Communist party Chairman Mao Tse-tung did not inform the Soviet leader of the impending military action. Eisenhower had long known of tensions between China and the Soviet Union and hoped to exacerbate them. But in this instance he apparently believed that Mao was acting as the agent of international communism when he threw down the gauntlet in the Taiwan Strait.

Mao, however, ordered the artillery barrage to influence American policy toward China. He desired the resumption of negotiations with American diplomats in Geneva, talks that had begun in the aftermath of the first offshore islands crisis and that the United States had suspended in early 1958 after the repeated refusal of PRC representatives to renounce the use of force against Taiwan. He also wanted to protest the Eisenhower administration's steps toward a two-Chinas policy, an effort to secure recognition of Taipei as well as Peking in such organizations as the International Red Cross and International Olympic Committee. ''We . . . will not accept . . . occupation of China's Taiwan as legal,'' one PRC official declared, ''nor will we tolerate the appearance of a situation of 'two Chinas' in any international conference or international organization in which we take part.'' Apparently Mao hoped that military pressure would make the United States more willing to accept these positions in future negotiations.[27]

If Mao, in Eisenhower's view, caused the crisis by opening the bombardment, Chiang ''helped complicate the problem.'' Not only did the generalissimo recklessly concentrate his troops on Quemoy and Matsu, but also he seemed frighteningly inclined toward action that might deepen the crisis. Chiang still nurtured hopes of overthrowing Communist rule, and, according to John Foster Dulles, apparently viewed the crisis ''as a golden opportunity for recovering the mainland as the outcome of a war between the U.S. and Red China.'' Because of such fears, Eisenhower carefully tried to prevent Chiang from seizing the initiative. For example, soon after the shelling commenced Eisenhower augmented the Seventh Fleet, which was stationed in the Taiwan

Strait. He also allowed American vessels to escort through international waters Nationalist supply ships bound for Quemoy and Matsu. But he was unwilling to give Chiang an unqualified statement of support because he thought that "Orientals can be very devious; they would then call the tune." Eisenhower's ethnocentric apprehensions must have deepened as American military and diplomatic officials reported that Chiang was distraught over American inaction and might be "planning something big," perhaps even an invasion of the mainland.[28] Restraining Chiang, Eisenhower later exclaimed in exasperation, "was not always easy."[29]

However much he preferred restraint, Eisenhower still seriously considered the possibility of using nuclear weapons. The president knew that in the event of a major assault against Quemoy or Matsu, he would almost certainly have to order retaliation with tactical nuclear weapons against PRC airfields. While fully aware that the United States would face worldwide condemnation, he nevertheless hoped that "relatively small detonations . . . [with] no appreciable fallout or large civilian casualties" would minimize the popular revulsion. While such a reaction was frightening, Eisenhower worried that the failure to hold the offshore islands and the subsequent toppling of Asian dominoes would unleash even more ferocious criticism from those who were determined to prevent any more territory from falling under Communist control. Eisenhower also realized that the use of tactical nuclear bombs might provoke Soviet intervention. Since the last offshore island crisis, the Russians had greatly increased their nuclear stockpile and had improved their capabilities of striking American targets. What began as a "small" nuclear war, Eisenhower recognized, would probably not remain limited.[30]

Because he faced such horrifying alternatives, Eisenhower hoped that stern public rhetoric and an offer to negotiate would end the crisis. When Secretary of State Dulles urged an atomic strike against PRC airfields on 4 September, Eisenhower demurred. The president was unmoved by Dulles's assertion that the failure to use atomic bombs "when the chips are down because of adverse public opinion" would require fundamental revision of the administration's basic national security policy, which emphasized nuclear capabilities at the expense of conventional forces. Instead he authorized Dulles to issue a warning that the president was prepared to use force, if necessary, to protect Quemoy, Matsu, and Formosa. At the same time, though, Dulles called on the Chinese Communists to renounce the use of force against Taiwan. Mao responded by announcing his willingness to resume the suspended talks with the United States. The shelling, however, continued.

197

To calm apprehensions both at home and on Taiwan that negotiations with the Chinese Communists were tantamount to appeasement, Eisenhower forcefully proclaimed American resolve. Speaking on national television on 11 September, Eisenhower maintained that the current crisis was part of a pattern of Communist aggression in East Asia that included the North Korean attack of 1950 and the revolutionary war in Vietnam. Underlying these separate actions, he insisted, was a Communist plan to "liquidate all of the free world positions in the Western Pacific area and bring them under captive governments." The United States would never acquiesce in Communist efforts to dominate the Western Pacific, but it did hope that diplomacy would "find a way out" of the current crisis. He assured the American people that "there is not going to be any appeasement." He also predicted that there would be no war. But if conflict did occur, he promised that "no American boy will be asked by me to fight *just* for Quemoy."[31]

The speech caused an avalanche of criticism. The mail received at the White House ran four-to-one against Eisenhower's handling of the crisis. In Congress, several leading Democrats denounced Eisenhower's actions as provocative and demanded the withdrawal of the Seventh Fleet from the Taiwan Strait. Eisenhower's assurances that no American would fight only for Quemoy was cold comfort, since as critics pointed out, the president thought that at stake on that tiny island was the credibility of the United States. Republicans also denounced the president. Members of the Old Guard, who had long been sympathetic toward Chiang, charged that Eisenhower had sold out Nationalist China by agreeing to talks with the Communists.

Even the closest allies of the United States had serious reservations about Eisenhower's actions. British Prime Minister Macmillan found the administration's policies unsettling. He had long considered American efforts to support the Nationalists and ostracize the Communists "unrealistic and almost childish." During the crisis, he admired Dulles's public pronouncements as "the most brilliant exposition of the art of 'brinkmanship,'" but shuddered at the possible consequences of the secretary of state's "militant diplomacy." Privately Macmillan informed Eisenhower that British public opinion would not support the United States in a war for Quemoy and Matsu.[32] Dulles condemned the failure of Britain and the other NATO countries to endorse American policies and worried that the alliance was disintegrating. Gloomily Eisenhower commented that "as much as two-thirds of the world, and 50 percent of U.S. opinion, opposes the course which we have been following."[33] The president found that action aimed at proving American reliability seemed only to demonstrate intemperance.

Eisenhower lashed out at his critics when he publicly replied to a hostile letter from Senator Theodore Francis Green (D., R.I.), chair of the Foreign Relations Committee. Writing on 29 September, Green summed up the principal objections to Eisenhower's handling of the crisis. Eisenhower had fastened American prestige to two islands that were not essential to the defense of either Formosa or the United States, Green asserted. Should war occur, the Eisenhower administration would lack allies "in fact or in heart" and the support of the American people. On 5 October Eisenhower reminded Green of his "dedication to peace," which was second only to a commitment "to the safety of the United States and its honorable discharge of obligations to allies." The president insisted that both domestic public opinion and friendly nations would unite behind the administration if war occurred. Then after responding to Green's arguments, he castigated the senator's judgment. "I deeply deplore the effect upon hostile forces of a statement that if we became engaged in battle, the United States would be defeated because of disunity at home. If that were believed, it would embolden our enemies and make inevitable the conflict which, I am sure, we both seek to avoid provided it can be avoided consistently with the honor and security of our country."[34] Weary of the onslaught of criticism, Eisenhower believed that Green—and, by implication, the administration's other detractors—were playing into the hands of adversaries of the United States.

The Quemoy-Matsu crisis finally ebbed in late October. Dulles visited Taipei and persuaded Chiang to release a statement forswearing the use of force to recover the mainland. The generalissimo's declaration was actually more equivocal than Eisenhower and Dulles desired. In subsequent proclamations, Chiang and other key officials made clear that they would simply place their hopes mainly on other means of overthrowing Mao's regime but would still resort to force, if appropriate. The generalissimo also resisted American pressure to withdraw his troops from the offshore islands and accept their demilitarization. However limited the Nationalist concessions, they may have helped persuade Mao to restrict the shelling to even-numbered days beginning on 25 October. Eisenhower muttered about "a Gilbert and Sullivan war," but he was pleased that tensions had subsided.[35] The president had avoided war, but none of the issues that had produced the crisis had been settled.

Public discontent with Eisenhower's actions in the Taiwan Strait and Lebanon added to Republican woes during the fall campaign. Never before had the Democrats had so many issues to use against the administration. If they were not hammering away at brinkmanship, they were decrying the corruption that forced Sherman Adams's resignation or the Eisenhower recession. By the time of the election, Eisenhower's approval rating had receded to 52 percent, matching the previous low for his presidency established eight months earlier. The Democrats scored a major victory in the congressional elections by increasing their control in each house almost to two-to-one majorities. No wonder Eisenhower considered the year 1958 "the worst of his life."[36]

Eisenhower had not yet recovered from the GOP's depressing performance at the polls when he learned of a new foreign policy crisis. At issue were Allied rights in Berlin, long the most potent symbol of Cold War divisions. "West Berlin has become a sort of malignant tumor," Khrushchev announced in November. "Therefore we have decided to do some surgery." The Russian leader gave the Western powers six months to negotiate an agreement that would end the occupation of Berlin. Khrushchev's ultimatum raised the specter of a Soviet-American confrontation that could rapidly escalate into nuclear war. Eisenhower appreciated this grave danger, and he calmly defended American interests without backing Khrushchev into a corner. Eisenhower's wise and firm leadership—far more imaginative and flexible than during the crises in Lebanon and the Taiwan Strait—helped turn a moment of danger into an opportunity to improve Soviet-American relations.[37]

For Khrushchev, Berlin had long been a source of irritation. That divided city was the lone Western enclave behind the iron curtain. The open borders of the city enabled hundreds of thousands of East Germans to flee the repression, inefficiency, and material deprivation of Communist rule. During the 1950s, the population of East Germany actually declined, and many of the defectors were professionals and skilled technicians whose abilities were essential to a sophisticated industrial economy. Because of this drain of talent and manpower, Khrushchev complained that Berlin was "a bone in my throat." Yet the Soviet leader knew that he had the power to exert pressure for change. Using a different anatomical analogy, he explained, "Berlin is the testicles of the West. Every time I give them a yank, they holler."[38]

In November 1958, Khrushchev yanked. No longer a symbol of Allied unity, Berlin was "a dangerous center of contradiction between the Great Powers," a Soviet note declared. The time had come to liquidate the Allied occupation and create instead a demilitarized free city in West Berlin, while East Berlin became the capital of East Germany. Should the Western powers not accept these arrangements, Khrushchev promised to conclude a separate peace with East Germany. Such an accord would transform the issue of access to West Berlin—110 miles behind the border between the two Germanys—into a matter no longer guaranteed by Allied agreement but determined by East German discretion.[39] Understandably, Western leaders hollered. They worried about a Berlin blockade like the one imposed by the Soviets a decade earlier and an incident that might trigger a military showdown.

Such apprehensions seemed justified when in mid-November, the Soviets stopped an American convoy bound for West Berlin. Although the Soviets released the vehicles after eight hours, Gen. Lauris Norstad, the Supreme Allied Commander in Europe, wanted to send another convoy along the autobahn immediately to test the Soviet response. Should the Soviets again interfere, Norstad proposed to use the "minimum force necessary" to secure the release of the convoy. Although the Joint Chiefs heartily endorsed Norstad's plan, Eisenhower demurred. He reminded his military advisers that Allied—not just American—rights were at stake in Berlin, and the United States should consult Britain and France before taking any action that might lead to a clash of arms. Such sensible counsel cooled the ardor of the uniformed officers and averted an incident that could have turned a crisis into a tragedy.[40]

Yet Eisenhower was as firm as he was temperate in meeting the Soviet challenge. He believed that in Berlin, just as in Lebanon and the Taiwan Strait, American credibility was at risk. The United States, he argued, had expressed its "solemn obligation . . . to the two million Germans of West Berlin and to the entire world to stand by a city that had freely chosen to stay with the West and the cause of freedom. If our word to them would be broken, then no one in the world could have confidence in any pledge we made." After meetings of the American, British, French, and West German foreign ministers and the NATO Council, the United States pledged to stand firm in Berlin and hold the Soviets to Allied agreements until they were terminated by mutual consent. Dulles and Eisenhower also made clear that they had no intention of negotiating with the East German government, a regime the United States did not recognize. The president was willing to consider the possibility of establishing a free city, but only if it included all of Berlin and the UN regulated the access routes from the West.[41]

To back up these positions, Eisenhower quietly authorized military preparations. The president ordered these measures to proceed without fanfare so they would not create a public stir, but he wanted them prominent enough so that they would be noted by Soviet intelligence. Eisenhower also insisted that the United States would not acquiesce in any transfer to the East Germans of responsibility for monitoring Allied traffic in and out of Berlin. Such actions, the president argued, would be strong enough to warn Khrushchev that the United States would defend its position in Berlin but not so provocative as to prevent the Soviet leader from moderating his position for fear of humiliation. Indeed Eisenhower spared no effort to assure Khrushchev a retreat with honor. Yet he also made clear that "in this gamble we are not going to be betting white chips, building up the pot gradually and fearfully. Khrushchev should know that when we decide to act, our whole stack will be in the pot."[42]

Eisenhower also recognized the importance of easing pressures at home for precipitous action. In press conferences and statements to congressional leaders, he took pains to emphasize that there was no cause for alarm. The situation in Berlin, he insisted, was not a crisis, but a continuing problem that required calm and deliberate action. To those who demanded stronger military measures, Eisenhower replied that their counsel was dangerous. A full mobilization of NATO forces, which one reporter suggested on 4 March, would only exacerbate tensions. To critics who thought he should build up even further American forces in NATO, he soberly responded, "We are certainly not going to fight a ground war in Europe." When asked if nuclear weapons would be used to liberate Berlin, he mused, "Well, I don't know how you could free anything with nuclear weapons."[43]

Eisenhower also had to rein in his own military advisers. He rejected, for example, the Joint Chiefs' recommendation that a division of troops be sent in to break any blockade of Berlin after the expiration of the Soviet ultimatum. Such a contingent was far larger than necessary to make a show of force and so might cast the United States in the role of the aggressor or panic the Soviets into even stronger action. A division, however, was not large enough to protect the entire 110-mile autobahn between West Germany and West Berlin. Should there be a blockade, Eisenhower wanted to make sure negotiations were possible before war erupted. He ordered the Joint Chiefs to ready a much smaller force for action.

The president also repeatedly told Congress that there was no need for emergency military spending to meet the challenge in Berlin. Eisenhower sent Congress in January 1959 a budget for the coming fiscal year of $77 billion, including $40.9 billion in national security expenditures. The budget was in balance, and Eisenhower was determined to keep it that way. Ultimately he did so, but only after accepting additional spending of $2 billion. The president did succeed, however, in paring army strength by 50,000, in spite of vehement congressional protests. Democratic Senators J. William Fulbright of Arkansas and Lyndon B. Johnson of Texas told Eisenhower that troop cuts would be hard to justify during a time of international tension. Eisenhower retorted that the soldiers would serve no useful purpose because of the administration's heavy reliance on its nuclear deterrent. He also reminded leaders of both parties that any effort to match the Soviets in conventional forces would lead to the establishment of a garrison state that would threaten American democracy.

No less important than domestic opinion to a successful resolution of the Berlin crisis was Western solidarity. Eisenhower did not worry much about French President Charles de Gaulle, even though he knew from painful experience during the Second World War that de Gaulle was a prickly egotist who usually cooperated only on his own terms. "He's a proud, stubborn man," Eisenhower commented. "But if the chips are down, he's going to be proud and stubborn on our side."[44] He had greater reservations about British Prime Minister Macmillan, even though they had been friends since the invasion of North Africa in 1942. Fearful that a blockade or, worse, a war was in the offing, Macmillan flew to Moscow in February. Eisenhower thought that the prime minister should have gone home after Khrushchev broke an appointment because of a toothache. But Macmillan persisted, and Khrushchev backed away from the six-month ultimatum he had issued in November. The Soviet leader insisted that his real goal was *de facto* Western recognition of East Germany. He suggested a Big Four summit meeting to settle the German question but agreed with Macmillan that an essential prerequisite was a gathering of foreign ministers.

Several weeks later, Macmillan came to Washington to report on his journey to the Kremlin. During a meeting with Eisenhower, Macmillan became emotional and blurted out that the British "were not prepared to face obliteration for the sake of two million Berlin Germans, their former enemies, especially over issues such as the color of passes for motor convoys and the nationality of those who stamped them." It would take only eight atomic bombs, the prime minister reminded Eisenhower, to kill 30 million British people and destroy their economy. Eisenhower retorted that even more Americans would die in a nuclear war.[45] Later during his visit, Macmillan and the president called on Dulles, who was dying of cancer at Walter Reed Army Hospital. The secretary of state launched into a tirade about spending $40 billion annually on defense and then compromising whenever the Soviets threatened. "If appeasement and partial surrender are to be our attitude," he told his visitors, "we had better save our money."[46] Macmillan thought that Dulles's illness had "made his mind more rigid and reverting to very fixed concepts."[47] Although by no means so truculent, Eisenhower protested that he would not be forced to attend a summit conference that had no prospect of success. At the president's insistence, Macmillan agreed that such a Big Four meeting could occur only after their foreign ministers had made substantial progress. On 30 March, only days after Eisenhower and Macmillan released their communiqué, Khrushchev announced that he was prepared to send Foreign Minister Andrei Gromyko to a meeting in Geneva. The Berlin issue was no closer to settlement, but the crisis had passed.

The day Khrushchev's Berlin ultimatum expired—27 May 1959—the Big Four foreign ministers came to Washington, along with other foreign dignitaries, to attend the funeral of John Foster Dulles. For President Eisenhower, it was a day of unspeakable sorrow. The secretary of state had resigned in mid-April, when the severity of his illness made it impossible for him to continue his duties. As a final gesture of loyalty and friendship, the president had created a special advisory post for Dulles. For the president, watching his secretary of state die was arduous and painful. After one visit to Walter Reed, Eisenhower came back to the White House in a "queer mood," according to his secretary, Ann C. Whitman. He "seemed to want only to be left alone [and] said he was 'talked out.'"[48] Eisenhower felt "an overpowering loss" at Dulles's death, for however much the secretary of state seemed gruff and forbidding to others, there was a closeness he shared with Eisenhower that could never be replaced.[49]

Dulles's successor, Undersecretary Christian A. Herter, never played a leading role in the administration's foreign policy. Herter quickly established a good working relationship with Eisenhower. Yet though he had the president's confidence, Herter never developed the intimate mutual understanding with the president that his predecessor had enjoyed. The old procedure of daily White House consultations between secretary and president continued, but now each meeting was monitored by at least one executive assistant—something Dulles never allowed. Herter's responsibilities centered less on shaping basic policy than communicating it to Congress and the public.[50]

After convening in April 1959, the Geneva foreign ministers' meeting—Herter's first major assignment—made no progress in resolving differences over Berlin. The Soviets demanded Western acceptance of the division of Germany and the withdrawal of occupation troops from Berlin. Herter replied that Berlin's status was inextricably tied to

German reunification, which could occur only after free elections. Pending such arrangements, the Western foreign ministers offered to limit their forces in West Berlin and refrain from arming them with nuclear weapons. Neither side budged, and as Eisenhower later recollected, "no agreement of even the smallest kind was reached."[51]

Also stalled were talks on an issue that generated much greater public concern—the testing of nuclear weapons. During the first five years of Eisenhower's presidency, the Soviet Union and the United States frequently exploded hydrogen bombs in the atmosphere. The dangers of fallout quickly became a source of international alarm. An incident following the BRAVO test at Bikini atoll in March 1954 dramatically revealed the consequences of atmospheric testing. Sailors on a Japanese vessel, the *Lucky Dragon*, inadvertently were exposed to fallout when their ship came too close to the point of detonation of an H-bomb. One of the crew died several months later from the effects of what Japanese journalists called "ashes of death." During the mid-1950s, congressional and public protests occurred regularly against the dangers of radioactive fallout, a peril that claimed victims indiscriminately according to prevailing winds and that endangered future generations by causing genetic damage. Reflecting these common fears was Nevil Shute's best-selling novel, *On the Beach*, published in 1957, which told of a doomed world whose atmosphere was contaminated by an apocalyptic nuclear exchange. By the late 1950s, Eisenhower faced strong pressure to halt nuclear testing.[52]

He also encountered unyielding counsel to continue it. Lewis L. Strauss, the chair of the Atomic Energy Commission, insisted that testing was essential for the maintenance of American superiority in nuclear weapons. Testing, he argued, had enabled the United States to develop superior weapons technology; under a test ban the Soviets would be able to catch up through espionage and an accelerated program of research and development. The Joint Chiefs of Staff also repeatedly reminded Eisenhower that any moratorium on testing required effective monitoring to ensure compliance, and the Soviets were not willing to agree to a suitable inspection system. Edward Teller, a leading nuclear physicist, warned that the Soviets would be able to violate secretly any test ban. Defense Department officials insisted that further testing was needed to develop weapons that could be used to blunt a Soviet attack by destroying the incoming missiles. Strauss and Pentagon officials told Eisenhower that further testing was necessary—ironically—to produce "clean" bombs free of fallout.

Electoral and bureaucratic politics complicated the debate over nuclear testing. Eisenhower considered Adlai Stevenson's call for a test ban during the 1956 presidential campaign the lowest form of partisanship. The president frequently expressed his desire to achieve a test moratorium but too often yielded to the arguments of hard-line advisers. He reined in his own disarmament adviser, Harold Stassen, who proposed a Soviet-American moratorium on testing as a first step toward disarmament. When Stassen committed a diplomatic blunder at an international conference on arms control in London, Eisenhower allowed Dulles, who resented Stassen's independent authority, to issue a reprimand. On 31 March 1958, the Soviet Union announced a unilateral suspension of testing. Although he was forewarned of the Soviet demarche, Eisenhower was unable to forge a consensus among his advisers that enabled him to forestall the Soviet initiative. Many critics, both in the United States and abroad, lamented the inability of Eisenhower to provide moral leadership on such a fundamental issue.

Several months later, Eisenhower finally halted American testing. He announced at the end of August that the ban would take effect two months later and last indefinitely, provided that negotiations yielded progress toward an arms control agreement. Eisenhower reached his decision despite the "permanent fundamental disagreement" of Strauss. The president considered such action an essential step toward an international agreement on atomic energy, a goal he had long cherished but had not vigorously enough pursued. However constructive the American moratorium, it did not lead to international action. During the Geneva talks in 1959, the negotiators made little more progress on disarmament than on Berlin.[53]

With talks on those two issues stalled, pressure built for a summit conference to break the East-West deadlock. Khrushchev had repeatedly indicated he was eager for such a meeting. Macmillan also favored such a gathering because he thought that only Khrushchev had the authority to make an agreement with the Western powers. Before his death, Dulles had consistently discouraged Eisenhower from responding favorably to Khrushchev's overtures. He warned that the Soviets would merely exploit a summit for propaganda purposes and advised the president not to risk his prestige by participating in such an event. Eisenhower, too, was cool toward a Big Four meeting, but by mid-1959 he was prepared to talk directly to Khrushchev. He insisted, though, that there would be no invitation to the Soviet leader to visit the United States unless the foreign ministers first made some progress on Berlin. In short, Khrushchev would get the meeting he wanted, but only after making concessions at Geneva.

Robert Murphy conveyed Eisenhower's terms—or at least what he thought were the president's conditions—to the Soviets. On 12 July, Murphy extended an invitation when he met Soviet Deputy Premier Frol Koslov, who was in New York City to open a Russian Exhibition, part of a program of Soviet-American cultural exchanges. After learning of Koslov's startling news, Khrushchev accepted the invitation with alacrity. Eisenhower was flabbergasted, however, when Herter cabled from Geneva that the foreign ministers were still deadlocked over Berlin. After talking to Murphy, Eisenhower discovered to his great dismay that Murphy had not understood that the invitation had carried a prerequisite and so failed to inform Koslov. Furious over the state department's blunder, Eisenhower rebuked his assistants for their sloppy procedures. Had Dulles still been in charge, he believed, such a mistake would never have occurred.

The difficulties of dealing with Khrushchev became apparent during a trip that Vice-President Richard M. Nixon made to Moscow in late July. Nixon's visit had been scheduled months before the announcement of the Khrushchev-Eisenhower summit. The vice-president made his journey not to engage in negotiations, but to open the American Exhibition. Nevertheless, Nixon had to deal with the Soviet leader's bluster throughout his goodwill mission. Khrushchev was in bad humor because of the recent passage in Congress of the annual Captive Nations Resolution, which condemned Communist oppression in the Eastern bloc nations. He vented his wrath by comparing the congressional resolution to "fresh horse shit, and nothing smells worse than that!" Engaging in scatological one-upmanship, Nixon shot back, "I am afraid that the Chairman is mistaken. There is something that smells worse than horse shit—and that is pig shit."[54] Khrushchev grinned and conceded his error, but gave no further ground during Nixon's sojourn. At the American Exhibition, the two leaders stopped at a model kitchen and traded barbs about the superiority of their respective systems. This "kitchen debate"—one of the great media events of the Cold War— seemed to underscore Dulles's warnings about the tendency of East-West meetings to degenerate into propaganda forums.

However great the problems of dealing with Khrushchev or flawed the circumstances of their meeting, Eisenhower was determined to use the opportunity to further the cause of peace. During his last two years in office, Eisenhower hoped that he could leave as one of his principal legacies as president a détente in the Cold War. He explained to congressional leaders that he intended to make "one great personal effort, before leaving office, to soften up the Soviet leader even a little bit."[55] To a reporter who asked whether he worried about eroding his prestige, he snapped back, ''We are talking about the human race and what's going to happen to it.'' He reminded his interrogator that ''we are putting now, just in the engines and the training and preparations of war something on the order of $41 billion every year.'' Any ''President that refused finally to use the last atom of his prestige or the last atom of his energy'' to make such enormous expenditures unnecessary should ''be condemned by the American people,'' he exclaimed.[56]

In the weeks before Khrushchev's arrival, Eisenhower tried to calm apprehensions about the meeting. So vociferous was the reaction among some conservatives that William F. Buckley, Jr., proposed using red dye to make the Hudson ''a river of blood'' in protest against a visitor who ''profanes the nation.''[57] Eisenhower, however, emphasized the enormous benefit of allowing the Soviet leader to become acquainted with American life. Khrushchev, he insisted, should see Americans doing what they ordinarily did in cities and suburbs, on farms and in factories; even traffic jams and the current steel strike could prove that the United States was an affluent, mobile, and unregimented society. Eisenhower also tried to allay foreign concerns about the impending summit. Just before Khrushchev's arrival in the United States, the president took a quick trip—his first jet flight—to England, France, and West Germany to assure the heads of those countries that no deals would be made with the Soviet visitor that compromised Western interests.

As soon as he set foot on American soil on 15 September, Nikita Khrushchev created a stir. Never the model of tact, the Soviet leader presented the president with a replica of the Soviet Union's latest space success, a lunar projectile, launched only days earlier. Eisenhower accepted the gift with all the grace he could muster because ''the fellow might have been sincere.''[58] In public and private, Khrushchev made remarks that sounded boastful, outrageous, and condescending. At the United Nations, he proposed the elimination of all weapons—nuclear and conventional—in four years. As he traveled across the nation, he attracted a swarm of reporters who gleefully recorded his outrage over his exclusion from Disneyland or his professed shock over the pornographic exposure of women on the set of the movie Can Can. Henry Cabot Lodge, the UN ambassador who accompanied Khrushchev on his cross-country tour, informed Eisenhower that the Soviet leader's exploits would ''fill a book.''[59]

At the end of his jaunt, Khrushchev spent two days with Eisenhower at the presidential retreat at Camp David, Maryland. According to Ann Whitman, Eisenhower approached these conversations ''not with great anticipation but . . . with some dread.''[60] The president was pleasantly surprised, though, because he found that Khrushchev actually "was very convivial . . . , especially eager to be friendly. He kept belittling most of our differences and gave every indication of wanting to find ways to straighten them out through peaceful compromise."[61] Earlier in Khrushchev's visit, Eisenhower had taken the Soviet leader aside and appealed to him to seize a "priceless opportunity to go down in history as one of the truly great statesmen of all time."[62] Yet Eisenhower's plea produced no significant results. The two leaders agreed to meet again at a Big Four summit and, after that, during a presidential trip to the Soviet Union. Khrushchev returned to Russia praising the "spirit of Camp David," but that feeling did not produce agreements on Berlin, nuclear testing, or any other Cold War issue.

At the end of 1959, Eisenhower engaged in his most ambitious effort at personal diplomacy. He made an extended tour in December of southern Europe, the Near East, and South Asia. Having long believed that personal contacts promoted international understanding, Eisenhower hoped that his prestige, directness, warmth, and simplicity would build confidence in what he saw as the quest of the United States for a peaceful world. As he explained to reporters,

> I decided to make an effort that no President ever was called on before to make. I do feel a compulsion to visit a number of countries, and through them hoping to reach many others, and tell them exactly what I believe the United States is trying to do: that our basic aspiration is to search out methods by which peace in the world can be assured with justice for everybody. I want to prove that we are not aggressive, that we seek nobody else's territories or possessions; we do not seek to violate anybody else's rights. We are simply trying to be a good partner in this business of searching for peace.[63]

The president's journey was a great personal success, but by no means a diplomatic triumph. Throngs greeted him in India, Pakistan, Italy, and elsewhere. Eisenhower returned to the United States exhilarated, his sense of mutual dependence among distant and diverse peoples reinforced by his extensive travels. Observers hailed a "new Eisenhower," a leader who no longer shared the diplomatic spotlight with his late secretary of state and who finally used his greatest asset— his personality—to advance international goals. Yet Eisenhower also returned empty-handed. Aiming at no diplomatic agreements, he concluded none. His trip indicated a desire to move beyond the rigidities of the Cold War, but his policies—especially those concerning Third World nations—had not kept pace with his sincere, simple, and genuine desire to foster peace.

9

★ ★ ★ ★ ★

BEYOND HIS GRASP

"Seven years ago I entered my present office with one long-held resolve overriding others," President Eisenhower declared in his state of the union address in January 1960. "I was then, and remain now, determined that the United States shall become an ever more potent resource for the cause of peace."[1] As his presidency neared its end, Eisenhower appeared to be within reach of achieving the goal of relaxing Cold War tensions. At home, despite facing a Congress with overwhelming Democratic majorities, he had been remarkably successful at holding the line against increased federal spending, especially in defense. He looked forward to his final year in office "full of drive, enthusiasm and a desire to attack on all fronts."[2]

Yet only months later, his hopes had collapsed. The Big Four summit in Paris, where the president had looked forward to signing an arms control agreement, ended in disarray after the Soviets shot down an American U-2 spy plane over their territory. Eisenhower's influence in Congress evaporated as Democrats—and even some Republicans—voted to increase spending to improve their chances in the fall elections. The final disappointment occurred when Vice-President Richard M. Nixon lost in his bid to succeed Eisenhower in the White House. A year that began with hopes of peace and prosperity ended with renewed Cold War tensions, recession, and repudiation.

Although Democrats enjoyed almost two-to-one majorities in both

211

houses of the Eighty-sixth Congress, Eisenhower demonstrated a surprising ability to achieve his goals during the first session in 1959. For some of his success, the president could thank the new Republican leadership. After William F. Knowland gave up his senate seat to make an unsuccessful run for governor of California, Everett M. Dirksen of Illinois succeeded him as minority leader. Although he often voted with the Old Guard, Dirksen consistently supported the president on economic issues. In the House, the new minority leader was Charles A. Halleck of Indiana, who deposed Joseph W. Martin. Like Dirksen, Halleck got along well with the president and skillfully mobilized GOP support for legislation that the White House considered essential.

Yet however much the Republican leadership helped him win important votes, the main reason for Eisenhower's success in 1959 was his own determination and vigor. He quickly recovered from the discouragement of the Democratic landslide in the election of 1958 and vowed to fight with all his energy against "the spenders" whom the voters had put in office. By identifying these legislators as his opponents, Eisenhower shrewdly left the door open to cooperation with conservative Democrats. He needed their cooperation to balance the budget and reduce inflationary pressures, the economic peril about which he worried most. To do so he also decided to carry out public appearances more aggressively to mobilize support for a balanced budget.

In defense of his fiscal 1960 budget, Eisenhower fought his most effective battle of the budget. When he presented his spending proposals to Congress in January 1959, the economy had only recently pulled out of a recession. One of the effects of that slump was a $12 billion deficit for fiscal year 1959, a new record for a budget shortfall in peacetime. Fearful that so much red ink would cause a rise in inflation, Eisenhower asked Congress to approve a balanced budget of $77 billion. Although Eisenhower asked for $3 billion less in expenditures than the previous year, the real savings came in resisting demands for substantial increases in domestic programs. During the next several months, he vetoed bill after bill—including housing and farm legislation twice—that he said the country could not afford. By the time it adjourned, Congress had hardly increased spending, and the budget ran a surplus—the third and last of Eisenhower's presidency—of $1.3 billion.[3] All in all, Eisenhower's ability in holding down spending was a resounding victory, all the more so because it was so unlikely.

The White House also counted as a success the enactment in September 1959 of Landrum-Griffin labor legislation. The original bill, whose principal sponsor was John F. Kennedy (D., Mass.), was far different. After sensational Senate investigations into labor racketeering, Kennedy introduced a bill protecting union finances, guaranteeing workers the right to vote by secret ballot on the question of union representation, and containing other provisions endorsed by organized labor. Eisenhower thought the bill did not go far enough to get gangsters out of the unions. Republicans and conservative Democrats insisted on a sweeping revision and got some support from Majority Leader Lyndon B. Johnson, who was thinking about a run for the White House and willing to try to diminish Kennedy's presidential prospects. The Landrum-Griffin Act imposed new restrictions on secondary boycotts and increased the power of states to regulate unions, provisions that organized labor condemned. Eisenhower, however, praised the law for its anticorruption provisions.[4]

One of the few major defeats Eisenhower suffered was Senate rejection of his nomination of Lewis L. Strauss to be secretary of commerce. In view of Strauss's long service on the Atomic Energy Commission, Eisenhower thought that there was no question about his nominee's qualifications. But some legislators had not forgotten Strauss's devious, disdainful answers during congressional investigation of the Dixon-Yates contract. Nor did they think that the AEC had acted properly in revoking the security clearance of J. Robert Oppenheimer. Strauss's combative, even truculent, manner won him no friends during his confirmation hearings. The Senate voted him down, forty-nine to forty-six, on 19 June 1959, the first time in a quarter century that a cabinet nominee had failed to be confirmed.

Although he was bitter about the Strauss defeat, Eisenhower was optimistic about the second session of the Eighty-sixth Congress. "The home stretch is upon us," he wrote to Press Secretary James C. Hagerty at the end of 1959, but "a thoroughbred tries to make his best effort in the last furlong."[5] Once more he told his cabinet that "the watchwords" should be frugality, economy, simplicity, and efficiency.[6] In accordance with those principles he presented Congress in January 1960 with a budget for the coming fiscal year that had only modest increases in spending—practically none overall in defense—and with a substantial surplus.

With unprecedented fury, Congress attacked the defense budget. In an election year, beefing up defense spending seemed to be a way of winning votes and, for some Democratic hopefuls, proving both their expertise and the inadequacies of Eisenhower's leadership. Senator Stuart Symington of Missouri, for example, renewed his charges that a missile gap had opened between the Soviet Union and the United States. Lyndon Johnson, the chair of the Senate Aeronautical and Space

Committee, provided a forum for Gen. Thomas Power, the head of the Strategic Air Command, to make public his case for more money for missiles and bombers. Gen. Maxwell Taylor, former army chief of staff, also appeared before Johnson's committee and demanded immediate and "heroic measures." What was needed was "men, money, and sacrifice. The alternative is military inferiority—and there is no living long with communism as an inferior."[7]

Angered by these challenges to his own military competence, Eisenhower lashed back at his critics. About the supposed missile gap, he told reporters on 3 February, "I am always a little bit amazed about this business of catching up. What you want is enough, a thing that is adequate. A deterrent has no added power, once it has become completely adequate, for compelling the respect of any potential opponent." Two weeks later, he put the matter more directly. "Our defense is not only strong," he assured the public, "it is awesome, and it is respected elsewhere." At the same time, he told reporters that he thoroughly resented the partisan charges that he had let economy take precedence over security. "If anybody—anybody—believes that I have deliberately misled the American people, I'd like to tell him to his face what I think about him. This is a charge that I think is despicable." The real problem, though, was that too many people simply thought that more money made for better defense. "I get tired of saying that defense is to be made an excuse for wasting dollars," he complained to the press. "I don't believe that we should pay one cent for defense more than we have to."[8]

While Eisenhower tried to hold the line in Washington against higher defense spending, he hoped that the Paris summit in May and his visit to the Soviet Union in June would produce an agreement that would slow the momentum of the arms race. Eisenhower considered détente with the Soviet Union a real possibility. In his state of the union address in 1960, he noted that Khrushchev now seemed genuinely ready to cooperate in "diminishing the intensity of past rivalry."[9] Eisenhower, too, wanted to reduce Cold War tensions, and he was determined to sign a nuclear test ban treaty before leaving office. In Geneva, Soviet, British, and American negotiators narrowed their differences over such an accord. At times, the president rejected the pleas of John A. McCone, the chair of the Atomic Energy Commission, to avoid making concessions. Instead he declared that he would "probe in every way the sincerity and intent of the Soviet declaration on disarmament."[10] Gaining an accord on nuclear testing was no favor to the Soviets, he asserted, but a "vital" American interest. It would provide "a ray of light in a world that is bound to be weary of the tensions brought about by mutual suspicion, distrust and arms races."[11]

Khrushchev also spoke optimistically about the prospects for peaceful coexistence. He returned from his summit meeting with Eisenhower in September 1959 extolling Soviet-American friendship and ebullient over the forthcoming Big Four summit and the president's visit to the Soviet Union. Khrushchev certainly saw successful East-West negotiations as a means of increasing his stature as a world statesman. But he was also quite serious about reducing the risk of war and, as Ambassador Llewellyn Thompson reported, making "progress in the reduction of armaments."[12] Khrushchev also hoped for cooperation in preventing West Germany and China from acquiring atomic arsenals. Traditional fears accounted for his opposition to a nuclearized Germany. So strong were his apprehensions that he might have been prepared to renounce his demands for Western recognition of East Germany in return for Eisenhower's agreement not to allow atomic weapons on German soil. Concern about Chinese challenges to Soviet leadership and distrust of Mao Tse-tung made him dread the prospect of a Chinese atomic bomb. Khrushchev thus saw détente as a way to increase Soviet security.

Yet however much he wanted détente with the United States, Khrushchev was not prepared to ignore violations of Soviet airspace by American U-2 spy planes. At altitudes of 60,000 feet, U-2s had been flying over the Soviet Union since 1956, their pilots photographing Soviet military installations. The Soviets had infrequently protested these violations of their airspace but had never publicly complained. To do so would only be to admit that Soviet armed forces were incapable of protecting their own territory. Khrushchev said nothing about the U-2 missions at the Camp David summit, but he did obliquely warn the Western nations in October 1959 to do nothing that might jeopardize the next Big Four meeting. At about the same time, the U-2 missions over Soviet territory ceased, but then one occurred on 9 April 1960. Khrushchev was outraged. He considered the intrusion an act of war. Furthermore, he thought that the resumption of the flights made him look like a fool in the eyes of Kremlin hardliners, who had long been skeptical of peaceful coexistence. Yet Khrushchev did not protest, for fear of only confirming once more that the U-2 flew too high and too fast for Soviet air defenses.

Despite Khrushchev's failure to complain, Eisenhower realized the dangers of the U-2 missions. The president had halted the missions for several months in 1959/60 precisely because of his desire to nurture the fragile prospects of détente. In the event that a U-2 went down in Soviet territory, he predicted that "a wave of excitement mounting almost to panic would sweep the world inspired by the standard Soviet claim of injustice, unfairness, aggression, and ruthlessness."[13] Secretary of State John Foster Dulles had been far more sanguine and had insisted that the Soviets would never admit the downing of a U-2 since they would have to concede that they had been unable to do anything about countless earlier violations of their territory. CIA Director Allen W. Dulles and his deputy Richard Bissell, who supervised the U-2 program, assured Eisenhower that the Soviets would never be able to recover a plane with its espionage instruments intact or its pilot alive. With a chorus of Democratic legislators crying "missile gap," it was essential to monitor Soviet air bases, Dulles and Bissell insisted, especially since the Russians appeared to be on the verge of deploying their first operational intercontinental ballistic missiles armed with nuclear warheads. Because of the importance of that information, Eisenhower authorized the 9 April U-2 flight and a second mission, provided it took place no later than 1 May 1960—just fifteen days before the opening of the Paris summit.

For the pilot of that last U-2 mission, Francis Gary Powers, May Day had a doubly disastrous meaning. After taking off from a base at Peshawar, Pakistan, and flying more than thirteen hundred miles into Soviet airspace, Power's plane went down near Sverdlovsk, probably because of damage caused by the near miss of a surface-to-air missile. Despite CIA assurances that the plane was so fragile that it would disintegrate in a crash, its electronic instruments survived the impact. Powers parachuted to safety and decided not to use his poison pin. The downing of the U-2 occurred on a great national holiday in the Soviet Union. Khrushchev heard the spectacular news while reviewing a parade of Soviet military might atop the Lenin-Stalin tomb in Red Square.

After receiving reports that the U-2 was missing and probably down, Eisenhower and his advisers tried to conceal the nature of its mission. On 3 May, the president authorized the release of a cover story that the CIA had prepared when the U-2 missions began. Few Americans probably even noticed a story in their newspapers the following day about a missing NASA plane that had been conducting high-altitude weather studies in eastern Turkey. But they certainly did notice reports about Khrushchev's sensational announcement on 5 May that the Soviets had shot down an American spy plane. Hagerty, who was unaware of the U-2 flights because they were so sensitive, pleaded with Eisenhower to meet with reporters and personally refute Khrushchev's allegations. The president refused, but he did authorize another statement that conceded only that the missing NASA plane might have strayed into Soviet territory.

Khrushchev then exposed the president's lie with an even more sensational disclosure. "Comrades, I must let you in on a secret," he told the Supreme Soviet on 7 May. "When I made my report two days ago, I deliberately refrained from mentioning that we have the remnants of the plane—*and we also have the pilot, who is quite alive and kicking!*" "Unbelievable," Eisenhower exclaimed when he found out that what the CIA had repeatedly promised could never occur had now happened. Even more unbelievable was the president's decision to keep on lying. While Eisenhower played golf in Gettysburg so as not to arouse public fears, Secretary of State Christian A. Herter supervised the drafting of a statement designed to get Eisenhower "off the hook." After obtaining the president's authorization, the State Department disclosed that U-2s had been flying along the Soviet border to gather intelligence, a practice made necessary by excessive Soviet secrecy that interfered with legitimate American efforts to protect against surprise attack. Yet even though these reconnaissance flights had been going on for four years, the State Department still asserted that no one in Washington had authorized the May Day mission. The statement revealed what no previous president had acknowledged: that the United States engaged in foreign espionage. What it did not concede was that the president approved—or, for that matter, even knew—about these intelligence missions.[14]

Eisenhower had a hunch that the statement might be a mistake, and the stormy reaction sustained his intuition. Editorial writers and columnists skewered the president. If Eisenhower had not authorized the doomed flight, they wondered, who had? If the president truly had not given the mission his approval, was it because he had abdicated his powers to Dulles or Herter or was simply too busy with golf? Had the president or his associates established a system that allowed a local commander or pilot to fly over the Soviet Union at his own discretion? And if an espionage mission over the Soviet Union could go forward without authorization from Washington, could a B-52 pilot launch a nuclear attack on his own initiative? So depressed was Eisenhower by the public reaction that he told his secretary, Ann C. Whitman, "I would like to resign."[15]

Instead he decided to take responsibility for the U-2 debacle. He told his son John on 9 May, "We're going to take a beating on this. And I'm the one, rightly, who is going to have to take the brunt."[16] Later that afternoon, the State Department issued yet another statement that justified aerial surveillance as a means of preventing the Soviet Union from making "secret preparations" that might force the United States to choose between "abject surrender or nuclear destruction." The State Department now revealed that the president had authorized the program of U-2 intelligence missions. But, again, the statement stopped short of full disclosure in an effort to shield Eisenhower. "Specific missions . . . ," the State Department asserted, "have not been subject to Presidential authorization." In reply to critics who predicted that the Paris summit would collapse, the statement concluded that the U-2 incident "should serve to underline the importance to the world of an earnest attempt . . . to achieve agreed and effective safeguards against surprise attack and aggression."[17]

The new statement made Khrushchev livid. Following the downing of Powers's plane, the Soviet leader found himself in a difficult situation. Exposing the Americans as aggressors would only destroy the chances for détente that Khrushchev himself had so carefully cultivated. Withholding information that Powers was alive might encourage the Eisenhower administration to issue false statements that Khrushchev could then refute, but at the cost of discrediting the Soviet leader's own repeated assertions that the president was the friend of the Soviet people. Khrushchev apparently hoped both to silence his critics, who charged that he was not tough enough with the West, and to soften up Eisenhower on the eve of the Paris summit. The Soviet leader knew that he was playing a dangerous game and became enraged when Eisenhower failed to cooperate. Rather than disavowing responsibility for the U-2 flights as Khrushchev had hoped, Eisenhower accepted it, albeit belatedly, and even justified the violation of Soviet airspace as necessary and legitimate. Khrushchev told reporters that his opinion of Eisenhower had changed and that he was horrified that the president authorized the U-2 missions. There was now no way to appease Khrushchev's honor without humiliating the president of the United States.

By the time the two leaders arrived in Paris in mid-May, there was little chance of salvaging the summit. As the aggrieved party, Khrushchev waited for Eisenhower to call on him before the beginning of formal sessions. The president had no intention of doing so, since he thought that he had nothing to be sorry about. He told reporters before departing for Paris that the real issues at the Big Four meeting were disarmament and Berlin—not the U-2. Khrushchev, however, said that settling the U-2 matter was a prerequisite to further negotiations. The Soviet leader told French President Charles de Gaulle that he demanded an American apology, punishment of those responsible for the U-2 flights, and a promise that there would be no further violations of Soviet sovereignty. When Eisenhower learned of these terms, he was convinced that Khrushchev was determined to wreck the summit. In anticipation of a crisis, he placed American armed forces on alert on the eve of the first formal meeting of the Big Four.

Khrushchev, Eisenhower, de Gaulle, and British Prime Minister Harold Macmillan met together for the first and last time in Paris in a stormy session on 16 May at the Elysée Palace. The Soviet leader demanded the floor and launched into a tirade against American aggression. His anger was more than official; he felt betrayed by a man whom he had until recently considered a friend. As Eisenhower listened to this indictment of his conduct, his neck and bald head turned ever darker shades of red as he struggled to control his temper. The Soviet people could no longer welcome Eisenhower, Khrushchev continued, and so must postpone his visit. The summit conference would also have to be deferred until Eisenhower was out of office unless the president complied with the Soviet ultimatum.

None of the three other leaders could persuade Khrushchev to relent. Eisenhower announced that there would be no further U-2 missions and revived a version of his Open Skies proposal for aerial surveillance flights conducted by UN aircraft. Macmillan urged Khrushchev to be realistic: espionage, however deplorable, was something that all nations practiced. Eisenhower, he thought, had gone a long way toward meeting Soviet objections by calling off further U-2 flights. De Gaulle ridiculed Khrushchev's complaints. He reminded his Soviet guest that the newest Sputnik, launched on the eve of the summit, was flying over French territory many times each day. Furthermore, if Khrushchev was so offended that he could not negotiate, why, de Gaulle asked, had he wasted everybody's time by allowing them to come to the summit under false pretenses? None of these statements, accusations, or questions mollified Khrushchev or encouraged him to yield. When the conference resumed the next day, Khrushchev simply refused to attend.

Although he regretted the breakdown of the summit, Eisenhower placed strict limits on American efforts to conciliate the Soviets. When he learned of Khrushchev's demands, he threw a fit. The Soviet leader was a "son-of-a-bitch," who was "completely intransigent and insulting to the United States." He had had his fill of Khrushchev's posturing. "I'm just fed up!" he yelled to his associates.[18] In the critical forty-eight hours between the presentation of Khrushchev's ultimatum and the collapse of the talks, there was no effort to try to work out a deal between Soviet and American officials. Bitterness, disappointment, and vindictiveness on both sides—and on the highest levels—made any such efforts impossible. Indeed throughout the U-2 incident there was a remarkable absence of Soviet-American diplomatic efforts to resolve the controversy.

After returning home, the president enjoyed a temporary spurt in popularity. At the airport, a cheering crowd gave him a reception reminiscent of those he had received at the end of World War II. Over the next few days, Eisenhower's rating in the Gallup Poll rose by 4 percent. A solid majority of 58 percent in the Gallup Poll believed that Eisenhower had effectively handled the U-2 crisis.[19] Reporting to the nation in a televised address, Eisenhower laid the blame for the failed summit squarely on Khrushchev. Soviet offense over the U-2 incident was nothing more than hypocrisy. Khrushchev had lodged no complaint about the flights at Camp David in 1959. Soviet agents were continuously trying to secure secret information about American defenses. Once again the president insisted that he had done the right thing by ordering the U-2 to enter Soviet airspace, even so soon before the Paris summit. Using a familiar, frightening, but hardly appropriate historical analogy, he declared, ''From Pearl Harbor we learned that even negotiation itself can be used to conceal preparations for a surprise attack.''[20]

Yet though he appeared to show no remorse about the breakdown of the summit, Eisenhower privately was despondent. He told his science adviser, George B. Kistiakowsky, that ''the stupid U-2 mess'' had spoiled all his hopes of ''ending the cold war.'' No temporary rise in the polls could compensate for the evaporation of his dreams of leaving a legacy of détente as his greatest achievement. He confided to Kistiakowsky that ''he saw nothing worthwhile . . . to do now until the end of his presidency.''[21]

Yet Eisenhower had to devote considerable energy to dealing with the repercussions of the U-2 incident. In an election year, the debacle of the U-2 and the Paris summit provided an extraordinary opportunity for the Democrats. On Capitol Hill, the Democratic leadership launched an investigation into the Eisenhower administration's handling of the crisis. Although the final report blamed bad luck for the downing of the U-2, the chair of the inquiry, Senator J. William Fulbright repeatedly faulted political officials for ineptitude.

Almost as if to test that conclusion, another American reconnaissance plane disappeared on a mission over the Barents Sea near the northern coast of the Soviet Union. The plane was an RB-47 based in Great Britain whose mission was electronic eavesdropping. When the aircraft vanished on 1 July, the Soviets again delayed making any announcement. But this time so did the Eisenhower administration. When the Soviets revealed ten days later that they had shot down the plane and captured two crew members, Eisenhower was furious. American radar stations had tracked the plane and indicated that it went down in international waters. As much as he wanted to expose the fraudulence of Khrushchev's claims that the United States had again violated Soviet sovereignty, he refrained from doing so because the existence of the radar stations was secret. Eisenhower suffered the insults, but he revealed to Herter that he now did not trust the Soviets "to the slightest degree."[22]

Just as frustrating was congressional action to increase the defense budget. Senate Majority Leader Johnson asserted, "I cannot help but feel that Mr. Khrushchev would not have felt so free to abuse and humiliate our President if he had more respect for our future military strength." Eisenhower's own succession of warnings about surprise attack in defense of the U-2 missions also seemed to prove to many legislators that American defenses required strengthening. Congress eventually approved expenditures of $41.7 billion, which exceeded the president's request by $700 million. The legislation provided for $394 million more than the administration budget for missiles launched from the Polaris submarine. It also provided additional funds for Atlas ICBMs, air defense, and the B-70 bomber, which Eisenhower had tried to cancel. The defense budget was a significant political victory for the Democrats. Indeed so popular was the issue of increasing defense spending that many Republicans broke with the president.[23]

The U-2 incident caused problems for Eisenhower not only in Washington, but also overseas. Eisenhower still intended to travel to Japan, where he had originally planned to stop after his visit to the Soviet Union. To make up for the cancellation of Khrushchev's invitation, the president added the Philippines, Taiwan, South Korea, and Okinawa to his itinerary. Eisenhower began this East Asian journey on 12 June, but he did not make all the stops. Demonstrators in the streets of Japan protested against the ratification of a Japanese-American mutual defense treaty and the use of a Japanese base for U-2 flights. When Hagerty arrived with an advance party, a crowd attacked his car, and he had to be rescued by a marine helicopter. Because of the ferocious opposition to Eisenhower's visit, the Japanese prime minister canceled the invitation. "Viewed from any angle," the president recollected, "this was a Communist victory."[24]

The shadow of the U-2 also hung over Eisenhower's journey to the United Nations in September. Khrushchev announced that he too would attend the General Assembly, and many observers wondered whether there would be another summit. Eisenhower, however, thought that talking to Khrushchev was now pointless. He also opposed—and ultimately helped defeat—a General Assembly resolution, sponsored by five neutral nations, calling for a meeting of the two leaders. Both separately addressed the General Assembly, as did Macmillan. Far more memorable than Khrushchev's speech was his reaction to Macmillan's address. The Soviet leader took off his shoe and pounded it on the desk in childish anger. Eisenhower had grown so disgusted with his Russian adversary that he told Herter that if he had absolute power, he would use it to "launch an attack on Russia while Khrushchev is in New York."[25] That remark was a sad measure of how thoroughly the prospects of détente had withered.

No less infuriating than Khrushchev was Fidel Castro. In January 1959, Castro and his revolutionary army overthrew Fulgencio Batista, a tyrant who had ruled Cuba since 1952 with lavish support from the United States. Until his last months in power, Batista had received military assistance and subsidies for Cuban sugar exports in return for his protection of U.S. investments on the island and support for the Eisenhower administration's anti-Communist initiatives. Only after Batista rigged elections and allowed his air force to bomb civilian areas while fighting against Castro's guerrillas did Eisenhower halt the flow of arms in March 1958. Batista rejected an eleventh-hour U.S. plan to cede power to a military junta to prevent Castro from taking control. Finally, in mid-December, the Eisenhower administration, convinced that Batista's days were numbered, withdrew support from its erstwhile client. Two weeks later, Batista fled, and Castro triumphantly entered Havana.

Although Eisenhower by no means welcomed Castro's success, he did try at first to cooperate with the new Cuban leader. The State Department promptly extended diplomatic recognition and conveyed its "sincere goodwill . . . toward the new Government and people of Cuba." Privately, administration officials fully expected Castro to implement an extensive program of social reform. Many Latin American experts considered such changes salubrious in view of the corruption and stagnation that had flourished under Batista. Because of overdependence on sugar production, for example, 25 percent of the island's work force was unemployed or underemployed, except during the busy harvest season. Poverty, malnutrition, illiteracy, and squalid working conditions all were common parts of Cuban life. Castro would undoubtedly impose reforms aimed at alleviating such harsh conditions. But in the reckoning of the CIA, Castro was no Communist.[26]

Even if Castro was not a Communist, Eisenhower soon found him unpalatable. Within weeks after seizing power, the Cuban leader drove moderates out of the government and postponed elections for at least two years. Particularly objectionable was the imposition of revolutionary justice, usually at the behest of impassioned crowds who cheered the gruesome work of the firing squads. So deplorable did Eisenhower consider these actions that the president left Washington to avoid meeting Castro, who toured the United States in April 1959 at the invitation of the American Society of Newspaper Editors. Nixon stood in and reported that the Cuban leader was emotional and volatile. But U.S. influence, properly applied, could push Castro "in the right direction," Nixon insisted.[27]

Such hopes were futile, Eisenhower concluded after traveling to Latin America at the beginning of 1960. Castro's lieutenants, he learned, were already in contact with leftist organizations in Panama, the Dominican Republic, and other nations. On returning to the White House, Eisenhower insisted that Castro was "a madman" who "is going wild and harming the whole American structure."[28] Further efforts to work with Castro would be futile, the administration decided. Eisenhower had come to view Castro much as he had Jacobo Arbenz Guzmán six years earlier.

On 17 March 1960, the president decided to bring down Castro. Following meetings with the NSC and a task force from the CIA, Eisenhower approved a memorandum entitled "A Program of Covert Action against the Castro Regime." It authorized a propaganda offensive against Castro and the creation of a Cuban exile government. To help this alternative regime gain power, Eisenhower also approved steps to develop "a paramilitary force outside of Cuba for future guerrilla action."[29] Drawing on its experience in Guatemala in 1954, the CIA prepared to overthrow another Latin American government.

The CIA even went so far as to try to have Castro assassinated. CIA technicians devised bizarre schemes to do away with the Cuban dictator. One involved a booby-trapped sea shell that would be planted in an area where Castro went skin diving. To carry out the execution, the CIA enlisted figures from organized crime. Eisenhower's involvement in this plotting is uncertain. CIA procedures on assassination aimed at providing the president with plausible deniability, the ability to maintain that he was unaware and unconnected with any such activities. Yet CIA actions seemed to accord with Eisenhower's wishes. Eisenhower repeatedly called Castro a madman and a "little Hitler."[30] Certainly assassination seemed an acceptable means of dealing with such a threat to U.S. security.

The Eisenhower administration also applied economic pressure against Castro. Angered by Soviet purchases of Cuban sugar, Eisenhower all but closed the U.S. market to the island's sugar exporters for the remainder of 1960. In October, the president imposed tight restrictions on Cuban-U.S. trade in hopes of disrupting the island's economy. Castro retaliated by nationalizing U.S.-owned properties in Cuba. And he deepened his ties with the Soviet Union. The Russians agreed to buy the sugar that had previously gone to U.S. markets. They also started furnishing Castro with military supplies. Eisenhower concluded that such transactions proved that Castro had become an agent of international communism.

Because economic sanctions and diplomatic pressure did nothing to weaken Castro's rule, the CIA's plans for covert action were crucial. By late 1960, the CIA had established secret bases in Guatemala for the training of Cuban exiles. Its goal was to build a guerrilla army of about 750 men who would invade the island and set off a general uprising against the Castro regime. Eisenhower wanted the CIA to be ready to launch the attack as soon as possible, since Castro was using Soviet military aid to strengthen his military forces.

Eisenhower's authorization of planning for the overthrow of Castro indicated how important interventionism had become in his Latin American policy. In his state of the union message in January 1960, Eisenhower had repeated an earlier promise that "the United States has no intention of interfering in the internal affairs of any nation." "We reject any attempt to impose . . . [a political] system . . . on other peoples by force or subversion."[31] Now, a year later, as his second term was ending, Eisenhower disregarded those pledges in dealing with Cuba.

By late 1960, Castro had learned of the CIA's clandestine training of an invasion force. Information about those activities also leaked out to several newspapers. President-elect Kennedy seemed generally to approve of the CIA's plans to invade Cuba when he learned of them in mid-November from Allen Dulles. During his last two months in office, Eisenhower decided to get even tougher with Castro. The State Department made plans to enlist the Latin American nations in a trade embargo. The CIA enlarged the guerrilla army and equipped it with heavier weapons. Castro applied pressure of his own. After the Cuban dictator announced new limitations on the number of Americans employed at the U.S. embassy in Havana, Eisenhower severed diplomatic relations on 3 January 1961. The president hoped that this step might provoke Castro into retaliatory action that would build support in the United States for even stronger measures to bring down the Cuban ruler.

Eisenhower's belligerent actions toward Castro were part of a shift in the administration's Latin American policy during Eisenhower's last year in office. As always, Eisenhower believed that the principal danger to U.S. security interests in Latin America was communism. The advent of Castro persuaded the president and his principal advisors that the Communist threat had become intolerable. Increasingly the president blamed the growth of communism on Latin American dictators, like Batista, who had frustrated all legitimate demands for reform and so had encouraged the growth of radical opposition. The Eisenhower administration thus no longer saw Latin American tyrants, no matter how strongly anticommunist or protective of U.S. investments, as desirable allies. At the same time that the CIA plotted against Castro, it also tried to depose the reactionary leader of the Dominican Republic, Rafael Trujillo. The Dominican dictator refused U.S. suggestions that he step aside by declaring, "You can come in here with the Marines, and you can come in here with the Army, and you can come in here with the Navy or even the atomic bomb, but I'll never go out of here unless I go on a stretcher." In May 1960, Eisenhower declared that he wanted to see Trujillo "sawed off." A year later he was. The dissidents who assassinated Trujillo had received arms from the CIA, although they may not have used those particular weapons in the murder.[32]

Another new part of the Eisenhower administration's Latin American policy was expanded economic assistance. In mid-1960, the president announced the creation of the Social Progress Trust Fund, a $500 million project to improve health, housing, and agriculture. The administration also altered its trade policies to conform to long-standing Latin American demands. Again, the goal of these steps was the containment of communism. Poverty, disease, and despair bred radicalism, the administration now believed. Although the Social Progress Trust Fund began only in the final months of the Eisenhower presidency, it provided the foundation for the Alliance for Progress during the Kennedy administration.

By the middle of 1960, Eisenhower believed that the Cold War had reached a new peak of danger. The breakdown of the Paris summit had brought mutual recriminations from the two leaders who months earlier had tried to forge détente. And, at the same time, the Communists had accelerated their efforts in the Third World, where nationalist movements generated demands for radical change. "The world has developed a kind of ferment greater than [I can] remember in recent times," Eisenhower told Herter. Much as they had in Cuba, Communists were everywhere trying to capitalize on this turbulence, the president thought.[33]

Another "Castro or worse," the Eisenhower administration feared, was Patrice Lumumba, the prime minister of the Congo. After receiving its independence from Belgium on 30 June 1960, the Congo was torn by factional strife and a secessionist movement in Katanga, a region rich in uranium. Lumumba tried to quiet the turmoil by welcoming a UN peacekeeping force and asking for American aid. Administration officials replied that they were channeling all their assistance to the Congo through the UN. While stressing that they declined to send assistance directly to the Congo to avoid interfering with UN efforts to restore stability, administration officials actually refused to help Lumumba because they were convinced he was a Communist. CIA Director Dulles told the National Security Council that it was safe to assume "that Lumumba had been bought by the Communists." Undersecretary of State C. Douglas Dillon declared that the Congolese prime minister was "working to serve the purposes of the Soviets." Lumumba's request for Soviet arms only seemed to confirm the speculation and extrapolation of Dulles and Dillon and to justify strong action against the Congolese leader.

In August 1960, a special committee that supervised CIA covert operations agreed to take steps to get rid of Lumumba and to do so without ruling out "any particular kind of activity." The participants knew that their euphemistic instructions sanctioned assassination. Nowhere did they leave any written proof of presidential involvement, but again many participants in the meeting believed that they were acting with Eisenhower's knowledge and approval. In September, a CIA agent known as "Joe from Paris" arrived in the Congolese capital of Leopoldville with poison for Lumumba's food or toothpaste that would produce a fatal disease. The plot was never carried out, and the Congo crisis abated. But once again, the Eisenhower administration acted mainly on suspicion and fear to turn nationalist turmoil into Cold War conflict.[34]

Frustrated in international affairs, Eisenhower hoped to find vindication at the polls. He thought that the results of the election of 1960 not only would determine the next chief executive, but also reveal whether the public considered *his* presidency a success. So even though he could not be a candidate, Eisenhower felt a keen sense of involvement in the campaign. He was determined to use his influence to elect a Republican successor.

Before the nominating convention, he used it ineptly. Although Nixon was the leading candidate for the GOP nomination, Eisenhower could not bring himself to endorse his own vice-president. He still harbored reservations about Nixon's character, partisanship, and maturity. Privately he hoped that Robert B. Anderson, the secretary of the Treasury, would seek the nomination. Anderson realized that his chances were close to nil. Early in the year, Eisenhower released a list of a dozen potential GOP candidates, and Nixon's name was last. Yet only Governor Nelson A. Rockefeller of New York mounted a serious challenge to Nixon, who was far and away the first choice of party regulars. Even though Rockefeller had previously worked in his administration, Eisenhower could not abide the governor's candidacy because of Rockefeller's call for higher defense spending. Thus, he was pleased—if only by default—with Nixon's nomination by the Republican National Convention in Chicago in July and the vice-president's choice of Henry Cabot Lodge for the second spot on the ticket. Yet his failure to issue an endorsement before the convention suggested that the president continued to have doubts about Nixon's qualifications for the White House.

Reports from the Nixon camp suggested that the reservations were reciprocal. Some of the Nixon people resented the president's persistent habit of keeping the vice-president at arm's length, and they were eager to run the campaign without Eisenhower's interference. They also worried about the difficulties of defending the president's record after the collapse of the Paris summit and the emergence of trouble in Cuba and the Congo. One high official at Nixon's campaign headquarters privately remarked that he wanted nothing more from Eisenhower except for him to "handle Khrushchev at the UN and not let things blow up there."[35] Obviously the results of the General Assembly meeting must have dismayed the Nixon strategists even more.

But the Nixon camp was far more upset by Eisenhower's blundering remarks at a news conference. Because Nixon was emphasizing that he had far more experience in governing than his Democratic opponent, Senator John F. Kennedy of Massachusetts, reporters asked Eisenhower for examples of the vice-president's contributions to major decisions. Eisenhower replied rather impatiently on 24 August that only the president could be responsible for the administration's actions. Once more the question arose, and once more Eisenhower replied with exasperation that Nixon was "not a part of decision-making. That has to be in the mind and heart of one man." A third time the issue came up, when a reporter inquired, "I just wondered if you could give us an example of a major idea of his that you had adopted in that role, as the decider and final—" Cutting off his interrogator, Eisenhower blurted out, "If you give me a week, I might think of one. I don't remember."[36]

When the statement was printed, Republicans grimaced and Democrats grinned. Eisenhower was angry at the reporters who pressed him, but he realized that the mistake was his own. The remark was the product of his famous temper, which he rarely showed in public, and, perhaps, his own long-standing reservations about Nixon. The president complained that his comment was blown wildly out of proportion, yet he knew that he had given the Democrats a line they would never stop repeating. Eisenhower's fantastically thoughtless gaffe—the most spectacular of his presidency—saddled Nixon with a burden he could never shed.

Eisenhower tried to atone for his mistake by offering Nixon several friendly campaign suggestions. He advised Nixon, for example, not to participate in televised debates with Kennedy. The "ins" should never take on the "outs" in a public debate, he argued. Moreover Kennedy would benefit from nationwide television exposure far more than the vice-president. Finally, he pointed out that Nixon would not be able to use classified security information in his responses to various issues raised during the exchanges. In the president's opinion, Nixon's subsequent performance in the debates with Kennedy confirmed his apprehensions.

Eisenhower also eagerly offered to campaign in Nixon's behalf. The president intended to concentrate his activity in the campaign's final days, and as the race came to a close Eisenhower wanted to expand his scheduled appearances so as to give Nixon as much help as possible in a race that was extraordinarily tight. "I had rarely seen Eisenhower more animated than he was when I arrived at the White House," Nixon recalled of their meeting on 31 October. The previous evening, however, the president's wife had telephoned Pat Nixon so that the vice-president would know that she feared for her husband's health if he tried to do too much campaigning. Acting on Mamie's wishes, Nixon declared that he did not want the president to make additional last-minute appearances. As Nixon recalled, "His pride prevented him from saying anything, but I knew that he was puzzled and frustrated by my conduct."[37] Not until years later did Eisenhower learn the real reason for Nixon's action.

Eisenhower's appearances generated enthusiasm, but not enough to counteract discontent over a new recession. The economy slumped during the campaign, and in October unemployment climbed to 6.3 percent of the work force. As early as March, Arthur F. Burns, the former chair of the president's Council of Economic Advisers, had warned Nixon that the economy would decline unless the administration immediately took corrective action. Burns made his prediction because he thought that Eisenhower's determination to balance the budget in fiscal year 1960—so soon after the recession of 1958—would abort the recovery. Nixon delivered Burns's warning to the president and his principal economic advisers, but they remained convinced that the greatest danger was inflation, not unemployment. Instead the president waited until the first signs of recession appeared in September before belatedly authorizing steps to stimulate the economy. In the campaign's final weeks, Kennedy made a third Republican recession one of his major issues. Nixon was sure that the slipping economy provided Kennedy with his thin margin of victory. "All the speeches, television broadcasts and precinct work in the world could not counteract . . . [the] hard fact" of rising unemployment, Nixon lamented.[38]

Nixon's defeat in one of the closest elections in American history plunged Eisenhower into despair. Reports of voting fraud in Illinois and Texas that had cost Nixon those critical states and, ultimately, the White House infuriated the president. Eisenhower instructed Attorney General William P. Rogers to investigate those polling irregularities, but Nixon opposed such an effort and Rogers quietly let the matter drop. Eisenhower's personal hopes for continuity in foreign and domestic policies lay shattered. "All I've been trying to do for eight years has gone down the drain," he remarked to his son.[39]

Despite his gloominess, Eisenhower contributed to a smooth and even friendly transfer of power to his successor. Earlier, Eisenhower had privately denigrated Kennedy's lack of experience in governing and his connections to machine politics. But since neither attacked the other directly during the campaign, there was no personal rancor when the two met at the White House on 6 December. The two covered a long list of topics—the organization of the National Security Council, problems with the balance of payments, Eisenhower's impressions of Macmillan and de Gaulle. No question, however, was more important than what to do about Castro. Eisenhower gave his successor a memorandum that described Cuba as the principal danger to U.S. goals in Latin America. At a second meeting on 19 January 1961—just a day before the inauguration—Eisenhower provided Kennedy the latest information about the training of the Cuban exile army in Guatemala and declared that the new administration had to do "whatever is necessary" to carry out the plans for invasion.[40] Throughout these two meetings, the conversations were cordial, and the two leaders established the foundation for cooperation in the future.

The most notable event of Eisenhower's last weeks in office was his farewell address, a final warning about the dangers of a garrison state. Speechwriter Malcolm Moos drafted the sentences that would be the most quoted of the Eisenhower presidency: the "conjunction of an immense military establishment and a large arms industry is new in the American experience. The total influence—economic, political, even spiritual—is felt in every city, every State house, every office of the Federal government. . . . In the councils of government, we must guard against the acquisition of unwarranted influence, whether sought or unsought, by the military-industrial complex. The potential for the disastrous rise of misplaced power exists and will persist." Eisenhower next cautioned about the potentially pernicious effects of government-sponsored research on institutions of higher education. "The free university," he pointed out, "historically the fountainhead of free ideas and scientific discovery, has experienced a revolution in the conduct of research. Partly because of the huge costs involved, a government contract becomes virtually a substitute for intellectual curiosity." Fearful that the military-industrial complex was developing an enormous power to absorb national resources, Eisenhower issued one last warning. "As we peer into society's future, we—you and I, and our government—must avoid the impulse to live only for today, plundering, for our own ease and convenience, the precious resources of tomorrow."[41]

Many commentators mistakenly thought that the president's valedictory revealed belated recognition of a problem he had done little to combat during his presidency. "It can be said, quite without irony," the *Nation* editorialized, "that nothing became Mr. Eisenhower's career in office like the leaving of it. . . . For eight years, Mr. Eisenhower has depressed his fellow Americans by a seeming inability to grasp the major problems of his era; but now in the closing days of his Administration he spoke like the statesman and democratic leader we had so long hungered for him to become."[42]

Nothing could have been further from the truth. Eisenhower constantly worried about balancing the needs of defense against the imperatives of economic health. His New Look aimed at protecting the economy while assuring adequate military power. In the aftermath of Sputnik, Eisenhower resolutely resisted calls for emergency defense spending, despite enormous pressure from the Pentagon, Congress, and defense contractors. Throughout his presidency, Eisenhower worried about a militarized United States that sacrificed social improvements and democratic liberties to the goals of absolute security. The farewell address was no last-minute revelation; it was his most eloquent expression of abiding principles.

During his waning days in the White House, the president discharged several final tasks. He arranged for the transfer of his public and personal papers to the new Eisenhower Library in Abilene, Kansas. At the urging of his staff, he awarded the Medal of Freedom to members of his cabinet and other close advisers. When he met reporters for his final news conference, he reviewed the highlights and disappointments of his administration. He signed one last treaty, for joint U.S.-Canadian use of the Columbia River. At the final meeting of the Eisenhower cabinet, the members talked about the recent election results, and Nixon urged them to work diligently for Republican causes. As the meeting adjourned, they gave the president a moving round of applause.

Dwight D. Eisenhower and John F. Kennedy made a striking contrast of age and youth as they rode down Pennsylvania Avenue toward the inaugural stand at the Capitol. Their conversation was far more cordial than the hostile remarks Eisenhower had exchanged with Truman eight years before. After the ceremonies ended, the president and his wife attended a farewell party, given in their honor by Lewis Strauss, and then drove off to their farm at Gettysburg.

The end of a presidency always is a bittersweet occasion, but Eisenhower turned over power to his successor with disappointment and remorse. His final year in office began with the highest hopes for peace and ended with an intensified Cold War. Eisenhower's cherished goal of an arms control agreement was unrealized. The former president could blame Khrushchev's opportunism or rigidity, but he knew that he too had to take responsibility. His disastrous decision to approve additional U-2 flights and his calamitous authorization of a string of patently false cover stories destroyed the possibilities of achieving the détente he desired. In the end Eisenhower could not bring his actions into accord with his aspirations. The goals he professed most dear were beyond his grasp.

10

★ ★ ★ ★ ★

EPILOGUE

Almost as soon as he left the White House, Dwight D. Eisenhower became a cultural anachronism. John F. Kennedy proclaimed in his inaugural address that the torch had been passed to a new generation, and Eisenhower seemed to personify those who had been left behind. The dynamism and glitter of Camelot stood in sharp contrast to the stolid, old-fashioned values of the squire of Gettysburg. As social norms underwent drastic change during the 1960s, Eisenhower appeared even more to be a figure of the distant past. It was hard for an aficionado of Fred Waring and the Pennsylvanians to get any satisfaction from the Rolling Stones. It was impossible for someone who was the model of military deportment to accept Beatle haircuts or love beads. Yet however much he deplored the values of the "me generation," Eisenhower continued to adjust his thinking to changing circumstances. As president, for example, he vehemently opposed suggestions that the federal government establish programs for birth control; in retirement, he spoke publicly about the great need for planned parenthood. Such statements notwithstanding, Eisenhower appeared out of step with the culture of the 1960s. In the popular mind, he represented values that seemed quaint, curious, or—the ultimate put-down of the decade—irrelevant.

Although the public paid Eisenhower little heed, his successor in the White House avidly sought his counsel. On many issues, Eisenhower and John F. Kennedy hardly saw eye-to-eye. Eisenhower had deplored Kennedy's demagogic cries of "missile gap" during the 1960 campaign, and he noted sourly that once in office the new president had found that the charge was myth. He also thought unwise Kennedy's precipitous dismantling of the White House staff system and appointment of his own brother as attorney general. JFK's decision to engage the Soviet Union in a race to put an astronaut on the moon endangered American prestige, Eisenhower insisted. Yet the former president reserved these criticisms for private audiences. He also felt an obligation—one that he had often wished his own critics had shared—to support the president whenever possible, particularly on matters of foreign policy. Kennedy, for his part, was extremely solicitous of Eisenhower, not only because the new president recognized the political value of his predecessor's support, but also because he increasingly realized that Eisenhower was one of only three people—the other two were Harry S. Truman and Herbert Hoover—who fully understood the enormous burdens of the office that he now filled.

Kennedy first called on Eisenhower's counsel in mid-April in the aftermath of the disastrous invasion at the Bay of Pigs. Kennedy had accepted Eisenhower's advice to carry out the CIA's attempt to overthrow Castro but had modified previous plans to attempt to conceal U.S. involvement. The result, as Eisenhower noted and almost everyone agreed, was a "debacle." The two architects of the disastrous covert operation met on 22 April at Camp David. Eisenhower was pleased to learn that Kennedy accepted "full responsibility" for the disaster and that the administration's postmortem investigation aimed at finding "lessons for possible future action" rather than a "scapegoat." Although he told Kennedy that the decision to withhold U.S. air support from the invaders was unwise, Eisenhower reserved his harshest criticisms for his diary. The story of Kennedy's handling of the invasion, he sneered, could be called "Profile in Timidity and Indecision."[1] So distressed was Eisenhower that he even ordered the alteration of the historical record so that he would not absorb any responsibility for what he thought was Kennedy's blundering. In June 1961, he had Gordon Gray, his former assistant for national security affairs, rewrite a critical document that had authorized "planning" for a covert operation to overthrow Castro.[2]

Although Kennedy drew on Eisenhower's advice on other occasions—most notably during the Cuban missile crisis—Lyndon Johnson courted Eisenhower even more assiduously. The two men had often worked together during Eisenhower's White House years, but they had never been close. Indeed in 1960, Eisenhower dismissed Johnson as "a small man, . . . superficial and opportunistic."[3] Yet the common experience of the presidency helped them overcome past differences. After

Kennedy's death, Eisenhower called on the new president and urged his long-time adversary to address Congress and the nation in a call for unity and cooperation. Johnson, in turn, replied that he hoped to be able to draw frequently on the former president's wisdom.

Eisenhower repeatedly expressed his opinions to the president on Vietnam, and his counsel was remarkably truculent. He endorsed Johnson's decisions during 1965 to begin the sustained bombing of North Vietnam and to commit American combat troops to the war. Like Johnson, he thought that American credibility rested on the preservation of an independent, non-Communist South Vietnam. Apparently Eisenhower forgot the warning he had drafted only a few years earlier while composing his memoirs about Southeast Asian jungles swallowing up division after division of American soldiers. "Once you appeal to force, you must win," he told his friend Arthur Larson.[4] The United States should seek victory, he thought, by using overwhelming force, enough to overawe the enemy and minimize American casualties.

Eisenhower's assessments grew more caustic as the war produced stalemate and dissent. The former president excoriated Johnson's strategy of gradualism, even though LBJ committed 500,000 troops to Vietnam and authorized bombing strikes that exceeded in magnitude those of World War II. He told reporters in October 1966 that he favored "any action to win." Asked if that included nuclear weapons, he replied, "I wouldn't automatically preclude anything. When you appeal to force to carry out the policies of America abroad, there is no court above you."[5] Although he shuddered when the news media reported that he advocated nuclear war in Vietnam, he privately told Larson that Chinese intervention would necessitate the resort to tactical nuclear weapons, at a minimum.[6] One year later, he appeared on television with another superannuated general, his old wartime comrade Omar N. Bradley, to generate support for an escalation of the war, perhaps by an invasion of North Vietnam or raids into Cambodia or Laos. He curtly dismissed the critics of the American war effort as "kooks" and "hippies" whose dissent bordered on treason.[7]

If the Vietnam war aroused his wrath, Republican politics caused him dismay. Always an advocate of Modern Republicanism, Eisenhower was justifiably worried as the 1964 elections approached that the party would again reject his advice. The leading candidate for the GOP nomination, Senator Barry Goldwater of Arizona, had taken ultraconservative and—in Eisenhower's view—unrealistic positions on Social Security and civil rights. Eisenhower thought Goldwater's candidacy would be a disaster for the Republican party. "My definition of the political road," he told an interviewer, "is all of its usable surface. That is where the road is highest and where the traction is best and where you can bring the most people along with you, as contrasted with the ruts and ditches on the extreme sides.''[8] Eisenhower gave sporadic encouragement to Henry Cabot Lodge and Governor William Scranton of Pennsylvania but issued no endorsement before the convention. Following Goldwater's nomination, Eisenhower made an unpersuasive declaration of support. Goldwater's only victory was in the hearts of conservative true believers; he lost in a landslide. Eisenhower's judgment may have been vindicated, but critics noted how inept and ineffective the former president was in trying to lead his party toward the middle of the road.

Although politics caused frustration, Eisenhower found personal satisfaction during his years of retirement. He now had time to enjoy the farm at Gettysburg and the pleasures of gatherings with family and friends. No one seemed to care how often he went to the golf course now, he wryly noted. And when he made his first hole in one at the age of seventy-seven, he pronounced it the thrill of a lifetime. He returned to Normandy for a documentary on the twentieth anniversary of D-Day and to West Point for the fiftieth reunion of his graduating class. With more time to travel, he visited the George C. Marshall Library in Lexington, Virginia, the Harry S. Truman Library, in Independence, Missouri, and his own library and museum in Abilene. With Mamie he finally took the slow voyage to Europe he had always wanted to make; he later returned to England for the funeral of his great friend Winston Churchill. Eisenhower was greatly pleased when former White House aide Andrew J. Goodpaster assumed his old post as commander of NATO forces and when his own son John was appointed ambassador to Belgium. Illness prevented him from personally participating in one of the happiest of family occasions—the marriage of his grandson David in December 1968 to Richard Nixon's daughter Julie.

During his final year, illness severely limited his public activities. Finally abandoning his customary neutrality, Eisenhower issued an early endorsement of Richard Nixon's presidential candidacy in 1968. After suffering heart attacks in November 1965 and April 1968, Eisenhower had to send his greetings by television to the Republican National Convention in August 1968. His image on the screen was shockingly frail, and the effort proved too much for him. The next morning he had yet another coronary. While the election campaign was under way that October, President Johnson proclaimed a ''Salute-to-Eisenhower Week.'' Nixon's narrow victory was comforting, though Eisenhower had hoped for a smashing Republican triumph.

His final months were an ordeal. The pocket of his dressing robe carried a familiar inscription, "feeling great again," but Eisenhower was losing weight and in early 1969 had to undergo surgery for a recurrence of intestinal blockage. He flashed the famous grin and gave the thumbs-up sign as he was wheeled into the operating room, but afterwards, for the first time anyone could remember, he seemed to despair. Evangelist Billy Graham talked with him about spiritual matters, and Eisenhower listened to a nurse read from the Bible. He declared to Mamie his abiding love of family and country and thanked Milton for his loyal counsel over the years. For a time, he thought of things that he still wanted to say to the American people, but finally he resigned himself to the end. Near midday on 28 March 1969, he softly gave his last command, "I want to go; God take me."[9]

"My place in history," Eisenhower predicted during his last year in office, "will be decided by historians. . . . And I don't think I will be around to differ with them."[10] Eisenhower, however, did live long enough to try to shape the judgments historians would make and to criticize those he was unable to influence. Soon after retiring to Gettysburg, he began writing his presidential memoirs. The first volume, *Mandate for Change, 1953–1956*, appeared in November 1963, and *Waging Peace, 1956–1961*, was published two years later. These thick volumes provided detailed accounts of the major events of Eisenhower's presidency. Not surprisingly, they also unfailingly justified the president's conduct. Many reviewers found the memoirs impersonal, officious, and less than candid. Far more popular was *At Ease: Stories I Tell to Friends*, an anecdotal evocation of his youth and military life published in 1967. Notably felicitous in style and content, *At Ease* offered an impression of the "Ike" most Americans wanted to remember—the warm, disarming, and modest military hero.

Many of the judgments of his presidency during the 1960s aroused his ire. Rated only an average chief executive in a poll of American historians, Eisenhower complained that his administration had faced many problems that were hardly routine and had handled them effectively. Eisenhower also bridled at critics who maintained that he was not in charge of his own administration. "It makes me sick when I see sometimes how history is written," he later told an interviewer.[11]

Eisenhower would have been far more pleased with the assessment of his presidency that dominated the historical literature during the Eisenhower Centennial Year of 1990. The consensus among students of his presidency was that Eisenhower had shrewdly used his power, often behind the scenes, to accomplish his purposes. Most historians also praised his restraint in the use of military power, particularly during the crises in Indochina in 1954, Suez in 1956, and Berlin in 1959. After a generation of growing budget deficits, high inflation, and persistent foreign trade deficits, Eisenhower's handling of the economy often received high marks. The most recent polls of historians ranked him ninth and eleventh, respectively, among chief executives.[12]

Eisenhower hoped to achieve the basic goals of peace and prosperity, and he attained mixed results. He entered office determined to contain what he considered the reckless spending of his predecessor, especially on Fair Deal programs. Yet he managed to balance the budget only three times—a record no better than Truman's—and he ran up what was then the largest peacetime deficit in American history—$12 billion in fiscal year 1959. Compared with the record of his successors, some of whom signed the nation's ledgers only with red ink, three of eight balanced budgets was an extraordinary achievement. Eisenhower worried about inflation, and he managed to keep it low, usually at a level of 2 percent or less. Yet his preoccupation with rising prices led to overzealous efforts to balance the budget in the aftermath of the 1958 recession. The result was the shortest period of recovery since the end of World War II and the onset of another recession. Although spending on domestic programs rose from 23 percent of federal expenditures in fiscal year 1954 to 38.6 percent six years later, Eisenhower resisted larger increases and enjoyed some major victories in his second term in the battles of the budget. The economy was healthy, if by no means robust, when Eisenhower left office.[13] But the president's fiscal policies did not redistribute the benefits of prosperity to those in low-income categories.

Eisenhower's greatest economic achievement was holding the line on defense spending. The president entered office with a clear conception of the relationship between defense and economy, and he consistently fought efforts to spend on national security more than he thought necessary. Eisenhower deserves high praise for framing defense issues not just in economic, but in moral terms. Security to him meant preservation of fundamental values, and he never forgot that weaponry was simply a means to that end. Few people may have fully appreciated the perils of the garrison state he so frequently decried, though. His ability to get his way on defense matters usually had more to do with his immense personal prestige as the nation's most trusted general. Still, Eisenhower's discussion of defense issues represented a rare blend of strategic competence and principled reflection.

Principle, though, too often produced rigidity and aggressiveness in prosecuting the Cold War. Eisenhower saw this struggle in moral terms, and he was determined not to yield any advantage to the Soviets.

Convinced of the righteousness of American purposes, he sanctioned unsavory methods—covert intervention, assassination attempts—to frustrate Communist designs. Although he recognized the power of nationalism, he could never truly alter his outlook to admit that anti-American hostility was unconnected to Cold War intrigue. Eisenhower simply could not adapt his Cold War principles sufficiently to an increasingly complex world, and so he intervened—in Iran, Guatemala, Lebanon, Cuba—too quickly and for the wrong reasons. He gave hopeful indications of wanting a détente at the end of his presidency. Yet he helped squander that opportunity and then began to prosecute the Cold War more fiercely than at any time during his presidency.

If Eisenhower used his powers too aggressively in pursuit of Cold War objectives, he used them too reluctantly to forge a political base. Certainly Eisenhower enjoyed considerable success on Capitol Hill, and his victories were often the result of careful planning, effective lobbying, and skillful maneuvering. Yet Modern Republicanism—an approach that the president thought was critical to the rejuvenation of the GOP—was more slogan than anything else. Too often, the president invoked this vision for the party's future only in moments of pique—after GOP setbacks in Congress or at the polls. He did not make a sustained effort to reshape the party, a task that required far more attention to state and local politics. Eisenhower failed to do so partly because he never overcame his distaste for partisanship. His inattention to building a Modern Republican movement also had much to do with the similarity of his views on domestic matters to those of most conservative Republicans. While Eisenhower maintained his popularity, the strength of his party declined. He neither invigorated the GOP, nor managed to nurture a potential successor other than Nixon, about whom he had continuing reservations.

Eisenhower probably won more political battles than he lost—at least on the issues he thought were most important. He used his power resourcefully—and often successfully—in domestic and foreign policy to accomplish his objectives. His greatest failures were not from lethargy or ineptness but lack of vision. His Cold War attitudes became increasingly outmoded in a world where nationalism was an ever more powerful force. His conservatism on domestic matters did little, if anything, to relieve inequities caused by race, class, or gender. To a great extent Eisenhower achieved what he wanted. He was not able to ask for more.

NOTES

PREFACE

1. Stephen E. Ambrose, *Eisenhower*, vol. 2: *The President* (New York: Simon and Schuster, 1984), pp. 17–18.

CHAPTER 1
DUTY AND AMBITION

1. Robert H. Ferrell, ed., *The Eisenhower Diaries* (New York: W. W. Norton, 1981), p. 204.

2. Ibid., p. 198.

3. Louis Galambos, ed., *The Papers of Dwight D. Eisenhower*, vols. 12–13: *NATO and the Campaign of 1952* (Baltimore: Johns Hopkins University Press, 1989), 12:522–23.

4. Dwight D. Eisenhower, *At Ease: Stories I Tell to Friends* (Garden City, N.Y.: Doubleday, 1967), p. 37.

5. Kenneth S. Davis, *Soldier of Democracy: A Biography of Dwight D. Eisenhower* (Garden City, N.Y.: Doubleday, Doran, 1945), p. 146.

6. Stephen E. Ambrose, *Eisenhower*, vol. 1: *Soldier, General of the Army, President-Elect, 1890–1952* (New York: Simon and Schuster, 1983), pp. 73–77.

7. D. Clayton James, *The Years of MacArthur*, vol. 1: *1880–1941* (Boston: Houghton Mifflin, 1970), p. 564.

8. Ambrose, *Eisenhower*, 1:95.

9. James, *The Years of MacArthur*, 1:485, 509.

10. Ferrell, *Eisenhower Diaries*, p. 20.

11. Forrest C. Pogue, *George C. Marshall: Ordeal and Hope, 1939–1942* (New York: Viking Press, 1966), pp. 237–40.

12. Ambrose, *Eisenhower*, 1:135.

13. Pogue, *George C. Marshall: Ordeal and Hope*, p. 338.

14. Dwight D. Eisenhower, *Crusade in Europe* (Garden City, N.Y.: Doubleday, 1949), p. 207.

15. Ferrell, *Eisenhower Diaries*, pp. 109–18.

16. Alfred D. Chandler, Jr., and Louis Galambos, eds., *The Papers of Dwight D. Eisenhower*, vol. 6: *Occupation, 1945* (Baltimore: Johns Hopkins University Press, 1978), p. ix.

17. Ibid., pp. 114–17, 357–61.

18. Martin J. Sherwin, *A World Destroyed: The Atomic Bomb and the Grand Alliance* (New York: Vintage Books, 1975), pp. 220–38.

19. Chandler and Galambos, *The Papers of Dwight D. Eisenhower*, 6:309–10.

20. Ferrell, *Eisenhower Diaries*, pp. 136–39.

21. Louis Galambos, ed., *The Papers of Dwight D. Eisenhower*, vols. 7–9: *The Chief of Staff* (Baltimore: Johns Hopkins University Press, 1978), 8:1717, 1752.

22. Robert Griffith, ed., *Ike's Letters to a Friend, 1941–1958* (Lawrence: University Press of Kansas, 1984), p. 30.

23. Ferrell, *Eisenhower Diaries*, pp. 137, 143.

24. Galambos, *The Papers of Dwight D. Eisenhower*, 8:1855–56; *Public Papers of the Presidents of the United States: Harry S. Truman: 1947* (Washington, D.C.: Government Printing Office, 1963), pp. 176–80; Chester J. Pach, Jr., *Arming the Free World: The Origins of the United States Military Assistance Program, 1945–1950* (Chapel Hill: University of North Carolina Press, 1991), p. 122.

25. Ferrell, *Eisenhower Diaries*, pp. 154–57.

26. Steven L. Rearden, *The Formative Years, 1947–1950*, vol. 1: *History of the Office of the Secretary of Defense*, ed. Alfred Goldberg (Washington, D.C.: Office of the Secretary of Defense, 1984), p. 373.

27. Griffith, *Ike's Letters to a Friend*, p. 54.

28. Galambos, *The Papers of Dwight D. Eisenhower*, 8:1737–38, 1775–76.

29. Kevin McCann, *Man from Abilene* (Garden City, N.Y.: Doubleday, 1952), p. 110.

30. Ambrose, *Eisenhower*, 1:459–60.

31. Galambos, *The Papers of Dwight D. Eisenhower*, 9:2191–94; Ambrose, *Eisenhower*, 1:464.

32. McCann, *Man From Abilene*, pp. 178–90.

33. Ferrell, *Eisenhower Diaries*, pp. 161–62

34. Louis Galambos, ed., *The Papers of Dwight D. Eisenhower*, vols. 10–11: *Columbia University* (Baltimore: Johns Hopkins University Press, 1984) 10:808–9.

35. Ferrell, *Eisenhower Diaries*, pp. 175–76.

36. Griffith, *Ike's Letters to a Friend*, p. 79.

37. Lawrence S. Kaplan, *A Community of Interests: NATO and the Military*

Assistance Program, 1948–1951 (Washington, D.C.: Office of the Secretary of Defense, 1980), p. 211.

38. Griffith, *Ike's Letters to a Friend*, pp. 82–83.

39. Galambos, *The Papers of Dwight D. Eisenhower*, 12:370.

40. Richard M. Fried, *Nightmare in Red: The McCarthy Era in Perspective* (New York: Oxford University Press, 1990), p. 128.

41. David M. Oshinsky, *A Conspiracy So Immense: The World of Joe McCarthy* (New York: Free Press, 1983), p. 196.

42. Ferrell, *Eisenhower Diaries*, p. 195.

43. Eisenhower, *At Ease*, pp. 371–72; Herbert S. Parmet, *Eisenhower and the American Crusades* (New York: Macmillan, 1972), pp. 35–36.

44. Galambos, *The Papers of Dwight D. Eisenhower*, 12:606.

45. H. W. Brands, Jr., *Cold Warriors: Eisenhower's Generation and American Foreign Policy* (New York: Columbia University Press, 1988), p. 189.

46. Galambos, *The Papers of Dwight D. Eisenhower*, 12:307.

47. Dwight D. Eisenhower, *Mandate for Change, 1953–1956* (Garden City, N.Y.: Doubleday, 1963), p. 18.

48. Galambos, *The Papers of Dwight D. Eisenhower*, 12:729–30.

49. John Robert Greene, *The Crusade: The Presidential Election of 1952* (Lanham, Md.: University Press of America, 1985), pp. 56–57.

50. Galambos, *The Papers of Dwight D. Eisenhower*, 13:971, 974.

51. Dwight D. Eisenhower (hereafter DDE), oral history transcript OH 11, p. 19, Dwight D. Eisenhower Library, Abilene, Kansas.

52. Peter Lyon, *Eisenhower: Portrait of the Hero* (Boston: Little, Brown, 1974), p. 390.

53. Henry Cabot Lodge, *The Storm Has Many Eyes: A Personal Narrative* (New York: W. W. Norton, 1973), p. 89.

54. James T. Patterson, *Mr. Republican: A Biography of Robert A. Taft* (Boston: Houghton Mifflin, 1972), pp. 519, 535–36.

55. Merriman Smith, oral history transcript OH 160, pp. 10, 13, Eisenhower Library.

56. *The Memoirs of Richard Nixon* (New York: Grosset & Dunlap, 1978), pp. 97–98.

57. Roger Morris, *Richard Milhous Nixon: The Rise of an American Politician* (New York: Henry Holt, 1990), pp. 818, 821–23; Richard Norton Smith, *Thomas E. Dewey and His Times* (New York: Simon and Schuster, 1982), pp. 601–2.

58. Richard M. Nixon, *Six Crises* (Garden City, N.Y.: Doubleday, 1962), p. 123; Ambrose, *Eisenhower*, 1:558–61.

59. *Time*, 17 Nov. 1952, p. 21.

60. Robert Smylie to W. Smylie, 13 Nov. 1952, Personal File, Robert E. Smylie Papers, Idaho State Archives, Boise; R. Heminger to Walt Horan, 26 Feb. 1953, Box 553, Political File, Walter F. Horan Papers, Washington State University Library, Pullman.

CHAPTER 2
ORGANIZING THE PRESIDENCY

1. Robert H. Ferrell, ed., *The Eisenhower Diaries* (New York: W. W. Norton, 1981), p. 225.

2. Robert H. Ferrell, ed., *Off the Record: The Private Papers of Harry S. Truman* (New York: Harper & Row, 1980), pp. 273-75, 287; Donald R. McCoy, *The Presidency of Harry S. Truman* (Lawrence: University Press of Kansas, 1984), p. 306; Stephen E. Ambrose, *Eisenhower*, vol. 2: *The President* (New York: Simon and Schuster, 1984), pp. 13-15; Louis Galambos, ed., *Papers of Dwight D. Eisenhower*, vols. 10-11: *Columbia University* (Baltimore: Johns Hopkins University Press, 1984), 11:1584.

3. McCoy, *The Presidency of Harry S. Truman*, pp. 165-87; Robert J. Donovan, *Tumultuous Years: The Presidency of Harry S Truman, 1949-1953* (New York: W. W. Norton, 1982), pp. 118-27.

4. Robert Griffith, "Dwight D. Eisenhower and the Corporate Commonwealth," *American Historical Review* 87 (Feb. 1982):90.

5. *New York Times*, 13 Oct. 1948.

6. Ferrell, *Eisenhower Diaries*, p. 231.

7. *New York Times*, 13 Oct. 1948.

8. Ibid., 6 Sept. 1949.

9. Robert Griffith, ed., *Ike's Letters to a Friend* (Lawrence: University Press of Kansas, 1984), p. 104.

10. *New York Times*, 13 Oct. 1948, 6 Sept. 1949; Griffith, "Dwight D. Eisenhower and the Corporate Commonwealth," pp. 89-94.

11. McCoy, *The Presidency of Harry S. Truman*, p. 180.

12. True D. Morse, oral history transcript OH 40, pt. 1, p. 25, Eisenhower Library.

13. *Public Papers of the Presidents of the United States: Dwight D. Eisenhower: 1953*, 8 vols. (Washington, D.C.: Government Printing Office, 1958-61), p. 542 (hereafter *Public Papers*).

14. Ferrell, *Eisenhower Diaries*, p. 218.

15. Townsend Hoopes, *The Devil and John Foster Dulles* (Boston: Little, Brown, 1973), pp. 128-30.

16. Ferrell, *Eisenhower Diaries*, p. 237.

17. Ibid.

18. Fred I. Greenstein, *The Hidden-Hand Presidency: Eisenhower as Leader* (New York: Basic Books, 1982), pp. 83-84.

19. Dwight D. Eisenhower, *Mandate for Change, 1953-1956* (Garden City, N.Y.: Doubleday, 1963), p. 110.

20. Don Paarlberg, oral history transcript OH 52, pt. 1/1, p. 13, Eisenhower Library.

21. Ferrell, *Eisenhower Diaries*, p. 267.

22. James C. Hagerty, oral history transcript OH 91, pt. 1, p. 56, Eisenhower Library.

23. Ferrell, *Eisenhower Diaries*, p. 238.

24. Kenneth W. Thompson, ed., *The Eisenhower Presidency: Eleven Intimate Perspectives of Dwight D. Eisenhower*, Portraits of American Presidents, vol. 3 (Lanham, Md.: University Press of America, 1984), pp. 65, 75.

25. Murray Kempton, "The Underestimation of Dwight D. Eisenhower," *Esquire* 68 (Sept. 1967):108.

26. Greenstein, *The Hidden-Hand Presidency*, pp. 58–65.

27. Paarlberg, oral history transcript OH 52, pt. 1/1, p. 62, Eisenhower Library.

28. Ferrell, *Eisenhower Diaries*, p. 218.

29. Griffith, *Ike's Letters to a Friend*, p. 111.

30. John S. D. Eisenhower, *Strictly Personal* (Garden City, N.Y.: Doubleday, 1974), p. 172.

31. H. Roemer McPhee, oral history transcript OH 145, p. 35, Eisenhower Library.

32. Robert J. Donovan, *Confidential Secretary: Ann Whitman's 20 Years with Eisenhower and Rockefeller* (New York: E. P. Dutton, 1988), p. 44.

33. Griffith, *Ike's Letters to a Friend*, p. 109.

34. Eisenhower, *Mandate for Change*, p. 171.

35. *Public Papers: 1947*, pp. 178–79.

36. U.S. Department of State, *Foreign Relations of the United States: 1950* (Washington, D.C.: Government Printing Office, 1977), 1:234–92 (hereafter cited as *FRUS*).

37. Elaine Tyler May, *Homeward Bound: American Families in the Cold War Era* (New York: Basic Books, 1988), pp. 3–7, 16–20.

38. U.S. Census Bureau, *Historical Statistics of the United States: Colonial Times to 1970*, 2 vols. (Washington, D.C.: U.S. Government Printing Office, 1975), pp. 9, 224, 297.

39. May, *Homeward Bound*, p. 11.

CHAPTER 3

PRESIDENT, PARTY, AND CONGRESS

1. Gary W. Reichard, *The Reaffirmation of Republicanism: Eisenhower and the Eighty-third Congress* (Knoxville: University of Tennessee Press, 1975), p. 181.

2. Letter, DDE to Mark W. Clement, 21 Dec. 1957, folder DDE, Dictation, Dec. 1957, DDE Diary Series, Ann Whitman File, Eisenhower Library.

3. Robert H. Ferrell, ed., *The Eisenhower Diaries* (New York: W. W. Norton, 1981), pp. 218, 226, 234, 239–40, 269–70.

4. DDE, oral history transcript OH 11, p. 72, Eisenhower Library.

5. Robert Griffith, ed., *Ike's Letters to a Friend, 1941–1958* (Lawrence: University Press of Kansas, 1984), pp. 132–33; Robert Griffith, "Dwight D. Eisenhower and the Corporate Commonwealth," *American Historical Review* 87 (Feb. 1982):89–94, 100–101.

6. Reichard, *The Reaffirmation of Republicanism*, p. 98.

7. Ferrell, *Eisenhower Diaries*, pp. 235–36.

8. Iwan W. Morgan, *Eisenhower versus "the Spenders": The Eisenhower Administration, the Democrats and the Budget, 1953–60* (New York: St. Martin's Press, 1990), pp. 60–69.

9. Reichard, *The Reaffirmation of Republicanism*, pp. 108–13.

10. Diary entry, 17 Feb. 1953, folder Diary—WER and DDE, William E. Robinson Papers, Eisenhower Library.

11. Griffith, "Dwight D. Eisenhower and the Corporate Commonwealth," p. 102.

12. Reichard, *The Reaffirmation of Republicanism*, p. 162; Griffith, "Dwight D. Eisenhower and the Corporate Commonwealth," p. 106.

13. *Public Papers: 1953*, p. 433; *Public Papers: 1955*, p. 859; letter, DDE to Robert W. Woodruff, 20 July 1959, folder Woodruff, R.W. (1), Name Series, Ann Whitman File, Eisenhower Library.

14. Duane Tananbaum, *The Bricker Amendment Controversy: A Test of Eisenhower's Political Leadership* (Ithaca, N.Y.: Cornell University Press, 1988), p. 221.

15. Duane A. Tananbaum, "The Bricker Amendment Controversy: Its Origins and Eisenhower's Role," *Diplomatic History* 9 (Winter 1985):79–80.

16. *Congressional Record*, 82d Cong., 1st sess., 1951, 97, pt. 6, pp. 8258, 8265.

17. Tananbaum, *The Bricker Amendment Controversy*, pp. 84, 118–19.

18. Tananbaum, "The Bricker Amendment Controversy," p. 82.

19. Tananbaum, *The Bricker Amendment Controversy*, p. 78.

20. *FRUS: 1952–1954*, 1, pt. 2: 1816–17.

21. Tananbaum, *The Bricker Amendment Controversy*, pp. 109–10.

22. Gary W. Reichard, *Politics as Usual: The Age of Truman and Eisenhower* (Arlington Heights, Ill: Harlan Davidson, 1988), p. 97.

23. Robert H. Ferrell, ed., *The Diary of James C. Hagerty: Eisenhower in Mid-Course, 1954–1955* (Bloomington: Indiana University Press, 1983), p. 43; David M. Oshinsky, *A Conspiracy So Immense: The World of Joe McCarthy* (New York: Free Press, 1983), p. 260.

24. Richard M. Fried, *Nightmare in Red: The McCarthy Era in Perspective* (New York: Oxford University Press, 1990), pp. 125–26.

25. Stephen E. Ambrose, *Eisenhower*, vol. 2: *The President* (New York: Simon and Schuster, 1984), pp. 56–61, 219.

26. Athan Theoharis, *Spying on Americans: Political Surveillance from Hoover to the Huston Plan* (Philadelphia: Temple University Press, 1978), pp. 209–11.

27. Ambrose, *Eisenhower*, 2:64–65; Gary May, *China Scapegoat: The Diplomatic Ordeal of John Carter Vincent* (Washington, D.C.: New Republic Books, 1979), pp. 273–78.

28. *Public Papers: 1953*, pp. 40, 447.

29. Oshinsky, *A Conspiracy So Immense*, pp. 266–85.

30. *Public Papers: 1953*, p. 415.

31. Griffith, *Ike's Letters to a Friend*, pp. 110–11.

32. Letter, DDE to William E. Robinson, 27 July 1953, folder Comments on Various Columnists and Authors, William E. Robinson Papers, Eisenhower Library; Ambrose, *Eisenhower*, 2:57.

33. Ferrell, *Diary of James C. Hagerty*, p. 27.

34. Oshinsky, *A Conspiracy So Immense*, p. 348.

35. Ibid., pp. 349–56.

36. Ferrell, *Eisenhower Diaries*, p. 259.

37. Ibid., pp. 259–61; Ferrell, *Diary of James C. Hagerty*, pp. 42–43.

38. Ferrell, *Diary of James C. Hagerty*, p. 20; *Public Papers: 1954*, p. 290–91.

39. Oshinsky, *A Conspiracy So Immense*, pp. 390–404.

40. *Public Papers: 1954*, p. 483.

41. Raoul Berger, *Executive Privilege: A Constitutional Myth* (Cambridge, Mass.: Harvard University Press, 1974), pp. 234–35.

42. Ferrell, *Diary of James C. Hagerty*, p. 58; Griffith, *Ike's Letters to a Friend*, p. 126.

43. Oshinsky, *A Conspiracy So Immense*, pp. 462–65.

44. Ibid. p. 491.

45. Ibid., p. 493.

46. Ferrell, *Diary of James C. Hagerty*, pp. 127–31; *Public Papers: 1954*, p. 1089.

47. Reichard, *The Reaffirmation of Republicanism*, p. 216.

48. Morgan, *Eisenhower Versus "the Spenders,"* p. 69.

49. Griffith, *Ike's Letters to a Friend*, p. 137–38.

50. Ferrell, *Diary of James C. Hagerty*, p. 129.

CHAPTER 4

WAGING COLD WAR

1. *Public Papers: 1953*, pp. 13–17.

2. *FRUS: 1950*, 1:245, 282.

3. Stephen E. Ambrose, *Eisenhower*, vol. 2: *The President* (New York: Simon and Schuster, 1984), p. 89.

4. *FRUS: 1952–1954*, 2, pt. 1:260–61.

5. Dwight D. Eisenhower, *Mandate for Change, 1953–1956* (Garden City, N.Y.: Doubleday, 1963), p. 129; Iwan W. Morgan, *Eisenhower versus "the Spenders": The Eisenhower Administration, the Democrats and the Budget, 1953–60* (New York: St. Martin's Press, 1990), p. 53.

6. *FRUS: 1952–1954*, 2, pt. 1:260, 278.

7. Robert H. Ferrell, ed., *The Eisenhower Diaries* (New York: W. W. Norton, 1981), pp. 235–36.

8. Anna Kasten Nelson, "The 'Top of the Hill': President Eisenhower and the National Security Council," *Diplomatic History* 7 (Fall 1983):307–11; Fred I. Greenstein, *The Hidden-Hand Presidency: Eisenhower as Leader* (New York: Basic Books, 1982), pp. 124–25; Stephen G. Rabe, *Eisenhower and Latin America: The*

Foreign Policy of Anticommunism (Chapel Hill: University of North Carolina Press, 1988), pp. 27–28.

9. X [George F. Kennan] "The Sources of Soviet Conduct," *Foreign Affairs* 25 (July 1947):566–82.

10. H. W. Brands, "The Age of Vulnerability: Eisenhower and the National Insecurity State," *American Historical Review* 94 (Oct. 1989):966–68; *FRUS: 1952–1954*, 2, pt. 1:388–93, 399–431 (emphasis in the original).

11. Brands, "The Age of Vulnerability," pp. 968–70; *FRUS: 1952–1954*, 2, pt. 1:514–20.

12. *FRUS: 1952–1954*, 2, pt. 1:519, 593.

13. Ibid., pp. 582, 593; Brands, "The Age of Vulnerability," p. 972.

14. Eisenhower, *Mandate for Change*, p. 452; John Lewis Gaddis, *Strategies of Containment: A Critical Appraisal of Postwar American National Security Policy* (New York: Oxford University Press, 1982), p. 171.

15. *Public Papers: 1953*, pp. 179–88 (emphasis in the original).

16. *FRUS: 1952–1954*, 2, pt. 1:579–80.

17. Ibid., p. 583.

18. Walter LaFeber, *America, Russia, and the Cold War, 1945–1984*, 5th ed. (New York: Alfred A. Knopf, 1985), p. 136.

19. *FRUS: 1952–1954*, 2, pt. 1:580.

20. Ibid., pp. 391, 581.

21. Brands, "The Age of Vulnerability," pp. 967, 973.

22. Ibid., p. 974.

23. *FRUS: 1952–1954*, 2, pt. 1:461.

24. Ferrell, *Eisenhower Diaries*, p. 262.

25. *FRUS: 1952–1954*, 2, pt. 2:1169–74; *Public Papers: 1953*, pp. 813–22.

26. Ferrell, *Eisenhower Diaries*, p. 261.

27. Robert A. Strong, "Eisenhower and Arms Control," in *Reevaluating Eisenhower: American Foreign Policy in the 1950s*, ed. Richard A. Melanson and David Mayers (Urbana: University of Illinois Press, 1987), pp. 247–48.

28. *Department of State Bulletin* 30 (25 January 1954):108.

29. Ferrell, *Eisenhower Diaries*, pp. 237, 306, 350.

30. Richard H. Immerman, ed., *John Foster Dulles and the Diplomacy of the Cold War* (Princeton, N.J.: Princeton University Press, 1990), p. 9.

31. Eisenhower, *Mandate for Change*, p. 95.

32. Edward C. Keefer, "President Dwight D. Eisenhower and the End of the Korean War," *Diplomatic History* 10 (Summer 1986):270.

33. Roger Dingman, "Atomic Diplomacy during the Korean War," *International Security* 13 (Winter 1988/89):50, 85–91.

34. Ferrell, *Eisenhower Diaries*, p. 223.

35. Ibid.

36. Eisenhower, *Mandate for Change*, pp. 160–61; Ambrose, *Eisenhower*, 2:109.

37. Ambrose, *Eisenhower*, 2:109.

38. Stephen E. Ambrose, *Ike's Spies: Eisenhower and the Espionage Establishment* (Garden City, N.Y.: Doubleday, 1981), p. 199.

39. *FRUS: 1952–1954*, 4:6–10.

40. Rabe, *Eisenhower and Latin America*, 33–36; Chester J. Pach, Jr., "The Containment of U.S. Military Aid to Latin America, 1944–49," *Diplomatic History* 6 (Summer 1982):225–43.

41. Richard H. Immerman, *The CIA in Guatemala: The Foreign Policy of Intervention* (Austin: University of Texas Press, 1982), p. 183.

42. *FRUS: 1952–1954*, 4:1065.

43. Ibid., p. 1096.

44. Ibid., p. 1093; Rabe, *Eisenhower and Latin America*, p. 47.

45. *FRUS: 1952–1954*, 4:1064.

46. Rabe, *Eisenhower and Latin America*, pp. 40, 43–46; Immerman, *The CIA in Guatemala*, pp. 68–75, 182–86.

47. Immerman, *The CIA in Guatemala*, pp. 155–58.

48. Robert H. Ferrell, ed., *The Diary of James C. Hagerty: Eisenhower in Mid-Course, 1954–1955* (Bloomington: Indiana University Press, 1983), pp. 68, 74–75.

49. Immerman, *The CIA in Guatemala*, pp. 178–80.

50. Ibid., pp. 197–98; Rabe, *Eisenhower and Latin America*, pp. 61–63.

51. *FRUS: 1950*, 6:747.

52. Ronald H. Spector, *Advice and Support: The Early Years of the U.S. Army in Vietnam, 1941–1960* (New York: Free Press, 1985), p. 175.

53. Ferrell, *Diary of James C. Hagerty*, p. 15.

54. Spector, *Advice and Support*, pp. 198–208.

55. Ferrell, *Eisenhower Diaries*, p. 190.

56. Richard H. Immerman, "Between the Unattainable and the Unacceptable: Eisenhower and Dienbienphu," in *Reevaluating Eisenhower*, p. 123.

57. *FRUS: 1952–1954*, 13, pt. 1:1261.

58. George C. Herring, "'A Good Stout Effort': John Foster Dulles and the Indochina Crisis, 1954–1955," in *John Foster Dulles and the Diplomacy of the Cold War*, pp. 217–18.

59. Townsend Hoopes, *The Devil and John Foster Dulles* (Boston: Little, Brown, 1973), p. 222.

60. Herring, "'A Good Stout Effort,'" p. 223.

61. *FRUS: 1952–1954*, 12, pt. 1:903–4.

62. Ibid., 13, pt. 2:1783, 2156.

63. Herring, "'A Good Stout Effort,'" p. 230.

64. *FRUS: 1952–1954*, 12, pt. 1:773.

65. *FRUS: 1955–1957*, 1:176.

66. For a different point of view, see Melanie Billings-Yun, *Decision against War: Eisenhower and Dien Bien Phu, 1954* (New York: Columbia University Press, 1988).

67. David L. Anderson, "J. Lawton Collins, John Foster Dulles, and the Eisenhower Administration's 'Point of No Return' in Vietnam," *Diplomatic History* 12 (Spring 1988):146.

68. This discussion of the Quemoy-Matsu crisis relies on two excellent, recent studies: Gordon H. Chang, ''To the Nuclear Brink: Eisenhower, Dulles, and the Quemoy-Matsu Crisis'' and H. W. Brands, Jr., ''Testing Massive Retaliation: Credibility and Crisis Management in the Taiwan Strait,'' both in *International Security* 12 (Spring 1988):96–151.

69. *FRUS: 1952–1954*, 14, pt. 1:585.

70. Ibid., pp. 558, 613–24.

71. Ibid., pp. 981–82.

72. Chang, ''To the Nuclear Brink,'' p. 99.

73. *FRUS: 1955–1957*, 2:69–80.

74. Eisenhower, *Mandate for Change*, p. 469.

75. *FRUS: 1955–1957*, 2:91.

76. Ibid., pp. 345–50.

77. Ibid., pp. 336–37.

78. Brands, ''Testing Massive Retaliation,'' p. 142.

79. *Public Papers: 1955*, p. 332.

80. Chang, ''To the Nuclear Brink,'' p. 117.

81. Eisenhower, *Mandate for Change*, p. 483.

82. Robert A. Divine, *Eisenhower and the Cold War* (New York: Oxford University Press, 1981), pp. 65–66.

83. Ambrose, *Eisenhower*, 2:245.

84. *FRUS: 1955–1957*, 2:284.

85. Ibid., pp. 345–50.

86. Brands, ''Testing Massive Retaliation,'' pp. 148–51.

CHAPTER 5
PERSONAL VICTORIES

1. *Public Papers: 1956*, pp. 1089–90.

2. Robert H. Ferrell, ed., *The Diary of James C. Hagerty: Eisenhower in Mid-Course, 1954–1955* (Bloomington: Indiana University Press, 1983), pp. 133, 204.

3. Dwight D. Eisenhower, *Mandate for Change, 1953–1956* (Garden City, N.Y.: Doubleday, 1963), pp. 499–500.

4. *Public Papers: 1955*, p. 282.

5. Ferrell, *Diary of James C. Hagerty*, pp. 198–99.

6. *Public Papers: 1955*, p. 674.

7. U.S. Census Bureau, *Historical Statistics of the United States: Colonial Times to 1970*, 2 vols. (Washington, D.C.: Government Printing Office, 1975), pp. 135, 210, 226–27, 1105.

8. W. W. Rostow, *Open Skies: Eisenhower's Proposal of July 21, 1955* (Austin: University of Texas Press, 1982), pp. 159–60.

9. Ibid., pp. 185–88.

10. Ibid., p. 46.

11. *Public Papers: 1955*, p. 703.

12. Ibid., p. 707.

13. Ibid., pp. 707–12.

14. Rostow, *Open Skies*, p. 108.

15. *Public Papers: 1955*, pp. 713–16.

16. John S. D. Eisenhower, *Strictly Personal* (Garden City, N.Y.: Doubleday, 1974), p. 178.

17. Charles E. Bohlen, *Witness to History, 1929–1969* (New York: W. W. Norton, 1973), p. 384.

18. *Public Papers: 1955*, p. 730.

19. *The Gallup Poll: Public Opinion, 1935–1971*, 3 vols. (New York: Random House, 1972), 2:1351.

20. Stephen E. Ambrose, *Eisenhower*, vol. 2: *The President* (New York: Simon and Schuster, 1984), p. 270.

21. *The Memoirs of Richard Nixon* (New York: Grosset & Dunlap, 1978), p. 166.

22. Ferrell, *Diary of James C. Hagerty*, p. 236.

23. *Public Papers: 1955*, p. 841.

24. Robert Griffith, ed., *Ike's Letters to a Friend, 1941–1958* (Lawrence: University Press of Kansas, 1984), p. 117.

25. Ibid., pp. 145–47.

26. Ferrell, *Diary of James C. Hagerty*, pp. 240–41.

27. Ibid., pp. 240–46.

28. Ibid., p. 246.

29. Griffith, *Ike's Letters to a Friend*, pp. 145, 157.

30. Lucius Clay, oral history transcript OH 56, pt. 2, p. 108, Eisenhower Library.

31. *Public Papers: 1956*, pp. 263–66.

32. Ibid., 273–79.

33. Ferrell, *Eisenhower Diaries*, pp. 306–7.

34. Sherman Adams, *Firsthand Report: The Story of the Eisenhower Administration* (New York: Harper, 1961), pp. 220–21.

35. *Memoirs of Richard Nixon*, p. 167.

36. Emmet John Hughes, *The Ordeal of Power: A Political Memoir of the Eisenhower Years* (New York: Atheneum, 1963), p. 173.

37. Ferrell, *Diary of James C. Hagerty*, pp. 244–45.

38. William Bragg Ewald, Jr., *Eisenhower the President: Crucial Days, 1951–1960* (Englewood Cliffs, N.J.: Prentice-Hall, 1981), pp. 184–88.

39. Ferrell, *Eisenhower Diaries*, p. 308.

40. Ewald, *Eisenhower the President*, pp. 197–98.

41. Ibid., pp. 186–87.

42. Michael R. Beschloss, *Mayday: The U-2 Affair* (New York: Harper & Row, 1986), p. 114.

43. DDE, oral history transcript OH 11, p. 91, Eisenhower Library.

44. *Public Papers: 1956*, pp. 266–67, 287.

45. Beschloss, *Mayday*, p. 114.

46. *Memoirs of Richard Nixon*, pp. 172–73.

47. *Public Papers: 1956*, p. 633.

48. Ibid., pp. 702–15.

49. Ferrell, *Diary of James C. Hagerty*, p. 198.

50. Mark H. Rose, *Interstate: Express Highway Politics, 1941–1956* (Lawrence: Regents Press of Kansas, 1979), p. 70.

51. Stephen E. Ambrose, *Eisenhower*, vol. 1: *Soldier, General of the Army, President-Elect, 1890–1952* (New York: Simon and Schuster, 1983), p. 566.

52. Ezra Taft Benson, *Cross Fire: The Eight Years with Eisenhower* (Garden City, N.Y.: Doubleday, 1962), p. 294.

53. Eisenhower, *Mandate for Change*, p. 557.

54. *Public Papers: 1956*, p. 705.

55. Robert A. Divine, *Blowing on the Wind: The Nuclear Test Ban Debate, 1954–1960* (New York: Oxford University Press, 1978), pp. 88–89, 98.

56. Griffith, *Ike's Letters to a Friend*, p. 173.

57. Eisenhower, *Strictly Personal*, p. 189.

58. Donald Neff, *Warriors at Suez: Eisenhower Takes America into the Middle East* (New York: Simon and Schuster, 1981), pp. 87–88.

59. Ferrell, *Eisenhower Diaries*, pp. 318–19.

60. William Stivers, ''Eisenhower and the Middle East,'' in *Reevaluating Eisenhower: American Foreign Policy in the 1950s*, ed. Richard A. Melanson and David Mayers (Urbana: University of Illinois Press, 1987), p. 213; Ferrell, *Eisenhower Diaries*, p. 320.

61. Neff, *Warriors at Suez*, p. 125.

62. Dwight D. Eisenhower, *Waging Peace, 1956–1961* (Garden City, N.Y.: Doubleday, 1965), p. 31.

63. Neff, *Warriors at Suez*, p. 258.

64. Stivers, ''Eisenhower and the Middle East,'' p. 196.

65. *The Memoirs of Anthony Eden: Full Circle* (Boston: Houghton Mifflin, 1960), pp. 467–74.

66. Eisenhower, *Waging Peace*, p. 36.

67. Memorandum for record, 12 Aug. 1956, folder Aug. 1956 Diary—Staff Memos, DDE Diary Series, Ann Whitman File, Eisenhower Library; Eden, *Full Circle*, p. 487.

68. Eisenhower, *Waging Peace*, p. 670.

69. Ibid., pp. 676–77.

70. Ibid., p. 59.

71. Neff, *Warriors at Suez*, p. 349.

72. Stephen E. Ambrose, *Ike's Spies: Eisenhower and the Espionage Establishment* (Garden City, N.Y.: Doubleday, 1981), pp. 237–39.

73. Eisenhower, *Waging Peace*, p. 95.

74. Neff, *Warriors at Suez*, p. 375.

75. Hughes, *The Ordeal of Power*, pp. 212–13, 216.

76. Eisenhower, *Waging Peace*, p. 85.

77. Hughes, *The Ordeal of Power*, p. 213.

78. Griffith, *Ike's Letters to a Friend*, p. 175.

79. *Public Papers: 1956*, p. 1072.

80. Eisenhower, *Waging Peace*, p. 73.

81. Ambrose, *Eisenhower*, 2:364.

82. Neff, *Warriors at Suez*, p. 385.

83. Eisenhower, *Waging Peace*, pp. 678–79.

84. Stivers, "Eisenhower and the Middle East," p. 198.

85. Hughes, *The Ordeal of Power*, pp. 223–24.

86. Neff, *Warriors at Suez*, p. 425.

87. David Carlton, *Anthony Eden: A Biography* (London: Allen Lane, 1981), p. 460.

88. Griffith, *Ike's Letters to a Friend*, pp. 173–74.

89. *Public Papers: 1956*, p. 1108.

CHAPTER 6
THE HAZARDS OF DELIBERATE SPEED

1. Herbert S. Parmet, *Eisenhower and the American Crusades* (New York: Macmillan, 1972), p. 553.

2. Donald R. McCoy and Richard T. Ruetten, *Quest and Response: Minority Rights and the Truman Administration* (Lawrence: University Press of Kansas, 1973), p. 100.

3. Stephen E. Ambrose, *Eisenhower*, vol. 2: *The President* (New York: Simon and Schuster, 1984), p. 125.

4. Morris J. MacGregor, Jr., *Integration of the Armed Forces, 1940–1965* (Washington, D.C.: Center of Military History, 1981), pp. 228–29.

5. *Public Papers: 1953*, p. 30.

6. Ibid., p. 556.

7. Robert Fredrick Burk, *The Eisenhower Administration and Black Civil Rights* (Knoxville: University of Tennessee Press, 1984), pp. 23–108.

8. Robert H. Ferrell, ed., *The Eisenhower Diaries* (New York: W. W. Norton, 1981), pp. 246–47.

9. Harvard Sitkoff, *The Struggle for Black Equality, 1954–1980* (New York: Hill and Wang, 1981), p. 22.

10. Ibid., p. 25.

11. William Bragg Ewald, Jr., *Eisenhower the President: Crucial Days, 1951–1960* (Englewood Cliffs, N.J.: Prentice-Hall, 1981), p. 81.

12. Arthur Larson, *Eisenhower: The President Nobody Knew* (New York: Charles Scribner's Sons, 1968), pp. 126–27.

13. *Public Papers: 1954*, pp. 491–92.

14. Emmet John Hughes, *The Ordeal of Power: A Political Memoir of the Eisenhower Years* (New York: Atheneum, 1963), p. 201.

15. E. Frederic Morrow, *Black Man in the White House* (New York: Coward-McCann, 1963), p. 47.

16. E. Frederic Morrow, oral history transcript OH 92, pt. 1, p. 27, pt. 2, pp. 102, 105, Eisenhower Library.

17. Numan V. Bartley, *The Rise of Massive Resistance: Race and Politics in the South during the 1950s* (Baton Rouge: Louisiana State University Press, 1969), pp. 82–107.

18. Steven F. Lawson, *Black Ballots: Voting Rights in the South, 1944–1969* (New York: Columbia University Press, 1976), p. 139.

19. Minutes of Cabinet Meeting, 9 Mar. 1956, by L. Arthur Minnich, folder C-30(4), Cabinet Series, White House Office, Office of the Staff Secretary, Eisenhower Library.

20. *Public Papers: 1956*, p. 724.

21. Ibid., p. 735.

22. *Public Papers: 1957*, p. 521.

23. William H. Chafe, *The Unfinished Journey: America since World War II* (New York: Oxford University Press, 1986), p. 157.

24. Taylor Branch, *Parting the Waters: America in the King Years, 1954–63* (New York: Simon and Schuster, 1988), p. 221.

25. Robert Griffith, ed., *Ike's Letters to a Friend, 1941–1958* (Lawrence: University Press of Kansas, 1984), pp. 186–87.

26. *Public Papers: 1957*, p. 546.

27. Virgil T. Blossom, *It Has Happened Here* (New York: Harper, 1959), pp. 25–26.

28. *Public Papers: 1957*, p. 659.

29. Burk, *The Eisenhower Administration and Black Civil Rights*, pp. 177–78.

30. Ferrell, *Eisenhower Diaries*, pp. 347–48.

31. Brooks Hays, *A Southern Moderate Speaks* (Chapel Hill: University of North Carolina Press, 1959), pp. 151–52 (emphasis added).

32. *Public Papers: 1957*, p. 674 (emphasis added).

33. Burk, *The Eisenhower Administration and Black Civil Rights*, p. 183.

34. Juan Williams, *Eyes on the Prize: America's Civil Rights Years, 1954–1965* (New York: Viking, 1987), pp. 105–6; Sitkoff, *The Struggle for Black Equality*, p. 32.

35. *Public Papers: 1957*, p. 689.

36. Blossom, *It Has Happened Here*, pp. 113–14.

37. DDE, oral history transcript OH 11, p. 82, Eisenhower Library.

38. *Public Papers: 1957*, pp. 689–94.

39. Ambrose, *Eisenhower*, 2:421.

40. Ibid., p. 409.

41. Blossom, *It Has Happened Here*, p. 127.

42. Burk, *The Eisenhower Administration and Black Civil Rights*, p. 189.

43. Larson, *Eisenhower*, p. 124.

44. Branch, *Parting the Waters*, pp. 233–36.

45. Burk, *The Eisenhower Administration and Black Civil Rights*, p. 246.

46. Sitkoff, *The Struggle for Black Equality*, pp. 35–36.

47. Burk, *The Eisenhower Administration and Black Civil Rights*, pp. 201, 249–50.

48. Larson, *Eisenhower*, p. 128.

CHAPTER 7
THE EROSION OF CONSENSUS

1. *Public Papers: 1957*, pp. 60–65.

2. U.S. Congress, Senate, *Executive Sessions of the Senate Foreign Relations Committee Together with Joint Sessions with the Senate Armed Services Committee (Historical Series)*, vol. 9, 85th Cong., 1st sess., 1957 (Washington, D.C.: Government Printing Office, 1979), pp. 1–35.

3. *Public Papers: 1957*, pp. 6–16.

4. *Executive Sessions of the Senate Foreign Relations Committee*, 9:20, 25, 327.

5. Ibid., p. 331.

6. Duane Tananbaum, "Not for the First Time: Antecedents and Origins of the War Powers Resolution, 1945–1970," in *Congress and United States Foreign Policy: Controlling the Use of Force in the Nuclear Age*, ed. Michael Barnhart (Albany: State University of New York Press, 1987), pp. 46–47.

7. William J. Burns, *Economic Aid and American Foreign Policy toward Egypt, 1955–1981* (Albany: State University of New York Press, 1985), p. 109.

8. William Stivers, "Eisenhower and the Middle East," in *Reevaluating Eisenhower: American Foreign Policy in the 1950s*, ed. Richard A. Melanson and David Mayers (Urbana: University of Illinois Press, 1987), p. 199.

9. Dwight D. Eisenhower, *Waging Peace, 1956–1961* (Garden City, N.Y.: Doubleday, 1965), pp. 185–86.

10. Harold Macmillan, *Riding the Storm, 1956–1959* (New York: Harper & Row, 1971), pp. 213–14.

11. Eisenhower, *Waging Peace*, p. 124.

12. Burns, *Economic Aid and American Policy toward Egypt*, p. 110.

13. Gail E. Meyer, *Egypt and the United States: The Formative Years* (Rutherford, N.J.: Fairleigh Dickinson University Press, 1980), pp. 185–86.

14. Ibid., pp. 187–91.

15. Burton I. Kaufman, *Trade and Aid: Eisenhower's Foreign Economic Policy, 1953–1961* (Baltimore: Johns Hopkins University Press, 1982), pp. 58–59, 63–68.

16. Chester J. Pach, Jr., "Military Assistance and American Foreign Policy: The Role of Congress," in *Congress and United States Foreign Policy*, p. 143.

17. Burns, *Economic Aid and American Policy toward Egypt*, pp. 48–49.

18. *Public Papers: 1957*, pp. 385–96.

19. Stephen E. Ambrose, *Eisenhower*, vol. 2: *The President* (New York: Simon and Schuster, 1984), pp. 377–78.

20. Robert Griffith, ed., *Ike's Letters to a Friend, 1941–1958* (Lawrence: University Press of Kansas, 1984), p. 183.

21. Kaufman, *Trade and Aid*, p. 104–12.

22. Sherman Adams, *Firsthand Report: The Story of the Eisenhower Administration* (New York: Harper, 1961), p. 364.

23. *New York Times,* 17 Jan. 1957.

24. *Public Papers: 1957,* p. 99.

25. Adams, *Firsthand Report,* p. 366.

26. Ibid., pp. 365, 371.

27. *Public Papers: 1957,* pp. 341–52.

28. Eisenhower, *Waging Peace,* p. 147.

29. *Public Papers: 1957,* pp. 354–55.

30. Ambrose, *Eisenhower,* 2:428.

31. Richard A. Aliano, *American Defense Policy from Eisenhower to Kennedy: The Politics of Changing Military Requirements* (Athens: Ohio University Press, 1975), p. 50.

32. H. W. Brands, "The Age of Vulnerability: Eisenhower and the National Insecurity State," *American Historical Review* 94 (Oct. 1989):988.

33. Walter A. McDougall, . . . *The Heavens and the Earth: A Political History of the Space Age* (New York: Basic Books, 1985), pp. 118–24.

34. *Public Papers: 1957,* pp. 719–32.

35. Ibid., pp. 789–99.

36. Ibid., pp. 807–16.

37. James R. Killian, Jr., *Sputnik, Scientists, and Eisenhower: A Memoir of the First Special Assistant to the President for Science and Technology* (Cambridge, Mass.: MIT Press, 1977), p. 98.

38. Griffith, *Ike's Letters to a Friend,* pp. 168–69.

39. Eisenhower, *Waging Peace,* pp. 227–28.

40. *The Memoirs of Richard Nixon* (New York: Grosset & Dunlap, 1978), p. 184.

41. George H. Gallup, *The Gallup Poll: Public Opinion, 1935–1971,* 3 vols. (New York: Random House, 1972), 2:1467, 1522, 1536, 1545, 1552, 1570, 1579.

42. Anonymous flyer, Washington State Federation of Labor Papers, University of Washington Library, Seattle.

43. Iwan W. Morgan, *Eisenhower versus "the Spenders": The Eisenhower Administration, the Democrats and the Budget, 1953–60* (New York: St. Martin's Press, 1990), pp. 93–100.

44. Robert H. Ferrell, ed., *The Eisenhower Diaries* (New York: W. W. Norton, 1981), pp. 352–53.

45. Morgan, *Eisenhower versus "the Spenders,"* pp. 103–5.

46. Eisenhower, *Waging Peace,* p. 306.

47. Willard W. Cochrane and Mary E. Ryan, *American Farm Policy, 1948–1973* (Minneapolis: University of Minnesota Press, 1976), p. 34.

48. Eisenhower, *Waging Peace,* p. 307.

49. *Public Papers: 1958,* p. 221, 251.

50. Ibid., 2–15.

51. Eisenhower, *Waging Peace,* pp. 246–53.

52. Notes on telephone call, 25 June 1958, folder June 1958—Telephone

Calls, DDE Diary Series, Ann Whitman File, Eisenhower Library; Kaufman, *Trade and Aid*, pp. 133–41.

53. Ambrose, *Eisenhower*, 2:458.

54. Adams, *Firsthand Report*, p. 444.

55. *Public Papers: 1958*, pp. 479–80.

56. *Memoirs of Richard Nixon*, p. 196.

57. *Public Papers: 1958*, p. 651.

58. Ibid., 758–60.

59. James C. Hagerty, oral history transcript OH 91, pt. 6, p. 486.

60. Ferrell, *Eisenhower Diaries*, pp. 356–58.

CHAPTER 8
INTERVENTION AND DIPLOMACY

1. Dwight D. Eisenhower, *Waging Peace, 1956–1961* (Garden City, N.Y.: Doubleday, 1965), p. 519.

2. *Public Papers: 1958*, p. 358.

3. John Prados, *Presidents' Secret Wars: CIA and Pentagon Covert Operations since World War II* (New York: William Morrow, 1986), pp. 128–48.

4. *The Memoirs of Richard Nixon* (New York: Grosset & Dunlap, 1978), p. 190.

5. *FRUS: 1955–1957*, 6:119–20, 194–200.

6. *Memoirs of Richard Nixon*, p. 191.

7. *Public Papers: 1958*, p. 395.

8. Stephen G. Rabe, *Eisenhower and Latin America: The Foreign Policy of Anticommunism* (Chapel Hill: University of North Carolina Press, 1988), p. 102.

9. Ibid., pp. 104–12.

10. *Department of State Bulletin* 40 (19 January 1959):90.

11. Rabe, *Eisenhower and Latin America*, pp. 114–16.

12. Roger J. Spiller, *"Not War But Like War"": The American Intervention in Lebanon*, Leavenworth Papers no. 3 (Fort Leavenworth, Kans.: Combat Studies Institute, 1981), p. 14.

13. Eisenhower, *Waging Peace*, p. 266.

14. William Stivers, "Eisenhower and the Middle East," in *Reevaluating Eisenhower: American Foreign Policy in the 1950s*, ed. Richard A. Melanson and David Mayers (Urbana: University of Illinois Press, 1987), p. 208; Spiller, *"Not War But Like War""*, p. 18.

15. *Public Papers: 1958*, pp. 556–57.

16. Stephen E. Ambrose, *Eisenhower*, vol. 2: *The President* (New York: Simon and Schuster, 1984), p. 470.

17. Eisenhower, *Waging Peace*, p. 290.

18. H. W. Brands, Jr., *Cold Warriors: Eisenhower's Generation and American Foreign Policy* (New York: Columbia University Press, 1988), pp. 104, 109.

19. Memorandum of telephone call, 16 July 1958, folder July 1958—Telephone Calls, DDE Diary Series, Ann Whitman File, Eisenhower Library.

20. Stivers, "Eisenhower and the Middle East," p. 209; Brands, *Cold Warriors*, pp. 104–9.

21. Michael B. Bishku, "The 1958 American Intervention in Lebanon: A Historical Assessment," *American-Arab Affairs* 31 (Winter 1989/90):116.

22. Memorandum of telephone call, 15 July 1958, folder July 1958—Telephone Calls, DDE Diary Series, Ann Whitman File, Eisenhower Library; Harold Macmillan, *Riding the Storm, 1956–1959* (New York: Harper & Row, 1971), p. 512.

23. Robert J. McMahon, "Eisenhower and Third World Nationalism: A Critique of the Revisionists," *Political Science Quarterly* 101 (1986):465–66.

24. Bishku, "The 1958 American Intervention in Lebanon," 116–19.

25. William J. Burns, *Economic Aid and American Foreign Policy toward Egypt, 1955–1981* (Albany: State University of New York Press, 1985), 112–20.

26. Eisenhower, *Waging Peace*, pp. 293, 691–93; Leonard H. D. Gordon, "United States Opposition to Use of Force in the Taiwan Strait, 1954–1962," *Journal of American History* 72 (Dec. 1985):645.

27. Thomas E. Stolper, *China, Taiwan, and the Offshore Islands: Together with an Implication for Outer Mongolia and Sino-Soviet Relations* (Armonk, N.Y.: M. E. Sharpe, 1985), pp. 114–17.

28. Gordon, "United States Opposition to Use of Force in the Taiwan Strait," pp. 644–48.

29. Eisenhower, *Waging Peace*, pp. 293–96.

30. Ibid., pp. 293, 691–93.

31. *Public Papers: 1958*, pp. 694–700.

32. Macmillan, *Riding the Storm*, pp. 540–49.

33. Ambrose, *Eisenhower*, 2:484.

34. *Public Papers: 1958*, pp. 723–25.

35. Ambrose, *Eisenhower*, 2:485.

36. *The Gallup Poll: Public Opinion, 1935–1971*, 3 vols. (New York: Random House, 1972), 2:1579; Ambrose, *Eisenhower*, 2:486.

37. Michael R. Beschloss, *Mayday: The U-2 Affair* (New York: Harper & Row, 1986), p. 162.

38. Frank A. Ninkovich, *Germany and the United States: The Transformation of the German Question Since 1945* (Boston: Twayne Publishers, 1988), pp. 122–23.

39. Ibid., pp. 123–24.

40. Eisenhower, *Waging Peace*, p. 331.

41. Ibid., pp. 331–38.

42. Ibid., pp. 338–41.

43. *Public Papers: 1959*, pp. 244–45; Ambrose, *Eisenhower*, 2:518–19.

44. Hagerty oral history transcript OH 91, pt. 3, p. 194, Eisenhower Library.

45. John S. D. Eisenhower, *Strictly Personal* (Garden City, N.Y.: Doubleday, 1974), p. 229.

46. Eisenhower, *Waging Peace*, p. 353.

47. Macmillan, *Riding the Storm*, p. 644.

48. Robert J. Donovan, *Confidential Secretary: Ann Whitman's 20 Years with Eisenhower and Rockefeller* (New York: E. P. Dutton, 1988), p. 134.

49. Eisenhower, *Waging Peace*, p. 373.

50. Beschloss, *Mayday*, pp. 245-46.

51. Eisenhower, *Waging Peace*, p. 398.

52. Richard G. Hewlett and Jack M. Holl, *Atoms for Peace and War, 1953-1961: Eisenhower and the Atomic Energy Commission* (Berkeley: University of California Press, 1989), pp. 271, 452; Robert A. Strong, "Eisenhower and Arms Control," in *Reevaluating Eisenhower*, p. 250.

53. Hewlett and Holl, *Atoms for Peace and War*, pp. 546-57.

54. *Memoirs of Richard Nixon*, p. 207.

55. Eisenhower, *Waging Peace*, p. 432.

56. *Public Papers: 1959*, p. 593.

57. Beschloss, *Mayday*, p. 184.

58. Eisenhower, *Strictly Personal*, p. 257.

59. Eisenhower, *Waging Peace*, p. 441.

60. Beschloss, *Mayday*, p. 204.

61. Sherman Adams, *Firsthand Report: The Story of the Eisenhower Administration* (New York: Harper, 1961), p. 454.

62. Eisenhower, *Waging Peace*, p. 432; Beschloss, *Mayday*, p. 192.

63. *Public Papers: 1959*, p. 786.

CHAPTER 9
BEYOND HIS GRASP

1. *Public Papers: 1960-61*, p. 3.

2. Letter, Hagerty to Dewey, 7 Jan. 1960, folder Personal—friends, Hagerty Papers, Eisenhower Library.

3. Iwan W. Morgan, *Eisenhower versus "the Spenders": The Eisenhower Administration, the Democrats and the Budget, 1953-60* (New York: St. Martin's Press, 1990), p. 182.

4. Gary W. Reichard, *Politics as Usual: The Age of Truman and Eisenhower* (Arlington Heights, Ill.: Harlan Davidson, 1988), 155-57.

5. Letter, Eisenhower to Hagerty, 29 Dec. 1959, folder Eisenhower, President and Mrs.—letters from, Hagerty Papers, Eisenhower Library.

6. Memorandum by Paarlberg, 27 Nov. 1959; and paraphrase of Eisenhower's remarks at Cabinet meeting, 27 Nov. 1959, both in folder Cabinet Meeting of 27 Nov. 1959, Cabinet Series, Ann Whitman file, Eisenhower Library.

7. Edward A. Kolodziej, *The Uncommon Defense and Congress, 1945-1963* (n.p.: Ohio State University Press, 1966), p. 316.

8. *Public Papers: 1960-61*, pp. 145, 198-99.

9. Ibid., pp. 3-4.

10. Richard G. Hewlett and Jack M. Holl, *Atoms for Peace and War, 1953-1961:*

Eisenhower and the Atomic Energy Commission (Berkeley: University of California Press, 1989), p. 560.

11. Michael R. Beschloss, *Mayday: The U-2 Affair* (New York: Harper & Row, 1986), pp. 7, 232. This section on the U-2 incident and Paris summit is based mainly on Beschloss's book.

12. Ibid., p. 232.

13. Dwight D. Eisenhower, *Waging Peace, 1956–1961* (Garden City, N.Y.: Doubleday, 1965), p. 546.

14. Beschloss, *Mayday*, pp. 58–65, 243–49.

15. Robert J. Donovan, *Confidential Secretary: Ann Whitman's 20 Years with Eisenhower and Rockefeller* (New York: E. P. Dutton, 1988), p. 155.

16. John S. D. Eisenhower, *Strictly Personal* (Garden City, N.Y.: Doubleday, 1974), p. 271.

17. Beschloss, *Mayday*, pp. 257–58.

18. Ibid., p. 290.

19. George H. Gallup, *The Gallup Poll: Public Opinion, 1935–1971*, 3 vols. (New York: Random House, 1972), 2:1661–62, 1672.

20. *Public Papers: 1960–61*, p. 439.

21. George B. Kistiakowsky, *A Scientist at the White House: The Private Diary of President Eisenhower's Special Assistant for Science and Technology* (Cambridge, Mass.: Harvard University Press, 1976), p. 375.

22. Stephen E. Ambrose, *Eisenhower*, vol. 2: *The President* (New York: Simon and Schuster, 1984), p. 585.

23. Morgan, *Eisenhower versus "the Spenders,"* pp. 155–56; Kolodziej, *The Uncommon Defense and Congress*, pp. 265, 311.

24. Eisenhower, *Waging Peace*, p. 563.

25. Ambrose, *Eisenhower*, 2:590.

26. Richard E. Welch, Jr., *Response to Revolution: The United States and the Cuban Revolution, 1959–1961* (Chapel Hill: University of North Carolina Press, 1985), p. 29; Stephen G. Rabe, *Eisenhower and Latin America: The Foreign Policy of Anticommunism* (Chapel Hill: University of North Carolina Press, 1988), pp. 119–22.

27. Rabe, *Eisenhower and Latin America*, p. 124.

28. Ibid., p. 128.

29. Ibid., p. 129.

30. Ibid., pp. 164, 166–67.

31. *Public Papers: 1960–61*, p. 5.

32. Rabe, *Eisenhower and Latin America*, pp. 156–62.

33. Ibid., pp. 139–40.

34. Madeleine G. Kalb, *The Congo Cables: The Cold War in Africa—From Eisenhower to Kennedy* (New York: Macmillan, 1982), pp. xi, 29, 53, 63–65; Robert J. McMahon, "Eisenhower and Third World Nationalism: A Critique of the Revisionists," *Political Science Quarterly* 101 (1986):469–70.

35. Theodore H. White, *The Making of the President, 1960* (New York: Atheneum, 1961), p. 309.

36. *Public Papers: 1960–61*, pp. 652–58.

37. *The Memoirs of Richard Nixon* (New York: Grosset & Dunlap, 1978), p. 222.

38. Morgan, *Eisenhower Versus "the Spenders,"* pp. 160–62, 175.

39. Eisenhower, *Strictly Personal*, p. 285.

40. Rabe, *Eisenhower and Latin America*, p. 171; Robert H. Ferrell, ed., *The Eisenhower Diaries* (New York: W. W. Norton, 1981), pp. 379–83.

41. *Public Papers: 1960–61*, pp. 1035–40.

42. *The Nation*, 28 Jan. 1961, pp. 69–70.

CHAPTER 10
EPILOGUE

1. Robert H. Ferrell, ed., *The Eisenhower Diaries* (New York: W. W. Norton, 1981), pp. 386–90.

2. Stephen E. Ambrose, *Eisenhower*, vol. 2: *The President* (New York: Simon and Schuster, 1984), pp. 638–40.

3. Ibid., pp. 596–97.

4. Arthur Larson, *Eisenhower: The President Nobody Knew* (New York: Charles Scribner's Sons, 1968), p. 190.

5. *New York Times*, 4 Oct. 1966.

6. Larson, *Eisenhower*, p. 191.

7. Ambrose, *Eisenhower*, 2:662–65.

8. Norman Cousins, *Present Tense: An American Editor's Odyssey* (New York: McGraw-Hill, 1967), p. 559.

9. John S. D. Eisenhower, *Strictly Personal* (Garden City, N.Y.: Doubleday, 1974), pp. 336–37.

10. *Public Papers: 1960–61*, p. 553.

11. DDE, oral history transcript OH 11, p. 89, Eisenhower Library.

12. Robert K. Murray and Tim H. Blessing, "The Presidential Performance Study: A Progress Report," *Journal of American History* 70 (Dec. 1983):540.

13. Iwan W. Morgan, *Eisenhower versus "the Spenders": The Eisenhower Administration, the Democrats and the Budget, 1953–60* (New York: St. Martin's Press, 1990) pp. 177–81.

BIBLIOGRAPHICAL ESSAY

Since the late 1970s, there has been an explosion in historical scholarship on the Eisenhower presidency. The boom has coincided with the opening of many collections of official documents and personal papers at the Eisenhower Library in Abilene, Kansas, and at the National Archives in Washington, D.C. For a description of the collections of the former repository, see *Historical Materials in the Dwight D. Eisenhower Library* (Abilene, Kans.: Dwight D. Eisenhower Library, 1989); for the holdings of the latter, consult *Guide to the National Archives of the United States* (Washington, D.C.: National Archives and Records Service, 1974). This essay will emphasize the most recent secondary works.

The most important collection of printed documents is *The Papers of Dwight D. Eisenhower* (Baltimore: Johns Hopkins University Press, 1970–   ), ed. Alfred D. Chandler, Jr., and Louis Galambos, vols. 1–13. To date this series covers Eisenhower's career from the beginning of World War II up to his inauguration as president. It is an essential source for Eisenhower's prepresidential years. Also revealing is Robert H. Ferrell, ed., *The Eisenhower Diaries* (New York: W. W. Norton, 1981). For Eisenhower's thoughts on a variety of issues as expressed in his correspondence with his boyhood friend, Edward E. (Swede) Hazlett, see Robert Griffith, ed., *Ike's Letters to a Friend, 1941–1958* (Lawrence: University Press of Kansas, 1984). For Eisenhower's public statements, see *Public Papers of the Presidents of the United States, Dwight D. Eisenhower*, 8 vols. (Washington, D.C.: Government Printing Office, 1958–61). Also useful is Robert L. Branyan and Lawrence H. Larsen, eds., *The Eisenhower Administration, 1953–1961: A Documentary History* (New York: Random House, 1971).

The president's account of his White House years is in *Mandate for Change, 1953–1956* (Garden City, N.Y.: Doubleday, 1963) and *Waging Peace, 1956–1961* (Garden City, N.Y.: Doubleday, 1965). For Eisenhower's reminiscences of earlier years, see *At Ease: Stories I Tell to Friends* (Garden City, N.Y.: Doubleday, 1967). Milton S. Eisenhower recollects in *The President Is Calling* (Garden City, N.Y.: Doubleday, 1974). A candid account by a family member is John S. D. Eisenhower, *Strictly Personal* (Garden City, N.Y.: Doubleday, 1974).

For the campaign of 1952, see John Robert Greene, *The Crusade: The Presidential Election of 1952* (Lanham, Md.: University Press of America, 1985); Henry Cabot Lodge, *The Storm Has Many Eyes: A Personal Narrative* (New York: W. W. Norton, 1973); John Bartlow Martin, *Adlai Stevenson of Illinois* (Garden City, N.Y.: Doubleday, 1976); and Richard Norton Smith, *Thomas E. Dewey and His Times* (New York: Simon and Schuster, 1982).

Any survey of the secondary literature on the Eisenhower presidency must begin with the magnificent biography by Stephen E. Ambrose, *Eisenhower*, vol. 1: *Soldier, General of the Army, President-Elect, 1890–1952* (New York: Simon and Schuster, 1983), vol. 2: *The President* (New York: Simon and Schuster, 1984). Another revisionist work, which stresses Eisenhower's political astuteness, is Fred I. Greenstein, *The Hidden-Hand Presidency: Eisenhower as Leader* (New York: Basic Books, 1982). Favorable assessments of his leadership are in Herbert S. Parmet, *Eisenhower and the American Crusades* (New York: Macmillan, 1972); and R. Alton Lee, *Dwight D. Eisenhower: Soldier and Statesman* (Chicago: Nelson-Hall, 1981). Reaching more critical judgments are Peter Lyon, *Eisenhower: Portrait of the Hero* (Boston: Little, Brown, 1974); and Piers Brendon, *Ike: His Life and Times* (New York: Harper & Row, 1986). An astute assessment of Eisenhower's political philosophy is Robert Griffith, ''Dwight D. Eisenhower and the Corporate Commonwealth,'' *American Historical Review* 87 (Feb. 1982). A brief but solid biography is Robert F. Burk, *Dwight D. Eisenhower: Hero and Politician* (Boston: Twayne Publishers, 1986). Also useful are Charles C. Alexander, *Holding the Line: The Eisenhower Era, 1952–1961* (Bloomington: Indiana University Press, 1975); and William Bragg Ewald, Jr., *Eisenhower the President: Crucial Days, 1951–1960* (Englewood Cliffs, N.J.: Prentice-Hall, 1981). Essays on many aspects of the Eisenhower presidency are contained in Joann P. Krieg, ed., *Dwight D. Eisenhower: Soldier, President, Statesman* (Westport, Conn.: Greenwood Press, 1987).

Among the many assessments of the literature on the Eisenhower presidency are Alan Brinkley, ''A President for Certain Seasons,'' *Wilson Quarterly* (Spring 1990); Murray Kempton, ''The Underestimation of Dwight D. Eisenhower,'' *Esquire* 68 (Sept. 1967); Mary S. McAuliffe, ''Commentary: Eisenhower, the President,'' *Journal of American History* 68 (Dec. 1981); and Arthur M. Schlesinger, Jr., ''The Ike Age Revisited,'' *Reviews in American History* 11 (Mar. 1983). For Eisenhower's ratings by historians, see Robert K. Murray and Tim H. Blessing, ''The Presidential Performance Study: A Progress Report,'' *Journal of American History* 70 (Dec. 1983); and William Pederson and Ann McLaurin, eds., *The Rating Game in American Politics* (New York: Irvington Publishers, 1987).

There is an extensive literature on individuals who held high positions in the Eisenhower administration. For the vice-president's recollections, see *The Memoirs of Richard Nixon* (New York: Grosset & Dunlap, 1978) and *Six Crises*

(Garden City, N.Y.: Doubleday, 1962). Two recent works about Nixon's early years in politics are Stephen E. Ambrose, *Nixon*, vol. 1: *The Education of a Politician, 1913–1962* (New York: Simon and Schuster, 1987); and Roger Morris, *Richard Milhous Nixon: The Rise of an American Politician* (New York: Henry Holt, 1990). For the early career of Eisenhower's first secretary of state, see Ronald W. Pruessen, *John Foster Dulles: The Road to Power* (New York: Free Press, 1982). The Dulles-Eisenhower relationship is explored in Louis L. Gerson, *John Foster Dulles*, The American Secretaries of State and Their Diplomacy, vol. 17 (New York: Cooper Square Publishers, 1967); Michael Guhin, *John Foster Dulles: A Statesman and His Times* (New York: Columbia University Press, 1972); and Townsend Hoopes, *The Devil and John Foster Dulles* (Boston: Little, Brown, 1973). Emphasizing the partnership between the president and secretary of state is Richard H. Immerman, "Eisenhower and Dulles: Who Made the Decisions," *Political Psychology* 1 (Autumn 1979). An exercise in Dulles revisionism is Richard H. Immerman, ed., *John Foster Dulles and the Diplomacy of the Cold War* (Princeton, N.J.: Princeton University Press, 1990). On Dulles's successor, see G. Bernard Noble, *Christian A. Herter*, The American Secretaries of State and Their Diplomacy, vol. 18 (New York: Cooper Square Publishers, 1970).

For information on other members of the cabinet, consult Nathaniel R. Howard, ed., *The Basic Papers of George M. Humphrey* (Cleveland: Western Reserve Historical Society, 1965); Ezra Taft Benson, *Cross Fire: The Eight Years with Eisenhower* (Garden City, N.Y.: Doubleday, 1962); Edward L. and Frank H. Schapsmeier, *Ezra Taft Benson and the Politics of Agriculture* (Danville, Ill: Interstate, 1975); E. Bruce Geelhoed, *Charles E. Wilson and the Controversy at the Pentagon* (Detroit: Wayne State University Press, 1979). Among the other high administration officials who wrote memoirs or kept diaries were Sherman Adams, *Firsthand Report: The Story of the Eisenhower Administration* (New York: Harper, 1961); Emmet John Hughes, *The Ordeal of Power: A Political Memoir of the Eisenhower Years* (New York: Atheneum, 1963); and Henry Cabot Lodge, *As It Was: An Inside View of Politics and Power in the '50s and '60s* (New York: W. W. Norton, 1976). Material about Eisenhower's personality is in Robert J. Donovan, *Confidential Secretary: Ann Whitman's 20 Years with Eisenhower and Rockefeller* (New York: E. P. Dutton, 1988); and Robert H. Ferrell, ed., *The Diary of James C. Hagerty: Eisenhower in Mid-Course, 1954–1955* (Bloomington: Indiana University Press, 1983). Many members of the cabinet and White House staff reminisce about the president in Kenneth W. Thompson, ed., *The Eisenhower Presidency: Eleven Intimate Perspectives of Dwight D. Eisenhower* (Lanham, Md.: University Press of America, 1984).

The most valuable printed primary source for the study of American foreign policy during the Eisenhower years is U.S. Department of State, *Foreign Relations of the United States: Diplomatic Papers* (Washington, D.C.: Government Printing Office, 1861–   ). Now available are most of the volumes for the 1952–54 and many for the 1955–57 trienniums. Also important are U.S. Congress, Senate, Committee on Foreign Relations, *Executive Sessions of the Senate Foreign Relations Committee (Historical Series), 1953–1961* (Washington, D.C.: Government Printing

Office, 1977–84); and U.S. Congress, House, Committee on Foreign Affairs, *Selected Executive Session Hearings of the Committee, 1951–1956* (Washington, D.C.: Government Printing Office, 1980).

For overviews of Eisenhower and the Cold War, see Stephen E. Ambrose, *Rise to Globalism: American Foreign Policy Since 1938*, 5th ed. (New York: Penguin Books, 1988); Blanche Wiesen Cook, *The Declassified Eisenhower: A Startling Appraisal of the Eisenhower Presidency* (New York: Penguin, 1984); the revisionist account by Robert A. Divine, *Eisenhower and the Cold War* (New York: Oxford University Press, 1981); John Lewis Gaddis, *Strategies of Containment: A Critical Appraisal of Postwar American National Security Policy* (New York: Oxford University Press, 1982); Gaddis, *The Long Peace: Inquiries into the History of the Cold War* (New York: Oxford University Press, 1987); relevant chapters of Walter LaFeber, *America, Russia, and the Cold War, 1945–1984*, 5th ed. (New York: Alfred A. Knopf, 1985); and Thomas G. Paterson, *Meeting the Communist Threat: Truman to Reagan* (New York: Oxford University Press, 1988). A provocative series of essays that stresses the influence of World War II on the outlook of Eisenhower and his closest foreign policy associates is H. W. Brands, Jr., *Cold Warriors: Eisenhower's Generation and American Foreign Policy* (New York: Columbia University Press, 1988). An interesting set of essays is in Richard A. Melanson and David Mayers, eds., *Reevaluating Eisenhower: American Foreign Policy in the 1950s* (Urbana: University of Illinois Press, 1987).

There are several significant works that examine Eisenhower's use of covert operations. Overviews are in Stephen E. Ambrose, *Ike's Spies: Eisenhower and the Espionage Establishment* (New York: Doubleday, 1981); and John Prados, *Presidents' Secret Wars: CIA and Pentagon Covert Operations since World War II* (New York: William Morrow, 1986). An insider account of the Eisenhower administration's first major covert intervention is in Kermit Roosevelt, *Countercoup: The Struggle for the Control of Iran* (New York: McGraw-Hill, 1979). A first-rate account of the Guatemalan coup is in Richard H. Immerman, *The CIA in Guatemala: The Foreign Policy of Intervention* (Austin: University of Texas Press, 1982).

On Eisenhower's summitry, see W. W. Rostow, *Open Skies: Eisenhower's Proposal of July 21, 1955* (Austin: University of Texas Press, 1982); and Charles E. Bohlen, *Witness to History, 1929–1969* (New York: W. W. Norton, 1973), for Geneva. The failed Paris summit is treated in Michael Beschloss, *Mayday: The U-2 Affair* (New York: Harper & Row, 1986). The reactions of foreign leaders can be found in Charles de Gaulle, *Memoirs of Hope: Renewal, 1958–62* (London: Weidenfeld and Nicolson, 1971); Nikita S. Khrushchev, *Khrushchev Remembers: The Last Testament* (Boston: Little, Brown, 1974); and three volumes of memoirs by Harold Macmillan, *Tides of Fortune, 1945–1955* (New York: Harper & Row, 1969), *Riding the Storm, 1956–1959* (New York: Harper & Row, 1971), and *Pointing the Way, 1959–1961* (New York: Harper & Row, 1972). For important issues involving European nations, see Edward Fursdon, *The European Defence Community: A History* (London: Macmillan, 1980); Frank A. Ninkovich, *Germany and the United States: The Transformation of the German Question since 1945* (Boston:

Twayne Publishers, 1988); and W. W. Rostow, *Europe after Stalin: Eisenhower's Three Decisions of March 11, 1953* (Austin: University of Texas Press, 1982).

General treatments of the United States and the Korean War can be found in Bruce Cumings, ed., *Child of Conflict: The Korean-American Relationship, 1943–1953* (Seattle: University of Washington Press, 1983); Rosemary Foot, *The Wrong War: American Policy and the Dimensions of the Korean Conflict, 1950–1953* (Ithaca, N.Y.: Cornell University Press, 1985); Max Hastings, *The Korean War* (New York: Simon and Schuster, 1987); Burton I. Kaufman, *The Korean War: Challenges in Crisis, Credibility, and Command* (New York: Alfred A. Knopf, 1986). Eisenhower's nuclear threats and the end of the war are discussed in Roger Dingman, "Atomic Diplomacy During the Korean War;" Rosemary J. Foot, "Nuclear Coercion and the Ending of the Korean Conflict"; and Marc Trachtenberg, "'A Wasting Asset': American Strategy and the Shifting Nuclear Balance, 1949–54," all in *International Security* 13 (Winter 1988/89).

Although the Vietnam War has generated an enormous body of scholarship, there are stills gaps in the literature for the Eisenhower years. A useful starting point is the standard survey by George C. Herring, *America's Longest War: The United States and Vietnam, 1950–1975*, 2d ed. (New York: Alfred A. Knopf, 1986). Detailed accounts of American policy during the 1950s are in Lloyd C. Gardner, *Approaching Vietnam: From World War II through Dienbienphu* (New York: W. W. Norton, 1988) and Ronald H. Spector, *Advice and Support: The Early Years of the United States Army in Vietnam, 1941–1960* (New York: Free Press, 1985). There is a concentration of studies on Eisenhower and Dien Bien Phu. The classic account is Chalmers Roberts, "The Day We Didn't Go to War," *Reporter* 11 (14 Sept. 1954). A more persuasive analysis is George C. Herring and Richard H. Immerman, "Eisenhower, Dulles, and Dienbienphu: 'The Day We Didn't Go to War' Revisited," *Journal of American History* 71 (Sept. 1984). Emphasizing Eisenhower's hidden-hand leadership is Melanie Billings-Yun, *Decision against War: Eisenhower and Dien Bien Phu, 1954* (New York: Columbia University Press, 1988).

On military operations, see John Prados, *"The Sky Would Fall": Operation Vulture, the U.S. Bombing Mission in Indochina, 1954* (New York: Dial Press, 1983). On the aftermath of Dien Bien Phu, three excellent studies are Richard H. Immerman, "The United States and the Geneva Conference of 1954: A New Look," *Diplomatic History* 14 (Winter 1990); David L. Anderson, "J. Lawton Collins, John Foster Dulles, and the Eisenhower Administration's 'Point of No Return' in Vietnam," *Diplomatic History* 12 (Spring 1988); and George McT. Kahin, *Intervention: How America Became Involved in Vietnam* (Garden City, N.Y.: Anchor Books, 1987).

Published works on American-Chinese relations during the Eisenhower years concentrate on the offshore islands crisis. Especially useful are H. W. Brands, Jr., "Testing Massive Retaliation: Credibility and Crisis Management in the Taiwan Strait;" and Gordon H. Chang, "To the Nuclear Brink: Eisenhower, Dulles, and the Quemoy-Matsu Crisis," both in *International Security* 12 (Spring 1988); Leonard H. D. Gordon, "United States Opposition to Use of Force in the

Taiwan Strait, 1954–1962,'' *Journal of American History* 72 (Dec. 1985); Thomas E. Stolper, *China, Taiwan, and the Offshore Islands: Together with an Implication for Outer Mongolia and Sino-Soviet Relations* (Armonk, N.Y.: M. E. Sharpe, 1985); and Nancy Bernkopf Tucker, ''John Foster Dulles and the Taiwan Roots of the 'Two Chinas' Policy,'' in Immerman, *John Foster Dulles and the Diplomacy of the Cold War*, cited above.

There is much work that needs to be done on United States policy in the Middle East. A valuable overview is William Stivers, ''Eisenhower and the Middle East,'' in *Reevaluating Eisenhower*, ed. Melanson and Mayers, cited above. Among the best works on the Suez crisis are Chester L. Cooper, *The Lion's Last Roar: Suez, 1956* (New York: Harper & Row, 1978); and Donald Neff, *Warriors at Suez: Eisenhower Takes America into the Middle East* (New York: Simon and Schuster, 1981). British views are in *The Memoirs of Anthony Eden, Full Circle* (Boston: Houghton Mifflin, 1960); and David Carlton, *Anthony Eden: A Biography* (London: Allen Lane, 1981). On Lebanon, see Michael B. Bishku, ''The 1958 American Intervention in Lebanon: A Historical Assessment,'' *American-Arab Affairs* 31 (Winter 1989/90); Alan Dowty, *Middle East Crisis: U.S. Decision-Making in 1958, 1970, and 1973* (Berkeley: University of California Press, 1984); and, for army planning and operations, Roger J. Spiller, *''Not War But Like War'': The American Intervention in Lebanon*, Leavenworth Papers no. 3 (Fort Leavenworth, Kans.: Combat Studies Institute, 1981). Critical analyses of Eisenhower's diplomatic dealings with Nasser are in William J. Burns, *Economic Aid and American Policy toward Egypt, 1955–1981* (Albany: State University of New York Press, 1985); and Gail E. Meyer, *Egypt and the United States: The Formative Years* (Rutherford, N.J.: Fairleigh Dickinson University Press, 1980). For American policy toward a critical Near Eastern nation, see Barry Rubin, *Paved with Good Intentions: The American Experience and Iran* (New York: Oxford University Press, 1980); and Roosevelt, *Countercoup*, cited above. American military aid to the region is treated in Paul Jabber, *Not by War Alone: Security and Arms Control in the Middle East* (Berkeley: University of California Press, 1981).

United States policy toward Latin America has produced some of the best scholarship on any topic in the Eisenhower presidency. Two outstanding works are Stephen G. Rabe, *Eisenhower and Latin America: The Foreign Policy of Anticommunism* (Chapel Hill: University of North Carolina Press, 1988); and Richard H. Immerman, *The CIA in Guatemala: The Foreign Policy of Intervention* (Austin: University of Texas Press, 1982). Also on Guatemala, see Stephen C. Schlesinger and Stephen Kinzer, *Bitter Fruit: The Untold Story of the American Coup in Guatemala* (Garden City, N.Y.: Doubleday, 1982). An idiosyncratic interpretation is in Frederick W. Marks III, ''The CIA and Castillo Armas in Guatemala, 1954,'' *Diplomatic History* 14 (Winter 1990). On Eisenhower's dealings with Castro, consult Richard E. Welch, Jr., *Response to Revolution: The United States and the Cuban Revolution, 1959–1961* (Chapel Hill: University of North Carolina Press, 1985); and Trumbull Higgins, *The Perfect Failure: Kennedy, Eisenhower, and the CIA at the Bay of Pigs* (New York: W. W. Norton, 1987). Other Latin American topics are treated in Stanley E. Hilton, ''The United States,

Brazil, and the Cold War, 1945–1960: The End of the Special Relationship,'' *Journal of American History* 68 (Dec. 1981); Marvin R. Zahniser and W. Michael Weis, ''A Diplomatic Pearl Harbor? Richard Nixon's Goodwill Mission to Latin America in 1958,'' *Diplomatic History* 13 (Spring 1989); and Thomas Zoumaras, ''Eisenhower's Foreign Economic Policy: The Case of Latin America,'' in *Reevaluating Eisenhower*, ed. Melanson and Mayers, cited above. Milton S. Eisenhower reflects on Latin American affairs in *The Wine Is Bitter* (Garden City, N.Y.: Doubleday, 1963).

Treatments of miscellaneous topics in foreign policy include Anna Kasten Nelson, ''The 'Top of the Hill': President Eisenhower and the National Security Council,'' *Diplomatic History* 7 (Fall 1983); Duane Tananbaum, *The Bricker Amendment Controversy: A Test of Eisenhower's Political Leadership* (Ithaca, N.Y.: Cornell University Press, 1988); and, by the same author, two articles, ''The Bricker Amendment Controversy: Its Origins and Eisenhower's Role,'' *Diplomatic History* 9 (Winter 1985), and ''Not for the First Time: Antecedents and Origins of the War Powers Resolution, 1945–1970,'' in *Congress and United States Foreign Policy: Controlling the Use of Force in the Nuclear Age*, ed. Michael Barnhart (Albany: State University of New York Press, 1987); Burton I. Kaufman, *Trade and Aid: Eisenhower's Foreign Economic Policy, 1953–1961* (Baltimore: Johns Hopkins University Press, 1982); and Chester J. Pach, Jr., ''Military Assistance and American Foreign Policy: The Role of Congress,'' in *Congress and United States Foreign Policy*, ed. Michael Barnhart, cited above. Calling attention to the deficiencies of Eisenhower diplomacy toward the developing nations is Robert J. McMahon, ''Eisenhower and Third World Nationalism: A Critique of the Revisionists,'' *Political Science Quarterly* 101 (1986). A case study that supports that critique is Madeleine G. Kalb, *The Congo Cables: The Cold War in Africa—From Eisenhower to Kennedy* (New York: Macmillan, 1982).

Badly needed is a book on the New Look based on recently-declassified archival material. Highly suggestive of the enormous value of such a study is H. W. Brands, ''The Age of Vulnerability: Eisenhower and the National Insecurity State,'' *American Historical Review* 94 (Oct. 1989). For older treatments of defense issues, see Richard A. Aliano, *American Defense Policy from Eisenhower to Kennedy: The Politics of Changing Military Requirements, 1957–1961* (Athens: Ohio University Press, 1975); Edmund Beard, *Developing the ICBM: A Study in Bureaucratic Politics* (New York: Columbia University Press, 1976); Norman A. Graebner, ed., *The National Security: Its Theory and Practice, 1945–1960* (New York: Oxford University Press, 1986); Edward A. Kolodziej, *The Uncommon Defense and Congress, 1945–1963* (n.p.: Ohio State University Press, 1966); Douglas Kinnard, *President Eisenhower and Strategy Management: A Study in Defense Politics* (Lexington: University Press of Kentucky, 1977); and Ernest J. Yanarella, *The Missile Defense Controversy: Strategy, Technology, and Politics, 1955–1972* (Lexington: University Press of Kentucky, 1977). The best study of space policy is Walter A. McDougall, . . . *The Heavens and the Earth: A Political History of the Space Age* (New York: Basic Books, 1985). For the recollections and contemporary reactions of Eisenhower's two science advisers, see James R. Killian, Jr., *Sputnik, Scientists, and Eisenhower: A Memoir of the First Special Assistant to the President for Science and Technology* (Cambridge, Mass.: MIT Press, 1977); and George B. Kistiakowsky, *A Scientist at the White House: The Private Diary of President Eisenhower's Special Assistant for Science and Technology* (Cambridge, Mass.: Harvard University Press, 1976).

Nuclear issues are treated in Richard K. Betts, *Nuclear Blackmail and Nuclear Balance* (Washington, D.C.: Brookings Institution, 1987); Robert A. Divine, *Blowing on the Wind: The Nuclear Test Ban Debate, 1954–1960* (New York: Oxford University Press, 1978); Richard G. Hewlett and Jack M. Holl, *Atoms for Peace and War, 1953–1961: Eisenhower and the Atomic Energy Commission* (Berkeley: University of California Press, 1989); Michael Mandelbaum, *The Nuclear Question: The United States and Nuclear Weapons, 1946–1976* (Cambridge, Eng.: Cambridge University Press, 1979); and Lewis Strauss, *Men and Decisions* (Garden City, N.Y.: Doubleday, 1962).

Emphasizing the similarities in politics during the Truman and Eisenhower presidencies is Gary W. Reichard, *Politics as Usual: The Age of Truman and Eisenhower* (Arlington Heights, Ill.: Harlan Davidson, 1988). Reichard makes the case for Eisenhower's conservatism in *The Reaffirmation of Republicanism: Eisenhower and the Eighty-third Congress* (Knoxville: University of Tennessee Press, 1975). Eisenhower's relations with the Old Guard are covered in David W. Reinhard, *The Republican Right since 1945* (Lexington: University Press of Kentucky, 1983). For a discussion of Modern Republicanism, consult Arthur Larson, *Eisenhower: The President Nobody Knew* (New York: Charles Scribner's Sons, 1968).

Works on Congress and legislative leaders include Anthony Champagne, *Congressman Sam Rayburn* (New Brunswick, N.J.: Rutgers University Press, 1984); James T. Patterson, *Mr. Republican: A Biography of Robert H. Taft* (Boston: Houghton Mifflin, 1972); Anne Hodges Morgan, *Robert S. Kerr: The Senate Years* (Norman: University of Oklahoma Press, 1977); and Charles L. Fontenay, *Estes Kefauver: A Biography* (Knoxville: University of Tennessee Press, 1980).

Among the many fine studies of McCarthyism are David Caute, *The Great Fear: The Anti-Communist Purge Under Truman and Eisenhower* (New York: Simon and Schuster, 1978); Richard M. Fried, *Nightmare in Red: The McCarthy Era in Perspective* (New York: Oxford University Press, 1990); Robert Griffith, *The Politics of Fear: Joseph R. McCarthy and the Senate*, 2d ed. (Amherst: University of Massachusetts Press, 1987); and David M. Oshinsky, *A Conspiracy So Immense: The World of Joe McCarthy* (New York: Free Press, 1983). On civil liberties and constitutional issues, see Athan Theoharis, *Spying on Americans: Political Surveillance from Hoover to the Huston Plan* (Philadelphia: Temple University Press, 1978); and Raoul Berger, *Executive Privilege: A Constitutional Myth* (Cambridge, Mass.: Harvard University Press, 1974). The effects of McCarthyism on the State Department are examined in E. J. Kahn, Jr., *The China Hands: America's Foreign Service Officers and What Befell Them* (New York: Viking Press, 1972); and Gary May, *China Scapegoat: The Diplomatic Ordeal of John Carter Vincent* (Washington, D.C.: New Republic Books, 1979).

The best analysis of Eisenhower and race relations, which emphasizes the president's commitment to policies of symbolism, is Robert Fredrick Burk, *The Eisenhower Administration and Black Civil Rights* (Knoxville: University of Tennessee Press, 1984). A similar interpretation is in James C. Duram, *A Moderate among Extremists: Dwight D. Eisenhower and the School Desegregation Crisis* (Chicago: Nelson-Hall, 1981). General surveys of the civil rights movement can be found in Taylor Branch, *Parting the Waters: America in the King Years, 1954–63* (New York: Simon and Schuster, 1988); Harvard Sitkoff, *The Struggle for Black Equality, 1954–1980* (New York: Hill and Wang, 1981); and Juan Williams, *Eyes on the Prize: America's Civil Rights Years, 1954–1965* (New York: Viking, 1987). Treatments of white southern resistance to desegregation include Numan V. Bartley, *The Rise of Massive Resistance: Race and Politics in the South during the 1950s* (Baton Rouge: Louisiana State University Press, 1969); Earl Black, *Southern Governors and Civil Rights: Racial Segregation as a Campaign Issue in the Second Reconstruction* (Cambridge, Mass.: Harvard University Press, 1976); and Neil R. McMillen, *The Citizens' Council: Organized Resistance to the Second Reconstruction, 1954–1964* (Urbana: University of Illinois Press, 1971).

Black efforts to secure the right to exercise the franchise can be followed in Steven F. Lawson, *Black Ballots: Voting Rights in the South, 1944–1969* (New York: Columbia University Press, 1976). For one of the major confrontations, see Elizabeth Huckaby, *Crisis at Central High, Little Rock, 1957–58* (Baton Rouge: Louisiana State University Press, 1980); and two contemporary accounts, Virgil T. Blossom, *It Has Happened Here* (New York: Harper, 1959); and Brooks Hays, *A Southern Moderate Speaks* (Chapel Hill: University of North Carolina Press, 1959). For an important case study, see Morris J. MacGregor, Jr., *Integration of the Armed Forces, 1940–1965* (Washington, D.C.: Center of Military History, 1981). Eisenhower's highest black assistant recollects in E. Frederic Morrow, *Black Man in the White House* (New York: Coward-McCann, 1963).

The literature on fiscal and economic policy is thin. An excellent, recent study of Eisenhower's efforts to hold the line on federal spending is Iwan W. Morgan, *Eisenhower versus "the Spenders": The Eisenhower Administration, the Democrats and the Budget, 1953–60* (New York: St. Martin's Press, 1990). In addition to the works by Benson and Schapsmeier and Schapsmeier cited above, good treatments of farm policy are in Willard W. Cochrane and Mary E. Ryan, *American Farm Policy, 1948–1973* (Minneapolis: University of Minnesota Press, 1976); and Theodore P. Kovaleff, *Business and Government during the Eisenhower Administration: A Study of the Antitrust Division of the Justice Department* (Athens: Ohio University Press, 1980). A new study of labor relations is R. Alton Lee, *Eisenhower and Landrum-Griffin: A Study in Labor-Management Politics* (Lexington: University of Kentucky Press, 1990).

Among the domestic matters that have received scholarly attention is highway construction in Mark H. Rose, *Interstate: Express Highway Politics, 1941–1956* (Lawrence: Regents Press of Kansas, 1979); and Richard O. Davies, *The Age of Asphalt: The Automobile, the Freeway, and the Condition of Metropolitan America* (Philadelphia: J. B. Lippincott, 1975). Federal support of education is examined in Barbara Barksdale Clowse, *Brainpower for the Cold War: The Sputnik Crisis and the National Defense Education Act of 1958* (Westport, Conn.: Greenwood Press, 1981). Environmental and energy issues are the subject of Elmo Richardson, *Dams, Parks and Politics: Resource Development and Preservation in the Truman-Eisenhower Era* (Lexington: University Press of Kentucky, 1973). On one of the scandals of the Eisenhower years, see Hewlett and Holl, *Atoms for Peace and War*, cited above; and Aaron Wildavsky, *Dixon-Yates: A Study in Power Politics* (New Haven, Conn.: Yale University Press, 1962). The connections between containment and family life are explained in Elaine Tyler May, *Homeward Bound: American Families in the Cold War Era* (New York: Basic Books, 1988). An engaging and witty analysis of dating is in Beth L. Bailey, *From Front Porch to Back Seat: Courtship in Twentieth-Century America* (Baltimore: Johns Hopkins University Press, 1988).

INDEX

Benson, Ezra Taft, 183; as secretary of agriculture, 35; and farm legislation, 55, 125, 177; unpopularity of, 167
Berger, Raoul, 71
Berlin, 187, 209, 238; crisis over, 200–204; negotiations over, 204–5, 206, 207, 218
Bermuda Conference, 163
Bikini atoll, 205
Bissell, Richard, 216
Bohlen, Charles E., 63–64, 87
Bonus March, 5
Bradley, Omar N., 86, 235
Bragdon, John H., 123
Brands, H. W., 19
BRAVO, 205
Bricker, John W., 59–63; and Eisenhower Doctrine, 162; election defeat, 184
Bricker amendment, 49, 59–62; defeat of, 61–62; and 1954 election, 73
Bridges, Styles, 168
Brown v. *Board of Education of Topeka*, 106; Supreme Court decision, 141, 142–43; Eisenhower's reaction to, 142–43, 153, 154, 155; white southern resistance to, 145
Brownell, Herbert, Jr., 147; chosen attorney general, 34; and selection of cabinet nominees, 34–36; and Bricker amendment, 60–61, 62; and Rosenbergs, 65; accusations against Harry Dexter White, 67–68; and 1956 presidential nomination, 116; and *Brown* decision, 143; and Civil Rights Act of 1957, 146; and Little Rock crisis, 151, 155
Brundage, Percival, 37, 167
Buckley, William F., Jr., 208
Budget, Bureau of the, 108
Budgets, federal, 139, 174, 175; 1954, 53, 76–77; 1956, 108; 1958, 167–69; 1959, 176; 1960, 202–3, 212
Bulganin, Nikolai A., 112, 125–26, 134
Burns, Arthur F., 37–38, 228–29
Byrnes, James F., 139, 140–41
Byroade, Henry A., 126

Cambodia, 93, 96, 235
Camp David summit, 208–9, 215
Canada, 58
Candor, Operation, 83–84
Captive Nations Resolution, 207
Carney, Robert B., 102
Carroll, Paul T., 38
Castillo Armas, Carlos, 92–93
Castro, Fidel, 222–25, 229

Central Intelligence Agency, 97, 134; intervention in Iran, 88–89; intervention in Guatemala, 89, 92–93; attempted bribe of Nasser, 126; intervention in Hungary, 131; and Khrushchev's secret speech, 131; intervention in Indonesia, 188; and communism in Latin America, 189; and U-2 incident, 216; plans of to assassinate Castro, 223; plans of to invade Cuba, 224; efforts of to assassinate Trujillo, 225; plot of to assassinate Lumumba, 226
Chamber of Commerce, U.S., 60
Chamoun, Camille, 190–91, 193, 194
Checkers speech, 25
Chehab, Fuad, 191, 193
Chiang Kai-shek, 46, 59, 64; and Quemoy-Matsu crisis (1954–55), 98–102; and Quemoy-Matsu crisis (1958), 195, 196–97, 198
Childs, Marquis, 41
China, 25; civil war in, 46, 93. *See also* China, People's Republic of; China, Republic of
China, People's Republic of, 45, 86, 96, 215; relations with Soviet Union, 82; and Quemoy-Matsu crisis (1954–55), 98–100, 102–3; recognized by Egypt, 127; and Quemoy-Matsu crisis, 195–99. *See also* China; China, Republic of; Mao Tse-tung; Quemoy-Matsu crisis (1954–55); Quemoy-Matsu crisis (1958)
China, Republic of: and Quemoy-Matsu crisis (1954–55), 98–100, 101–2; and mutual defense treaty with U.S., 99; and Quemoy-Matsu crisis (1958), 195–99; Eisenhower's visit to, 221. *See also* Chiang Kai-shek; China; China, People's Republic of; Quemoy-Matsu crisis (1954–55); Quemoy-Matsu crisis (1958)
Chou En-lai, 96, 102
Churchill, Winston S., 7, 59; at Yalta Conference, 9; and Third World nationalism, 87; and United Action, 95; death of, 236
Civil rights, 137–57, 235
Civil Rights Act of 1957, 145–48
Civil Rights Act of 1960, 156–57
Clay, Lucius D.: and Eisenhower's nomination for president, 18, 20; and cabinet selections, 34–36; on second term of Eisenhower, 115; and highway construction, 123–24; and federal appointment of Warren, 141

INDEX